The Transatlantic Century

This is a fascinating new overview of European-American relations during the long twentieth century. Ranging from economics, culture, and consumption to war, politics, and diplomacy, Mary Nolan charts the rise of American influence in Eastern and Western Europe, its mid-twentieth-century triumph and its gradual erosion since the 1970s. She reconstructs the circuits of exchange along which ideas, commodities, economic models, cultural products, and people moved across the Atlantic, capturing the differing versions of modernity that emerged on both sides of the Atlantic, and examining how these alternately produced cooperation, conflict, and ambivalence toward the other. Attributing the rise and demise of American influence in Europe not only to economics but equally to wars, the book locates the roots of many transatlantic disagreements in very different experiences and memories of war. This is an unprecedented account of the American Century in Europe that recovers its full richness and complexity.

MARY NOLAN is Professor of History at New York University. She is the author of *Visions of Modernity: American Business and the Modernization of Germany* (1994) and co-editor of *Crimes of War: Guilt and Denial in the Twentieth Century* (2002).

New Approaches to European History

Series editors
William Beik *Emory University*
T. C. W. Blanning *Sidney Sussex College, Cambridge*
Brendan Simms *Peterhouse, Cambridge*

New Approaches to European History is an important textbook series, which provides concise but authoritative surveys of major themes and problems in European history since the Renaissance. Written at a level and length accessible to advanced school students and undergraduates, each book in the series addresses topics or themes that students of European history encounter daily: the series embraces both some of the more "traditional" subjects of study and those cultural and social issues to which increasing numbers of school and college courses are devoted. A particular effort is made to consider the wider international implications of the subject under scrutiny.

To aid the student reader, scholarly apparatus and annotation is light, but each work has full supplementary bibliographies and notes for further reading: where appropriate, chronologies, maps, diagrams, and other illustrative material are also provided.

For a complete list of titles published in the series, please see:
www.cambridge.org/newapproaches

The Transatlantic Century
Europe and America,
1890–2010

Mary Nolan

CAMBRIDGE
UNIVERSITY PRESS

CAMBRIDGE UNIVERSITY PRESS
Cambridge, New York, Melbourne, Madrid, Cape Town,
Singapore, São Paulo, Delhi, Mexico City

Cambridge University Press
The Edinburgh Building, Cambridge CB2 8RU, UK

Published in the United States of America by Cambridge University Press,
New York

www.cambridge.org
Information on this title: www.cambridge.org/9780521692212

First published 2012

Printed and bound in the United Kingdom by the MPG Books Group

A catalogue record for this publication is available from the British Library

Library of Congress Cataloguing in Publication data
Nolan, Mary, 1944–
The transatlantic century : Europe and America, 1890–2010 / Mary Nolan.
    pages   cm. – (New approaches to European history; 46)
ISBN 978-0-521-87167-9 (hardback)
1. Europe – Relations – United States.   2. United States – Relations – Europe.
3. Europe – Civilization – American influences.   4. United States – Civilization –
European influences.   5. Europe – Civilization – 20th century.   6. United
States – Civilization – 20th century.   I. Title.
D1065.U5N65   2012
909′.09821082–dc23
                                                                    2012007520

ISBN 978-0-521-87167-9 Hardback
ISBN 978-0-521-69221-2 Paperback

Contents

Illustrations

Maps

Tables

Acknowledgments

For the last twenty-five years I have been reading, thinking, and writing about transatlantic relations of all sorts, but this work relies on much more than my own research. The writing of history is always a collective project, and a synthetic work like this one relies particularly heavily on the recent scholarship of experts in European, American, and transnational history.

I am particularly fortunate to have had Michael Watson as my editor. He read and critiqued each chapter and was enormously patient with the delays in completing the project. Two friends and colleagues, Tom Bender and Marilyn Young, read and critiqued every chapter, sometimes more than once. They offered invaluable advice, saved me from many mistakes, and offered consistent encouragement when I doubted the book would ever be finished. I cannot thank them enough. I am grateful to Fred Block and Sasha Disko for reading early chapters of the manuscript and to Michael David-Fox for getting me up to speed on recent Soviet historiography. I appreciate helpful comments received when presenting parts of this project at the Atlantic History seminar at New York University, at the Northeast Working Group on German Women's History and Culture, and at the Davis Center in Princeton.

Writing requires time away from teaching and two institutions provided that. A fellowship from the Remarque Institute at New York University provided a semester's leave at the early stages of the project. The Shelby Collum Davis Center for Historical Studies at Princeton gave me a most productive and enjoyable year with access to Firestone Library and stimulating colleagues when the book was well underway. My thanks to Dan Rodgers, the director of the Davis Center, for his support for my work and for transnational history more generally.

Without help from my graduate student Laura Honsberger, this book would not have the images that enrich it. I am deeply grateful for her tireless work in tracking down both pictures and permissions.

A final thanks is owed to my friends and fellow peace activists in Brooklyn For Peace with whom I have worked for the past twenty-five years. They have constantly reminded me of the real-world stakes in understanding transatlantic relations and of the importance of combining scholarship with activism.

This book is dedicated to my students, past and present. My graduate students have been a constant source of intellectual stimulation and a joy to teach. Both they and the undergraduates in my Cold War course provided welcome feedback as I developed my arguments for various parts of *The Transatlantic Century*.

Introduction

"There are at the present time two great nations in the world ... the Russians and the Americans ... each of them seems marked out by the will of heaven to sway the destinies of half the globe."[1] Alexis de Tocqueville's prescient 1835 observation is often cited as a succinct summary of European-American relations in the twentieth century. According to the standard story, the multipolarity of the nineteenth century gave way to bipolarity by the middle of the twentieth century and then to unipolarity after 1989. As European power – economic, military, cultural, and moral – waned, America replaced Britain as the hegemonic nation in the global capitalist order, and European culture, politics, and economics were Americanized. As European colonial empires fractured and fell, new American forms of global economic and political integration and dominance emerged. Whereas Europe had once developed the Western values shared by America, America came to define the transatlantic commitment to liberal democracy and consumer capitalism. If the nineteenth century was European, the twentieth was American.

Tocqueville's observation and sweeping narratives of the decline of Europe and rise of America capture elements of the shifting relationship between Europe and America in the twentieth century, but they do justice neither to the complexity of the exchanges of goods, people, institutions, and ideas in both directions across the Atlantic nor to the ambivalent and contradictory attitudes of Europeans and Americans toward one another. A history of shifting transatlantic power relations, of provisional outcomes and ongoing indeterminacies, of cooperative projects and competing visions of capitalism, modernity, and empire cannot be reduced to the inevitable triumph of the United States; that history is much more nuanced, contingent, and contradictory. It begins with the stop-and-start rise of American influence in Europe in the early decades of the twentieth century, continues with the mid-century assertion of American hegemony in all fields, and then proceeds to the slow erosion of American

---

[1] Alexis de Tocqueville, *Democracy in America*, vol. I (New York: Vintage, 1954), 452.

1

economic, cultural, and political power from the1970s on and the emergence of an integrated and more autonomous Europe. American economic might did not automatically translate into political power or cultural influence, and hard military and diplomatic power and soft economic and cultural power did not always move in tandem. Transatlantic perceptions of shared interests, incompatibilities, and animosities were seldom clear-cut or stable.

Our story opens in the decades before World War I when European-American exchanges in both directions were multiplying but America's ascendancy was not evident and Europe's eclipse not preordained. Despite its growing economic might, the United States was not a military power, and Europeans did not consider the United States a major global player or a model to emulate. World War I tipped the uncertain transatlantic balance of economic, political, and cultural power decisively in America's favor. In the 1920s, however, America was deeply ambivalent about assuming a dominant political role in Europe, even as its economic entanglements multiplied. Despite Europeans' growing fascination with Fordist economic models, Hollywood films, and jazz, Europe did not become Americanized. The depression and the rise of fascist regimes in the 1930s ended four decades of globalization, turned nations inward, and curtailed the movement of capital, commodities, and people between Europe and America. Moreover, it tarnished the image of America as an economic model. As governments sought to cope with the devastating economic crisis, regimes with antithetical politics embraced similar programs; ideological divisions seemed at once sharper and more blurred. And neither the United States nor any single European nation emerged as the dominant transatlantic power.

During and after World War II, which ended Germany's attempt at European hegemony and devastated European economies and polities, the United States displayed a new determination to exert European and world leadership. This new global vision was articulated in 1941, when *Life* magazine publisher Henry Luce wrote an impassioned essay condemning isolationism and promoting an *"American* internationalism." His title, "The American Century," named the aspirations that he and others had for the nation's global mission.[2] While acknowledging that "America cannot be responsible for the good behavior of the entire world," he urged Americans

to accept wholeheartedly our duty and our opportunity as the most powerful and vital nation in the world and in consequence to exert upon the world the full impact of our influence, for such purposes as we see fit and by such means as we see fit.[3]

---

[2] The term was coined by H. G. Wells.
[3] Henry Luce, "The American Century," *Life*, Feb. 7, 1941. Italics in original.

American politicians, pundits, and scholars have readily adopted the label, most proudly endorsing the economic might, military prowess, and cultural influence of the United States, not merely in Europe but also globally. Many in Europe followed suit, albeit with considerably more ambivalence and at times anger. All too often American hegemony is read backward into the late nineteenth century and forward to the present; in deterministic and triumphalist arguments it emerges as the necessary result of America's impressive industrialization or its irresistible mass consumption and mass culture or its political values and virtuous foreign policy, any and all of which destined the United States for European and global leadership

In fact, America's desire for and achievement of hegemony in much of Europe and the globe was the product of two world wars and the Cold War, which divided Europe for four decades and shaped and warped transatlantic political, military, cultural, and ideological interactions. America's mid-century hegemony rested on five pillars. The first was America's economic prowess, embodied in Fordist mass production, technological innovation, unmatched productivity, and high wages that enabled the mass consumption of cars, consumer durables, and mass culture. The second was America's unchallenged military might, conventional and nuclear, and its military presence across Western Europe and around the world. The third was the Cold War domestic consensus on both sides of the Atlantic about anti-communism, containment, and isolation of the Soviet Union but also about Keynesianism and social policies of a much more extensive sort than before the war. The fourth pillar was widespread Western European sympathy and admiration for America's political values, global presence, and popular culture. Finally, there was Western Europe's willingness to be the junior partner in an American empire built largely by invitation in Western Europe but supplemented by American pressure, threats, and covert intervention when necessary.

During the high point of the American Century from the late forties to the early seventies, the United States reshaped the European and global economic order, helped restructure political regimes across Western Europe, and experimented with both containment and rollback toward the Soviet bloc. American businessmen, soldiers, and aid officials, American commodities, movies, music, and high culture flooded into Europe. Never had the American presence and influence been greater, but even at the highpoint of America's preponderance of power, there were significant tensions between the United States and its Western European allies over welfare and warfare, nuclear weapons and economic policies, attitudes toward the Soviet bloc, and relations with the Third World. There were numerous conflicts between the United States and the

Soviet Union both within Europe and outside. Europeans engaged in complex negotiations with American ideas, cultural products, and commodities and created hybrid forms of mass culture and modern living.

From the seventies onward, American influence began to erode. The protest movements of the late 1960s challenged both American hegemony and the Cold War categories central to it, and growing antinuclear movements further contested United States leadership. The multiple economic crises of the 1970s – the gold drain, oil shocks, and the exhaustion of Fordism – weakened America's domination of the global economy. Détente as practiced by the United States and the Soviet Union on the one hand, and European states on the other, took different forms that reflected Western Europe's increasing autonomy. In the eighties the United States and much of Europe grew still further apart, as America, along with Britain, embraced neoliberalism, while continental European states defended many of their social democratic social policies and their particular varieties of more regulated capitalism.

For many Americans the fall of communism represented the longed-for American Cold War victory, the end of a troubled history of challenges to liberalism and capitalism, and the beginning of United States unilateral global dominance. For Europeans the series of events for which 1989 is shorthand were more complex; far from ending history, they opened a new era in which Europe had to redefine its identity and institutions. As America turned away from Europe, Europe intensified its economic and political integration, and European states frequently dissented from American global projects. At home, European countries continued to borrow from America while creating their own distinctive versions of modernity.

The end of the Cold War did not lead to closer United States-European relations due to growing United States attention to non-European areas, the geographic expansion and institutional deepening of the European Union, and transatlantic conflicts over issues such as market fundamentalism, multilateralism, military interventions, and relations with the global South. Despite the pressures of globalization, most European states have not embraced neoliberalism; while their economies are less regulated than before, the European social model has persisted. Far from restoring the American Century in Europe, 1989 slowed but did not stop its decline. European prosperity, economic integration, and cultural vibrancy led Europeans to look increasingly to themselves rather than America to define identities, develop conceptions of the just society, and build versions of the good life.

As this brief sketch suggests, America was a very real presence in Europe, due both to the strengths and appeals of the United States economy and to the internecine wars that weakened and divided

Europe. This presence repeatedly raised the questions of whether Europe became or wanted to become Americanized and what was meant by that elusive term. Americanization as used here refers to the adoption abroad of American forms of production and consumption, technology and techniques of management, political ideas and social policies, high and mass cultural goods and institutions, gender roles and leisure practices. Americanization includes not only what was and was not adopted, but also how such borrowings were selectively appropriated and negotiated, how they functioned and acquired particular meanings. Americanization was (and is) in turn shaped by the images and discourses that present America as a model of economic, social, and cultural development, as one possible, extremely powerful, and appealing model of modernity. Americanization, real or imagined, hoped for or dreaded, was central to European-American relations in the twentieth century. It was what American business and government sought to export and promote; it provided many of the concrete images and practices in and through which Europeans debated modernity in ways that more abstract categories of modernization, rationalization, or secularization did not.

Americanism meant very different things to different European nations, classes, genders, and generations. American ideas, goods, and practices were not imperialistically imposed on a willing or reluctant but always-passive Europe; rather Europeans selectively resisted, adapted, and modified things American. Of equal importance, they recontextualized them within distinctive European state structures and policies, economic institutions, and value systems. Thus, American economic, military, and cultural power did not readily translate into wholesale Americanization. Americanization was most evident in mass consumption and mass culture, more limited in political and intellectual life, and scarcely present in social policy. It was intense in the three decades after World War II, the high point of American power globally and of the presence of things American in Europe. Most Europeans were unconcerned about an Americanization of Europe in the decades before World War I and debated but did not adopt American products and practices extensively in the interwar years. In the last decades of the twentieth century, Europeans have looked more to one another than to the United States to define their identity, culture, and everyday life.

Throughout the twentieth century the flow of ideas, investments, commodities, and people was not simply from west to east, from the new world to the old. Except in the 1930s and first post-1945 decades, Europeans invested in the United States, sold goods there, and often set up production facilities. European films dominated the globe before Hollywood became hegemonic in the twenties. For European migrants in the decades before

World War I and for refugees in the thirties and forties, the United States was the preferred although not the only destination, and many returned to Europe. Europeans in the 1920s and 1950s traveled to America to study the United States economy, but Americans were equally eager to study European history, culture, and social thought, and American tourists have traveled in their millions to enjoy European culture.

Even from 1945 to the mid 1970s, when United States influence in Europe was greatest, Europeans borrowed from and were influenced by one another, not simply by American goods and practices. From the late nineteenth century on, there were complex circuits of exchange, movement, and negotiation among European nations, including across the Iron Curtain during the Cold War. After 1989 Eastern and Western Europe were reknit as Western Europe funded the economic restructuring of former communist states and integrated them into the European Union and NATO. These all contributed to the creation of distinctive European ways of life. Over the course of the twentieth century, Europeans developed alternative fascist, communist, and social democratic versions of modernity that were not simply pale imitations of the American model.

The ways Europeans adopted and adapted things American, in turn, have been shaped by European varieties of capitalism and varieties of socialism. Across the twentieth century, European states developed forms of capitalism that distinguished themselves from the American model in terms of business organization, labor rights, investment strategies, and relations between the state and capitalism. Ironically, the state and economy that looked most like the United States in its organization of production, infatuation with technology, and faith in modernization was the Soviet Union.

Different conceptualizations of the social and of social rights as well as distinctive social policy regimes were integral parts of Europe's distinctive varieties of capitalism and versions of modernity. In the decades before World War I, Europe was the teacher and leader in social thought and practice. Although the transatlantic social policy gap narrowed in the 1930s in response to the depression, it widened again after 1945. Even in the heyday of Keynesianism and the welfare state from the fifties through the seventies, Europe and America differed in the extent and kinds of social rights they recognized and in the place accorded the state in the economy and everyday life. The transatlantic social policy gap widened much more from the 1980s on as the United States and Britain embraced neoliberalism and launched a full-scale assault on social rights and the "nanny state." These different varieties of capitalism and social policy regimes generated disputes between more social democratic Europe and the United States that at times were nearly as intense as the conflicts between communist and capitalist states.

War was as central to shaping and reshaping European-American relations as economics. The fundamentally different experiences of the two world wars in Europe and the United States were central to the crisis and decline of Europe after 1914 just as they were to the rise of America economically and politically. Wars fought on European soil not only destroyed political regimes and devastated economies; they also led to massive death, social and cultural dislocation, and demoralization, while America was spared all of these. After 1945 the experiences and memories of war led Western Europeans to emphasize multilateralism, diplomacy, and international law and the Soviets to fear a renewed major war. The United States, by contrast, defended international institutions and laws, while simultaneously emphasizing American exceptionalism and engaging in unilateral interventions. The lessons learned from the world wars and the lived experience of the Cold War were more similar to one another across Europe than across the Atlantic and led to many of the conflicts about foreign and domestic policies that shaped not only United States relations with the Soviet Union but also with Western Europe. Although war did as much as economics to create American dominance at mid century, by the late twentieth century military spending and controversial military interventions undermined it, as the United States wars in Vietnam, Iraq, and Afghanistan have shown. After 9/11 America has turned away from the post-World War II order that it had been instrumental in establishing and to which most of Europe remains committed.

The transatlantic twentieth century has flexible chronological boundaries. Many historians conceptualize a "short" twentieth century, which begins with World War I and ends with 1989 and whose central dynamic is the struggle among liberalism, fascism, and communism. My "long" twentieth century begins in the 1890s and continues through the first decade of the twenty-first century. It focuses not only on ideological competition and warfare across the Atlantic world but also on the changing character of transatlantic and global capitalism and consumer culture, on competing approaches to social rights and policy, and on shifting forms of empire. By opening with the late nineteenth century rather than World War I, this book captures the multiple contenders for transatlantic and global power in that phase of intensive globalization and suggests how contingent the rise of America and decline of Europe were. Continuing the story past the mid 1970s illustrates the limits of the American Century and the complex transatlantic renegotiations resulting from the erosion of American power and the divergent sociopolitical paths taken on different sides of the Atlantic. The long-twentieth-century approach avoids determinism and false triumphalism.

"Europe" and "America" cry out for definition every bit as much as "the twentieth century" does. America refers to the United States and the two terms are used interchangeably. Although it is politically incorrect to appropriate America for only one nation on the two vast American continents, I have adopted the term because it pervades the discussions and debates on both sides of the North Atlantic from the late nineteenth century on. Europe is more elusive. To begin with, America and Europe are not equivalent entities, for America refers to a politically unified, territorially delimited entity, while Europe denotes an idea, an aspiration, and a contested identity. Its geographic and cultural borders have been and still are shifting and disputed. Sometimes Europe refers to states acting as separate nations, sometimes to post-World War II processes of integration. And even now the European Union and Europe do not completely overlap. So why and how is Europe used here?

Throughout the long twentieth century, Europe featured in discourses about transatlantic relations, assuming great prominence after 1945. European politicians, writers, social reformers, businessmen, and labor leaders spoke for and about both particular national entities and broader continental ones, while Americans imagined a Europe with which they could trade or lend or which they hoped to reform or save, even as they engaged primarily with individual nations. Europe increasingly became an imagined frame of reference used by those living on the continent – and sometimes in Britain as well – to define themselves over and against the United States, just as Americans, particularly at times of conflict, defined themselves as not like Europeans. From the 1970s on Europe has become an increasingly thick and powerful institutional entity with coordinated and interconnected economies, a shared currency, and movement toward political, military, and foreign policy cooperation. These shifting constructions of Europe and America and the gradual emergence of transnational European institutions, practices, and identities are central components of European-American relations.

Europe is also obviously a collection of nation-states and this study defines that collection expansively rather than focusing on the major Western European powers as many works on twentieth-century transatlantic relations do. It is time to overcome the long-standing Euro-American ambivalence about whether Russia/the Soviet Union was and is part of Europe. It is time to abandon the Cold War geographic imaginary that divided Europe firmly in half with Soviet specialists studying the East and students of transatlantic relations looking only at Western Europe. America had long-standing interests and exchanges of all sorts with the East as well as the West, and Europeans east and west borrowed and learned from one another, even during the most frigid decades of the

Cold War. Russia/Soviet Union has long been a Eurasian power (just as the United States is both an Atlantic and a Pacific one), but it looked west and engaged with Europe and America as part of the West rather than as an outsider offering a complete alternative to it. The Soviet Union was particularly fascinated with economic Americanism and borrowed from America and collaborated with Americans as well as competing with the United States. It is thus necessary to reconstruct the complex circuits in Eastern and Western Europe and across the Atlantic along which capital, commodities, cultural borrowings, social policy discussions, and memories of war moved.

Relations and exchanges between the United States and various European states always involved competing visions not only of how to order domestic economies and polities and transatlantic relations but also of the global order. The changing forms and fortunes of empire have been as important to shaping transatlantic relations as has the ebb and flow of globalization. From the 1890s on the United States, like many European countries, had become an imperial power, even if America then, as later, disliked the concept while nonetheless seeking political and economic influence abroad. But various European states and America had different kinds of empires, ranging from Western European colonial empires in the late nineteenth and first half of the twentieth centuries to the new empires of Nazi Germany and Japan in the thirties and forties to America's post-1945 empire of bases and free trade. In the increasingly global twentieth century, Europeans and Americans never gazed only across the Atlantic, and transatlantic relations were triangulated and complicated by competition and conflicts in the Middle East, Asia, and Africa.

A decade into the new millennium, the future of the transatlantic century is uncertain. A multipolar global order has replaced the bipolarity of the Cold War decades and the unipolar moment of the 1990s. The North Atlantic no longer contains all the global players, nor is it central to all networks and exchanges. The United States enjoys military dominance, but that is no longer bolstered by economic and cultural hegemony, and it does not guarantee success in America's numerous limited wars. Of equal importance, the severe financial crises and deep recession that began in 2008 threaten economies on both sides of the Atlantic and, many believe, may threaten the European Union itself. This has exacerbated transatlantic disagreements about economic policy, cultural norms, and military interventions abroad. The transatlantic market gap, God gap, and war gap continue to contribute to a widening Atlantic. For neither Europe nor the United States will the twenty-first century be transatlantic as the twentieth was.

1   An uncertain balance, 1890–1914

In the decades before World War I transatlantic relations were paramount neither for the United States nor for states across Europe. The world was multipolar and rapidly globalizing. Britain remained the dominant economic and colonial power. While exchanges of goods, capital, ideas, and people across the Atlantic were increasing rapidly, for both Europe and the United States, the North Atlantic world was just one arena of economic and political interest and interaction, and transatlantic relations were often triangulated through imperial concerns in Asia, Latin America, and Africa. The American Century had not yet begun. But was it visible on the horizon?

Many historians view the twentieth-century rise of the United States as preordained due to America's economic might, geography, or purported political and cultural exceptionalism. Likewise, the end of European hegemony appears predictable due to imperial overreach, nation-state rivalries, and less robust economies. In the decades before World War I, however, the new world did not dominate the old, and the United States was a nation among nations. It was unclear how the transatlantic balance of economic, political, and cultural power would evolve.

A survey of the varied interactions and exchanges across the Atlantic suggests that America's industrial might was growing exponentially, but Germany offered stiff competition and Britain dominated global trade, investment, and finance. The United States was not yet the locus of unrivaled prosperity and consumption that it would later become. Americans and Europeans were increasingly involved in networks of intellectual and cultural exchange, but Europe played the leading role, and most Europeans did not view America as an economic, cultural, or political model. The prewar world was one of empires, continental and colonial, and the United States was very much a part of this wave of imperialism. Yet, militarily it remained insignificant.

The global economy

The turn of the century witnessed extraordinary economic growth, technological progress, and an expansion of foreign trade and investment and labor migration that laid the groundwork for twentieth-century economic life. These sweeping changes raise three questions about European-American economic relations. Did the United States emerge as the global economic hegemon in these years? Did the capitalist economies on both sides of the Atlantic increasingly resemble one another, or did they display distinctive characteristics? Did European politicians, businessmen, and labor leaders envy, fear, or seek to emulate the American economic model? Let us begin with the abundant data on national economies and transnational economic connections that suggest a complex global economy in which the United States was a key player but by no means the undisputed leader.

European and American economies, whether large or small, substantially industrialized or barely so, were part of a British-dominated global capitalist order in which Europe and America occupied a privileged place. They were the core or, in the case of less developed European states such as Spain or Greece, the semi-periphery, and enjoyed much greater wealth and economic power than the colonial and neocolonial economies of Latin America, Asia, and Africa. In 1880 the leading industrial powers, Britain, the United States, Germany, France, Russia, and Italy produced over three-fifths of world manufacturing output; by 1913 that had risen to over three-quarters. Trade and population reveal similar imbalances as Table 1.1 shows. In 1870 the average Gross Domestic Product (GDP) per capita for Europe, the United States, Canada, Australia, and New Zealand was roughly three times that of the rest of the world; by 1914 it was over four times greater. Urbanization accompanied industrialization and by 1900 Europe had six cities with over a million people and North America had three, while Latin America and Asia had only two each.[1]

Europe and America shared many institutions and policies, for international agreements on everything from postal services and underwater cables to railroads and the law of the sea regulated the global economy. Each nation followed the economic progress of others through the mass press, travel, and migration as well as the widely attended and well-publicized international exhibitions in Paris in 1889 and 1900, Chicago

---

[1] Paul Kennedy, *The Rise and Fall of the Great Powers* (New York: Vintage, 1987), 202. Alice Amsden, *The Rise of the Rest: Challenges to the West from Late-Industrializing Economies* (Oxford University Press, 2001), 9. Geoffrey Barraclough, *Introduction to Contemporary History* (Baltimore: Penguin, 1967), 89.

Table 1.1 *Percentage world trade and population, 1914*

World exports and imports		Population
Europe	58	25 (32 with Russia included)
United States and Canada	14	5

Rondo Cameron, *A Concise Economic History of the World* (Oxford University Press, 1993), 324, 340.

in 1893, and St. Louis in 1904. States across Europe and the Americas followed Britain's lead and abandoned bimetallism or the use of both gold and silver to back currencies in favor of the gold standard. This international monetary system, in which British sterling was the central currency, required governments to back their dollars or marks or francs with gold, maintain stable exchange rates, protect property, and at least partially open their economies. An additional prerequisite for currency stability among major powers was an active colonial policy. The gold standard facilitated international trade and investment but prevented states from using fiscal and monetary policy to promote social welfare or respond to economic crises. Although American populists and others protested against the social costs of the gold standard, governments and business considered stability more important. The gold standard and efforts to replace it were to trouble transatlantic relations throughout the twentieth century.

The Great Depression of 1873–96 brought financial crises, slower growth, diminished investment, falling prices, rising unemployment, and heightened economic anxiety on both sides of the Atlantic. It also encouraged similar responses – economic concentration, protectionism, and imperialism. While small and medium-sized firms persisted and prospered, new large-scale, horizontally and vertically integrated firms emerged. Capitalists also sought monopolies and formed trusts in America and cartels in Germany that concentrated vast economic resources, coordinated production and prices, and exerted significant political influence. United States Steel, Standard Oil, Krupp, Siemens, General Electric (GE), the Tobacco Trust, and the handful of large German investment banks embodied this trend. In the United States, Belgium, France, Germany, Russia, and Italy statesmen, bankers, and industrialists encouraged trade and investment abroad as well as formal colonization or informal economic intervention. While Britain retained free trade at home, although not in its colonies, continental Europe and the United States imposed barriers. By 1914 tariffs on industrial goods averaged

4 percent in Holland, 13 percent in Germany, 18 percent in Italy, 20 percent in France and Sweden, and reached a high of 32 percent in the United States and 38 percent in Russia. Agrarian tariffs were particularly high in Germany, France, Austria-Hungary, and Italy.[2]

Despite tariffs and colonial expansion, capital, labor, primary products, and manufactured goods moved in much greater quantities and with many fewer restrictions than previously. The causes were diverse. Railroad building, the advent of steamships, and the opening of the Suez Canal in 1869 and the Panama Canal in 1914 dramatically reduced transportation costs. International lending, expanded foreign investment, and offshore production promoted global economic integration. Millions of European and Asian workers and peasants migrated overseas or within Europe.

This was not the first age of globalization, but it did represent a break from earlier forms of multi-centered "archaic globalization," to employ Chris Bayly's term, which were built around universalizing kingship or cosmic religion. Modern globalization was centered on North Atlantic nation-states and empires and linked through economic exchanges and networks. It was a product of the turn-of-the-century political and economic conjuncture and retreated when that collapsed. From the 1890s until World War I, however, the global economy experienced "a high point of international economic integration" and came closer to establishing free markets in goods, labor, and capital than it would for another hundred years. The United States was every bit as involved in this moment of globalization as were such European countries as Britain, Germany, Sweden, and Russia. But different national economies were situated differently in this increasingly interconnected and interdependent global economy.[3]

Transatlantic differences

Historical statistics on growth rates, productivity, and wages are difficult to calculate and compare, but available data show enormous differentiation among European countries (not to mention within them). They also reveal the strength and limits of the American economic challenge to Europe. GDP per capita provides one useful measure as Table 1.2 shows. Britain, which had dominated the global economy unchallenged in the mid

---

[2] Sidney Pollard, *Peaceful Conquest: The Industrialization of Europe, 1760–1970* (Oxford University Press, 1981), 258. Angus Maddison, *The World Economy in the 20th Century* (Paris: OECD Development Centre, 1989), 47.

[3] C. A. Bayly, *The Birth of the Modern World, 1780–1914* (Oxford: Blackwell, 2004), 42. Jeffry A. Frieden, *Global Capitalism: Its Fall and Rise in the Twentieth Century* (New York: Norton, 2006), 16.

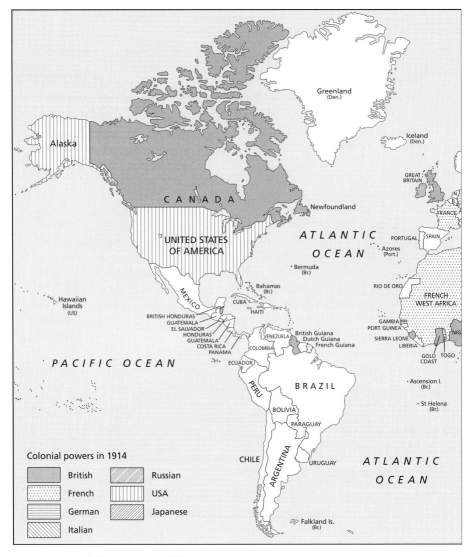

Map 1 The world in 1914

nineteenth century, lost it lead to America but held its own, and Germany made substantial progress. From 1900 on the small economies of Belgium, the Netherlands, and Switzerland ranked higher than Germany, France, Austria, and Sweden, while Russia along with Japan occupied the distant last places among industrializing countries.

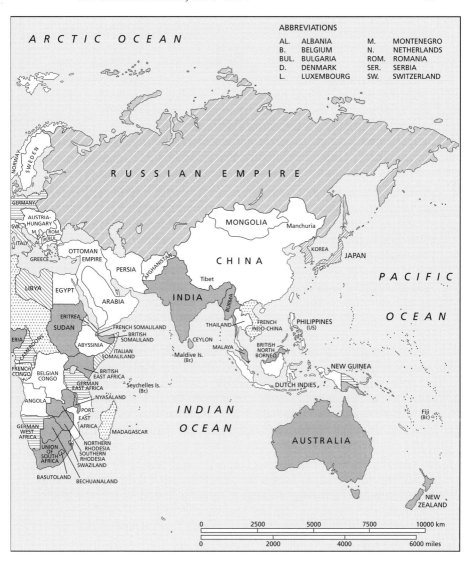

ABBREVIATIONS

AL.	ALBANIA	M.	MONTENEGRO
B.	BELGIUM	N.	NETHERLANDS
BUL.	BULGARIA	ROM.	ROMANIA
D.	DENMARK	SER.	SERBIA
L.	LUXEMBOURG	SW.	SWITZERLAND

In terms of absolute size, the American economy surged ahead; by 1913 United States GDP was more than twice that of Britain or Russia, and three and half times larger than that of France or Germany, foreshadowing the shape of the twentieth-century economic order. Moreover, labor productivity, measured in terms of GDP per hour worked, was higher in

Table 1.2 *GDP per capita at 1970 United States prices*

	1870	1913
United States	$764	$1813
Britain	$972	$1491
Germany	$535	$1073

Alfred D. Chandler, Jr., *Scale and Scope: The Dynamics of Industrial Capitalism* (Cambridge, MA: Harvard University Press, 1990), 52.

the United States than anywhere except Australia, and the gap between the United States and Western Europe was widening.[4]

Growth rates tell a similar story. Between 1900 and 1913 American GDP per capita grew at an average rate of 2 percent per annum; only Denmark and Italy equaled that, while Germany and Russia's growth rate was 1.6 percent and Great Britain's only 0.7 percent. In absolute terms America's GDP grew at 4 percent annually, while rates for the top three European nations – Russia, Denmark and Germany – were in the 3–3.5 percent range. This was far more robust growth than Britain's 1.5 percent or France's 1.7 percent. In both absolute and per capita terms, however, the highest growth rates were in Canada and Argentina.[5] If GDP data suggest impressive United States economic development, they also indicate the rapid transformation of multiple European economies, large and small, a European as well as a transatlantic challenge to Britain's industrial prominence, and the emergence of rapidly developing economies in Canada, Australia, Japan, and parts of Latin America. And size alone did not answer the question of whether the United States could or wanted to translate economic might into global political leadership.

Manufacturing data reinforce the picture of Britain's loss of dominance to America and Germany as Table 1.3 shows. In 1880 it was the leading producer of iron and steel; by 1890 the United States was producing more iron and by 1910 four times as much steel, while Germany made nearly twice as much. America was the world's premier industrial producer by 1913, but it was not in a league by itself. The major industrial powers of Europe still accounted for nearly 50 percent of the world's total. At that time, however, few inside or outside Europe thought in terms of European as opposed to national aggregates.

---

[4] Alfred E. Eckes and Thomas W. Zeiler, *Globalization and the American Century* (Cambridge University Press, 2003), 161.
[5] Maddison, *World Economy*, 35–36.

Table 1.3 *Distribution of world's industrial production in %*

	1880	1900	1913
Britain	2.9	18.5	3.6
United States	14.7	23.6	32.0
Germany	8.5	13.2	14.8
France	7.8	6.8	6.1
Russia	7.6	8.8	8.2
Austria-Hungary	4.4	4.7	4.4
Italy	2.5	2.5	2.4
Japan	–	–	1.0

Paul Kennedy, *The Rise and Fall of the Great Powers* (New York: Vintage, 1989), 202. Alfred D. Chandler, *Scale and Scope: The Dynamics of Industrial Capitalism* (Cambridge, MA: Harvard University Press, 1990), 4.

Outside of the industrial sector, the picture is more complex. The decline of Britain was only relative, for between 1870 and 1913 the British economy doubled in size and grew by 50 percent per capita. With the world's largest merchant fleet and a far-flung empire Britain continued to be the world's shipper, carrying one-third of American imports and two-thirds of American exports at the turn of the century. Of greater importance it was the world's banker. By 1910 British banks had 5,000 branches and affiliates around the globe, while France had a mere 140 and Germany and the Netherlands half that number. It was also the world's primary insurance agent, despite the movement of major American insurance companies abroad from the 1890s on. Britain still dominated global trade, for although its share fell from 23 percent in 1880 to 16 percent in 1913, America's share increased only from 10 percent to 11 percent and Germany's from 10 percent to 12 percent. British exports per capita remained well ahead of France, Germany, and the United States, although by 1913 Britain had ceded first place to Argentina.[6]

Information on incomes is scarcer and more difficult to interpret. In 1914 per capita income in the industrialized core, measured in current dollars, ranged from $377 in the United States, through $244 and $184 for Britain and Germany to $57 for Austria-Hungary and $41 for Russia. These figures hid enormous differences among regions, between urban

---

[6] Frieden, *Global Capitalism*, 107. Fred McKenzie, *The American Invaders* (New York: Arno, 1976), 33. Michel Beaud, *A History of Capitalism, 1500–2000* (New York: Monthly Review, 2001), 143–44, 159.

and rural areas, and between classes, races, ethnic groups, and genders. White industrial workers in the United States undoubtedly received higher wages and enjoyed a better standard of living, but European observers disagreed about whether the transatlantic gap was widening or narrowing. In his 1906 study, *Why Is There No Socialism in the United States?* Werner Sombart, a leading German economic historian and sociologist, emphasized the higher standard of living of American workers, concluding "All Socialist utopias came to nothing on roast beef and apple pie." Even he, however, saw a marked division between rich and poor. Writing at the same time, the English writer H. G. Wells noted how prosperous American workers seemed, but nonetheless believed that the income and wealth differentials were growing within the United States and might indicate the Europeanization of America. Some historians argue that persistent labor shortages in the United States kept wages higher and enabled more consumption; others see Europe as having become more like America, arguing that commodity market integration and migration promoted a convergence of real wages between the core Western European countries and Scandinavia on the one hand and the United States on the other hand. British real wages rose from one-quarter of United States ones in 1851 to nearly three-fifths in 1913, for example. Eastern and Southern Europe were excluded from these trends, however, and both this convergence and the globalizing forces that promoted it were to be reversed in the interwar years.[7]

Differences among European economies were greater than those between the most developed core European nations and the United States. Britain had nearly as much reason to worry about German competition and pressure from other European countries in foreign markets as about the United States. Although commodities, capital, and labor traveled back and forth across the Atlantic, different varieties of capitalism were emerging in Europe and America.

Varieties of capitalism

In the decades before World War I all transatlantic economies were influenced by the second industrial revolution in which steel, chemicals, and the electrical industries emerged, oil began to challenge coal as the

---

[7] Kennedy, *Rise and Fall of the Great Powers*, 243. Werner Sombart, *Why Is There No Socialism in the United States?* (White Plains: International Arts and Sciences Press, 1976), 106. H. G. Wells, *The Future in America: A Search after Realities* (New York: St. Martin's Press, 1987), 60–62. Kevin O'Rourke and Jeffrey G. Williamson, *Globalization and History: The Evolution of a Nineteenth-Century Atlantic Economy* (Cambridge, MA: MIT, 1999), 21.

principal power source, and science became more closely linked to technological innovation. Yet, national economies developed different production profiles, investment strategies, marketing, and relations among business, the state, and labor. New forms of integrated mass production and the first assembly lines emerged, but less technologically advanced factories, craft production, small manufacturing shops, and homework continued to thrive not only in less industrialized countries like Russia, Spain, and Italy, but also in Britain, Germany, and the United States. New economic forces interacted with very different states and national economies at very different levels of development. The resulting distinctive varieties of capitalism were to persist throughout the twentieth century.

The timing of a country's industrialization determined some of these differences. Britain industrialized first and alone between 1780 and 1840, the United States in the early and mid nineteenth century, Germany between 1850 and 1870, France more slowly over the course of the nineteenth century, and the Scandinavian countries from the 1890s on. Italy and Russia, along with the Austrian half of the Austro-Hungarian monarchy, had more partial industrial revolutions in the two decades before World War I, while the Iberian Peninsula and the Balkans showed barely any signs of development. Textiles and railroads dominated early industrialization, thereafter iron, steel, and machine making, and at century's end electrical equipment and petrochemicals. Britain excelled at the first two but failed to make the transition to the new industries of the second industrial revolution, whereas the United States performed outstandingly at each stage. Some later industrializers like Germany pioneered newer industries, while others like Italy or Russia mixed textiles and basic heavy industry.

Different starting points led to distinctive class structures and employment patterns. By 1913, 44 percent of Britain's population was employed in manufacturing and mining and a comparable proportion was in the service sector. The United States with extensive agricultural employment had just under 30 percent in manufacturing and just over 42 percent in service. Two-fifths of Germans worked in manufacturing and mining but one-third remained in agriculture, while in France the figures were reversed. Russia had pockets of modern industry but remained overwhelmingly agrarian, as did Italy, where industrialization was concentrated in the north.[8]

Capitalism was organized and managed quite differently across the transatlantic world. There was a general tendency for firms to become

---

[8] Angus Maddison, *Monitoring the World Economy, 1892–1992* (Paris: OECD Development Centre, 1995), 39.

larger and more hierarchical and use technology and new managerial practices, such as Taylorism with its time and motion studies, to control the labor process. These transformations proceeded fastest in the United States and among some late industrializers, while Germany displayed a diversity of firms and managerial styles, France retained a plethora of smaller, less mechanized firms, and Britain had fewer technologically integrated plants and left more control in workers' hands. Family firms prevailed in some countries but corporate firms came to dominate in others, especially the United States and Germany. European capitalism, especially in Germany, was more organized than its American counterpart; in addition to cartels, industrialists formed associations to regulate production, manage marketing, resist unions, and bargain with the state. American capitalists were more individualistic, the American populace and state less tolerant of trusts. As the costs of industrial development escalated greatly due to technological and organizational advances, new mechanisms for financing industrialization – investment banks, the stock market, international lending and foreign direct investment – emerged. States promoted economic development, protected national economic interests abroad, and regulated labor, but to markedly different degrees.

In his seminal essay, "Economic Backwardness in Historical Perspective," Alexander Gerschenkron argued persuasively that precisely because nations that industrialized after Britain were in every respect less developed and started when costs were higher, they could not imitate Britain's laissez-faire approach. Rather they needed to mobilize capital, create a labor force, and build an infrastructure by other than small-scale and private means. Investment banks played key roles in France and Germany, while the state dominated in countries like Russia. Mobilizing ideologies of industrial development, ranging from Saint Simonianism through Marxism, were necessary to overcome obstacles. The resulting configurations of state, finance, and industry were distinctive and set these countries down a path of development on which they remained.[9]

If backwardness carried disadvantages, it also enabled later industrializers to skip stages and adopt the most modern technologies and organizational forms. Germany did this most advantageously, Russia and Italy more partially and disruptively. While the Scandinavian periphery of Europe successfully industrialized before 1914, the Balkans, Spain, and Portugal failed to, even though the northern and southern peripheries of Europe shared residues of feudalism and serfdom, poor transportation, a lack of resources, and low levels of urbanization. A different agrarian

---

[9] Alexander Gerschenkron, *Economic Backwardness in Historical Perspective*, (Cambridge, MA: Belknap Press, 1962), 5–30.

structure, a better education system, better transportation opportunities, and Protestantism all contributed to Scandinavian success.

Being the first to industrialize was no guarantee of lasting success, as Britain learned. But why were the United States and Germany able to surge ahead? Alfred Chandler argues that America excelled because United States entrepreneurs invested in production facilities to get economies of scope and scale, transformed marketing and distribution, and recruited and organized managers effectively. By World War I America came to embody "competitive managerial capitalism" that enabled United States businesses to integrate horizontally and vertically, expand geographically, and produce new goods. By contrast British firms retained "personal capitalism," while German ones adopted some American organizational forms and production technologies but retained a "co-operative managerial model." Only the American model of capitalism promised success.[10] Others, however, insist that a variety of managerial styles, technologies and production processes, and marketing strategies was economically rational and profitable.

These distinctive varieties of capitalism were rooted in different political and social orders and values. Europe was less democratic and more hierarchical, its elites claimed and received more deference, and its states were more developed and regulatory. America, by contrast, was more democratic and egalitarian (at least among whites), and its elites lacked an organic relationship to the diverse immigrant population. The result was popular anti-elitism and anti-statism that led to minimal economic regulation and social policy. Before World War I it was not clear whether the American variety of capitalism was destined to triumph over its European counterparts or whether there were several viable roads to economic prosperity that entailed different logics and embodied different social values. Debates about these issues were to haunt European-American relations throughout the long twentieth century. So too was the closely related question of consumption.

Consumption new and old

The path-breaking achievements and distinctive characteristics of American mass consumption have been analyzed in celebratory tones in recent works with titles such as *An All-Consuming Century, The Consumers' Republic, Sold American,* and *Irresistible Empire: America's Advance through Twentieth-Century Europe.* Viewed from the middle of

---

[10] Alfred D. Chandler, *Scale and Scope: The Dynamics of Industrial Capitalism* (Cambridge, MA: Harvard University Press, 1990), 21–40, 235–36, 393–95.

the twentieth century, European perspective of three decades of depression, wars, and genocide, American consumer capitalism seemed distinctive and enviable, but the midcentury transatlantic consumption gap cannot be read back into the late nineteenth century.

Industrialization, urbanization, rising real incomes, and expanding trade transformed consumption in the decades before World War I. New goods abounded. Homemade food and clothes gave way to store-bought goods. People moved around by mechanized public transportation, bicycle, and after the turn of the century, car as well. The telegraph, the telephone, mass newspapers, nickelodeons, and silent films sped communication and expanded entertainment. The sewing machine, the typewriter, and the harvester transformed homes, offices, and farms across America and Europe. The elevator and the electric light made their debut, as did synthetic fibers and plastic, although these would spread most rapidly in the interwar years and after 1945.

Americans consumed more goods and prided themselves on so doing, but Europeans in urban and industrial areas did not live in a radically different culture of consumption. Los Angeles, for example, had the most phones per capita, but eight of the top fourteen cities were European, including Stockholm and St. Petersburg. Europe consumed over 57 percent of the world's newsprint in the 1880s, North America only 37 percent. Consumers on both sides of the Atlantic enjoyed the rapidly expanding global output of tropical goods like tea, cocoa and coffee, sugar and bananas, rubber and cotton as well as a variety of oils. America did far surpass Europe in one area – automobiles. In 1913 Great Britain had 106,000 cars, France 91,000, Germany 61,000, and Italy 22,000, while the United States had 1,190,000.[11]

Automobiles were a harbinger of the new form of American mass production and mass consumption that after World War I would catapult America far ahead of Europe and enable rural as well as urban households and all classes, but not all races, to purchase a new array of consumer durables, including refrigerators, washing machines, vacuum cleaners, radios, and cars. Before 1914, however, class shaped consumption patterns more than nationality. Middle-class consumption on both sides of the Atlantic bore many resemblances, in part because middle-class Europeans and Americans traveled, read about other countries, and emulated the styles, cuisines, and furniture they encountered. Working-class consumption was very sensitive to income, but everywhere mixed necessities with as much fashion and entertainment as possible.

[11] Eric Hobsbawm, *Age of Empire* (New York: Vintage, 1989), 346–48. Maddison, *World Economy*, 72.

Everywhere men had more discretionary income and consumption pos-
sibilities than women. Rural dwellers, especially in Eastern and Southern
Europe and the American South, lacked money and access to most of
these new goods, but sewing machines were sold surprisingly widely.
    Goods were marketed in similar ways on both sides of the Atlantic.
Department stores spread across Europe and the United States, with
European ones modeling themselves on the pioneering Parisian Bon
Marche. Sears and Roebuck was the largest and most famous catalogue
company, but the Parisian Bon Marche sent out 1.5 million catalogues in
1894, for example, and even Moscow's Muir and Mirrielees department
store had a mail-order business. The United States pioneered one-price
stores like Woolworth's Five and Dime, but they found few imitators in
prewar Europe. New forms of marketing drew public attention, yet the
traditional small store, where goods were displayed behind the counter
and purchases were negotiated with the owner or employee, continued to
dominate. Their position was weakest in the United States, but what
Victoria de Grazia has called the "Fordist mode of distribution," in
which mass-produced and widely advertised goods are sold in self-service
stores, would not fully triumph there until the interwar years.[12]

People and money in motion

Commodities and capital, labor and technology, management practices
and marketing techniques moved in multiple circuits within Europe,
across the Atlantic, and in varied directions around the globe. Fully
formed national economies did not venture out into the world, transforming what they encountered but remaining untouched themselves;
rather, they were constituted by these global encounters. How did people,
goods, and capital create European-American connections?
    Between 1820 and 1918 approximately 60 million Europeans crossed
the Atlantic. During the 1880s and 1890s, on average 600,000 migrated
each year, after 1900 over a million annually.[13] Some fled poverty, others
political or religious persecution; some came in families, others alone. In
the standard narrative, the United States was the preferred destination for
migrants who came first from Western and Northern Europe, then from
the East and South, above all the Russian Empire and Italy, and who

---

[12] Victoria de Grazia, "Changing Consumption Regimes in Europe, 1930–1979: Comparative
Perspectives on the Distribution Problem," in Susan Strasser, Charles McGovern, and
Matthias Judt, eds., *Getting and Spending: European and American Consumer Societies in the
Twentieth Century* (Cambridge University Press, 1998), 59.
[13] O'Rourke and Williamson, *Globalization and History*, 119–20.

stayed and assimilated, albeit at differential rates. Immigration and high rates of geographic mobility were key to building a robust national economy and distinguished America from Europe.

Recent works on global migration complicate this story. Over 30 percent of European migrants returned between the 1890s and the early 1920s. Italians were most likely to, the Irish and Jews from the Russian Empire least so. Although migrants moved in search of better jobs and wages, they did not necessarily want to become modern and urban; many migrated abroad temporarily in order to maintain their family and future in more traditional European agrarian regions. Although over two-thirds of European migrants went to the United States, many others chose Latin American destinations, and Canada had sizable foreign communities.[14]

Europeans also moved en masse within Europe. Between 1876 and 1914, for example, 44 percent of Italian migrants moved within Europe, while only 31 percent went to North America and 24 percent to South America.[15] England, the Netherlands, Belgium, France, lower Austria, Bohemia, Switzerland, and above all the western and central parts of Germany attracted labor from Eastern and Southern Europe. Britain and Germany also continued to export labor, although France did not. In Austria-Hungary, Slovaks, Poles, Serbians, Czechs, and Romanians went to Vienna, Prague, or Budapest rather than abroad. Ruhr towns were filled with Poles and Mazurians as well as German rural migrants, and Paris attracted Poles, Russians, Jews from Eastern Europe, and German and Italian workers as well as large numbers of migrants from within France. Most non-national migrants eventually returned home. Europe thus had highly mobile, multiethnic cities and proletariats, just as the United States, Canada, and parts of Latin America did. The pressures for and possibilities of assimilation were, however, significantly less.

Capital moved as freely as labor and in multiple directions. The United States had not made loans to foreign governments in the early and mid-nineteenth century and was not a major player in the turn-of-the-century upsurge in foreign direct and portfolio investment. Britain continued to be the global hegemon, accounting for 43 percent of the world's total foreign investments in 1914. French investors were responsible for another 20 percent, Germans for 13 percent, and the Swiss, Dutch, and Belgians combined for another 12 percent, while the United States held only 7 percent. Although the United States began exporting capital after

---

[14] Dirk Hoerder, *Cultures in Contact: World Migrations in the Second Millennium* (Durham: Duke University Press, 2002), 347.
[15] Donna Gabaccia, *Italy's Many Diasporas* (Seattle: University of Washington Press, 2000), 68.

1900, it borrowed much more than it lent or invested and remained, along with Russia, Canada, China, and the Ottoman Empire, among the major debtor nations until World War I.[16]

Global foreign investment went primarily to industrialized and indus-trializing countries, with Europe absorbing over one-fourth and North America just under one-fourth, while Latin America got nearly one-fifth. Foreign investment made Europe more Europeanized and Central America subordinate to the United States, while colonies were monopo-lized by their metropoles, which by and large failed to invest heavily in them. Investment across the Atlantic remained predominantly a one-way British venture. On the eve of World War I, for example, 37 percent of British foreign investment went to its white-settler colonies, 21 percent to the United States, and 9 percent to India, while only 5 percent went to continental Europe. Britain accounted for three-fifths of the foreign investment in the United States. The United States put 20 percent of its foreign investment into Europe, but that amounted to only one-seventh of what Britain invested in the United States. Although roughly one-third of German foreign investments were in the United States and Canada with small amounts in South America, most went to Austria-Hungary, the Balkans, and Russia. Belgian and Dutch foreign invest-ments followed a similar pattern. France invested very little in North America, focusing instead on Russia and Mediterranean countries. The increasing United States foreign investment after 1900 went primarily to the Western Hemisphere, but British investments still exceeded American ones except in Mexico, Cuba, and Central America.[17] In terms of investment, the world was not becoming Americanized, as some alarmist commentators feared. If we turn from foreign investment to trade, however, the picture shifts.

An American empire of commodities

World trade grew rapidly from the 1870s on. While Britain's share declined from its mid-nineteenth-century high point, the centrality of Britain and Germany to foreign trade and that trade to their economy is

---

[16] Rondo Cameron, *A Concise Economic History of the World* (Oxford University Press, 1993), 287–90. Karl Erich Born, *International Banking in the 19th and 20th Centuries* (New York: St. Martin's Press, 1983), 134–35.

[17] Cameron, *Concise Economic History*, 288–90. Eckes and Zeiler, *Globalization*, 22. Born, *International Banking*, 117–18. Mira Wilkins, *The Emergence of Multinational Enterprises: American Business Abroad from the Colonial Era to 1914* (Cambridge, MA: Harvard University Press, 1970), 110, 201. Raymond F. Mikesell, *United States Private and Government Investment Abroad* (Eugene: University of Oregon Books, 1962), 24.

Table 1.4 *1913 world trade*

	share of global exports in manufactured goods as %	foreign trade as % GDP
Britain	30.2	17.7
France	12.1	8.2
United States	13.0	3.7
Germany	26.6	15.6

Michel Beaud, *A History of Capitalism, 1500–2000* (New York: Monthly Review, 2001), 175. Alfred E. Eckes and Thomas W. Zeiler, *Globalization and the American Century* (Cambridge University Press, 2003), 18.

clear in Table 1.4. So too is America's more modest role. Yet, from 1873 to 1913, American exports to Europe increased from $346 million to nearly $1.5 billion in 1913 prices, and their composition changed dramatically. In the 1870s over four-fifths of American exports to Europe were raw materials, mainly cotton, and crude and manufactured foodstuffs. Thereafter cotton remained the single largest export, but food declined due to tariff restrictions and Europe's growing reliance on imports from Russia, Canada, Argentina, New Zealand, and Australia. Americans increasingly exported semi-manufactured and finished manufactured goods (excluding foodstuffs). By 1913–14, 40 percent of the machinery Europe imported came from the United States.[18] Although raw materials continued to account for two-thirds of American exports to Europe, European observers were struck by the visible presence of American manufactured goods from London to Moscow. Was this, as some feared, an American commercial invasion?

All major American corporations began selling abroad in the late nineteenth and early twentieth centuries, and Canada and Europe were their preferred markets. Initially commercial agents sold American commodities, but firms soon set up their own sales offices, usually in London first, then on the continent. The three big insurance companies, New York Life, Mutual, and Equitable, followed this pattern. Manufacturing firms often moved from sales outlets to production facilities in an effort to circumvent legal restrictions and tariff barriers or to cut costs and be closer to markets. Between 1890 and 1914 thirty-seven American firms

[18] Matthew Simon and David E. Novack, "Some Dimensions of the American Commercial Invasion of Europe, 1871–1914: An Introductory Essay," *Journal of Economic History* 24/4 (Dec. 1964): 593, 599–603. Mary Lock Eysenbach, *American Manufactured Exports, 1879–1914: A Study of Growth and Comparative Advantage* (New York: Arno, 1976), 208–9.

bought or built plants in at least one European country (all but one of these firms had plants in Canada as well, but only six had factories in Central or South America). There were twenty-two American plants in Britain alone and fourteen in Germany. Most were machinery firms such as Singer, International Harvester, American Radiator, Gillette, International Steam Pump, and Westinghouse, but there were three food processors, Coca-Cola, Quaker Oats, and Heinz, and two pharmaceutical firms. Foreign sales and production proved extremely profitable for Singer, International Harvester, New York Life, and Standard Oil, but not for many others. Nonetheless, as the pioneering work on American multinationals concluded, "foreign business was *not* peripheral in terms of the aspirations of the nation's key industrial leaders."[19]

Singer Sewing Machines was the first and most famous American company to move into Europe, beginning in the 1850s. From the 1880s Singer produced its machines via what was known as the "American system," that is mass production with interchangeable parts, and marketed them aggressively throughout Europe, especially to women and working-class families. By 1906 Singer had 754 shops that sold machines and taught buyers how to use them in Russia, over 600 each in Germany and Britain, over 200 each in France, and Italy, and a few dozen in smaller countries like Belgium and Sweden. In each European country a small army of sales agents went door to door, plying their wares and collecting installment payments. By World War I Singer supplied 60 percent of the American market and 90 percent of the foreign one, much of which was in Europe. Singer established a major factory in Glasgow in the mid 1880s that employed over 10,000 by 1911; other factories followed in Russia and Germany. German sewing machine manufacturers such as Ludwig Loewe tried unsuccessfully to pressure the government to restrict Singer, which dominated the German market, and then tried to compete against Singer in Russia. Singer continued to dominate the Russia market, however, and its sales rose from 68,788 in 1895 to 678,986 in 1914.[20]

American firms penetrated European farms just as they did households. McCormick Reaper moved into Europe tentatively in the 1870s and aggressively thereafter, focusing on both areas with large-scale grain agriculture similar to the American Great Plains, and those with more diversified farming. By 1902 International Harvester, formed by a merger of

[19] Wilkins, *Emergence of Multinational Enterprises*, 64, 67, 101, 212–13. Quote 207, italics in original. Chandler, *Scale and Scope*, 160.
[20] Mona Domosh, *American Commodities in an Age of Empire* (New York: Routledge, 2006), 24, 32, 36. Wilkins, *Emergence of Multinational Enterprises*, 37–43. Robert Bruce Davies, *Peacefully Working to Conquer the World: Singer Sewing Machines in Foreign Markets, 1854–1920* (New York: Arno, 1976), 161.

McCormick and its main competitors, had sales offices in England, Russia, the Netherlands, Italy, Germany, Switzerland, Finland, Norway, France, Greece, Portugal, and Romania as well as in South Africa, India, Australia, Argentina, and Uruguay. By 1901 there were over 11,000 McCormick machines in use in Russia. Between 1905 and 1910 International Harvester built plants in Sweden, France, Germany, and Russia, and by 1914 nearly half of its sales came from overseas.[21]

Three other American firms had a major presence in Europe. Standard Oil became synonymous with America's power in the increasingly important world oil industry. It transported, refined, and marketed oil across Europe and had ties to foreign subsidiaries in Britain and Germany. The United States was far from the sole power in the diverse and decentralized oil industry, however, for Britain and the Netherlands had major oil firms, and Galicia was the world's third largest oil producer, with wells financed by the French, British, and Belgians. Eastman Kodak set up sales offices in London in the 1880s and Paris and Berlin in the following decade. After 1905 it established branch offices and subsidiary companies in Italy, Austria, Belgium, Switzerland, Denmark, the Netherlands, Spain, and Russia and built manufacturing plants in England and France. American Tobacco, founded by James Duke, began by exporting to Europe, and then entered into joint ventures and set up subsidiaries in such countries as Germany. When Duke bought a manufacturing plant in England, British tobacco interests protested. Instead of excluding American competition, however, they agreed to carve up the world tobacco market.[22] American firms also had a visible presence in the markets for office machines of all sorts, ranging from typewriters and cash registers to calculators, made by the predecessor of IBM. They did well in elevators and telephones.

Despite these highly visible American successes, European, especially German, firms offered stiff competition. Take electrical equipment. GE had plants and subsidiaries in England, Germany, Italy, and Russia, and Westinghouse had factories in Germany, France, and Russia, but the German firms Siemens and AEG were global corporations as well. AEG had affiliates in London, St. Petersburg, Paris, Stockholm, Genoa, Brussels, Vienna, and Milan as well as in several American cities. In 1913 Germany controlled 46.9 percent of the world's electrical

---

[21] Domosh, *American Commodities*, 28. George Sherman Queen, *The United States and the Material Advance in Russia, 1881–1906* (New York: Arno, 1976), 140.

[22] Wilkins, *Emergence of Multinational Enterprises*, 62–64, 91–93. Alison Fleig Frank, *Oil Empire: Visions of Prosperity in Austrian Galicia* (Cambridge, MA: Harvard University Press, 2005), 3–4. Domosh, *American Commodities*, 30.

equipment market, while Britain had 22 percent, and the United States only 15.7 percent. Mannesmann Pipe Company sold worldwide from the late nineteenth century on, even though it concentrated production in Europe. In the category of non-electrical machinery, Germany, Britain, and the United States were running neck and neck, with 29.1 percent, 28.4 percent, and 26.8 percent of world production respectively. The German Automatengesellschaft dominated the global vending-machine market. The United States supplied railroad cars to Canada but not to Europe. It sold machine tools and machines to Cuba but Germany, France, and Britain did better in Argentina. And the United States imported most of its textile machines from Britain. Although German chemical firms did not produce abroad, they controlled 28.5 percent of the world chemical market versus 15.6 percent for British businesses and 9.7 percent for American companies. In industries such as Swiss watches, German and British shirtwaists, and bicycles all over Europe, American competition initially triumphed, but Europeans then learned from American methods and won back markets. Europe's car plants were owned exclusively by national capital.[23]

While Europeans found some American mass-produced goods appealing, they complained that American firms often pushed standardized items and failed to attend to the particular interests of foreign buyers as, for example, the Germans did. According to one American observer, American businessmen lacked foreign-language skills and sufficient knowledge of European societies and geography.[24] Moreover, the United States was not the undisputed leader in science and technology that it later became.

The American presence across Europe was very uneven. Britain was the main recipient of American investment and commodities, with Germany in second place. Yet, Germany remained Britain's main foreign supplier and customer. In Russia, where roughly half of total capital was foreign, France, Britain, Germany, and Belgium dominated in descending order of their investments. Although the United States provided Russia with nearly half the agricultural machinery it imported, German trade with Russia far surpassed that of the United States, which accounted for less than 5 percent of Russian imports. American trade with France was minimal. In Latin America and Canada, British and American trade and

---

[23] Wilkins, *Emergence of Multinational Enterprises*, 94–96. Beaud, *History of Capitalism*, 159. Chandler, *Scale and Scope*, 70, 175, 213–17, 400, 410.
[24] Frank A. Vanderlip, *The American "Commercial Invasion" of Europe* (New York: Arno, 1976), 21–23.

investment competed, and outside of Liberia, Europeans controlled African investment.[25]

Although there were no European firms of the stature of Singer, International Harvester, and Kodak in the United States, many European multinationals operated there. In the late 1890s, for example, foreign firms produced 25 percent of American copper, and a British multinational controlled the entire borax mining industry. British, German, French, and Swiss firms manufactured thread, yarn, carpets, and lace goods, and a subsidiary of British Courtaulds Ltd. monopolized the production of rayon. Germans invested extensively in the chemical industry, and British, Belgian, Swiss, French, and Austrian firms also produced chemicals and fertilizer. Michelin made tires; Daimler manufactured Mercedes cars, and Fiat opened a production facility. Germans owned the largest manufacturer of surgical instruments in America.[26]

There was an "American invasion" of certain types of goods, but overall commodities, investments, and labor moved across the Atlantic and around the globe in many directions. Nonetheless, many Europeans worried about the impact of American investments and commodities. With much rhetorical passion they posed a question that would be debated throughout the twentieth century. Was Europe becoming Americanized?

The Americanization debate, round one

The British journalist W. T. Stead coined the phrase "Americanization of the world" in his 1902 book that in alarmist tones detailed the impact of America on Europe and the British Empire. America pioneered cheap journalism and preached new ideas about women's rights and church–state relations, which Europeans were imitating. Cities such as Hamburg and Berlin were becoming "American in the rapidity of their growth, American in their nervous energy, American in their quick appropriation of the facilities for rapid transportation." "American commercial supremacy," however, was the key vehicle of Americanization, above all "ingenious inventions" like the typewriter, the sewing machine, the linotype, the

---

[25] Reiner Pommerin, *Der Kaiser und Amerika: Die USA in der Politik der Reichsleitung, 1890–1917* (Cologne: Böhlau Verlag, 1986), 202–3. Born, *International Banking*, 158. John P. McKay, *Pioneers for Profit: Foreign Entrepreneurship and Russian Industrialization, 1885–1919* (University of Chicago Press, 1970), 379. Queen, *United States in Russia*, 106–8, 140.

[26] Mira Wilkins, "European Multinationals in the United States: 1875–1914," in Alice Teichova, Maurice Lévy-Beboyer, and Helga Nussbaum, eds., *Multinational Enterprise in Historical Perspective* (Cambridge University Press, 1986), 55–64.

phonograph, the elevator, and electrical lights. Around the globe Americans were competing in industries Britain once dominated, such as locomotives, and J. P. Morgan's purchase of the Leyland fleet suggested that the United States wanted to challenge Britain's dominance in shipping.[27]

In his 1902 book *The American Invaders*, Fred A. McKenzie insisted that American manufactured goods were shaping everyday life "from Madrid to Saint Petersburg," and no country was affected more deeply than Britain. "The real invasion goes on unceasingly and with little noise or fuss in five hundred industries at once. From shaving soap to electric motors, and from tools to telephones, the American is clearing the field." Indeed, everywhere one turned, one encountered things American. It is worth quoting McKenzie's lengthy lament:

The average citizen wakes in the morning at the sound of an American alarum [*sic*] clock; rises from his New England sheets, and shaves with his New York soap, and a Yankee safety razor. He pulls on a pair of Boston boots over his socks from West Carolina, fastens his Connecticut braces, slips his Waterbury watch into his pocket and sits down to breakfast. Then he congratulates his wife on the way her Illinois straight-front corset sets off her Massachusetts blouse, and begins his breakfast at which he eats bread made from prairie flour ... tinned oysters from Baltimore, and a little Kansas City bacon ... The children are given Quaker Oats.

Concurrently he reads his morning paper, set up by American machines, printed with American ink, by American presses, on American paper ...

Rising from his breakfast table the citizen rushes out, catches an electric tram make in New York to Shepherds Bush, where he gets into a Yankee elevator, which takes him on to the American-fitted railway to the city. At his office of course everything is American. He sits at a Nebraskan swivel chair, before a Michigan roll-top desk, writes his letters on a Syracuse typewriter, signing them with a New York fountain pen, and drying them with a blotting sheet from New England. The letter copies are put away in files manufactured in Grand Rapids.

When evening comes he seeks relaxation at the latest Adelphi melodrama or Drury Lane startler, both made in America ... For relief he drinks a cocktail or some California wine and finishes up with a couple of "little liver pills" made in America.[28]

This depiction of what is a distinctly middle-class English existence undoubtedly exaggerates the American goods that any one family would own, but it does capture their presence in everyday life and reflects an interconnected set of economic and cultural anxieties. If one became what one consumed, were European countries losing their national identities

[27] W. T. Stead, *The Americanization of the World* (New York and London: Horace Markley, 1902), 164 (quote), 214–15, 312–32, 348–79.
[28] McKenzie, *American Invaders*, ix–x, 2, 142–43.

along with their national industries? The British articulated these fears most strongly in the prewar years; Germans would do so in the interwar era and the French after World War II.

Prewar fears were exaggerated. Not all the commodities that Stead and McKenzie enumerated were identified with America, even if they were manufactured there or by United States firms in Europe. According to Mona Domosh, the Singer man on horseback was "a common, everyday sight" in tsarist Russia and Singer shops were in towns large and small. Yet,

in many cases, the fact that the product was American – whatever that meant – was not part of the conversation. Many of the machines, in fact, were produced in Russia at Singer's factory in Podolsk, just outside Moscow. Although decorated with the Singer logo, these machines were stamped with the Kompaniya Singer mark and were sold by Russian agents.[29]

Germans, Englishmen, or ethnic minorities from Russia, in turn, supervised the agents. Singer advertising, like that of International Harvester, depicted American machines as agents of modernization and civilizational uplift, but those linkages were likely more persuasive to Americans than Europeans. Even when goods were identified as American, they were not necessarily used in the same ways nor did they carry the same cultural meanings as in the United States. Class, nationality, culture, and gender all influenced how a given commodity was appropriated. American goods did not create homogeneous consumers and consumer cultures abroad any more than they did at home.

The potential or actual Americanization of Europe was counterbalanced by a "globalization of the United States." In 1914 when the United States was exporting $2.4 billion in goods, it was importing $1.9 billion. As Kristin Hoganson argues, these imports reshaped everyday life. While immigrants brought their own European foods with them, cookbooks and women's magazines introduced middle-class American women to a host of exotic dishes ranging from Hungarian goulash and German liver dumplings to Chinese rice and French hors d'oeuvres. The new bourgeois "culinary cosmopolitanism" conveyed geographic and ethnographic information about Europe and the non-European world and enabled American middle-class women to see themselves as integrally related to the European and global order, and yet different from and in ways superior to those from whom they borrowed.[30]

[29] Domosh, *American Commodities*, 42.
[30] Kristin Hoganson, *Consumers' Imperium: The Global Production of American Domesticity, 1865–1920* (Raleigh: University of North Carolina, 2007).

Americans viewed imported goods with more equanimity than many Europeans. Because American culture was less homogeneous, ethnically defined, and historically rooted than its European counterparts and because many felt the lack of a high cultural tradition, they welcomed things foreign. Most seemed confident that imports would enrich American identity without diluting its essence. A few saw growing international exchanges as a harbinger of a new cosmopolitanism. W. E. B. Du Bois, for example, optimistically proclaimed in his commencement address at Fisk University in 1898 that

On our breakfast table lies each morning the toil of Europe, Asia, and Africa and the isles of the sea; we sow and spin for unseen millions and countless myriads weave and plant for us; we have made the earth smaller and life broader by annihilating distance, magnifying the human voice and the stars, binding nation to nation, until today, for the first time in history, there is one standard of human culture as well in New York as in London, in Cape Town as in Paris, in Bombay as in Berlin.[31]

While some Europeans focused on the American penetration of everyday life, others pondered the threat the United States posed to European economic and imperial interests. Those most fearful deployed a rhetoric that was martial, Darwinian, and at times apocalyptic. Many English observers spoke of an American commercial invasion; the German press of economic rivalries and threats. Count Goluchowski, the Austrian foreign minister in the mid 1890s, feared that "the twentieth century will be a struggle for existence in the domain of economics," while Prince Albert of Belgium regrettably concluded in 1898 that "Alas! You Americans will eat us all up." In his 1902 pamphlet on *The American Invasion*, Benjamin Thwaite claimed "the wolf is really amongst us this time, and the industrial flock is in serious danger of being torn to pieces." Adding imperial concerns to economic ones, Stead lamented that hegemony within the Anglo-Saxon race had already passed from Westminster to Washington.[32]

Not every country was equally fearful. There was no talk of an American invasion in Russia or France. Although critical of American trusts and

---

[31] Quoted in "Introduction," in Gary W. Reichard and Ted Dickson, eds., *America on the World Stage: A Global Approach to United States History* (Urbana: University of Illinois Press, 2008), xvii.

[32] David E. Novack and Matthew Simon, "Commercial Responses to the American Export Invasion, 1871–1914: An Essay in Attitudinal History," *Explorations in Entrepreneurial History*, Second Series, 3 (1966): 135. Stead, *Americanization*, 15, 179. Benjamin Howarth Thwaite, *The American Invasion or England's Commercial Danger* (London: S. Sonnenschein, 1902), 3.

imperial expansion, some French observers felt that France's relative economic underdevelopment protected it from the competition Britain and Germany experienced. German industry and large-scale agriculture may not have believed in an American danger, but they invoked it to lobby for lower social insurance costs and higher tariffs. To some Europeans the German danger seemed more immediate than the transatlantic one. At the 1900 Paris exhibition, for example, German machines, dynamos, and cranes dazzled observers and made the French feel humiliated on the economic battlefield as they had been thirty years before on the military one. And according to Stead, a few Europeans "would delight to see a much greater Americanization of Europe than anything likely to take place."[33]

When Europeans compared themselves to Americans, they attributed American economic success to a combination of institutional and attitudinal factors. Sergei Witte, Russian minister of finance at the turn of the century, emphasized the initiative of its businessmen and the absence of high military spending that so burdened European states. Stead foregrounded the interaction of a "vigorous race" and a "virgin continent," and admired the United States education system and democracy along with Americans' single-minded focus on making money. While some European observers stressed entrepreneurial energy and openness to new ideas, others singled out the work ethic. According to British commentators, Americans worked longer and harder than their British counterparts, but whether this was due to closer supervision, higher wages, or more secure employment was unclear. German analysts praised the faster work pace, superior technology, and more extensive division of labor and noted the beneficial effects of the American belief that "work ennobles."[34]

Those perceiving an American challenge were divided about how to respond. Admiral Canevaro, who had served in the Italian foreign ministry, urged Europeans "to consider the possibility and the necessity of uniting against America, as the future of civilization would require them to do." But economic, military, and colonial rivalries made such unity "a vain dream," according to Stead, who favored merging the entire British Empire with the United States to create a vast English-speaking United States of the World. If not, he predicted, Britain would be superseded by America, loose its empire, and be reduced to the status of Belgium.[35]

[33] Stead, *Americanization*, 162. Frieden, *Global Capitalism*, 57–58.
[34] Vanderlip, *American "Commercial Invasion,"* 2. Stead, *Americanization*, 381–84. McKenzie, *American Invaders*, 16–23, 157, 222–32. Pommerin, *Kaiser und Amerika*, 207–12.
[35] Stead, *Americanization*, 176–81, 396–97.

Most recommended adopting some American practices while maintaining distinctive national economies. Thwaite believed Britain could meet American competition if it encouraged inventions by Americanizing its patent system and railroads and borrowing from American and German technical education. He urged trade unions to promote worker efficiency, but the only means suggested was curbing drinking on the job. McKenzie urged British capitalists to adopt American technology to enhance competitiveness. Georg Freiherr von Rheinbaban, who was sent by the Kaiser to report on the American economy, recommended that German firms imitate some American methods of organizing production and labor but warned that many highly mechanized American factories were inflexible. Overall, he was confident that Germany would withstand the American challenge as it had the British one. German and French engineers looked favorably on American technology, and in 1913 Bosch in Stuttgart and Renault at Billancourt introduced Taylorism, with its time and motion studies and minute subdivision and supervision of the labor process. Engineers were enthusiastic, but workers opposed these American methods, demanding shorter hours and higher pay as compensation.[36]

Even those who admired American productivity and work ethic did not see America as a model to be emulated; rather, they assumed that Europe operated on different principles. After traveling to the United States in 1905, for example, Philipp Harjes concluded:

There is no need to fear that our German industry will be endangered by America as long as we remain true to ourselves and keep our eyes open, for our strengths lie in other areas, and due to national character and relationships, will always lie there.

A few optimistically argued that Germany might become the leader of an economically united Europe. The secretary of the German League of Industrialists, Wilhelm Wendtland, even predicted that the American danger to Europe would soon be replaced by the European threat to America.[37]

American observers did not see an economic danger arising across the Atlantic. Indeed, some felt economic primacy was already securely in United States hands. After touring Europe in 1901–2, Frank Vanderlip, vice president of National City Bank of New York and a former assistant secretary of the Treasury, dismissed most of Europe as "unmodern and unprogressive." He confidently described a "mature America, the

---

[36] Thwaite, *American Invasion*, 29–38. McKenzie, *American Invaders*, 224–32. Pommerin, *Kaiser und Amerika*, 212.
[37] Alexander Schmidt, *Reisen in die Moderne: Der Amerika-Diskurs des deutschen Bürgertums vor dem Ersten Weltkrieg im europäischen Vergleich* (Berlin: Akademie Verlag, 1997), 131, 278. Pommerin, *Kaiser und Amerika*, 220.

exemplar of modern industrial methods, perfected mechanical ideas, and ripe economic policy."[38] In the decades before World War I, however, the core countries of industrialized Europe did not accept these claims.

Transatlantic networks

Economies were not the only sites and subjects of transatlantic exchanges. Social and cultural ideas, goods, policies, and practices moved between Europe and America, and individuals and institutions developed dense networks to share ideas and experiences and foster international cooperation. Education and social reform, urban development and poverty, the status of labor and the rights of women were central to these multiple "Atlantic crossings." Transatlantic interactions involving labor movements, social reform, high art, and popular culture show that Western Europe generally played the leading role. It was not yet the American Century.

There were multiple connections as well as revealing differences among labor movements in Europe and America. Working-class parties on both sides of the Atlantic joined the Second International, which provided a forum for socialist and labor parties to debate everything from the mass strike and colonialism to social insurance, protective legislation, and the relationship of trade unions and socialist political parties. Through meetings, journals, newspapers, letters, and translations of theoretical works, members created "a unique experiment in international political discourse and organization."[39] Unfortunately, the experiment failed, for national and ideological divisions tore the Second International apart long before its members overwhelmingly supported their warring nations in 1914.

Immigration also linked European and American labor movements as the German case illustrates. When the German Social Democratic Party (SPD) was outlawed between 1878 and 1890, German workers in America as well as the Socialist Labor Party there offered political and material support. After 1890, the SPD's national newspaper *Vorwärts* regularly carried letters from German workers in America, and union newspapers reported on the American Federation of Labor annual conventions and the state of the economy.

---

[38] Vanderlip, *American "Commercial Invasion,"* 36, 38.
[39] Moira Donald, "Workers of the World Unite?" in Martin H. Geyer and Johannes Paulmann, eds., *The Mechanics of Internationalism: Culture, Society and Politics from the 1840s to the First World War* (London: German Historial Institute, 2001), 177–203. Quote, 202.

European labor leaders studied the United States more than American ones did Europe. A few leading socialists, such as Edward Averling, Eleanor Marx, James Keir Hardie, and Wilhlem Liebknecht visited the United States, and many others like Karl Kautsky, the principal theorist of the Second International, Jules Guesde, a prominent French socialist, and H. M. Hyndman, founder of the Social Democratic Federation in Britain, commented extensively on it. All agreed with Kautsky that

> The United States are today unquestionably the most important and the most interesting of the modern culture lands. Not England, but America shows us our future, in so far as one country can reveal it at all to another, since each has its own peculiar development. In America capitalism is making its greatest progress; it rules there more absolutely . . . than anywhere else.[40]

They differed, however, in their assessments of American workers. In the 1880s Liebknecht emphasized working-class prosperity, while Averling and Marx painted a more somber picture. After the turn of the century, the moderate Belgian socialist leader Èmile Vandervelde insisted that American workers lived much better than European ones even though class divisions were widening. For moderate German Social Democrat Ludwig Quessel conditions in the United States showed how effective trade union activity could be; for John Marlin of the British Independent Labour Party, national parks and free towels and soap in public baths were evidence of a practical socialism. More orthodox Marxists disagreed. Kautsky insisted that under ruthless American capitalism "the class struggles are sharpening there to the highest possible degree." French socialists perceived a diffuse working-class radicalism in America. They, like Kautsky and SPD head August Bebel, felt that American capitalist development, rather than its workers' movement, put socialist revolution on the agenda. Europeans often projected their reformist or radical proclivities onto conditions about which they knew little, but whether they saw American capitalism as ruthless and headed for revolution or prosperous and able to integrate workers, they did not see it as unique. As socialist and labor parliamentary representation grew rapidly in Germany, France, Austria, Belgium, and Italy, European labor movements lost interest in America. American workers thought in class terms, and shop-floor labor relations were confrontational, even violent, yet, American workers lived in a different institutional milieu, where craft unions focused primarily on wages and hours, and mainstream, multi-class parties, of a sort Europe lacked, attracted workers.

---

[40] Laurence R. Moore, *European Socialists and the American Promised Land* (New York: Oxford University Press, 1970), 58–59.

After 1905, many European socialists transferred their revolutionary hopes to Russia.

Nineteenth-century women's movements also developed international connections. An international women's rights congress met in conjunction with the 1878 Paris exhibition, and a decade later the American National Women's Suffrage Association convened an International Council of Women in Washington, DC. By 1914 Germany, Britain, Sweden, Denmark, Italy, the Netherlands, Switzerland, Hungary, Norway, Belgium, Bulgaria, Greece, Finland, Serbia, and Portugal all had National Councils of Women, as did several non-European countries. The regular international congresses discussed women's history, employment, morality, and public health, sparking lively transnational debate about protective legislation and social purity campaigns. Because these congresses avoided the most divisive issue, suffrage, the International Alliance of Women was established in 1904 to focus only on that. Although many bourgeois European women's movements joined, the socialist women's organizations, strong in countries like Germany, remained apart.

Social reformers ranging from American Progressives and members of the German Verein für Sozialpolitik to the British Fabian Socialists and associates of the French Musée Social developed dense informal networks. These were a response to urbanization and industrial capitalism that created excessive hours and low wages, unsafe factories, sprawling slums, deteriorating health, and insecurity in old age on both sides of the Atlantic. In earlier decades Americans believed that their liberal constitutionalism and republicanism were far superior to European monarchism, authoritarianism, and militarism, and although many Europeans admired America's freedoms and small federal state, they were repulsed by machine politics and corruption. Neither side was eager to learn from the other. By 1900, however, social policy came to dominate the transatlantic agenda for reform-minded economists, social workers, lawyers, politicians, architects, and urban planners who sought to preserve capitalism while limiting exploitation and commodification.

In wide-ranging discussions that spanned the Atlantic and also included countries like Japan and Argentina, ideas moved in many directions, but overwhelmingly, Europe was the teacher, America the pupil. As Walter Weyl, American Progressive and cofounder of the *New Republic* wrote in 1912, "America no longer teaches democracy to an expectant world ... our students of political and industrial democracy repair to the antipodes, to England, Belgium, France, to semi-feudal Germany." From the 1880s on many Americans studied at German universities, where they were exposed not only to new ideas about higher education and history but also to critiques of laissez-faire. At the 1900 Paris exhibition, proud displays of industrial prowess were accompanied by social exhibits, revealing new anxieties and policy initiatives. Many Americans traveled to Europe to meet reformers, visit new institutions, and study social legislation. Like the delegates to a prewar meeting of the International Association of Labor Legislation, they discovered that the United States was "put in a category with rather backward countries." To be sure, Europeans got ideas about public education and playgrounds from the United States, but "the list of social-political experiments drawn westward from the European nations to the United States outstrips by severalfold the corresponding movement in the opposite direction."[41]

Although North Atlantic states shared a social policy discourse, the resulting social projects took specific national forms. Improving urban services was a transatlantic concern, but while Europeans developed municipal ownership of gas, electricity, and transit, United States cities only took over transit and otherwise settled for public utilities commissions to oversee private firms. Everywhere there was a commitment to improving housing stock, but the British built municipal housing and new towns, and Germans channeled money into cooperative housing associations and subsidized some private contractors, while Americans strongly opposed public housing.

Germany led the way in health, accident, and old age social insurance programs in the 1880s, and Britain passed a National Insurance Act in 1911. Other European states subsidized mutual aid societies and pensions for the poor. Although American social reformers worried about poverty, they were unable to promote state social insurance. Here as in other social policy arenas, the United States started later than European countries, and reformers were unable to challenge private sector dominance in health or gas and water or housing. Women's organizations pushed reform in America more than labor did, and improving homes and families often took priority over transforming workplaces. American social policies were at the laissez-faire, anti-statist end of a transatlantic spectrum of ideas and policies. Then and later these differences implied alternative understandings of economic and social justice and of the desirable relationship between the individual and society.

Culture high and low

Europe unquestionably dominated transatlantic high culture, and America saw itself as Europe saw America – a nation of business and materialism,

---

[41] Daniel T. Rodgers, *Atlantic Crossings: Social Politics in a Progressive Age* (Cambridge, MA: Harvard University Press, 1998), 70, 74–75.

opportunity and energy, not of art, music, and architecture. In debating how the United States could become cultured, American magazines like *the Nation, Century* and *World's Work* drew on the dichotomies that structured European criticisms of American society from the late nineteenth century on – culture versus economy, depth versus superficiality, spirituality versus materialism, quality versus quantity, history versus the present.

Americans regarded art collecting as a key means to overcome their cultural deficit, partake in the heritage of Western civilization, and raise the nation's stature. And collect they did with astonishing energy and money. J. Pierpont Morgan, financier, banker, and founder of United States Steel, for example, transferred innumerable European paintings, decorative objects, sculptures, books, and furniture into his private collection. The industrialist Henry Clay Frick paid over a $1 million for three paintings, and the banker Otto Kahn spent $400,000 for one Frans Hals. Kahn was also a major patron of the Metropolitan Opera with its European repertoire. These "businessmen with taste" shared American novelist Henry James's belief that "We can deal freely with forms of civilization not our own, can pick and choose and assimilate and in short (aesthetically, etc.) claim our property wherever we find it." Europeans, especially the British and French, protested vociferously against the purchase of their cultural patrimony. Collectors and the American press, however, insisted that art was a legitimate object for market transactions.[42]

European governments, artists, intellectuals, and cultural entrepreneurs also brought European art and music to the United States, competing against one another for cultural preponderance. The French government promoted French art, the dealer Goupil established galleries along the east coast, and by 1906 over half of all paintings imported into the United States came from France, while Britain, Italy, and Germany accounted for one-third. German and Austrian composers, musicians, and conductors dominated the classical music scene. Germany and France sought to attract American students, but Britain was more successful.[43]

---

[42] *The Selected Letters of Henry James*, ed. Leon Edel (New York: Farrar, Straus, and Giroux, 1999), 23. Neil Harris, *Cultural Excursions: Marketing Appetites and Cultural Tastes in Modern America* (University of Chicago Press, 1990), 258, 261. Flaminia Gennari Sartori, "The Taste of Business: Defining the American Art Collector, 1900–1914," in Luisa Passerini, ed., *Across the Atlantic: Cultural Exchanges between Europe and the United States* (Brussels: Peter Lang, 2000), 87–88.

[43] Jessica C. E. Gienow-Hecht, "Trumpeting Down the Walls of Jericho: The Politics of Art, Music and Emotion in German-American Relations, 1870–1920," *Journal of Social History* 36/39 (Spring 2003): 585–613.

Americans traveled to Europe not only to study but also, and in much larger numbers, to tour or live for a few months or years. London, Paris, Rome, and Florence were initially the preferred destinations, but after 1900 Munich and Berlin became increasingly popular. Some explored art, architecture, music, and history seriously, others naïvely, as novels such as Henry James's *The Americans* reveal. One of the few to venture into Eastern Europe was George Kennan, who investigated the Russian system of penal exile in Siberia.

European travelers to America pursued quite different itineraries. Many were fascinated by the American West and natural wonders such as Niagara Falls, but most socialists, capitalists, politicians, and academics wanted to see the American present of steel mills, slaughterhouses, and New York skyscrapers. Chicago was singled out as distinctively modern and quintessentially American. For H. G. Wells it represented "the dark disorder of growth" and "the almost perfect presentation of nineteenth century individualistic industrialism," but its playgrounds and community centers offered hope of amelioration. While Maxim Gorky condemned it as "a monstrous city," where "people have never seemed so insignificant to me, so enslaved," many other Russian visitors saw this raw, dynamic, and imposing metropolis as a model for their country's development.[44]

Europeans ignored American high culture but were intrigued by everyday life. Americans were simultaneously materialistic and religious. In contrast to the state-sanctioned religions of Europe, churches and sects proliferated and church attendance was high for all classes, even if religion often seemed more about sociability and social services than spirituality. French and German visitors often commented on the American woman, who was described as free and independent, but also cold and inaccessible. She enjoyed camaraderie with men but sacrificed romance and mystery in the process. She dominated the family but failed to educate and discipline her children properly. She had more opportunities for education and cultural influence than her European counterparts and was unquestionably more modern, yet she thereby called male privileges into question. The European fascination with and anxiety about American religion and gender relations were to persist throughout the twentieth century.

Few Europeans traveled to the American West, but many saw Buffalo Bill Cody's Wild West Show. In the late 1880s, the Wild West Show toured

---

[44] Wells, *Future in America*, 43–44. Olga Peters Hasty and Susanne Fusso, *America through Russian Eyes, 1874–1926* (New Haven: Yale University Press, 1988), 135.

England, where it gave a command performance before Queen Victoria, as well as Italy, where Pope Leo XII attended, and France, where it played next to the 1889 Paris exhibition. It also played in Germany, Greece, Denmark, and Belgium. The show presented the conquest of the American West through fast-paced action, colorful costumes, horses, buffalos, the most modern American guns, and a troupe that included ninety-seven Native Americans. By the turn of the century, tales of colonial adventures, performed by Zulu tribesmen in European productions, Filipinos in an American one, and Arabs on both side of the Atlantic, were added.

Like the wildly popular American Indian novels of Karl May in Germany or the western adventure stories of Gustave Aimard in France and of Mayne Reid in Britain, the Wild West Show offered appealing alternatives to modern urban industrial society. Europeans could project fantasies of exoticism, adventure, male bonding, and racial harmony onto the American West. Yet civilization always conquered, for no matter how noble, the savage was always doomed. The Wild West Shows made "the story of the American west merge with the story of European expansion," and legitimated ideas of imperial mission.[45]

Movies developed independently on both sides of the Atlantic. Hollywood was to become synonymous with the global movie industry from the twenties on, but before 1914 European countries dominated the silent film industry. France, Germany, and Italy produced over half of the four thousand melodramas, romances, and adventures made annually. The French company Pathé, with offices around the world from Berlin, Barcelona, and Moscow to Calcutta and Singapore, was the largest single supplier for America's growing number of nickelodeons and theaters. In 1909 it augmented its sales office in New York with a United States production studio. American films did well in Britain, were competitive in Belgium, Holland, and Norway, and accounted for a third of new releases in Germany, but they sold poorly in France and Italy, and the French dominated the Eastern European market. American films did well in Australia and South Africa, but not in India, Turkey, or China. In short, America was one player among many.[46]

---

[45] Robert W. Rydell and Rob Kroes, *Buffalo Bill in Bologna: The Americanization of the World, 1869–1922* (University of Chicago Press, 2005), 107–9, 111.

[46] Rydell and Kroes, *Buffalo Bill in Bologna*, 79. Kristin Thompson, *Exporting Entertainment: America in the World Film Market, 1907–34* (Tonbridge, UK: BFI, 1985), 5, 18, 29–45, 47.

An Age of Empires

These unprecedented Euro-American economic and cultural exchanges occurred in an Age of Empires – colonial, continental, and informal. Imperial aspirations and representations permeated politics and economics, high culture and everyday life. How did competing visions of empire, collaborative colonial projects, and shared assumptions about Euro-America and its multiple others shape transatlantic relations?

Empires long predated the late nineteenth century, but formal colonization reached its highpoint then. By 1900 Europe and the United States formally controlled 90 percent of Africa, 98 percent of Polynesia, and 57 percent of Asia. European states alone had 115 colonies that covered over 20 million square miles and dominated more than 530 million people. Britain had the largest and most global empire, followed by France, while Germany and Italy entered the colonial scramble late and with limited success, and Belgium notoriously misruled its one colony, the Congo. The United States began acquiring colonies late but by 1914 controlled the Philippines, Puerto Rico, the Virgin Islands, eastern Samoa, Guam, and the Panama Canal Zone and exercised de facto control over Cuba, the Dominican Republic, Nicaragua, and Haiti. Industrializing Japan also joined the ranks of the imperial powers by annexing Taiwan in 1895 and Korea in 1910.

This vast expansion of formal, colonial empires was motivated by actual or anticipated economic gain, strategic considerations, and great-power rivalries as well as altruistic desires to civilize the indigenous. These varied motives were inextricably intertwined, for imperialists saw their mission as a project of total reconstruction. The absence of private property, productive agriculture, bourgeois individualism, or ordered family life provided compelling rationales for colonizing projects. While the colonized found the means used to spread capitalism and Christianity self-serving, coercive, and often violent, colonizers emphasized good intentions and mutual benefits. What Thomas Bender wrote about the United States applies to Europeans as well: "The core of empire as a way of life is precisely this incapacity to see oneself as a potential enemy."[47]

Sprawling continental empires covered Central, Eastern and Southern Europe. The German, Austro-Hungarian, Ottoman, and Russian empires all suffered from relative economic underdevelopment, illiberal politics, and emerging nationalism among their multiethnic populations, and none were to survive World War I. The other major continental empire, the

---

[47] Thomas Bender, *A Nation among Nations: America's Place in World History* (New York: Hill and Wang, 2006), 192.

United States, fared better. Over the nineteenth century it had acquired territories by purchase or warfare from Native American tribes, France, Mexico, and Russia. In the 1890s, when Frederick Jackson Turner proclaimed the closing of the American frontier, the United States expanded into the Caribbean and toward Asia, becoming a Pacific as well as an Atlantic power. It was "well experienced in taking territory and in the affairs of empire."[48] Yet, then and later Americans overlooked the connections between westward and overseas expansion and defined United States interventions abroad as just and necessary but not imperial.

Empire could come without territorial control. The United States pioneered liberal developmentalism, and Britain dominated the Southern Cone of Latin America and ran the lucrative opium trade in China. Germany invested in ambitious infrastructure projects like the Berlin–Baghdad railroad, while France bankrolled Russian industrialization. States lent money to needy governments, encouraged private investment, and aggressively insisted on the repayment of loans made by private banks, all without the burdens of colonial administration.

No country articulated the idea of informal empire more elaborately than the United States, and none practiced it more coercively. Some Americans deemed colonies too costly, others judged the colonized racially incapable of Americanization, and still others viewed imperialism as incompatible with American republicanism. Yet, virtually all saw expansion as necessary for economic prosperity and domestic stability. Dollar diplomacy in the Caribbean and Central America combined with racial paternalism to cast a variety of economic and military interventions in a benevolent light. If countries in which the United States had economic and strategic interests failed to stabilize their economies, adopt the gold standard, collect customs and taxes efficiently, pay their debts to American lenders, and thereby create conditions favorable for foreign investment, the United States would act as an "international police power." It deployed private bankers and businessmen as "financial missionaries" to advise countries like the Dominican Republic, Haiti, Nicaragua, and Liberia on how to reorganize their governments and economies. If that failed, the United States Marines would intervene; between 1898 and 1920 they did so twenty-two times in Central America and the Caribbean.[49]

Imperial rivalries were most frequent and intense among European powers, and although the United States entered the global stage, it did

[48] Bender, *Nation among Nations*, 191.
[49] Emily S. Rosenberg, *Financial Missionaries to the World: The Politics and Culture of Dollar Diplomacy, 1900–1930* (Durham: Duke University Press, 2003).

not disrupt the existing hierarchies of colonial power. It was not involved in the scramble for Africa from the 1880s on, for it had no interests outside of Liberia. It directed its imperial gaze toward the Caribbean, the Pacific Islands, and China. In 1898 the United States fought Spain over Cuba and Puerto Rico, which lay within the vast area covered by the 1823 Monroe Doctrine's prohibition of direct European interference in the Western Hemisphere and represented nearby and desirable targets of economic expansion. No European power rose to Spain's defense.

All believed that America had become an empire among empires. Germans viewed 1898 as a continuation of America's continental expansion and an indication that it, like Germany, sought colonies to enhance its global status. The French criticized America's colonial ventures as one-sidedly economic and lacking any political vision or cultural mission. America hypocritically proclaimed the Monroe Doctrine while trying to Americanize the world. The British initially judged American actions more positively, for in the late 1890s the United States regarded Britain as an imperial model and invoked the shared ideology of Anglo-Saxonism to link their infant empire and Britain's mature one. An 1898 American cartoon, for example, depicted Uncle Sam as the Colossus of the Pacific, straddling the ocean exactly as Cecil Rhodes had been depicted striding from Cape Town to Cairo. The romance of supposed racial-nationalist affinities and empires of liberty quickly cooled, however, as Britain criticized American rule in the Philippines and the United States distanced itself from Britain's Boer War policies.

Britain, France, Germany, Russia, Japan, and America directly confronted one another in China, for each nation wanted to invest in infrastructure and lend to the state and each fantasized controlling the potentially vast Chinese market. None could hope to rule the sprawling, politically divided, and economically underdeveloped nation alone. European states negotiated spheres of influence, but in 1899 America secured the Open Door policy, which guaranteed both Chinese territorial integrity and equal access to trade and investment in China for all nations. This did not, however, bring the anticipated economic benefits. In China the United States pursued imperial economic expansion while claiming to be anti-colonial, a pattern it would repeat throughout the twentieth century.

Imperial cultures

The Age of Empire was characterized by cooperation as well as conflict. Colonizers shared the "tools of empire" that were the precondition for the new imperialism, such as steamships and quinine, the Maxim gun,

THE RHODES COLOSSUS
STRIDING FROM CAPE TOWN TO CAIRO.

Illustration 1   The Rhodes Colossus: striding from Cape Town to Cairo.
Punch. December 10, 1892.

and transoceanic telegraph cables. Colonial policymakers, administrators, and businessmen encountered one another in far-flung places and
at international conferences and studied one another's achievements
and mistakes. These exchanges created a transnational discourse of
categories and policies from which colonizers could borrow as they
developed their local variant of indirect or direct rule, labor exploitation,
and racial law. Britain, for example, which had dominated trade and
banking in the Philippines before 1898, continued to do so, thereby

COLOSSUS OF THE PACIFIC.

Illustration 2 Colossus of the Pacific. *Chicago Tribune.* August 24, 1898.

linking the American colony to British ones in Asia. The French in
Indochina borrowed techniques for dealing with those of mixed race
from the Dutch in Batavia. In Samoa the first American governor modeled his policies on those of the neighboring German colony. In Togo
borrowings moved in the opposite direction. German cotton farmers
and colonial officials invited a delegation from the Tuskegee Institute to
Togo to teach new agricultural methods and labor discipline and reform
Ewe families by reducing the economic power of women. In the
Philippines, Americans first looked to the British for guidance and
then developed their own colonial experts. These were often engineers,
who saw colonial rule as a series of technical problems that could be
solved without knowledge of culture, history, or language. This "engineers' imperialism," as Michael Adas termed it, would henceforth char-
acterize American interventions.

A broader culture of imperialism linked metropoles with their colonies and with one another. Colonial images and issues pervaded Europe and the United States. The penny press in France, Britain, and the United States, for example, avidly followed Stanley and Livingstone in Africa, Teddy Roosevelt and the Rough Riders in Cuba, and the Boer War. Imperial adventurers like Savorgnan de Brazza in Central Africa became popular heroes in France. Celebratory poetry and prose on imperial themes found ready audiences in every colonial country. Rudyard Kipling with his admonition to "take up the white man's burden" and his stirring portrayal of the adventures of Kim during the Great Game of Russian and British imperial rivalry in Afghanistan, was the most famous, but he was hardly alone. Women and men wrote widely read colonial travel narratives that mixed adventure, exoticism, and eroticism while portraying native cultures in terms of absence, lack, and passivity.

Ethnographers, colonial agents, and entrepreneurs across Europe and America avidly collected, categorized, and exhibited both colonial objects and bodies. Ethnographic museums displayed tools, weapons, clothes, domestic items, and bones. Colonial exhibitions, world's fairs, and commercial shows brought colonized people to enact their ostensibly authentic and ahistorical cultures for the edification, entertainment, and racialized voyeurism of Europeans and Americans. The World Columbian Exhibition held in Chicago in 1893, for example, opened and closed with a procession, headed of course by Americans, which included Turks, Bedouins, Algerians, and Sudanese, as well as residents of the Amazon and the South Sea Islands. The 1900 exhibition in Paris reconstructed a Tunisian souk with a variety of craftsmen displaying their skills and wares. The 1896 German Colonial Exhibition, a commercial venture, included Tunisian and Togolese dancers and Abyssinian and Masai villagers. Appealing to middle-class and working-class audiences of both sexes, these exhibitions enabled Europeans and Americans to see themselves as part of a multinational colonial project and imagine that they possessed a dazzling variety of exotic cultures within their consuming gaze.

Empire came to the forefront of domestic politics at times of colonial crisis and war, such as Fashoda, the Spanish-Cuban-American War, the Boxer Rebellion, the Boer War, and the German genocide against the Herero in Southwest Africa. But colonial questions never fell off the political radar because colonial organizations, such as the British Empire League, the Primrose League, and the Pan German League steadily promoted colonialism, while naval leagues, commercial associations, missionary organizations, and geographic societies mobilized politicians, monies, and personnel for particular colonial ventures. Many appealed in general terms to the white man's burden or the Western civilizing mission, while others spoke of a national need to restore lost imperial glory or claim a new place in the sun. The Russians couched expansionist aims in the language of pan-Slavism, while Americans preferred Manifest Destiny. German social imperialists, such as Friedrich Naumann and Max Weber, optimistically insisted that expansion abroad and reform at home were mutually reinforcing, while Cecil Rhodes argued more pessimistically "If you wish to avoid civil war then you must become an imperialist."[50] Some dissented from the imperial consensus. The British journalist E. D. Morel campaigned to reform the Belgian Congo; many German Social Democrats protested colonial atrocities; Jane Addams advocated internationalism, and William James wrote of the need to find a moral equivalent of war to combat the appeals of militaristic masculinity, which was integral to imperialism. But these were minority voices. On both sides of the Atlantic, empire had become a way of life, part of the accepted order of the world.

Imperialism shaped Europe and America just as it did the colonies. Ideas about inclusion and exclusion in rights and social policies and projects for disciplining labor and reforming education were worked out in circuits of knowledge and policy experimentation that moved from colony to metropole and back as often as the other way. Workhouses in Eastern Westphalia borrowed techniques employed in German East Africa. French colonies in Indochina, Madagascar, and Morocco were laboratories of modernity, where architects, urban planners, and social reformers could experiment with solutions to social, political, and aesthetic problems that existed at home as well. Workers in the East End of London and the Lower East Side of New York City were described in the same derogatory terms as natives in colonies – wild, dangerous, primitive, other; they failed to practice proper domesticity and sexual respectability. Class, race, and gender came to be defined in and through each other.

Armed peace

Despite the shared culture of imperialism and successful adjudication of many colonial conflicts, imperial competition contributed significantly to the division of Europe into the British, French, and Russian Triple Entente on the one hand and the German, Austro-Hungarian, and Italian Triple Alliance on the other. America was not drawn into these entangling alliances – as much from a lack of interest on the part of the

---

[50] Heinz Gollwitzer, *Europe in the Age of Imperialism: 1880–1914* (New York: Norton, 1979), 136.

European powers as from an American desire to remain uninvolved. European states did transform their ministers in Washington to full ambassadors in the 1890s, and they recognized both America's new imperial presence and its growing industrial might. Nonetheless, the United States lacked a military of the sort deemed requisite to serious great-power status.

Although Europe avoided wars at home, militaries and defense budgets expanded exponentially. Intra-European rivalries between Germany and Britain over naval building and between France and Germany over the size of armies fueled the arms race, as did pervasive fears that a major war was inevitable. America joined in, but on a small scale. In 1890 when France and Germany had over half a million army and navy personnel, the United States had only 39,000; by 1914 United States forces had grown to 164,000, but Russia had over 1.3 million men in arms, France and Germany were just above and just below the 900,000 mark respectively, and Britain had over half a million. Every country had military conscription, except Britain and America. All European countries had a professional officer corps and a General Staff, but only in 1904 did the United States, with an eye on the successful Prussian model, establish a General Staff and an Army War College.[51]

The United States moved more assertively on the naval front, inspired in part by American naval officer Alfred T. Mahan's 1890 book *The Influence of Sea Power in History* that saw the navy as the key to British imperial power and a prerequisite for American global influence. Yet, even though the United States had the world's third largest navy by 1914, the German navy was a third again as large and the British one nearly three times bigger. The American military budget was smaller than that of European countries, representing less than 1 percent of GDP, as opposed to 2.5 percent for Britain and Germany, over 4 percent for France, and 6.1 percent for Japan.[52] Defense spending represented a larger proportion of the American federal budget than in European states – over half as opposed to one-third for France and Britain, but that reflected America's smaller state apparatus and less developed social programs. American military men played less prominent roles in politics and diplomacy, and there were not the close connections between industry and the military that existed in Germany. Despite its economic prowess and size,

[51] Kennedy, *Rise and Fall of the Great Powers*, 203. Chalmers Johnson, *The Sorrows of Empire: Militarism, Secrecy and the End of the Republic* (New York: Metropolitan Books, 2004), 45–46.
[52] Jari Eloranta, "Military Spending Patterns in History," http://eh.net/encyclopediaarticle/eloranta.military, 11–12.

America was "a Great Power. But it was not part of the Great Power system."[53]

For all the talk of old Europe and young America in the decades before 1914, few predicted either the twilight of European hegemony or the ascendancy of an interventionist America. It took war and revolution to dramatically redraw the ideological, political, and economic map of Europe and alter America's role in it.

---

[53] Kennedy, *Rise and Fall of the Great Powers*, 248.

2 World War I: European crisis and American opportunity

In August 1914 war engulfed the European continent. Each belligerent anticipated a quick and glorious end to hostilities but instead experienced four years of brutal, mechanized warfare that required total mobilization of the home front. When the troops returned from the battlefields in late 1918, they found their prewar worlds profoundly shaken. In the wake of war and contentious peace negotiations, old empires collapsed, new nation-states and fledgling democracies emerged, and colonial possessions were reshuffled. Among victors and vanquished alike, economies lay in tatters, traditional gender norms were in disarray, and social conflicts and revolutionary upheavals spread over Russia, Germany, Italy, Austria, Hungary, and Britain. The war, which killed, injured, and psychologically maimed millions of soldiers, began what many have called the Thirty Years War of the twentieth century. Europeans experienced and remembered the war as a horrific trauma, which destroyed lives, states, economies, and ways of life and began an extended period of conflict, loss of confidence, and decline.

For America, the war had a quite different meaning. Although essentially a European conflict, the Great War, as it was then called, offered the United States the opportunity to intervene economically and militarily and the prospect of rescuing and reforming Europe politically. It also presented the danger of entangling alliances. The United States attained a new kind of presence in Europe, while enjoying economic prosperity and suffering comparatively few social conflicts and military losses. Some Americans came to see the United States as Europe's savior, guide, and sole bulwark against Bolshevism; Europeans, however, sought to chart their own course, and many Americans were ambivalent about assuming new European and global roles.

War, revolution, and the Versailles peace settlement raise two central questions about European-American relations. How and why did war and its aftermath make Europe and America both more entangled and more distant, at once more similar and more distinct? Did World War I mark the permanent eclipse of Europe and the dawn of the American Century?

American neutrality

Europe's hundred-year peace (which to be sure had seen the Crimean War, the limited wars of Italian and German unification and innumerable colonial conflicts) ended in August 1914, as the Central Powers – Germany, Austria-Hungary, and the Ottoman Empire – fought the Entente of Britain, France, Russia, and later Italy. Each nation portrayed its actions as defensive; each condemned the expansionist aims and autocratic governments of the opposing alliance; each claimed to defend European civilization against barbarism. Bitter debates about war guilt and war aims raged during the conflict, at the Versailles peace conference, and among historians ever since. Some argue that Germany, alone or in league with the Austro-Hungarian Empire, was to blame and that both saw war as inevitable, desirable for foreign policy reasons, and useful as a diversion from domestic pressures for democratization and national autonomy. Others claim that all powers bore responsibility for raising tensions to the breaking point due to economic and colonial rivalries, an increasingly rigid and armed alliance system, and a desire to divert attention from conflicts at home.

In 1914 the United States, which was free from entangling alliances with the belligerent powers, remained aloof from both the hostilities and the debates about responsibility for war that so preoccupied European publics. From across the Atlantic the causes of war seemed simple – European militarism, autocracy, imperialism, and a cynical balance of power politics. The war was Europe's disaster, and America should remain uninvolved. Initially Europeans neither solicited nor expected American military participation or financial support. No one anticipated that the war would last over four years, require total economic as well as military mobilization, and be deeply influenced by American loans, munitions, and food. No one envisioned that the United States, whose army was only the nineteenth largest in the world in 1913, would deploy a major military force in 1917.

While some Americans favored intervention, most did not, and the government's official policy was neutrality. Although President Woodrow Wilson and many of his closest supporters were more sympathetic to Britain than Germany, many Americans were critical of both sides, citing reports of German atrocities, the illegal naval blockade of Germany, British repression of the Irish, and brutality on all sides. Military and diplomatic arguments for non-involvement were bolstered by the domestic political risks of taking sides, for allying with the British, which was the only serious alternative to neutrality, threatened to alienate America's large German and Irish populations. Moreover, the influential Progressive movement initially saw war as an obstacle to domestic reform, although it gradually came to support it. Although the Allies, especially Britain, complained about American neutrality, Wilson insisted this policy was the best way to save white, Western civilization.

Neutrality, however, did not mean complete disengagement from Europe's war, for as American businessmen and politicians quickly realized, war offered economic opportunities. United States exports increased from $2 billion in 1913 to $6 billion in 1916. As Mira Wilkins has shown, "United States parent corporations retained direct communications with their subsidiaries and affiliates in Europe – *on both sides of the war ...*"[1] GE, for example, made war *matériel* for the Entente and Central Powers alike. Singer's Scottish factory switched to war production for Britain, while its German facility continued to manufacture sewing machines that assisted the German war effort. More importantly, America bankrolled the Entente war effort. J. P. Morgan & Co. signed the Commercial Agency Agreement with the British government and bought $3 billion in United States goods for the Allies between January 1915 and April 1917. To pay for these war goods, Britain sold off its foreign investments, sent gold to America, and borrowed $2.7 billion from United States banks. As Britain and France became dependent on the United States for money, weapons, and supplies, the United States moved from being a debtor nation to being the world's number one creditor.[2]

Economic opportunities were not restricted to Europe. American businessmen took advantage of Europe's self-involvement and growing financial plight to increase American investments in Central and South America, Canada, and to a lesser extent east of Suez. United States manufacturing firms bought up supplies of raw materials, investing in Cuban sugar, Chilean copper, Australian and Latin American meat packing, and oil reserves in the Western Hemisphere, and thereby created vast integrated firms. As in the prewar period, the United States government encouraged foreign direct investment and dollar diplomacy, and when more peaceful advice went unheeded, took quasi-colonial financial and military control in Haiti, the Dominican Republic, Nicaragua, and Liberia and intervened militarily in Mexico's civil war. In November 1915 major industrial and financial firms formed the American International Corporation to direct investment and trade with the non Euro-American world, including Europe's colonies. As Frank Vanderlip, head

---

[1] Mira Wilkins, *The Maturing of Multinational Enterprise: American Business Abroad from 1914 to 1970* (Cambridge, MA: Harvard University Press, 1974), 7–8. Italics in original.
[2] Robert Zieger, *America's Great War: World War I and the American Experience* (Lanham, MD: Rowman and Littlefield, 2000), 16, 30.

of National City Bank, optimistically stated, "We have an opportunity now to become the wellspring of capital for the world."[3]

Neutrality, however profitable economically, was not a long-term political option, due to Germany's aggressive naval warfare and growing domestic pressure for intervention. When German submarines sank the British luxury liner *Lusitania* in 1915, many Americans turned against Germany both because 114 Americans died and because the sinking of civilian ships violated the rules of war. Although Germany agreed to refrain from such actions, as it grew more desperate, it resumed unlimited submarine warfare in January 1917. American anger was further exacerbated when German Foreign Minister Zimmermann sent a note to the German ambassador in Mexico in February 1917, instructing him that in the case of war between Germany and the United States, Mexico should be asked to join with the Central Powers and reclaim territory lost to America. In April the United States Congress voted overwhelmingly to declare war on Germany, and Wilson stressed that America was fighting to make the world safe for democracy and had no selfish aims. Criticism of European militarism and imperialism, once applied to all European states, now focused exclusively on Germany and Austria-Hungary. Yet, siding against the Axis did not mean identifying completely with the Entente. Indeed, as Alan Dawley has argued,

The more Americans contemplated intervention in the Old World, paradoxically, the more they defined themselves *against* Europe. Insisting that America was not just different from the Old World, but altogether exceptional, they held the United States to be a nation outside the limitations of history with a duty to redeem history's sins.[4]

Like so many Europeans in August 1914, Americans entered the conflict in 1917 believing that war could be redemptive.

The bulk of the nearly 1,400,000 American troops who were to see combat in France did not arrive until the spring of 1918. By that point all European countries except Spain, the Netherlands, Switzerland, and the Scandinavian countries had been fighting for nearly four years, and Entente states had had to augment their armies with soldiers from Australia, New Zealand, and Canada as well as British and French colonial troops from Africa and India. Americans fought only on the Western Front, infamous for its brutal trench warfare, not on the equally barbaric but lesser-known Eastern Front.

How crucial to the Entente victory were "Pershing's crusaders," as these soldiers were called with American messianic enthusiasm?

---

[3] Zieger, *America's Great War*, 31.
[4] Alan Dawley, *Changing the World: American Progressives in War and Revolution* (Princeton University Press, 2003), 134.

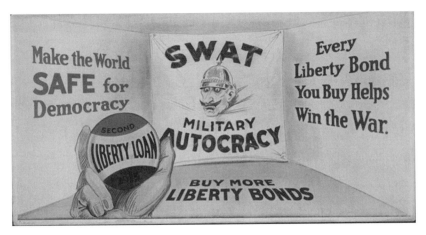

Illustration 3 Make the world safe for democracy, 1917.

Although they boosted the Entente war effort in its final six months, it was American war loans and war production that made the decisive difference. By war's end, Britain had borrowed $3,696 million from United States banks and after April 1917 from the United States government as well; France had $1,970 million in loans, Italy, $1,031 million, and Russia $188 million. In 1913 Germany and Austria-Hungary accounted for 19.2 percent of world manufacturing production while the figure for Britain, France, and Russia was 27.9 percent. The Central Powers, however, outproduced the Allies in steel, and even though the Allies blockaded Germany, it was nearly self-sufficient in food. The balance of economic power shifted dramatically when the United States joined the Entente, and America more than compensated for the withdrawal of Russia from the war in January 1918. By November 1918 the GDP of Britain, France, and the United States was two and half times larger than that of the Central Powers; if all of the Allies are included, the GDP was nearly five times larger. In 1913 Britain, France, and the United States accounted for just over half of world manufacturing and produced more than double the amount of steel the Axis powers did. Wilson and many other Americans prided themselves on America's contributions in men, money, and *matériel* to the Entente cause. Imbued with a sense of mission, they felt entitled to design the new European and international order. Before exploring the contradictory and destabilizing consequences of such efforts, however, we need to look at the political, economic, and social effects of the war itself, for these created vastly different transatlantic experiences of war, huge postwar power differentials, and sharply conflicting visions of the desired postwar order.[5]

Mobilizing for total war

Unlike wars of the nineteenth century, prolonged total war required a vast expansion of military and state power and the mobilization of the economy for war production. Each belligerent faced escalating demands for manpower, munitions, and food; each struggled to finance the most costly war ever and maintain popular morale or at least repress dissent. However reluctantly, every major power moved in the direction of organized capitalism and war collectivism, developed state propaganda machines, policed dissent, and mobilized the home front, including women. States failing to meet these challenges, like Germany, Austria-Hungary, and Russia, risked defeat, imperial disintegration, and revolution. Although Americans mobilized, regulated, propagandized, and protested just as Europeans did, the American war lasted scarcely a year and a half, and its reverberations were shallower and much less disruptive and divisive.

During World War I roughly 65 million soldiers from over thirty countries were mobilized. Russia with 12 million soldiers, Germany with 11 million, Britain and its empire with over 9 million, France with 8.5 million and Austria-Hungary with nearly 8 million led the way. The United States mobilized over 4 million, ranking just behind Italy, but well ahead of Turkey, Bulgaria, Romania, and Japan. Even smaller states mobilized proportionally large numbers – over 700,000 in Serbia, 267,000 in Belgium, and 100,000 in Portugal.[6] Countries with military conscription drafted a much higher percentage of men than before 1914; those, such as Britain and the United States, which had relied on volunteers, implemented compulsory service.

Training, supplying, and fielding such vast forces cost unprecedented amounts. Britain spent over $23 billion in 1913 dollars on the war, while Germany spent nearly $20 billion and the United States $17 billion. Overall, the Allies outspent the Central Powers by over $30 billion. Government spending during the entire war was equivalent to over half of GDP in France and Germany, over one-third in Britain but only one-sixth in the United States. In 1918 alone 80 percent of the British state

---

[5] Gerd Hardach, *The First World War, 1914–1918* (Berkeley: University of California Press, 1977), 148. Kennedy, *Rise and Fall of the Great Powers*, 258–59, 266–71. Stephen Broadberry and Mark Harrison, "The Economics of World War I: An Overview," in Stephen Broadberry and Mark Harrison, eds., *The Economics of World War I* (Cambridge University Press, 2005), 11

[6] www.worldwar1.com/tlcrates.htm.

budget went to defense, and the figure was even higher in Germany. That same year, France spent $234 per person on defense, Britain $187, Germany $131, and the United States $67. States raised such vast sums by selling war bonds at home, borrowing abroad, or raising taxes. The last option, especially income tax, was politically divisive in countries such as France and Germany and unpopular everywhere, and only a small proportion of war expenses were covered this way. Governments preferred loans. The Allies ran up huge debts to the Americans and to one another and floated waves of war bonds at home, successfully in Britain, much less so in impoverished and increasingly antiwar Russia. The Central Powers, who were cut off from global financial markets, ran up huge domestic debts. Every belligerent abandoned the gold standard, most ran large trade deficits, and if necessary printed money to fund the war in the short run. No one contemplated the long-term consequences of such acts, counting instead on victory to pay the bill.[7]

The economic challenges of total war hardly ended with financing, for it quickly became clear that victory would be determined on the home front as much as on the battlefield. Each belligerent faced the challenges of allocating manpower between the front and the factories, producing sufficient munitions, and securing an adequate food supply, and all resorted to new forms of state intervention. The transatlantic story of World War I reveals some remarkably similar developments in different national contexts, yet, the overall impact of the war proved radically different in Europe than in the United States.

In order to produce sufficient guns and shells and cut nonessential production and civilian consumption, states began to purchase and allocate raw materials through new institutions like Germany's raw materials board, run by the electrical entrepreneur Walther Rathenau. More expansive legislation and regulatory bodies quickly followed in 1915 and 1916. In order to allocate resources and manpower and regulate prices and wages, Britain passed the Defence of the Realm Act in 1914 and the Munitions of War Act in 1915; France put the socialist Albert Thomas in charge of the newly established Ministry of Munitions, and by 1916 the dictatorship of Generals Hindenburg and Ludendorff was running both the German war economy and the state. To drum up support for such regulations and restrictions as well as to publicize war aims, every belligerent developed elaborate propaganda machinery. Leading intellectuals rallied behind their nation's war effort, and the press, radio, and movies

[7] Hardach, *First World War*, 153. Broadberry and Harrison, "Economics of World War I," 15. Kennedy, *Rise and Fall of the Great Powers*, 267. Eric Rauchway, *Blessed among Nations: How the World Made America* (New York: Hill and Wang, 2006), 167.

cooperated with governments. The United States came late to the war but quickly established a panoply of state regulatory bodies, of which the most important were the War Industries Board, led by Bernard M. Baruch, and the Committee on Public Information, headed by George Creel.

While all countries learned from one another, war economies displayed national peculiarities. Everywhere industry became a major ally and beneficiary of government regulation, but nowhere was property nationalized (except the United States railroads temporarily). Prices and wages were regulated but profits were not. In no case was the label "war socialism" – whether used positively or pejoratively – appropriate for these new forms of state intervention. In Britain trade unions gained recognition in return for cooperation in war production, while in the United States and Germany workers' councils with union representatives achieved some voice, but unions were not formally recognized. In Russia, Italy, and France, however, no such concessions were made. Italy and France implemented state regulation under democratic auspices, albeit of a very consensual and attenuated sort, but in Germany the military played the leading role and in Russia the tsarist autocracy. Every belligerent dramatically increased its production of arms – Britain manufactured 100,000 rifles in 1914 for example, and 1,100,000 in 1918, while Russian munitions production increased from 43,000 tons in 1913 to nearly 400,000 in 1916. But none could meet the voracious demands of their armies. The United States mobilized soldiers more efficiently than munitions production, and American troops in Europe relied on the British and French for supplies and transportation.[8] The Russian and Italian governments became more politically authoritarian without becoming more economically efficient. Even the highly interventionist and autocratic German state was unable to meet the economic challenges of a two-front war.

For European nations, mobilizing manpower was as difficult as securing resources and proved much more destabilizing to class and gender relations. As hundreds of thousands of men were drafted or volunteered in the fall of 1914, industries crucial to the war economy were thrown into chaos, and states found it necessary to decide who was an essential worker and who could be sent to the front. France militarized its factories, Britain negotiated agreements with its trade unions, Germany passed the Auxiliary Service Law to allocate civilian manpower, and the United States set up the National War Labor Board. Across Europe states debated conscripting women for war work and then discarded the possibility. Yet women flocked

---

[8] Zieger, *America's Great War*, 58, 64.

into newly opened factory and government jobs, for however strenuous, or, in the case of shell production, dangerous, these positions were far better than the sweatshops, domestic service, and textile factories to which most had been relegated. Women were over one-third of German workers by 1918, while in France they formed one-quarter of the labor force in war industries. In Britain female employment in metals and chemicals increased from just over 200,000 to nearly 1 million over the course of the war. White women also moved into new jobs in the United States because immigration declined sharply, but they were not central to the war economy as they were in Europe and would become in the United States in World War II.[9] Everywhere, women moved into male sectors, but not into the exact jobs or same pay as men, for skilled jobs were "diluted," that is, broken up into a series of unskilled tasks. Male workers were often hostile and employers skeptical toward these new women workers, who breached, albeit temporarily, prewar gender occupational segregation.

Women in Europe were mobilized for other wartime economic roles as well. Middle-class women escaped the private sphere through paid or volunteer work as tram drivers, factory social workers, nurses, and clerical staff. Some moved into agriculture, increasingly vital as trade diminished and male farmers fought. Britain established the Women's Land Army, for example, while the Germans conscripted women for agricultural labor in occupied France. A few prominent feminists, such as Elisabeth Lüders in Germany or Anna Shabanova in Russia, served in government war offices, advising on women's issues. Only the military remained an entirely male bastion, except in Russia where several thousand women fought, including in the all-women battalion of Maria Bochkareva, and in Britain, where a Women's Army Auxiliary Corps was formed. Everywhere women, employed or not, were admonished to support the war by encouraging men to fight and buy war bonds, and every nation claimed to be defending its women, homes, and families against the danger of rape and pillage by the enemy. Women were admonished to be committed mothers, thrifty housewives, loyal spouses, and morally proper single women. In Western and Central Europe as well as the United States, the state took on new economic and familial roles, paying separation allowances to soldiers' wives and pensions to war widows.

The wartime mobilization of women had contradictory effects. Male workers, fearing a long-term loss of skills, pay, and bargaining power, insisted women workers were there for the duration only. Allowances and

---

[9] Geoff Eley, *Forging Democracy: The History of the Left in Europe, 1850–2000* (Oxford University Press, 2002), 132. Susan R. Grayzel, *Women and the First World War* (London: Longman, 2002), 28–34.

pensions brought some women material benefits, even as they subjected them to state scrutiny, tied social support to male military service, and opened recipients to criticism from others who suffered without government aid. In France war blurred gender roles yet polarized gender representations; in Britain, it seemed to immobilize and demoralize men while giving women a new freedom and confidence, and thus fueled misogyny. Everywhere women participated more fully in national politics, resumed demands for social rights and political citizenship, and in Germany, Italy, and Russia took to the streets, joining the waves of protest that escalated as the war dragged on. In the United States, where the mobilization of women was more partial, such politicization and gender destabilization hardly occurred. Social unrest in the United States was likewise less threatening.

When war broke out, prewar social, political, and national conflicts subsided, governments proclaimed political truces, and parties and publics united behind their nation's war effort. Before 1914 the French socialist Jean Jaurès had thundered against war; the German Social Democratic Party, the largest in parliament, promised "not a man and not a penny to this system"; and the socialist Second International instructed its members to use all appropriate means to oppose war. Yet, in August 1914 socialists supported the war and identified with the national cause everywhere except Italy and Bulgaria. As the war dragged on for months and years, mobilization, deprivation, and the occasional aerial bombardment of cities eroded consensus. Older conflicts about trade union rights, political democracy, and state social policies revived, and new tensions around war financing and war aims, food shortages, and war profits, new forms of state intervention and new roles for women emerged.

In the face of horrendous military casualties, skyrocketing food prices, acute food shortages, rampant inflation, and the evident inequality of sacrifices demanded, soldiers deserted and mutinied, women protested, and workers struck. Nearly half the French Army mutinied in 1917 and Britain executed a few hundred soldiers for desertion. In the wake of the February 1917 democratic revolution in Russia, the army rapidly disintegrated, as the Austro-Hungarian Army was to do in the fall of 1918. From 1916 on working-class and lower-middle-class women took to the streets in Berlin to demand food and peace, and women in St. Petersburg and Turin staged similar protests in 1917. There was extensive labor unrest in Britain throughout the war; millions of American workers struck between 1916 and 1918; and in 1917 labor protest across Europe escalated and became politicized. As the economic crisis worsened, the military stalemate continued, and Bolsheviks publicized the existence of secret treaties with expansive war aims. Hundreds of thousands of workers took to the streets. In Germany metalworkers struck, demanding democratization, lower food prices, and peace without annexations and indemnities. In Britain workers called for higher wages, the end of dilution, and the abrogation of secret treaties. Like French and Italian workers, they called for immediate peace.

Governments in Western Europe both repressed protest, sending some demonstrators to the front, and reluctantly made concessions that quelled social unrest but failed to restore consensus. In Russia the tsarist autocracy was overthrown in February and replaced by the liberal democratic regime of Alexander Kerensky, which, in turn, was overthrown by the Bolsheviks in October. Far from stabilizing the old order, war had led to revolution – and of a new communist sort. As British Foreign Secretary Gray had warned Germany and Austria in the summer of 1914, modern war would "mean a state of things worse than that of 1848 . . . irrespective of who were victors in the war, many things might be completely swept away."[10] Americans, however, remained convinced their war would save Western civilization.

The costs of war

Just as the war required greater mobilization from Europe than America, it extracted far greater costs in terms of productive assets and markets lost, casualties suffered, and political systems undermined. World War I decisively weakened European economies, while strengthening the American one. At war's end on both sides of the Atlantic, states rapidly dismantled their regulatory institutions and policies. Despite this attempt to return to the *status quo ante bellum*, governments, businesses, and labor movements found themselves living in a different economic and social world.

War took perhaps the greatest long-run and structural toll on victorious Britain. To fund the war, it liquidated its foreign assets; in the United States alone British investment plunged from $7.2 billion to $3.3 billion. It lost colonial markets in Asia to India and Japan and in Latin America to the United States. Even before the war, Britain had fallen behind Germany and America in industrial production, technology, and business organization but had made up for these handicaps by being the world's banker, shipper, and insurer. Those positions, along with profitable industries such as shipbuilding, declined postwar, and the 1920s were an economically bleak decade for Britain. To be sure, in comparison to the continent Britain remained relatively well off. In 1918–19, for

---

[10] Arno Mayer, "The Domestic Causes of the First World War," in Fritz Stern, ed., *The Responsibility of Power* (London: Macmillan, 1968), 286–93.

example, most European countries got relief aid from the American Relief Administration (ARA), while Britain provided nearly 40 percent of the funding for the American led effort. It still had the highest GDP per capita in Europe in the mid twenties.[11]

In the short run Germany and France suffered more than Britain. The Treaty of Versailles deprived Germany of 13 percent of its territory and 10 percent of its population as well as its navy and merchant marine. Germany lost 5–6 billion marks in investments in Russia and the successor states of East Central Europe, and after having been the world's third largest creditor prewar, became the world's biggest debtor. Yet, German industrial areas were undamaged, unlike France whose mines were flooded and whose key prewar industrial regions had been devastated. France lost its extensive prewar investments and loans in Russia and became a debtor nation as well. Although France regained Alsace-Lorraine after the war, its population was 2.5 million smaller than before 1914. Overall France lost three-fifths of its prewar human and physical capital and half of its overseas assets. The collapse of the Austro-Hungarian Empire and emergence of new states broke apart a once integrated economic unit, severing producers from resources and markets, disrupting food supplies, and causing high unemployment and starvation. Poland and Austria were the hardest hit and became the largest recipients of American aid after Germany and Belgium.[12]

No county was more economically devastated than Russia both before 1917 and as war morphed into a brutal civil war that lasted from 1917–20. The Russian Civil War, like World War I, paved the way for dramatic state interventions in the economy. Some, such as food rationing and forced requisitions, were built on tsarist practices; others, such as the nationalization of all manufacturing, the establishment of some collective farms, and efforts to organize poor peasants against better-off ones, were Bolshevik innovations. The results of militarized and coercive War Communism were catastrophic – deindustrialization, deurbanization, and deproletarianization as the number of industrial workers declined from 3.6 million to 1.5 million between 1917 and 1920. The population of Petrograd shrank from 2 million to 740,000. War was declared on markets, producing empty shops, long lines, barter, and black markets. The exact death tolls from

[11] Alfred E. Eckes and Thomas W. Zeiler, *Globalization and the American Century* (Cambridge University Press, 2003), 22. Margaret MacMillan, *Paris 1919: Six Months that Changed the World* (New York: Random House, 2003), 61. Gerold Ambrosius and William H. Hubbard, *A Social and Economic History of Twentieth-Century Europe* (Cambridge, MA: Harvard University Press, 1989), 145.

[12] Born, *International Banking*, 230. Ambrosius and Hubbard, *Social and Economic History*, 6. Broadberry and Harrison, "Economics of World War I," 28.

combat, terror, famine, and epidemics are impossible to determine. Estimates range from 3–5 million total, to 5 million famine deaths alone in a total of 9–10 million, to nearly 20 million on top of the 11 million who died between 1914 and 1917.[13]

The United States economy, by contrast, had surged ahead on all fronts. At war's end, America had become the world's number one creditor; its manufacturing production had tripled during the war and continued to grow rapidly thereafter, whereas Britain and Germany did not reach 1913 levels until the mid twenties. Even during the war the consumption of cars and other consumer durables increased. During the war, the United States, which had been dependent on British shipping, built a substantial merchant marine that carried a growing portion of America's expanding exports. The United States did lose up to $200 million in investments in Russia, for firms like Singer were expropriated immediately after the Bolshevik Revolution and others, like International Harvester, were taken over in 1924, but America's Western European investments survived and those outside Europe and Mexico remained profitable.[14]

World War I reshaped the international economy, making it both less Eurocentric and less interconnected than before 1914. Colonies took advantage of Europe's sale of overseas assets and inability to trade and invest and both increased their industrial base and expanded their economic autonomy. The United States became the main economic partner of countries formerly within the British orbit in Latin America, while Japan moved into Asian markets. America emerged from the war with a trade surplus, but every European country had a trade deficit in addition to huge war debts. In contrast to the prewar period, the United States exported slightly less to Europe and imported substantially less from it, while Britain exported more to Europe than before 1914, but mainly relied on its empire for markets, and Germany's economy remained overwhelmingly European centered.[15] War severed production, labor migration, and infrastructural links within the former Austro-Hungarian, Russian, and Ottoman empires and disrupted trade and investment patterns across Europe and the world. Transatlantic migration, so vital to both European countries and the United States, virtually ceased.

---

[13] William Rosenberg, "Problems of Social Welfare and Everyday Life," in Edward Acton, Vladimir Iu. Cherniaev, and William Rosenberg, eds., *A Critical Companion to the Russian Revolution, 1914–21* (Bloomington: Indiana University Press, 1997), 633.

[14] Jeffry A. Frieden, *Global Capitalism: Its Fall and Rise in the Twentieth Century* (New York: Norton, 2006), 130–32. Wilkins, *The Maturing of Multinational Enterprise*, 40, 43–45.

[15] Barry Eichengreen, *Golden Fetters: The Gold Standard and the Great Depression 1919–1939* (Oxford University Press, 1995), 82–83, 89–90.

The staggering casualty figures of World War I tell an even more horrific story of the differential costs of war. While estimates vary, most place the military death toll at between 9 and 10 million soldiers. Germany lost over 2 million soldiers and Russia over 1,800,000, while France saw over 1,300,000 die and Austria-Hungary 1,100,000. Britain lost over 700,000. Roughly 900 Frenchmen, 1,300 Germans, and over 1,400 Russians died every day from August 1914 to the November armistice of 1918. On the first day of the Battle of the Somme, 20,000 British soldiers died and nearly 40,000 were wounded. By contrast, in the entire war the United States lost between 116,000 and 126,000 soldiers, of whom 53,000 were combat deaths. In proportional terms smaller countries such as Romania suffered most, losing over 40 percent of those mobilized. Nearly half of French soldiers and around two-fifths of Russian, German, and Austro-Hungarian ones were wounded by shells or gas or suffered disease or shell shock. By war's end there were 5 million POWs on the Eastern Front. These unprecedented military casualties devastated economies, societies, and families as a generation was lost to death, physical disability, and psychological trauma. By contrast just over 5 percent of American soldiers were wounded and just under 3 percent died.[16]

World War I, particularly in the East, saw a blurring of the line between home front and battlefront that foreshadowed their fusion in World War II. Both sides deported and interned enemy aliens, and Germany used camps in France and the East both to punish and to meet labor shortages. In Central and Eastern Europe, refugees fled the fighting that moved back and forth across vast territories, and impoverishment and dislocation occurred everywhere. World War I became a testing ground for horrific new forms of warfare against civilians. London and Paris were bombed on a limited scale. More importantly, total war provided the context and pretext for mass murder, as 1.5 million Armenians in the Ottoman Empire were killed in the twentieth century's first genocide.

America suffered nothing comparable during World War I on the home or battlefronts, and parallels between the European struggle and America's devastating Civil War would have been a part of living memory only for older Americans. Because Americans were largely spared the shocking brutality of the war and the burden of the disabled and traumatized, because they experienced neither revolution nor counterrevolution, they did not reflect obsessively on World War I or war in general as Europeans did. After 1918 Americans focused their criticism on the peace treaty, not

---

[16] Broadberry and Harrison, "Economics of World War I," 27. Stéphane Audoin-Rouzeau and Annette Becker, *14–18: Understanding the Great War* (New York: Hill and Wang, 2003), 23. John Keegan, *The First World War* (New York: Knopf, 2000), 295.

on the conduct of the war itself. They retained an optimism about technological warfare that contrasted sharply with a growing European pessimism. To a much greater degree than Americans, many Europeans memorialized the war dead in every town and village, longed for the romanticized prosperity and stability of the prewar order, and developed a deep aversion to any and all war. Others urged preparation for an anticipated future conflict over national borders or political ideologies, while still others, prevalent in Germany and Italy, glorified the struggle and hardness of war, disdained democracy and bourgeois masculinity, and sought a new militarized, expansionist order.

In Europe war proved as fatal to states and political regimes as to soldiers and civilians. Although colonial empires survived the war, continental ones did not, and by November 1918 the Russian, German, and Austro-Hungarian empires had collapsed, the first under the strains of total war and revolution, the second as a result of defeat, and the last from nationality conflicts and military failures. Their rulers were dead or in exile, their territories to varying degrees dismembered, and the nature of the successor states contested. The partially dismembered Ottoman Empire was to limp along until 1923, when the Turkish Republic replaced the Caliphate. While Western European states survived intact, disputes about their internal order and future course raged. An age of political and social uncertainty had begun. Would regimes in old states and new be democratic, authoritarian, communist, or fascist? Would wartime economic regulation be retained, social policy expanded, and women enfranchised? Would a new American-led international order replace the old diplomacy and colonial system?

Wilson versus Lenin

"Vive Wilson! Vive Lenin!" chanted many on the streets of Paris in early 1919. Like others on both sides of the Atlantic, they looked to one or another of these charismatic figures to play a key role in redrawing the map of Europe and reordering its polities and economies. Wilson's liberal internationalism and Lenin's revolutionary socialism both rejected the prewar political and diplomatic order and promised a new world. But they represented competing visions of national and international order, as Wilson and Lenin clearly recognized. Each claimed universal validity; each sought to win the allegiance of the European left; each strove to shape the postwar European order in its image. Which leader and ideology would triumph?

The years 1918–19 have been termed "the Wilsonian moment" and Wilson "the first world leader of the twentieth century." In many respects he was an unlikely person to dominate the postwar settlement. A southern Democrat who had been a professor and then president of Princeton

University, he entered New Jersey politics as an anticorruption candidate, an opponent of big government, and supporter of racial segregation. He was a staunch Presbyterian, who saw America as a Christian nation, and was a firm believer in American exceptionalism. Elected president in 1912 and reelected in 1916, he brought to the office a "political millenarianism" that deepened as America's international involvement expanded. However reluctant initially to intervene in Europe's internecine struggle, Wilson was convinced from 1914 on that the world should take "moral inspiration" from America and hoped that the stars and stripes would be "the flag not only of America, but of all humanity." For Wilson and many others, America's national interests were humanity's interests. In the words of the American progressive Walter Weyl, Wilsonianism represented "a new and broader Americanism; an Internationalism." Wilson himself succinctly articulated this purported intertwining of the national and the international, the political and the economic in a 1916 speech in Detroit: "You are Americans and are meant to carry liberty and justice and the principles of humanity wherever you go," he told his audience of salesmen. "Go out and sell goods that will make the world more comfortable and more happy and convert them to the principles of America."[17]

The most expansive and famous statement of Wilsonian liberal internationalism came in his address to Congress on January 8, 1918, made after the Russians had laid out their principles for a peace settlement and the Germans had rearticulated their war aims. The Fourteen Points, as Wilson's statement of "purpose and principle" is known, outlined the "remaking of the map of the world as we would have it," to borrow a phrase from his closest advisor Colonel Edward House. Wilson made new claims for open treaties and "a general association of nations" and called for a marked reduction in armaments. He reiterated many principles of the older liberal internationalism, including a reduction of tariffs and freedom of the seas. This linkage of a liberal economy to a liberal political order would be a hallmark of twentieth-century American foreign policy. Calling for justice for "all peoples and nationalities," Wilson insisted the Germans evacuate Russia, Belgium, and France, demanded "autonomous development" for the nationalities of Austria-Hungary as well as for the non-Turkish parts of the Ottoman Empire, and championed an independent Poland. Determining the exact nature of autonomy and the

---

[17] The term Wilsonian moment is from Erez Manela, *The Wilsonian Moment: Self-Determination and the International Origins of Anticolonial Nationalism* (New York: Oxford, 2007). Dawley, *Changing the World*, 182, 191. Edward Hallett Carr, *The Twenty Years' Crisis, 1919–1939* (New York: Harper Torchbooks, 1964), 234. N. Gordon Levin, *Woodrow Wilson and World Politics: America's Response to War and Revolution* (New York: Oxford University Press, 1968), 18.

borders of new nations, however, proved extremely contentious. And on colonial issues Wilson's language was more equivocal. "A free, open-minded, and absolutely impartial adjustment of all colonial claims" must give equal weight to "the interests of the populations concerned" and "the equitable claims of the government whose title is to be determined." Colonialism was put on the agenda and self-determination was proclaimed as a general principle, but like John Hobson, Norman Angell, and E. D. Morel of the anti-colonial British Union of Democratic Control, Wilson was against imperialism but assumed an Anglo-American guiding role in the rest of the world. For Wilson this was to be exercised by economic more than military or colonial means.[18]

Wilson and the Americans were neither the only critics of the old diplomacy nor the only champions of national self-determination. The February Revolution, which brought the liberal government of Kerensky to power in Russia, also saw the rise of the Petrograd Soviet and ushered in a period of dual power in which parliament and workers and soldiers councils competed for control. While Kerensky was determined to con-tinue fighting on the Entente side, the Petrograd Soviet demanded the publication of the secret treaties signed by the Allies and called for a peace without annexations and indemnities. Lenin and other Bolsheviks were initially ambivalent about nationalism and uncertain about the possibility of turning a bourgeois liberal revolution into a communist one in back-ward Russia. In the face of massive peasant and worker unrest and grow-ing opposition to Kerensky's efforts to continue the war, however, the Bolsheviks called for "Peace, Land and Bread." They came to power in October 1917, more as a result of pervasive popular unrest, social polar-ization, and a popular program than of conspiracy, charisma, and a coup. Russia dropped out of the war and signed the punitive Treaty of Brest-Litovsk with Germany. Whether from conviction or a recognition that multinational empires were disintegrating across Europe, the Bolsheviks became vocal champions of national self-determination.

Lenin combined his vision of a radically restructured domestic political and economic order with a call for the reordering of both the European and the global political system. Whereas liberal proponents of national self-determination focused on Central and Eastern Europe and stressed issues of arbitration, disarmament, and international institutions, Lenin and the Bolsheviks insisted that national self-determination should be applied globally. They hoped it would promote decolonization and social

[18] Michael Hunt, *The American Ascendancy: How the United States Gained and Wielded Global Dominance* (Chapel Hill: University of North Carolina Press, 2007), 57, http://wwi.lib.byu.edu/index.php/President_Wilson%27s_Fourteen_Points.

РЕВОЛЮЦІЙНИЙ ТРИМАЙТЕ КРОК!

Illustration 4 Lenin, 1917.

revolution in the non Euro-American world. American Secretary of State Lansing believed that the Bolshevik program threatened "the existing social order in all countries" as well as the global order envisioned by the United States.[19]

This dual threat was enhanced not only by the survival of the Bolshevik Revolution in the face of domestic opposition, civil war, economic collapse, and the draconian policies of War Communism, but also by the postwar social upheavals across Europe and the United States. In late 1918 and 1919 there were democratic revolutions in Germany and Austria, an unsuccessful communist uprising in Berlin, a massive movement for workers' control and the socialization of mines in the Ruhr, a short-lived communist government in Munich, and the four-month Soviet Republic, led by Bela Kun, in Hungary. In Italy radical socialists protested and ultimately occupied factories but hesitated to seize power, while in Paris workers struck and in Britain radical trade unionists unsuccessfully demanded workers' control. In the United States over 4 million workers or roughly 20 percent of the labor force went out on strike, and race riots occurred in Chicago in 1919 and in Tulsa two years later. In no Western European country did the radical left come close to taking power

---

[19] Arno Mayer, *Political Origins of the New Diplomacy, 1917–1918* (New York: Vintage, 1970), 303–4.

as it had in Russia. Yet, in 1918–19 the threat to Wilson's vision of a liberal capitalist global order in which the United States would exert economic and moral leadership seemed very real.

The prerequisite for realizing Wilson's ambitious program of implementing national self-determination in Central Europe, bolstering French security, reintegrating Germany, and establishing a concert of nations was the containment or possibly even elimination of Bolshevism. France, Britain, and Italy shared America's anti-communism and preoccupation with the Russian question. Allied intervention in Russia to bolster the Entente war effort had begun in the spring and summer of 1918 with British and American troops landing in Archangel, and American troops supporting the Japanese in Siberia. At war's end over 180,000 foreign troops remained in Russia and were deployed against Bolshevik forces. British Prime Minister David Lloyd George, French Premier Georges Clemenceau, and Wilson disagreed about which White faction they favored in the Civil War, whether a liberal democratic regime could be restored or a more authoritarian one was preferable, and whether a large non-communist Russia or one stripped of territory would provide the most security for Western Europe, but they were united in their opposition to Lenin. Britain and France were unable to commit substantial troops, however, and America was unwilling. While some American officials such as House and William Bullitt came to favor de facto recognition of the Bolsheviks, neither White Russians nor Wilson were willing to negotiate, for anti-communism was becoming an entrenched pillar of American foreign policy. Intervention wound down by 1920 without influencing the outcome of the Civil War or destabilizing Bolshevik power.

Thereafter, American efforts to shape developments in Russia took the form of massive famine relief. Herbert Hoover's American Relief Administration (ARA), roughly half of which was funded by the government, sent 750,000 tons of supplies to Russia, and its 18,000 kitchens fed 10 million people a day in 1922. All supplies were purchased from American farmers, who were suffering from crop surpluses, and farm prices did rise as a result. In Hoover's view, it was a happy confluence of American ideals and self-interest. The Russians were considerably more critical, for Americans, who saw Russians as, in the words of one official, "mute millions of muzhiks," incapable of caring for themselves, delivered aid in a condescending manner. The Russian government wanted diplomatic recognition and help with economic reconstruction, not just relief aid, while Hoover preferred to keep Russia in an economic vacuum until the Bolsheviks fell.[20]

---

[20] David Engerman, *Modernization from the Other Shore: American Intellectuals and the Romance of Russian Development* (Cambridge, MA: Harvard University Press, 2003), 108.

The United States was able to isolate Russia economically and politically, at least for a few years, but not to overthrow the Bolshevik regime. Of greater importance from the perspective of the United States, Britain, France, and Italy, European states proved able to rule and, if necessary, repress protesters and potential revolutionaries, despite the toll of total war, the collapse of several monarchies and their replacement by weak republics. Workers' movements across Europe were divided between moderate socialists and more radical supporters of either Bolshevism or local variants of council communism, and the postwar economic depression eroded labor's bargaining power and ability to strike. Everywhere, the forces of order reasserted themselves. In France postwar elections brought the conservative Bloc National to power, while in Britain an alliance of liberals and conservatives won an overwhelming victory on an anti-labor, anti-welfare, anti-Irish home rule and pro-punitive peace platform. In Germany the social democratic government used the imperial police and military to repress rebellious workers while failing to democratize the new republic fully. In the United States new legislation restricted speech and dissent and the Bureau of Investigation tracked over two hundred thousand individuals and organizations, arresting many and deporting radical aliens. In Italy the widespread worker protest, which culminated in the 1920 occupation of factories by over half a million socialists and anarchists, collapsed due to strategic divisions among leaders and the political and geographic isolation of the workers' movement. Defeat was followed by a preemptive fascist counterrevolution. In Hungary, as elsewhere in Central and Eastern Europe outside Czechoslovakia, White terror and conservative autocracy ruled.

Versailles

The hostile relations and intransigent leaders of America and the Union of Soviet Socialist Republics (USSR), as Russia was renamed in 1922, were to have a significant long-term influence on European-American relations. In the short run, however, the attention of politicians, the press, and the public across Europe and the United States focused on the Paris Peace Conference from which Russia was excluded. Although anti-Bolshevism was a prominent theme there, it was only one element of the comprehensive American vision of a revamped Europe, whose positive counterparts were national self-determination, political and economic liberalism, and the establishment of a concert of nations. The conference opened in January 1919 with representatives from the victors, including Japan, as well as from smaller European states, new nations such as Czechoslovakia and Poland, British Commonwealth states, Latin

American countries, and China. All key decisions, however, were made by the Council of Four – Wilson, Lloyd George, Clemenceau, and the Italian Prime Minister Vittorio Orlando. Wilson, the first sitting American president to visit Europe, arrived in Paris full of optimism after having been greeted by wildly enthusiastic crowds in Britain, France, and Italy. Problems arose immediately. The American delegation found itself mired in innumerable territorial and economic disputes, about whose technical details and political stakes it knew little, and relations among Lloyd George, Clemenceau, and Wilson were marred by differences of style and substance. Although Lloyd George and Clemenceau shared Wilson's commitment to combat communism at home and abroad, for example, they regarded him as a naïve idealist. Despite personal animosities, they proved able to pursue security for France, reparations from Germany, and defense of the colonial order at the expense of the spirit of the Fourteen Points. In 1919 America lacked the preponderance of power it was to have after 1945, and Wilson could not impose his vision. When he sailed home in June 1919, sent off by only a small and somber crowd, Germany had reluctantly signed the Treaty of Versailles, which violated many of the principles of liberal internationalism. As Wilson himself recognized, "no one is satisfied." According to Harold Nicolson of the British delegation, instead of supplanting the past, "the new order had merely fouled the old."[21]

Were such criticisms justified? National self-determination, a theoretically universal principle, was the central pillar of Wilson's peace plan, yet the Big Four focused only on East Central Europe and the Balkans, and even there did not accommodate the wishes of all nationalities. Poland became independent, Czechoslovakia was carved out of the former Austro-Hungarian Empire, and Yugoslavia was formed from Serbia and remnants of Austria-Hungary. A rump, German-speaking Austria was prohibited from joining Germany, while Hungary gained its independence but lost territory to a vastly expanded Romania. The claims of Croats, Catalans, Estonians, Albanians, and Sinn Fein advocates of Irish independence, among others, were not recognized. Overall, the treaties signed at Versailles put 60 million people in new nation-states, but also created 25 million minorities. Versailles strove for "the rationalization of global space according to discrete national interests," but the principle of national self-determination could not be reconciled with the ethnic geography of the region, nor with the Anglo-French desire for a cordon sanitaire on Russia's western edge and determination to punish Germany, Austria, and Hungary with territorial losses. "The rhetoric was Wilsonian," noted one historian,

[21] MacMillan, *Paris 1919*, 467, 487.

"but the practice remained that of British imperialism" – a new balance of power and spheres of influence.[22] The redrawn map laid the seeds for nationality claims and conflicts that were to persist throughout the twentieth century and beyond. To forestall such contestation, Wilson agreed that the League of Nations would recognize the territorial integrity and political independence of existing states, but this did not prevent ethnic minorities and colonial subjects from asserting their rights, even if they lacked legal recourse.

Although representatives from Asia and the Middle East failed to get Wilson to read their petitions, let alone grant them representation at Versailles, Wilsonianism seemed to offer encouragement to established and emerging anti-colonial nationalists in Asia and the Middle East. While some historians see Lenin and Wilson competing for the allegiance of such anti-colonial movements from 1918 on, others argue that in 1918 and early 1919 Wilson alone "seemed to stand for mankind," in the words of H. G. Wells. The Treaty of Versailles and the League Covenant, however, limited self-determination to Europe. Rather than breaking up colonial empires, the Peace Conference merely redistributed the colonies of the defeated to the victors along the lines agreed upon in wartime secret treaties. These colonies were renamed mandates, and the European mandate holders were assigned the task of supervising the gradual evolution of non-Western populations toward self-determination. Germany's African colonies went to Britain, its Polynesian ones to Australia, and its Chinese settlement to Japan. The non-Turkish Ottoman territories, including Palestine, referred to by Versailles delegates as "the much promised land," were divided up into British and French mandates. Japan tried to insert a racial equality clause in the League Covenant, but Britain and America, worried about race problems in the colonies and at home, prevented its passage. Wilson accepted these arrangements, for he assumed that colonial peoples needed to be under Western trusteeship; he had supported the annexation of the Philippines; and his "racism was a matter of intellectual and social habit." His secretary of state, Lansing, thought it dangerous and misleading to put the idea of self-determination "into the minds of certain races" such as the Irish, Indians, Egyptians, and Boers. In addition, for Wilson, Lansing, and most Americans colonial issues were of marginal import. By consolidating colonial empires, Versailles fueled anti-colonial movements in Egypt, India, Indochina, Korea, and China and opened them to the communist influence. It discredited America's liberal

---

[22] Ivan T. Berend, *Decades of Crisis: Central and Eastern Europe before World War II* (Berkeley: University of California Press, 1998), 153.

anti-imperialism, for the emerging revolt against the West closely associated America with European colonialism.[23]

The Peace Conference found it even harder to legislate internal political relations than to draw national borders. Wilson envisioned a Europe of politically liberal democracies and free market economies. States such as Germany and Poland did write formally democratic constitutions, but others such as Hungary quickly reverted to authoritarianism. Across Europe, the franchise was expanded to include all men, and women received the vote as well, except in France, Italy, Spain, Switzerland, Greece, and Belgium. Whether formerly liberal institutions would be filled with democratic substance and acquire legitimacy, whether old elites would regain control or newer forces would win political influence would only be determined in the course of the tumultuous economic crises and political battles of the interwar decades.

Wilson's greatest victory at Versailles, albeit a pyrrhic one, was the creation of the League of Nations, which embodied liberal internationalism. Committed to international cooperation, the League proclaimed the principle of collective security and established mechanisms for arbitrating disputes. An International Labour Organization was established in conjunction with the League. Although the French wanted a League with "teeth," Wilson successfully opposed an international military force and secured a reservation stating that nothing in the Covenant invalidated the Monroe Doctrine.

Some on the right and left in Europe rejected the League, and others sought to modify it, but the major European powers accepted the League Covenant. Americans proved much more hostile. Some objected to German reparations, others to concessions to Britain, France, and Japan on colonial questions, but the largest and most vocal group condemned the League as an infringement of American sovereignty. Article X with its promise to defend the territorial integrity and political independence of member states abridged Congress's right to determine foreign policy and declare war, claimed people like Henry Cabot Lodge on the right, while Progressives complained that Article X upheld an inequitable global status quo and threatened to make the United States a world policeman for the House of Morgan. Wilson refused to modify Article X; Congress refused to ratify the League Covenant; and the United States remained outside the organization so central to Wilson's liberal internationalist vision. It was not ready to participate in international institutions as one nation among equals.

---

[23] Manela, *Wilsonian Moment*, 3, 27. Levin, *Woodrow Wilson*, 247–48.

World War I marked a crucial turning point in European-American relations. As Europe threw itself into internecine war and civil wars, America claimed a new political and military prominence in Europe and the globe. As European production and consumption plummeted, trade shrank, and finances collapsed, America enjoyed not only prosperity but also a new power position in the global economic order. However much states and societies on both sides of the Atlantic mobilized and reorganized for total war in similar ways, the impact and costs of the war were longer and significantly deeper for Europe. World War I was a traumatic experience and bitter memory for Europeans, while for Americans it was either a triumphant intervention or one proving that entangling alliances were best avoided.

World War I greatly intensified European-American interconnections, redirected exchanges overwhelmingly in a west-to-east direction, and created European economic, military, and political dependencies on the United States. Yet, it did not put the United States in a hegemonic position. Europe was weakened, but not fatally, and America was reluctant to claim a major political role in Europe and the globe. It did not become isolationist, but it did become wary of political involvements abroad. It turned its back on the League but not on Europe, for in the 1920s America's economic and cultural presence grew exponentially. World War I created the potential for the American Century, but that potential was to be unevenly and incompletely realized in the decade that followed.

3   Ambivalent engagement

The specter of Americanism haunted Europe in the 1920s. The United States enjoyed unprecedented economic prosperity and political stability of a sort that war had destroyed in Europe, and the transatlantic balance of power had shifted decidedly in its favor. It was the de facto global hegemon, even though the United States was deeply ambivalent about exerting transatlantic leadership. Instead, America oscillated between isolationism and unilateralism, economic engagement and political distancing. It provided loans, exported its movies and music, and championed the Fordist model of production, but transatlantic exchanges about social reform dwindled and social policy differences magnified. And the United States remained on the margins of European political developments and outside the internationalism of the League of Nations.

Europeans evinced a much greater interest in the United States than in the prewar decades. As lender, purveyor of mass culture, economic competitor, and model of modernity, America became the focus of European hopes and fears, the site of intense debates about Europe's present problems and possible futures, about shifting global power relations and new forms of empire. The European century was in crisis, but Europeans were deeply divided about whether it could be revived or whether the future lay with America, Russia, or both. How did Europeans in different nations and classes assess the perils and promise of Americanism? What roles did American business and government play in the building of a new postwar European order? Why did the Fordist model of mass production and mass consumption find many admirers but few emulators, while American popular culture was more influential?

Towards a new economic order

Leading American politicians and businessmen shared Wilson's view "that global integration, prosperity, and cooperation depended on United States leadership, above all in Europe itself," but they disagreed about how to exercise such leadership.[1] American economic involvement was not only a choice but also a necessity because the Treaty of Versailles held Germany responsible for starting the war and demanded the payment of substantial reparations; these reparations, in turn, were inextricably intertwined with the huge Allied war debts to the United States. Repayment of these multiple obligations proved extraordinarily difficult due to war damage, postwar inflation and deflation, the collapse of the Russian economy, and the structural weaknesses of economies across East Central Europe. Political conflicts within and among major powers further hampered repayment. Wilsonian peacemaking had secured capitalism outside of Russia but did not guarantee capitalist stability, European prosperity, or democracy. Attempts to achieve these dominated European-American relations in the 1920s.

At war's end, economic demobilization proceeded quickly in Western Europe and the United States, as women were pushed out of war work, soldiers reentered civilian life, and states dismantled wartime regulatory institutions and policies. In the successor states of the Habsburg monarchy and Russia, disintegration and collapse more accurately describes the immediate post-armistice situation. Returning to prewar conditions, however desirable to many, was impossible, for four years of war had destroyed production facilities, disrupted trade, wreaked havoc with financial institutions, and profoundly changed the transatlantic balance of economic power. While in 1920 American manufacturing had expanded by one-fifth since 1913, for example, European manufacturing had shrunk by nearly one-quarter and Russian production was at a mere 13 percent of the prewar level.[2]

Despite its advantageous economic position, even the United States emerged from World War I worried about agricultural surpluses, declining prices, market opportunities, and workers' demands. World trade had dwindled, and although America had a trade surplus, Europe played a smaller role in its imports and exports than before 1914. Wilson had championed economic liberalism as a necessary adjunct to political democratization, but only Britain and the Netherlands had anything close to free trade. Germany and France were moderately protectionist, the new states in Eastern Europe erected substantial trade barriers, and by 1925 the United States had the highest tariffs in the world. Transatlantic migration, so vital to both European countries and the United States, dwindled during the war, and the 1924 United States Immigration Act

---

[1] Michael Hunt, *The American Ascendancy: How the United States Gained and Wielded Global Dominance* (Chapel Hill: University of North Carolina Press, 2007), 68.

[2] Paul Kennedy, *The Rise and Fall of the Great Powers* (New York: Vintage, 1987), 280.

limited it to a trickle. Only population poor France continued to import over 2 million foreign laborers in the 1920s.

The key institutions that had regulated the global financial system were in tatters. While every belligerent had gone off the gold standard during the war, only the United States returned to it in 1919, displaying little understanding of why European nations could not follow suit. London was no longer capable of stabilizing and coordinating the global financial system, but Washington was unwilling to assume that role, refusing the requests of Montagu Norman, the governor of the Bank of England, that central banks in Europe and the Federal Reserve in the United States meet regularly to coordinate policy in the volatile postwar environment. And volatile it was. Currencies were unstable as acute inflation plagued Germany, Austria, Hungary, Czechoslovakia, Finland, Bulgaria, Romania, Estonia, Greece, and Yugoslavia. Countries like Britain and the United States that pursued deflationary policies, suffered high unemployment, while Italy saw its liberal center erode.

The economically and politically contentious issues of war debts and reparations were at the heart of problems of recovery. In 1921, 30 percent of British government expenditure and 23 percent of the French budget went toward servicing debt. Both nations faced huge bills for veterans' benefits and widows' pensions, and France needed to fund reconstruction of the territories Germany had occupied. Both states viewed war debts as a result of the joint Entente war effort and asked the United States to forgive them; American banks and the government regarded debts as commercial obligations and refused. The United States accused France of mismanaging its economy, while France suspected America of imperial aspirations, and Britain feared American competition. As one of Lloyd George's advisors noted with concern, "if we have to carry this sacrifice and America has to carry no sacrifice, we may have fought for the greatness of America."[3]

Britain and France insisted that if debts had to be paid in full, then reparations must be as well. The Treaty of Versailles mandated an initial German payment of 20 billion gold marks, and in 1921 the London Ultimatum presented the total bill of 132 billion gold marks or $31 billion. Germans, especially on the nationalist right, were shocked and angry, for they viewed reparations as politically objectionable and economically ruinous. Contemporaries and historians have debated whether the terms

---

[3] Barry Eichengreen, *Golden Fetters: The Gold Standard and the Great Depression 1919–1939* (Oxford University Press, 1995). Frank Costigliola, *Awkward Dominion: American Political, Economic and Cultural Relations with Europe, 1919–1933* (Ithaca: Cornell University Press, 1984), 34.

were fair to Germany or, as John Maynard Keynes famously argued, catastrophic for all. Some blame French and British intransigence and others German bad faith for Germany's failure to meet its full obligations. Meeting those obligations may well have been economically possible, but no proposal for so doing garnered sufficient support from Germany's deeply divided political parties. Germany did pay three-fourths of its obligations from 1920–22, and the accompanying moderate inflation wiped out debt and promoted economic reconstruction. In late 1922, however, Germany abandoned compliance and embarked on a fatal course of resistance that culminated in the French occupation of the Ruhr, the infamous hyperinflation of 1923, and putsch attempts from both the Communist left and Hitler's far-right National Socialist Party. The mark, which exchanged at 4.2 to the dollar in December 1918, stood at 4.2 trillion to the dollar in December 1923. Hyperinflation brought economic and political chaos, wreaked havoc with traditional class, gender, and generational relations, and left lasting scars on the German psyche. Of most importance for European-American relations, hyperinflation meant that neither reparations nor war debts were being paid.

The German government finally stopped the hyperinflation by inventing a new currency, ending the eight-hour day, and scaling back social policy. American intervention was still required, however, in order to restart reparations, assure debt payments, and revive Western European economies on the open door basis the United States wanted. It came in the form of economic diplomacy by informal business means. American financial experts, such as Edwin Kemmerer, traveled to Germany, Poland, and Britain; private banks brokered loans; and the Federal Deposit Bank of New York (FDBNY) coordinated stabilization efforts. In effect, private businessmen, such as Thomas Lamont of J. P. Morgan, Owen Young of GE, and Benjamin Strong, head of the FDBNY, ran "semi-independent foreign policies." Although President Calvin Coolidge grandiosely announced that the government must "afford protection to the persons and property of their citizens, wherever they may be," state involvement was of a discreet and unofficial sort. This was a European variant of the dollar diplomacy that America had long practiced in Latin America.[4]

The centerpiece of American non-governmental financial involvement was the 1924 Dawes Plan, named after Chicago banker Charles Dawes, which restructured the reparations settlement and arranged an 800 million

---

[4] Costigliola, *Awkward Dominion*, 56, 59, 61, 148–49. Emily S. Rosenberg, *Financial Missionaries to the World: The Politics and Culture of Dollar Diplomacy, 1900–1930* (Durham: Duke University Press, 2003), 140, 154.

Illustration 5 The first American gold for Germany, December 23, 1924.

gold mark loan to Germany, half of which was floated by the United States, a quarter by Britain, and the rest by France and smaller European countries. German reparations were negotiated downward to 1 billion marks per year, to rise gradually to 2.5 billion per year, and the French withdrew from the Ruhr. Britain was to get 28 percent of the payments and France 52 percent with the rest divided among smaller nations. The Dawes Plan proved workable until the late 1920s, when payments were renegotiated once again under the Young Plan.[5]

As part of the mid-twenties settlement, the United States offered Britain and France a revised debt agreement, with full payment to be completed over sixty-two years, and made signing a prerequisite for any private American loans. Britain reluctantly accepted but the French government refused, and Parisians harassed American tourists in Paris to show their disapproval. Only in 1926 did France sign the Mellon–Bérenger Accord, agreeing to pay war debts but over more years and at more advantageous terms than initially stipulated. After the Dawes Plan and war debt agreement, American private bankers, with United States

---

[5] Eichengreen, *Golden Fetters*, 150. Costigliola, *Awkward Dominion*, 112.

government approval, sent economic advisors and loans to stabilize the chronically troubled Polish economy. Only Austria was stabilized under League of Nations auspices rather than by American informal economic diplomacy.

Recovery and warning signs

The Dawes Plan and subsequent United States loans meant that America's economic health was partially dependent on Europe's well-being. The Dawes Plan did enable European countries to pay their obligations to one another and the United States and return to that symbol of prewar stability and prosperity, the gold standard, as the United States had urged. From 1925 to 1929 European economies, with the exception of Britain, grew at a healthy rate, and production and trade surpassed prewar levels. Inflation was curbed and capital flight in countries like France stopped, while German economic recovery lessened political tensions. The Treaty of Locarno, which guaranteed the French, German, and Belgian borders, and Germany's membership in the League of Nations further promoted confidence and prosperity.

Yet, even before the Great depression began, there were signs that economic recovery was fragile. Contrary to expectations, the return to the gold standard neither stabilized prices nor eliminated deficits, and the British insistence on restoring prewar parity overvalued sterling and hurt trade. Without a hegemon, the global financial order depended on the personal relations between the leading central bankers in the United States and Britain, Benjamin Strong, and Montagu Norman. When Strong died in 1928, "the intimacy of the transatlantic relationship evaporated."[6] Moreover, informal cooperation worked best in crisis situations but not for everyday problems. After decades of robust growth, global trade ceased to expand, due in part to tariffs, in part to the industrialization of new countries, and in part to declining demand for raw commodities in industrializing countries, which in turn curbed the ability of primary producers to buy manufactured goods. America's share of world trade increased somewhat, while those of Britain and Germany, for whom exports were vital, declined.

The picture for individual countries was mixed. Germany resumed its place as Europe's leading economy, but both private prosperity and public finance depended on American banks, which provided three-fourths of the money borrowed by local governments and over half of

---

[6] Eichengreen, *Golden Fetters*, 209.

that borrowed by large corporations. Many loans were invested in long-term projects, even though they could be recalled on short notice. While some in the United States warned that too much capital was flowing to Germany, the United States government, true to its hands-off policy, refused to limit loans. British trade to its empire rebounded, but the domestic economy remained sluggish, and unemployment, above all in mining, textiles, and shipbuilding, consistently ran over 1 million throughout the decade. Through a combination of tariffs, American loans, and repression of the labor movement, Fascist Italy stabilized the lira and stimulated industry in the late 1920s but failed to modernize the economy as Mussolini had promised. New states fared least well. Czechoslovakia, Romania, and Yugoslavia borrowed heavily with little hope of being able to repay their loans; all attempted import substitution industrialization but had underdeveloped domestic markets. Poland lost all of its former export markets when high tariffs were imposed throughout the region. As the Yugoslav Foreign Minister Marinkovitch lamented in 1927, Balkan countries could not compete agriculturally with Canada, the United States, or Argentina. They were "already in the throes of disaster."[7]

The United States inhabited a different economic universe. From 1925 to 1929 its GDP, which was already far larger than any single European country and almost as large as all of Europe combined (excluding Russia), increased 23 percent. Productivity rose, and one-quarter of the finished goods produced were consumer durables, above all cars and household appliances. In 1929 American GDP per capita was well ahead of Switzerland, the Netherlands, and Britain, the most well-off European countries, nearly double that of France, well over twice that of Germany, and four times that of the Soviet Union. The United States had three-and-a-half times as many radios, eight times more phones, and twenty-six times more cars per capita than Europe (excluding Russia). The United States accounted for 40 percent of global production, while Europe, excluding Russia, accounted for 42 percent.[8]

The United States gave priority to its domestic markets and investments and raised tariffs steadily, culminating in the Smoot–Hawley Bill of 1930, which increased duties on thousands of industrial and agricultural goods to unprecedented heights. Yet, the United States remained

[7] Edward Hallett Carr, *The Twenty Years' Crisis 1919–1939* (New York: Harper Torchbooks, 1964), 57–58.
[8] W. Arthur Lewis, *Economic Survey, 1919–1939* (London: George Allen and Unwin, 1949), 39. Angus Maddison, *The World Economy in the 20th Century* (Paris: OECD Development Centre, 1989), 19. Daniel T. Rodgers, *Atlantic Crossings: Social Politics in a Progressive Age* (Cambridge, MA: Harvard University Press, 1998), 372–73.

intimately tied to the European and global economies by $15 billion in loans and direct foreign investments, roughly one-third of which went to Europe, while another third of them were in Latin America and one-quarter of them were in Canada. American banks lent an average of $500 million a year to businesses and governments across Europe between 1924 and 1928, while multinationals had over $1.3 billion in foreign direct investments there. Over 1,300 firms in Europe were owned or controlled by American capital; the largest portions were in Britain, followed by Germany and France. Italy, Spain, and Belgium received modest amounts of American investment, but Poland was the only Eastern European country to do so. Investments ranged from older shoe, camera, and sewing-machine factories to a new Coca-Cola bottling plant in Germany. The Big Three American automakers became multi-nationals in the 1920s. General Motors bought Vauxhall in England and Opel in Germany, introducing American assembly-line production; Chrysler built an assembly plant in Germany, while Ford opened a major factory in Dagenham, England, and a smaller one in Cologne. GE bought into the German giants AEG and Siemens, while Western Electric produced telephone equipment in several cities across Europe. RCA purchased Victor Talking Machine Company and had operations in six European countries. American oil firms expanded refining and marketing in Britain, Germany, Poland, Norway, Italy, and Belgium, but only Jersey Standard ranked on a par with the European giants Royal Dutch Shell and Anglo-Persian.[9]

While financial stabilization improved European economies, it did not bring the anticipated expansion of trade and production. Politicians, economists, and historians disagreed about why. Many contemporary Europeans focused on American economic diplomacy and America's excessive faith in the gold standard, which imposed harsh deflationary pressures on European nations. Others blamed American tariffs; one contemporary economist viewed them as "a declaration of economic war by the strongest economic power against the whole of the civilized world."[10] The United States refused to discuss tariffs, immigration restrictions, or war debts, holding, as do some historians, that European problems had European causes, ranging from low wages to high social spending and a lack of industrial competitiveness. Many on both sides

[9] Jeffry A. Frieden, *Global Capitalism: Its Fall and Rise in the Twentieth Century* (New York: Norton, 2006), 141. Mira Wilkins, *The Maturing of Multinational Enterprise: American Business Abroad from 1914 to 1970* (Cambridge, MA: Harvard University Press, 1974), 56, 72–89, 155.
[10] Emily Rosenberg, *Spreading the American Dream: American Economic and Cultural Expansion, 1890–1945* (New York: Hill and Wang, 1982), 163.

of the Atlantic prescribed emulation of the American model of mass production and mass consumption as a solution.

Fordism

The American economy as material reality and model of modernity confronted Europeans in multiple ways. Wherever American firms invested, "they communicated concepts of mass production, standardization, and scientific management."[11] Singer sewing machines, Kodak cameras, Ford tractors, and International Harvester farm machinery, those icons of the empire of commodities, continued to be sold across the continent. Europeans of all classes and political persuasions traveled to the United States to see America's gleaming new factories first hand; those staying home could read innumerable travel reports. From Britain to Russia Europeans debated their current economic problems and future prospects, as well as the cultural concerns accompanying them, in the language of Americanism and Fordism. Some Europeans adopted the American discourse on productivity, technology, and technocracy; others defended Europe's distinctive forms of production, consumption, culture, and class relations. Why was the American model of modernity appealing to some and appalling to others? And why did European enthusiasm for Fordism rarely translate into new assembly lines, mass-produced appliances, or higher wages?

Throughout the twenties, Western European industrialists and trade unionists, politicians and feminists, engineers and academics crossed the Atlantic. Unlike their nineteenth-century counterparts, they were not fascinated by Niagara Falls or the Wild West; rather, they sought out Pittsburgh with its integrated steel mills, producing day and night, Chicago with its stock yards and the Sears and Roebuck catalogue business, and New York with its soaring skyscrapers, glittering boulevards, and "American tempo." Detroit, however, was the most essential stop, for Ford's vast, integrated, ultramodern River Rouge automobile factory was the awe-inspiring embodiment of the American model. According to the German engineer Franz Westermann:

I have long gone through life with perceptive eyes, a thinking soul, and an open heart, enthusiastic about everything beautiful, be it nature, art, sport, or productivity. Nonetheless, my most powerful experience was a visit to the Ford works.[12]

---

[11] Wilkins, *Maturing of Multinational Enterprise*, 91.
[12] Franz Westermann, *Amerika, wie ich es sah: Reiseskizzen eines Ingenieurs* (Halberstadt: H. Meyer, 1926), 99.

Illustration 6 Ford Motor Company River Rouge Plant Dearborn, 1927.

Some European travelers were primarily interested in American technology, others in the effects of scientific management and the assembly line on work and wages. Still others inspected the myriad of mass-produced goods, asking if they were shoddy or solid, oppressively homogeneous or wonderfully inexpensive and sufficiently diverse. In hundreds of books, articles, and lectures, European travelers debated the secrets of American economic success and the possibility and desirability of European emulation. Industrialists argued that American economic prowess was due to its abundant natural resources and large domestic market as well as the intense work pace and lack of protective labor legislation and social policy. Trade unionists countered that it was built on advanced technology and a high wage strategy, which fueled mass consumption that in turn promoted further economic growth and technological development.

Europeans studied American economic writings. Frederick Taylor's prescriptions for reorganizing work by separating planning and execution, minutely subdividing tasks, and enhancing productivity by means of time and motion studies had circulated in Europe before World War I and been applied in a few German and French factories. The expense of introducing scientific management, trade union opposition to it, and divided views in engineering circles, however, limited the spread of Taylorism after the war. Fordism garnered much broader support, for unlike Taylorism, which focused on extracting more from the individual worker, Fordism claimed to optimize all factors of production through mechanization, rationalization, standardization, and factory integration. Henry Ford laid out the purported promise in vivid and accessible fashion in his autobiography, *My Life and Work*, which became a European bestseller and was reviewed in the daily press, technical journals, political magazines, and government publications. By 1924 it had been translated into every major European language, with Germans buying over two hundred thousand copies and the Soviet Union going through four editions. But if *My Life and Work* popularized Fordism, it did not clarify its essential character. The book could be read as a bible of productivism, which prescribed new technology, the assembly line, factories integrated from raw materials through final assembly, and a standardized, mass-manufactured product. It could also be interpreted as a blue print for a radically new form of mass consumption, in which supply created demand by producing consumer durables sold at low prices to workers paid high wages. Finally, some academics and engineers emphasized the Fordist ideology of service, entrepreneurial leadership, and a society dominated by ostensibly apolitical business elites – what some Europeans called "white socialism."

Reactions to the American economic model in Europe were decidedly mixed. In France, for example, the bourgeois engineer André Siegfried opposed Fordism for its promotion of labor control and product uniformity. Middle-class Europeans saw the American preoccupation with consumption, materialism, and the single-minded pursuit of the almighty dollar as a threat to their understanding of culture and individualism. In oft-repeated tropes, Europeans claimed to value quality over quantity, distinction over homogeneity, and hierarchy over equality. Bourgeois opposition was also rooted in economic and political concerns. Industrialists feared competition from American firms both within Europe and globally and sought to carve out a space for the more specialized products in which Europe excelled. They did not completely reject Fordism but rather argued that Europeans could only adopt selected parts of it. German industrialists, for example, claimed they could only rationalize production, standardize parts, and increase productivity in order to foster further production reforms and exports. Perhaps, down the line, wages could be raised and consumer durables mass-produced, but not in impoverished postwar Europe. In Britain, the costs of retooling small-scale, technologically backward industries that were in any case in deep crisis proved prohibitive. In France some circles initially welcomed the assembly line, but by the mid 1920s it was viewed as a symbol of America's culturally inferior mass society and, along with war debts, a part of America's aggressively anti-French economic policies. As Richard Kuisel has argued, "progress to most French capitalists was not to be found in America."[13]

Americanism did have a heterogeneous group of supporters. Some politicians and businessmen hoped that a purportedly scientific organization of work would dampen class conflict, while others saw increased production and consumption as a way out of zero-sum conflicts. Most Europeans, however, had more modest expectations.[14] Engineers admired the Fordist commitment to technology and productivity and hoped an emulation of American methods would enhance their professional status as well as their power within the factory and society. German feminists and home economists admired the modern, rationalized American home, replete with electric appliances and canned goods, even as they believed that German women should strive to become more efficient without the aid of expensive consumer durables or prepared foods. The French metalworker H. Dubreuil claimed the assembly line made work easier, but German social democratic trade unionists worried about its intensity and monotony, which was the antithesis of German "quality work." Other Social Democrats were concerned that mass consumption might lure workers away from political work and serious self-improvement. Nonetheless, most urged capital to embrace the full Fordist model, for the promise of material betterment and technological progress outweighed other concerns.

Ironically, the most enthusiastic proponents of Fordism were to be found in the Soviet Union, while communists elsewhere in Europe saw Americanism as both admirable and dangerous. For the jailed Italian Communist Antonio Gramsci, Americanism and Fordism represented an extreme rationalization of production and sexuality that were harbingers of a new culture and new man; they created a system in which hegemony was born in the factory. While they challenged the outmoded European bourgeois order, they also impeded the workers' movement. In *Ford or Marx? The Practical Solution to the Social Question*, the German Communist Jakob Walcher urged the left to extract practical lessons

---

[13] Richard Kuisel, *Capitalism and the State in Modern France: Renovation and Economic Management in the Twentieth Century* (Cambridge University Press, 1981), 89.

[14] Charles S. Maier, "Between Taylorism and Technocracy: European Ideologies and Visions of Productivity in the 1920s," *Journal of Contemporary History* 5/2 (April 1970): 27–61.

about the struggle for material betterment from Ford's autobiography but insisted that under capitalism, high wages and mass consumption could not be realized. Communists in Russia admired and sought to emulate with no such ambivalence. Even as it received equipment and technical advice from Germany, the Soviet Union turned toward America as a source of inspiration and concrete knowledge about everything from electrification to mechanized agriculture. America provided both a goal and the means to get there; as one American visitor to the Soviet Union noted, "the word for industrialization is Americanization." Even in the countryside the American model was well known and peasants named their children after Ford. Soviet Communists were confident that technology was separable from the economic system and culture in which it was embedded and could serve quite different social ends from those it had in the United States. As Leon Trotsky optimistically predicted in 1924: "Americanized Bolshevism will triumph and smash imperialist Americanism."[15]

Shared assumptions and commitments underlay Soviet admiration for Americanism. For both the United States and the Soviet Union, production and productivity were primary, unlimited growth laudable, and the exploitation of nature unproblematic. Technology and science with their principles of efficiency, quantification, and calculability were valorized. There was a cult of the machine in both nations, even if it preceded extensive mechanization in the Soviet Union. The factory was the central institution in society and a model for society in its emphasis on rationalized work and productivity. The economic system America was realizing and the one the Soviet Union imagined differed less in terms of technology, labor process, and industrial visions than in terms of the political goals, which productivism was to serve.

Despite the diverse support for Fordism across Europe, the American model did not come close to being realized anywhere. To be sure, automobile production increased and the ratio of American cars to European ones sank from 10:1 to 5:1 over the decade. Yet, Daimler-Benz, Morris, Fiat, Renault, and Citroën neither introduced the assembly line nor produced a European equivalent of Ford's Model T. Middle-class markets for vacuums and washing machines developed in Western Europe, but few were produced by American assembly-line methods, and nowhere

---

[15] Antonio Gramsci, "Americanism and Fordism," in *Selections from the Prison Notebooks* (New York: International Publishers, 1972), 277–318. Jakob Walcher, *Ford oder Marx: Die praktische Lösung der sozialen Frage* (Berlin: Neuer Deutscher Verlag, 1925). Hans Rogger, "*Amerikanizm* and Economic Development in Russia," *Comparative Studies in Society and History* 23/3 (1981): 382, 385.

did cross-class mass consumption of the American sort emerge. Britain, still Europe's most prosperous nation, had industrialized first and was saddled with an outmoded industrial plant. German industrialists preferred to develop their specialized export industries. German firms introduced Taylorist time and motion studies, developed job-training programs, promoted government norms for thousands of goods, and rationalized the organization of firms, but German factories remained a far cry from River Rouge. German workers saw their wages rise, but as a result of political bargaining, not American-style productivity increases or wage policies. Everywhere political divisions, the slower growth of chain stores and credit purchasing, and the lack of a vast integrated market, such as United States capitalists enjoyed, hindered the development of mass consumption. In production methods but above all in consumption patterns, Europe and America diverged much more markedly than they had in the prewar decades.[16]

The Soviets were least able to emulate Fordism. The ravages of War Communism had been followed by the New Economic Policy, which reversed collectivization and dismantled state ownership, reintroduced markets, and postponed industrialization until the necessary capital could be accumulated. Although Germany, Britain, and other European countries made loans to the Soviets, the United States officially banned economic dealings with them and refused diplomatic recognition as well. Nonetheless, American as well as British and German exports to the Soviet Union increased throughout the decade. American engineers provided technical assistance, introducing, for example, American methods in Kuzbas coal mines, and United States communists helped their Soviet comrades improve tractor factories. Sidney Hillman and the Amalgamated Clothing Workers set up the Russian American Industrial Corporation to run several garment factories in Moscow. American businessmen such as Ford and GE's Owen Young saw potential in the Soviet Union, and financier W. Averell Harriman arranged long-term loans in 1927 and 1928. In the late 1920s over two hundred United States firms were giving short-term credits. The Soviet Union welcomed such aid, but given underdevelopment and wartime devastation, it did little to create a more modern economy, let alone one resembling America.[17]

---

[16] Frieden, *Global Capitalism*, 159. Edgar A. Mowrer, *This American World* (New York: J. H. Sears and Co., 1928), 138–52.
[17] Costigliola, *Awkward Dominion*, 158–61. Alan Dawley, *Changing the World: American Progressives in War and Revolution* (Princeton University Press, 2003), 305. Antony C. Sutton, *Western Technology and Soviet Economic Development, 1917–1930* (Stanford University Press, 1968), 184, 278.

Efforts to spread American business culture were seemingly more successful. Rotary Clubs that embodied the business values, service ethic, and social mores of Main Street America moved abroad vigorously, and by the end of the 1920s, there were branches of Rotary International in major cities from England to Germany. Although Rotary sought to promote the idea of American consumer culture and class relations, Europeans modified Rotary so that it expressed the class cultures, national politics, and economic conceptions of various European countries. In Germany Rotarians adopted the American organizational forms, but modified them according to national and class associational norms. They used Rotary to criticize Americanism as well as to affirm parts of that often-amorphous ideology.[18]

Mass culture

Unlike mass production and mass consumption, mass culture did spread across Europe in the 1920s – movies and motorcycling, jazz and the Charleston, amateur and professional sports of all sorts, and mass enthusiasm for aviation. Some of these products, practices, and passions were American imports; others had national roots but were shaped by transatlantic exchanges moving in both directions. All built on transformations of everyday life that proceeded in similar ways, albeit at different paces, on both sides of the Atlantic.

People had more leisure time, for the prewar ten- to twelve-hour day was replaced by the eight-hour day everywhere in the North Atlantic except Britain and the United States. Although European wages were well below American ones, both blue-collar and white-collar male workers had more discretionary income for watching movies and bicycle races or motoring in cars, or more likely motorcycles. Even single women, who had once dutifully turned over their pay packet to parents, kept a share of their income to spend on movies, dance halls, and modern fashion. The pervasive popularity of eugenics and the perceived need to compensate for the rigors of repetitive, fast-paced factory work fueled concerns about health and fitness. Both women and men did gymnastics, swam, rode bikes, and hiked, often in one of the thousands of sports clubs that sprang up everywhere. For example, tens of thousands of women joined the British Women's League of Health and Beauty to practice standardized precision movements. There was a marked shift from leisure organized around family, friends, political parties, and churches to more

[18] Victoria de Grazia, *Irresistible Empire: America's Advance through 20th Century Europe* (Cambridge, MA: Harvard University Press, 2005), 15–74.

commercialized forms of participation and spectatorship. The Tour de France became a big business, with corporate sponsorship for teams, generous prize money, and extensive coverage by the mass press and by decade's end radio as well. Germany's flourishing interwar motorcycling culture offered races and rallies, clubs and magazines, abundant accessories for machines of every size and price, and fashions for motorcycling men and women. All blurred the line between leisure and consumption in new modern ways.

Some elements of the twenties mass culture were made in America and transplanted to Europe. Jazz arrived with the United States Army and returned with postwar bands that toured the continent to very mixed reception. The British king, the Pope, the Archbishop of Paris, and German musicians all condemned jazz as did many bourgeois Europeans. Jazz represented American modernity and black primitivism and was a harbinger of degeneration; it was "the muse of mass-produced men."[19] Others dissented, lauding jazz for mixing high and low culture and providing a vital alternative to decadent Europe. The popularity of jazz grew, especially among the young, as did those American dances, the Charleston and the Shimmy. Josephine Baker and the American Revue Nègre played to packed houses in London, Paris, and Berlin, while the Tiller Girls, a female synchronized dance troupe, was the sensation of Berlin. To Europeans Baker embodied vitality, exoticism, and primitivism, while the Tiller Girls represented rationalization, mechanization, discipline, and a deeroticized athleticism. Both were seen as quintessentially American and enabled Europeans to partake of America's Roaring Twenties.

Movies were the most popular part of postwar mass culture and their production, distribution, and reception became a battleground for Europeans and Americans. Between World War I and the Great Depression, Hollywood forced the once powerful European film industries on the defensive as it conquered first non-European markets, then European ones, pioneered new film technologies, and dominated the production of new feature films, be they comedies, melodramas, or Westerns. Hollywood studios eclipsed the prewar French film giants Pathé and Gaumont, while Weimar's most famous film company, UFA, enjoyed brief success but then fell into severe financial straits. By the late 1920s Hollywood produced over half of all feature films made worldwide and accounted for over 90 percent of the feature films shown globally.

---

[19] Jeffrey H. Jackson, "The Meanings of American Jazz in France," in Carl J. Guarneri, ed., *America Compared: History in International Perspective*, vol. II: *Since 1865* (Boston: Wadsworth, 2005), 241–48.

America controlled film markets in Scandinavia, Eastern Europe, and in small Western European countries like the Netherlands. By the mid twenties over 40 percent of the films shown in Germany and France and double that in Britain were American. Thereafter these numbers declined because European governments required that a certain percentage of films shown were to be made domestically. Even in the Soviet Union half of box-office receipts were from American films; Douglas Fairbanks in *The Thief of Baghdad* was especially popular.[20]

European filmmakers from London to Moscow borrowed American techniques and themes; directors, such as Ernst Lubitsch, F. W. Murnau, and Jacques Feyde, migrated to Hollywood, as did actors such as Charlie Chaplin and Greta Garbo. To be sure, movement was not only in one direction. The German producer Erich Pommer, for example, worked on both sides of the Atlantic, seeking inspiration from Hollywood even as he sought to turn UFA into a rival. The Kansas-born silent film star Louise Brooks began her career in Hollywood and continued it in Germany before returning to America. A few American directors and actors moved across the Atlantic permanently, but for most Hollywood was the preferred destination. Anxious Europeans, recognizing the need for a coordinated response, advocated a Film Europe to compete with Film America, but the project was always more aspiration than concrete achievement. The triumph of Hollywood and the decline of European cinema – whether narrated with smug pride or anxious dismay – was undeniable.

But why did Hollywood triumph? Some see World War I as pivotal, for while Europeans engaged in fratricidal struggle, the United States moved into the global markets that France, Britain, and Germany had once controlled, and New York replaced London as the global distribution center for American films. This paved the way for Hollywood's conquest of Europe. Others focus on the postwar years when Hollywood pioneered longer films and the star system and consolidated production. As production costs rose, Europe was unable to compete. America had twice as many cinemas as Britain, France, and Germany combined and received state aid via the Webb–Pomerene Act, which exempted studios from antitrust legislation and thereby promoted coordinated American expansion abroad. But content was every bit as important. Europeans liked

---

[20] Andrew Higson and Richard Maltby, "Introduction," in Andrew Higson and Richard Maltby, eds., *"Film Europe" and "Film America": Cinema, Commerce and Cultural Exchange, 1920–1939* (University of Exeter Press, 1999), 7. Kristin Thompson, *Exporting Entertainment: America in the World Film Market, 1907–34* (Tonbridge, UK: BFI, 1985), 129–33, 147. Susan Buck-Morss, *Dreamworld and Catastrophe: The Passing of Mass Utopia in East and West* (Cambridge, MA: MIT, 2000), 158.

Westerns and Buster Keaton comedies. Germany tried to market art films, such as Fritz Lang's expressionist drama *Metropolis*, while the French government stressed the educational and artistic merits of its national cinema. As Erich Pommer noted, however, "the mentality of the American film . . . apparently comes closest to the taste of the international movie audience." Hollywood's "lack of complexity . . . made it a winner on the international market."[21]

The Soviets proved most open to American films. As Susan Buck-Morss has argued:

> Not only cinema but mass culture generally had a positive meaning in the United States and the Soviet Union that it lacked in the ethnically constructed imaginaries of Western European nations, where "masses," a visual phenomenon, and "culture," a literary one, tended to be viewed as antithetical extremes.[22]

In Western Europe, by contrast, American films threatened identity, culture, and morality. Germans were most vocal about the dangers to the literary and theatrical culture in which the educated middle classes took such pride. The French viewed the influx of American films as cultural imperialism that would dilute the nation's cultural patrimony. When the French government sought to limit them, however, the American Motion Picture Producers and Distributors Association boycotted France, and the government quickly capitulated. Despite linguistic and cultural affinities, the British were equally concerned. According to the London *Morning Post*, "The film is to America what the flag was once to Britain. By its means Uncle Sam may hope someday, if he be not checked in time, to Americanize the world." A conservative British MP claimed that movie viewers "talk America, think America, and dream America. We have several million people, mostly women, who, to all intent and purpose are temporary American citizens."[23]

Across Europe, religious and political leaders and cultural arbiters projected their fears about gender and generational disarray at home onto American movies. To be sure, prewar American Progressive reformers had shared similar fears about the effects of film on the masses, and churches continued to harbor them postwar. But in Europe war,

---

[21] Gerben Bakker, "America's Master: The Decline and Fall of the European Film Industry in the United States, 1907–1920," in Luisa Passerini, ed., *Across the Atlantic: Cultural Exchanges between Europe and the United States* (Brussels: Peter Lang, 2000), 228–29, 233. De Grazia, *Irresistible Empire*, 313

[22] Buck-Morss, *Dreamworld and Catastrophe*, 148.

[23] Higson and Maltby, eds., *"Film Europe" and "Film America,"* 9. Richard Maltby and Ruth Vasey, "'Temporary American Citizens': Cultural Anxieties and Industrial Strategies in the Americanization of European Cinema," in Higson and Maltby, eds., *"Film Europe" and "Film America,"* 34.

revolution, political divisions, and economic instability heightened social anxieties about independent, sexually assertive new women, who might never marry and have children, and troubled youth, who challenged authority, shunned work, and hung out on street corners. America was hardly the sole source of a new youth culture or independent women with short hair and short shirts. Weimar Germany's "Girl Kultur" had domestic roots as well as American role models, and the French traced the disturbing possibility of a "civilization without sexes" to the war. Nonetheless the new woman and to a lesser extent youth were coded American. Many feared that Europeans would adopt the American products, social relations and values that Hollywood films advertised. In *This Our Country* British Major Tawdon Hoare lamented that American cinema "is creating a race of youths belonging to all classes whose experience of life is based largely on the harrowing and frequently sordid plots of American films." According to a German Protestant cleric and youth expert, "it is not socialism but Americanism that will be the end of everything as we have known it."[24]

Those fears were overblown. Although the American State Department confidently claimed, "the people of Europe now consider America as the arbiter of manners, fashion, sports, customs and standards of living," reception was more complex. Europeans imagined America in and through their own countries. Film details were often altered for different national contexts, and in the age of silent movies, which lasted through the 1920s, language did not immediately brand a film as American. Many Europeans, like many Americans, wanted to be like Hollywood stars such as Greta Garbo or James Cagney, but this did not mean they wanted to become American. Rather, Hollywood was "a familiar foreign country" they enjoyed visiting.[25]

Social policy

If Hollywood successfully invaded Europe, American social thought did not; ideas and policy innovations continued to flow primarily from east to west. Europe and America shared similar concerns about transforming or transcending capitalism, democratizing the firm and factory, and guaranteeing social security. Social policy occupied a prominent place on the transatlantic political agenda due to the ideological challenge that the Russian Revolution posed to capitalist democracies and to the social

---

[24] Maltby and Vasey, "Temporary American Citizens," 34. Detlev Peukert, *The Weimar Republic* (New York: Hill and Wang, 1993), 178.
[25] Maltby and Vasey, "Temporary American Citizens," 41–50.

problems that hundreds of thousands of war widows, orphans, and disabled veterans presented to every European nation. Yet, social policy discourses took on different national forms, and Europe distinguished itself by translating social thought into public policy on a scale unimaginable in the United States. Unlike mass production and mass consumption, American politics and social policy aroused little interest among Europeans.

Transatlantic exchanges were fostered by both old and new informal and institutional channels. A growing number of Americans studied abroad, and tourism increased from 15,000 a year before the war to a quarter of a million per year in the twenties. An estimated 80,000 expats settled in cities like Berlin and above all Paris, the favored haunt of the "lost generation" of American writers such as Gertrude Stein and Ernest Hemingway, who were seeking an alternative to conservative, provincial America. Britain supplanted Germany as the favored destination for American Progressives in search of models, while the Soviet social experiment drew the curious and skeptical as well as the enthusiastic and ideologically committed. Visitors included W. E. B. Du Bois, Lincoln Steffens, Robert La Follette, and John Dewey. Americans traveled across Germany, Scandinavia, the Low Countries, and Britain to discuss everything from housing to agricultural cooperatives and adult education.[26]

Transatlantic labor contacts continued, but on a diminished scale. The prewar Second International was replaced by the short-lived Two and a Half International and the Moscow dominated Third International. The American Federation of Labor's attempt to build an Alliance for Labor and Democracy that would convert European labor to American business unionism found little resonance and quickly died. Labor on both sides of the Atlantic did mount a highly visible but ultimately unsuccessful international campaign against the execution of Italian-born American anarchists Sacco and Vanzetti, accused of bank robbery and murder. Overall, however, European workers' movements were absorbed with domestic issues and the acrimonious divisions between communists and social democrats; American labor's distinctive ideology, strategy, and legal situation were of little relevance.

New institutional channels to promote international exchange emerged in the 1920s, but few of the American ones involved Europeans. The American Council of Learned Societies did try to develop ties to scholarly societies abroad, but groups like the Social Science Research Council and the Council on Foreign Relations focused solely on shaping American

---

[26] Rodgers, *Atlantic Crossings*, 313, 319–43, 381.

policy. The League of Nations was the main international forum for exchanging ideas and influencing policy debates; although individual Americans participated, there was no official United States involvement in the important International Committee on Intellectual Cooperation or in the International Labour Organization. America was thus marginal to the liveliest international discussions of cultural affairs, labor, and social policy, and women's issues.

Progressive Europeans and Americans sought to link politics and economics, foreground social justice, and enhance the power of trade unions, and American social thought developed a postcapitalist imagination that was similar to European social democratic visions. American arguments about making corporations responsible to society at large, which Adolf Berle and Gardiner Means developed most strongly, resembled European theories of organized capitalism and economic democracy, which the German Social Democrats Rudolph Hilferding and Fritz Naphtali advocated. In addition, some American reformers overcame their prewar aversion to class politics and began to imagine broader cross-class coalitions. But even though American left liberals and journals such as *The Nation* and *The New Republic* were operating on the same discursive terrain as continental social democrats or British Labourites, they existed in a very different sociopolitical and ideological context. American left liberals lacked the established left political parties, access to government office, and political systems open to government regulation that enabled European social democrats to undertake social policy initiatives. The United States did not develop the social rights and welfare states that many European countries began to construct, as the divergent histories of social insurance and housing policy illustrate.

Social insurance programs predated World War I, but after 1918 new states, categories of citizens, and risks were covered. Before 1914 all Western and Southern European countries, Austria-Hungary, Romania, and Norway and Sweden had accident insurance for workers; by the mid 1920s Finland, Yugoslavia, Poland, and Bulgaria did as well. Compulsory sickness insurance programs existed in Germany, Norway, Britain, the Netherlands, Austria, Hungary, and Romania before 1914 and were put in place in East Central Europe, Italy and France over the course of the decade. Sweden, Denmark, Germany, France, Britain, the Netherlands and Romania had state old-age pensions prewar, and Belgium, the Habsburg successor states, and Southern Europe established them postwar. Britain pioneered unemployment insurance in 1911, and in the 1920s Italy, Austria, Poland, Hungary, Germany, and Yugoslavia followed suit, while Denmark, France, Belgium, and Switzerland had voluntary unemployment programs. Family allowances, much discussed as a pronatalist strategy, came only in the 1930s in Belgium and France. Building on the pioneering insurance policies established by Bismarck, Weimar Germany not only expanded the number of social programs and the size of benefits but also enshrined social rights in the constitution.[27]

These programs were far from perfect. State insurance was increasingly bureaucratic and impersonal; it both provided vital material benefits and imposed disciplinary norms on recipients. Many insurance programs were geared to the normative male worker and excluded women. Social insurance depended on capitalist prosperity, or at least stability, and began to collapse when the depression began. Nonetheless, Europe was far ahead of the United States.

Most Americans, who remained committed to low taxes and minimal regulation and were hostile to trade unions, rejected federal government insurance programs of any kind. To be sure, most individual states had set up workmen's compensation programs by the 1920s and most had pensions for widowed mothers (although other forms of insurance were woefully lacking). European observers, however, looked primarily at the national level and cared most about unemployment, sickness, and old-age insurance. European businessmen saw American employee representation plans as an alternative to trade unions and collective bargaining and admired private insurance. Yet, only one in five American workers had employer group life insurance, one in eight a company pension, one in twenty group health and accident insurance, and only one in 100 unemployment coverage. America's private approach to social policy was politically irrelevant in European countries where unions were recognized, left parties prominent, states strong, and social problems abundant. Small wonder most Europeans found American commodities more impressive than American industrial democracy and welfare capitalism.[28]

In housing as in social insurance, Europe and America looked less like one another in the 1920s than before the war, for although there was a housing boom on both sides of the Atlantic, American construction was entirely private, while in Europe half of the 6 million new units were state subsidized or cooperatively financed. Britain built council housing with indoor toilets, better-equipped kitchens, and more private space in new working-class suburbs. In Berlin and Frankfurt socially minded modern architects such as Ernst May, Martin Wagner, and Bruno Taut designed vast working-class housing projects with functional apartments filled with

[27] Gerold Ambrosius and William H. Hubbard, *A Social and Economic History of Twentieth-Century Europe* (Cambridge, MA: Harvard University Press, 1989), 118–19.
[28] Rodgers, *Atlantic Crossings*, 378.

light, air, and sun and surrounded by greenery. J. J. P. Oud built what he called "dwelling Fords" for the city of Rotterdam. "Red" Vienna constructed ambitious housing complexes, like the Karl-Marx Hof, which housed 12 percent of the population and had nurseries, kindergartens, public baths, and libraries as well as meeting rooms and playgrounds. Although not always well received by their working-class clientele, these modernist social housing projects were simultaneously a practical answer to Europe's acute housing shortage, the expression of modern architecture's desire to engineer new, rationalized ways of living, and "a project of 'anticipatory socialism,' designed to express collectivist goals and an integrated communal life."[29] They had no counterpart in the United States, where modernist aesthetics took root without social democratic politics or utopian aspirations.

There is a vast and contentious literature on why welfare states developed differently. Some stress the logic of industrialization; others national values and political dynamics, still others state capacity and interests. Some see business as the driving force, others labor or feminism. No one theory adequately explains the distinctive evolution of European and American social policy before and after World War I, for varied mixtures of working-class power, business opposition or tolerance, feminist activism, and national and political party attitudes toward public versus private initiatives were at play in each nation. Yet, there was a noticeable transatlantic difference that must be stressed, for it was to continue in varied forms throughout the twentieth century and be a source of European and American self-definition and contention.

Eugenics, pronatalism, and the woman question

From Moscow to New York, birthrates, sexuality, and contraception were hotly debated, as new discourses about companionate marriage and pervasive anxieties about family stability circulated widely, and eugenic theories gained popularity. Europeans and Americans shared similar emancipatory hopes, eugenic assumptions, and gender worries, and they developed similar policies regarding population, contraception, and abortion.

Economic, gender, racial, and national security anxieties all focused attention on biopolitical issues. The staggering death tolls of World War I led many to anguish over how to repopulate the nation as quickly as possible; so too did prewar beliefs that national strength depended on

---

[29] Geoff Eley, *Forging Democracy: A History of the Left in Europe, 1850–2000* (Oxford University Press, 2002), 212.

large armies and growing populations, a particular concern in France. Although birthrates varied from a high of thirty-two per thousand in Bulgaria to a low of seventeen to eighteen per thousand in Western Europe in the late twenties, women everywhere were having fewer children, and the transition to the modern small family was underway.[30] The emergence of the "new woman," who sought independence, income, and greater sexual freedom, sparked fears that marriage rates would plummet (which they did not), that maternity would be rejected and the gender order disrupted (which it was). Biopolitical debates swirled around quality as well as quantity, and a new eugenics discourse reframed older anxieties about degeneration, workers unfit for military service, and middle-class refusal to have large families.

Eugenics, now discredited by its association with Nazi racism and genocide, enjoyed scientific respectability and broad popularity in the twenties. The International Congress for Eugenics, first held in 1912, resumed its deliberations about nature versus nurture, positive measures to improve health and sexuality, and negative means to prevent those deemed unfit from reproducing. The British Eugenics Society campaigned unsuccessfully for voluntary sterilization, while Denmark approved it for the mentally handicapped. German proponents of racial hygiene debated the genetic value of different groups and measures to prevent the mentally ill and alcoholics from reproducing, while social democratic, communist, and feminist doctors and sex reformers talked of responsible motherhood, eugenic health, and rationalized sexuality. Racial hygienists favored compulsory intervention, but were not able to restrict marriage or legalize sterilization, while sex reformers, preferring voluntary means, set up sex education and birth-control clinics, and advocated abortion and better wages and living conditions. In the Soviet Union, scientists and doctors weighed the relative merits of the Mendelian emphasis on nature/genes over nurture and the Lamarckian insistence on the inheritance of acquired characteristics. Only in the 1930s did the Soviets emphatically reject eugenics as incompatible with the Soviet project of building a new man, while in Germany the most racist and radical variant of eugenics triumphed.

The United States was central to these biopolitical preoccupations. New York City hosted the 1921 International Conference for Eugenics; the Rockefeller Foundation funded German racial hygiene research, and key works in American eugenic and racial theory, such as Madison Grant's *Passing of the Great Race*, were translated into German. Many

---

[30] Bonnie G. Smith, *Changing Lives: Women in European History since 1700* (Lexington, MA: D. C. Heath, 1989), 434.

Europeans admired America's willingness to restrict marriage and reproduction along racial lines as well as those of ostensible fitness. Throughout the twenties the United States led in negative eugenic measures, averaging 200–600 forced sterilizations per year, and the Supreme Court declared compulsory sterilization constitutional in 1927.[31]

Progressive policies such as sex education, childrearing advice, and housing reform had a eugenic edge, for alleviating social need, spreading scientific knowledge, and improving the genetic stock were seen as integral parts of the same project. On both sides of the Atlantic, childbirth was medicalized, and governments in the Soviet Union and Austria launched campaigns to teach scientific childrearing. In England, Mothercraft Training Centres were established; France introduced compulsory public school courses for girls on modern childrearing, and the United States passed the 1921 Sheppard–Towner maternal and infant health bill, which provided mothers with educational advice but no services. Social democrats and communists, and feminists concerned with the plight of working-class families, provided instruction in modern hygienic living, as did states eager to apply ostensibly apolitical scientific solutions to social problems.

Pronatalism and improved childrearing were transatlantic projects. Politicians, priests, businessmen, and labor leaders valorized the family, prescribed maternity as a duty, and celebrated motherhood as women's highest calling. Many countries introduced Mother's Day – though as much to aid florists as the birthrate. Some maternalist feminists in Britain like Eleanor Rathbone fought for a motherhood endowment to be paid directly to women to enable them to stay home and raise their children without depending on husbands. In the United States the vast majority of states paid pensions to widowed mothers, but these supported only children, thus encouraging, indeed requiring, women to work. Although the French anguished about their low birthrate, the state did not introduce such positive pronatalist measures as family allowances and factory crèches until the 1930s.

Only the Bolsheviks sought to improve motherhood by restructuring marriage. The Family Code of 1918 made marriage a civil institution, abolished community property, enabled either spouse to request divorce, determined alimony by need, and abolished the concept of illegitimacy. In theory family was thus separated from marriage, women were equal to men, and all children had the same rights and benefits. Practice proved much messier. Housework was considered socially necessary labor but

---

[31] Stefan Kühl, *The Nazi Connection: Eugenics, American Racism and German National Socialism* (Oxford University Press, 1994), 17–25.

remained unpaid. Women could not leave peasant marriages because alimony provisions were impossible to apply where property was scant and largely non-cash. Divorce rose, but women had difficulty collecting alimony from husbands who often had children by more than one woman. The state failed to provide the promised collective childcare and housework, giving priority instead to aiding the over 7 million needy children, many orphaned, others with one parent unable to support them, who roamed the countryside and cities. The 1926 Marriage Law modified earlier libertarian provisions to accord with material reality. The Soviet state lacked both the ideological commitment and the monetary resources to restructure family, motherhood, and the sexual division of labor radically.

Given strained state budgets in Europe and opposition to state social policy in America, restrictions on women's rights to control reproduction were easier to implement than positive inducements. Britain, Germany, and the Scandinavian countries allowed contraception and birth-control clinics, but France, Belgium, Ireland, and Italy passed new laws against the sale of contraceptives and the circulation of information about birth control, while the older American Comstock Law did the same. States such as France made abortion laws more stringent, and Communist efforts to legalize abortion in Germany failed. Abortion was legal only in the Soviet Union, but there it was considered a regrettable necessity due to poverty and social disruption, not an inherent right of women to control their own bodies. Finally, in 1930 Pope Pius XI issued the encyclical *Casti Conubii*, condemning all non-procreative sex and any form of family limitation and endorsing large, patriarchal families. Despite laws and proscriptions, women continued to have abortions – an estimated 500,000 a year in France and up to 800,000 annually in Germany.[32] Altering women's reproductive rights proved much harder than improving their political ones, for states wanted larger populations, churches desired stable patriarchal families, and men feared gender equality.

These repressive practices stood at odds with lively transatlantic discussions of companionate marriage and mutually satisfying heterosexuality and with the erosion of prewar homosociality and emergence of heterosocial leisure, sports, and cultural consumption. Whether or not World War I opened a new era in sexual mores, there was an eroticization of everyday life, evident in new fashions, dances, athletics, and images. Sex was talked about much more openly. Educated classes read Sigmund Freud and Helene Deutsch, who offered conservative

---

[32] Mark Mazower, *Dark Continent: Europe's Twentieth Century* (New York: Vintage, 2000), 84–85.

views on women. More popular were the British sex educator Marie Stopes and her Dutch counterpart, Theodor van de Velde, whose widely translated books on *Married Love* and *Ideal Marriage: Its Physiology and Technique* offered practical advice on birth control and sexuality. Feminists and non-feminists debated whether empowerment and happiness could be achieved by emphasizing individualism, sexual liberation, and the sameness of women and men or by focusing on difference, family, and motherhood. Neither Europeans nor Americans could reconcile the contradictions between new attitudes and practices and traditional ones, between emancipatory visions and disciplinary state policy.

The Americanization debate, round two

"Who will be master, Europe or America?" asked the conservative French journalist and historian Lucien Romier in his 1927 book, which warned of the dangers that homogenizing, materialistic America presented to European culture, society, and families and which was translated into English a year later. Many on both sides of the Atlantic echoed his question. The issue was not whether Europe had become Americanized in its production methods, consumption patterns, cultural preferences, politics, and gender relations, for despite American economic incursions and European borrowings, Europe remained distinctive. Indeed in many respects Europe and America looked less like one another in the 1920s than they had before the war or were to after 1945. The concern was whether Europe would inevitably become Americanized. The American journalist Edgar Mowrer, who spent the twenties in Europe, drew a parallel between spreading American influence and the Roman Empire, arguing that Europe would become outwardly but not inwardly Americanized. The Englishman Bertrand Russell predicted that America would attempt to become a world empire, while the German Count Keyserling lamented that decaying Europe would become Americanized unless it developed "a new decisive culture type."[33]

Many socialists, communists, feminists, and apolitical engineers embraced America's factories and commodities, its informal social relations, and greater gender equality. Conservatives, clerics, capitalists, and intellectuals were more critical, condemning America as flat, homogeneous, collectivist, without history and culture, and hopelessly materialistic. European publications were filled with stereotypes of American men single-mindedly pursuing the almighty dollar, of workers casually chatting

---

[33] Lucien Romier, *Who Will Be Master, Europe or America?* (New York: Macaulay, 1928). Mowrer, *This American World*, 201, 211–12, 219, 237.

with foremen and dressing as the middle classes did, of women dominating culture and neglecting domesticity, and of shoddy, standardized goods flooding the market. But even the most critical cultural pessimists recognized that America could no longer be patronized or dismissed as irrelevant, as the Spanish philosopher Ortega y Gasset did. Many shared the feelings of the Dutch intellectual Johan Huizinga, who after his 1928 trip to the United States said: "We admire your strength, but we do not envy you."[34]

As many Germans, Italians, French, and Dutch wrestled with the material power and cultural seductions of Americanism and Fordism, they began to use Europe as "a frame of reference." To be sure, Europe was often imagined in nationally inflected ways and never included the Soviet Union, but people began to define their opposition to America – and thus themselves – in terms of Europe. The French statesmen Aristide Briand and Edouard Herriot even called for a United States of Europe to prevent the continent from becoming an American colony.[35]

For all the loans, commodities, and movies that flowed from America to Europe over the decade, however, Europe was in no danger of being Americanized, let alone colonized. Despite its economic crises and political divisions, Europe was not in a state of collapse such that massive United States intervention was possible or necessary. Of equal importance, America remained ambivalent about its role in Europe. Private business, with government encouragement, aggressively pursued every possible opportunity to invest and sell commodities and cultural products from Britain to the Soviet Union. Americans in and out of public life preached the virtues of the American model of modernity from capitalism to prohibition. But the American government remained officially aloof from European involvements as well as international organizations. America saw itself as both exceptional and as a model, which could and should nonetheless be emulated, but it was unwilling to offer inducements or to assume responsibilities. Had the spectacular American economic boom or the real but fragile European recovery of the mid and late twenties lasted, there is little reason to think America would have changed its policies or Europe would have become more Americanized. What then happened when American prosperity and European recovery collapsed dramatically?

---

[34] Rob Kroes, *If You've Seen One, You've Seen the Mall: Europeans and American Mass Culture* (Champagne/Urbana: University of Illinois Press, 1996), 18–23. For the German version of these debates, see Mary Nolan, *Visions of Modernity: American Business and the Modernization of Germany"* (Oxford University Press, 1994), 58–127.

[35] Kroes, *If You've Seen One*, 84. Costigliolo, *Awkward Dominion*, 155.

4　The depression and transatlantic new deals

The Roaring Twenties came to an abrupt end with the American stock market crash in the fall of 1929, which ignited a downward spiral of United States bank collapses, home foreclosures, currency instability, and acute price deflation. As the financial crisis spread to the real economy, production dropped precipitously, millions were thrown out of work, businesses closed, farmers went bankrupt, and confidence evaporated. America ceased to be the exceptional exemplar of unprecedented prosperity and the alluring, if disturbing, model of modernity that it had been. And it could no longer aid European economies, which lurched into crises that devastated agriculture, industry, and finance and destroyed the tenuous political and social stability of the mid and late twenties. Transatlantic economic conflicts and political tensions multiplied. Only the Soviet Union remained immune from the ravages of the depression, but the growth and modernization achieved through forced industrialization and collectivization proved enormously socially disruptive, politically divisive, and, for many, fatal.

The depression was not the final crisis of capitalism, as many on the communist left hoped and initially predicted. But it was, in the words of the economist John Maynard Keynes, "the greatest catastrophe due almost to entirely economic causes of the modern world." The depression destroyed the institutions, ideas, and networks that had structured transatlantic relations. Laissez-faire ideology, self-regulating markets, and the noninterventionist liberal state were called into question. Globalization, already slowed by war, economic turmoil, and political restructuring in the 1920s, virtually stopped, as the gold standard collapsed and trade and capital flows diminished significantly. By 1931 Montagu Norman, governor of the Bank of England, feared that "unless drastic measures are taken to save it, the capitalist system throughout the civilized world will be wrecked within a year."[1]

---

[1] Liaquat Ahamed, *Lords of Finance: The Bankers Who Broke the World* (New York: Penguin Press, 2009), 4–5.

How were European-American economic relations affected by these unprecedented events? What kinds of economic interventions and social policy experiments did desperate governments adopt? In this decade of kaleidoscopic changes, answers varied by country and crisis year, but certain trends emerged. The depression heightened economic nationalism everywhere, and it diminished the American economic presence in much of Europe. Regimes with antithetical politics embraced surprisingly similar programs to deal with the crisis, while similar polities took distinctive policy paths. Political divisions and ideological cleavages seemed at once sharper and more blurred, as governments, politicians, businessmen, and intellectuals sought to decipher the possible contours of the emerging postliberal order at home and abroad.

The global crisis

The depression of the 1930s, like its predecessor in the late nineteenth century, was not one crisis but several different and reinforcing ones; everywhere agriculture, industry, trade, and finance suffered from structural weaknesses, cyclical downturns, and global shifts in relative power. The depression was simultaneously a set of distinctive national phenomena and an interconnected global event. Its chronology is complex, its scope enormous, and its causes and cures disputed to this day.

Take the seemingly simple question of when the depression started. In the United States it began with a dramatic precipitating event, in much of Europe with creeping price deflation or persistent recession. Between 1929 and 1933 most countries went through a long period of sharp downturns in prices, production, trade, and employment, punctuated by brief upswings and then renewed crisis. Most historians of the United States cite Black Tuesday, October 29, 1929 as the fateful beginning, when 16 million shares were traded and the Dow lost 80 points, bringing its value to half what it had been six weeks before. Stock prices continued to fall precipitously thereafter; industrial production dropped 10 percent by year's end; and unemployment rose from 1.5 to 3 million.[2]

For European countries, the crisis began earlier and hit hardest later. In Eastern and Southern Europe, the depression started in agriculture. Europe faced expanded global production of a host of primary products, especially agricultural ones. As prices fell, farmers and governments tried desperately to export still more in order to stay afloat and service the huge foreign debt

---

[2] Ahamed, *Lords of Finance*, 359–61.

countries like Poland had. This only worsened a bad situation, and agricultural prices dropped an astonishing 52 percent between 1929 and 1933.[3] For Germany, heavily dependent on loans, recession hit in 1928, as changes in United States interest rates drew funds from Europe to the American stock market, fueling speculation there. Britain had suffered from diminished foreign trade, uncompetitive industries, and high unemployment for a decade, and these problems simply deepened.

The stock market crash in the United States did not have an immediate catastrophic impact across the Atlantic. Indeed, it "was greeted in Europe with a combination of schadenfreude and relief," for Europe hoped that American funds would flow back across the Atlantic.[4] Those hopes were dashed, and the depression worsened in Germany, Austria, Britain, and Sweden. (France remained unaffected until mid decade.) Problems began in the real economy, but financial crises soon followed. The fateful year was 1931: in May the Creditanstalt, the principal bank of Austria and East Central Europe, collapsed; in July the German banking system unraveled as the Danatbank went under, and in September, Great Britain abandoned both the gold standard and free trade. Most other countries followed suit. As production plummeted, trade shrank, and unemployment soared, politicians debated where to cut government spending, what level of social suffering was politically bearable, and whether alternatives to austerity were possible.

The economic toll of these years was staggering. Overall the GDP of the industrialized countries fell by 18 percent between 1929 and 1932 and in the United States alone by 28 percent. As prices plummeted and demand and loans dried up, factories and workshops downsized or closed. In the United States, 85,000 businesses failed. In Britain, Germany, and the United States, manufacturing production dropped below 1913 levels; for the United States the fall from late-twenties prosperity was breathtakingly sharp, while for Germany it cruelly ended the modest recovery after 1925. By the end of 1933 half of American banks, many of them small, local institutions, had collapsed. The more centralized European banking systems saw fewer failures, but suffered severe liquidity problems. Due to newly erected tariff barriers and lack of effective demand, exports fell by nearly half between 1929 and 1932 in the United States and Germany, the hardest hit among developed industrial economies, and by one-third in

---

[3] Ivan T. Berend, *An Economic History of Twentieth-Century Europe* (Cambridge University Press, 2006), 61–62. Jeffry A. Frieden, *Global Capitalism: Its Fall and Rise in the Twentieth Century* (New York: Norton, 2006), 175.

[4] Ahamed, *Lords of Finance*, 369–70.

Illustration 7 Breadline at McCauley Water Street Mission under the
Brooklyn Bridge, New York, early 1930s.

Britain. Imports of raw materials and agricultural goods sank correspond-
ingly and overall world trade diminished by half.[5]

The social costs were even more devastating. At its worst point in 1932–
33, unemployment stood above 20 percent in Britain and Belgium, at 24
percent and 27 percent respectively in Sweden and the United States, and
above 30 percent in Norway and Denmark. In Germany unemployment
hit a staggering 44 percent.[6] Hundreds of thousands of others were under-
employed or uncounted. Britain and Germany cut unemployment insurance benefits dramatically, while most countries had none.

The experience of being without work for weeks, months, and years was
similar on both sides of the Atlantic. It was evocatively captured in the bleak
descriptions of life on the dole in Northern England in George Orwell's
Road to Wigan Pier or in Paul Lazersfeld and Maria Jahoda's grim portrait of
the Austrian textile town of Marienthal, whose one and only industry had
utterly collapsed. Or in Dorothea Lange's famous photographs of gaunt
men and haggard women struggling to maintain dignity in the face of
immense rural poverty in the American South and West. Unemployment

---

[5] Stanley Buder, *Capitalizing on Change: A Social History of American Business* (Chapel
Hill: University of North Carolina Press, 2009), 258. Paul Kennedy, *The Rise and Fall of
the Great Powers* (New York: Vintage, 1987), 299. Frieden, *Global Capitalism*, 182.
Angus Maddison, *The World Economy in the 20th Century* (Paris: OECD Development
Centre, 1989), 53, 55.
[6] Eric Hobsbawm, *Age of Extremes: A History of the World 1914–1991* (New York: Pantheon,
1994), 92–93.

bred anger among many, especially young men with no prospects for work or marriage, but it led to resignation or despair in many others. Many saw unemployment not so much as a matter of shame, Orwell noted, but as a fact of life, the fate you shared with your cousin, your neighbor, your former workmates. In Britain crisis encouraged political passivity, in the United States and Sweden protest, organization, and a new militancy, and in Germany and Austria political polarization and an opening for the radical right. Millions of women in working-class neighborhoods and on farms were left to manage families on little or no income. Or they juggled the double burden of waged work and housework, while men took to the road in search of a job or sat despondently at home, unwilling to suffer the further humiliation of doing housework or childcare. Those who could move – drought-stricken Oklahoma farmers fleeing to California or French workers returning to live with rural relatives – did so. Migrant labor had no choice, as the United States expelled Mexicans and the French pushed out Algerians, Spaniards, Poles, and Italians.[7]

Recovery was halting and uneven, with the German economy rebounding first, Scandinavia and Britain following by mid decade and the United States first recovering and then lapsing back into renewed recession in 1937. And recovery was only partial. In 1938 exports remained below 1929 levels in all countries but Japan, GDP was still below 1929 levels in the United States and France, and unemployment stood above 10 percent in the Netherlands, Britain, and the United States. The American stock exchange did not regain its 1929 level until 1954. By 1938 American industrial output moved to just above 1929 levels, but the United States accounted for only 31.4 percent of world manufacturing as opposed to 39.3 percent in 1929. German indus-trial production rose more robustly and its share of world manufacturing crept up one point to 12.7 percent, while the British share rose to 10.7 percent, and Sweden and Italy held their own at around 1 percent and 2.8 percent respectively. The Japanese broke the 5 percent mark and the Soviets had 9 percent, nearly double the proportion a decade earlier.[8]

Keynes versus Hayek

Contemporary observers and later economic historians have been deeply divided about the causes and nature of the depression and their conflicting

---

[7] Maria Jahoda, Paul F. Lazarsfeld, and Hans Zeisel, *Marienthal: The Sociography of an Unemployed Community* (Chicago: Aldine, 1971). German original 1933. George Orwell, *The Road to Wigan Pier* (New York: Harcourt Brace Jovanovich, 1958).

[8] Maddison, *World Economy*, 55. Buder, *Capitalizing on Change*, 258. Gerold Ambrosius and William H. Hubbard, *A Social and Economic History of Twentieth-Century Europe* (Cambridge, MA: Harvard University Press, 1989), 191.

narratives reflect commitments to competing economic theories and political programs. The battles of the 1930s pitted those continuing to believe in the tenets of classical economic liberalism against those articulating social democratic alternatives; they would be fought again during post 1945 European reconstruction and again in the 1970s and 1980s, when market fundamentalism was on the ascendancy on both sides of the Atlantic, and once more in the wake of the 2008 global financial crisis. Battle lines ran within and among countries, alliances for and against laissez-faire shifted, and the issues raised by the depression and responses to it would trouble European-American relations nearly as much as conflicts between communism and capitalism.

As economic crisis swept the globe, those prescribing austerity had the upper hand. Policymakers and politicians were nearly unanimous that only drastic budget cuts, especially in social spending, and a strict policy of state nonintervention would protect national currencies and speed recovery. Few were as brutal as United States Secretary of the Treasury Andrew Mellon, who famously urged President Hoover to "liquidate labor, liquidate stocks, liquidate the farmers, liquidate real estate ... purge the rottenness out of the system ... People will work harder, live a more moral life." Yet most, like German Chancellor Heinrich Brüning, insisted on harsh budget cuts. Labor objected but seldom offered alternatives. German Social Democrats, for example, refused to slash the social benefits they had fought so hard to achieve in the twenties, leaving the coalition government in 1930 instead. A handful of innovative trade union economists proposed a public works program focusing on housing and highway construction, arguing, "People do not want to die just because the world's credit mechanisms no longer work." But the Social Democratic Party and trade union leadership refused to consider such unorthodox measures.[9]

The Labour government in Britain was unwilling to cut unemployment benefits but remained deeply divided about running the budget deficits necessary to support them and thereby forcing sterling off the gold standard. During the 1931 European financial crisis, Labour dithered and was finally replaced by a National Government that quickly abandoned the gold standard. "Nobody told us we could do that," lamented Tom Johnston, former Labour parliamentary secretary for Scotland, showing the lack of imaginative thinking characteristic of the early depression.[10]

[9] Ahamed, *Lords of Finance*, 364. Mary Nolan and Charles F. Sabel, "The Social Democratic Reform Cycle in Germany," *Political Power and Social Theory* 3 (1982): 156–57.
[10] Barry Eichengreen and Peter Temin, "The Gold Standard and the Great Depression," *Contemporary European History* 9/2 (July 2000): 202.

To be sure, Sweden was more open to unorthodox experiments, but elsewhere on both sides of the Atlantic more innovative and interventionist policies only came when new governments replaced those discredited by the depression.

The two economists whose theories would dominate twentieth-century policy debates, John Maynard Keynes and Friedrich Von Hayek, evolved antithetical explanations for the crisis and prescriptions for its cure. Hayek, an Austrian economist, who came to England in 1931, was a staunch defender of laissez-faire. He attributed the crisis to the overexpansion of credit and overinvestment. The cure was to increase savings and allow the economy to stabilize at a new equilibrium of lower prices and wages. Keynes, a Cambridge economist, member of the British delegation to the Versailles Conference, prolific public intellectual, and academic theorist, sought a middle way between unfettered capitalism and Bolshevism. He blamed the crisis on a lack of effective demand and as early as the 1929 British election enthusiastically endorsed the proposal of Liberal politician David Lloyd George for a large public works program. His ideas were most fully elaborated in his 1936 magnum opus, *The General Theory of Employment, Interest and Money*, but key points were popularized in the press, in his testimony before government committees, and in essays such as "The Means to Prosperity," circulated widely in both Britain and America in 1933. Keynes insisted that there was no natural cure for the depression, as Hayek and others asserted. Rather, only state spending could reemploy idle men and plants and create a level of demand sufficient for full employment. For Hayek unemployment came from "sticky" wages that labor organizations or state action prevented from falling sufficiently to restore profitability and hence employment. For Keynes, it was the lack of effective demand. Hayek prescribed a higher rate of savings, while Keynes pointed to "the paradox of thrift," that is, in conditions of economic uncertainty, more savings could lead to stagnation and an underemployment equilibrium. Keynes's star was on the ascendency in the 1930s and would dominate post-World War II economic policy, but the ideas of Hayek, embodied in his 1944 *Road to Serfdom*, were to challenge Keynesianism from the 1970s on.[11]

Keynes, Hayek, and their followers focused on policy, but structural problems contributed to the crisis as well. Some were particular to national economies, such as Germany's overdependence on exports or Britain's failure to modernize. One was shared by all – the gold standard to which Europe and the United States clung until 1931. Keynes called it "golden

[11] Robert Skidelsky, *John Maynard Keynes 1883–1946: Economist, Philosopher, Statesman* (New York: Penguin, 2003), 430–31, 483.

fetters," for the gold standard heightened the fragility of the international financial system in the twenties and mandated price deflation instead of currency devaluation in the early thirties and thereby transmitted and magnified instability. It constrained policymakers from effectively respond-ing to bank crises and financial panics. When the Fed raised interest rates in 1928, for example, this drew capital to the United States and France and provoked monetary contractions and tightened fiscal policies across Europe and Latin America, so currencies there would meet gold standard require-ments. In Germany outward flows of capital as well as reduced loans and diminished exports led to a downward spiral of monetary contraction and domestic austerity, as the Reichsbank fought in vain to maintain the legal minimum of gold required by the gold standard. Because Germans, still traumatized by the 1923 hyperinflation, feared inflation above all, the government was unwilling to depreciate the currency and thereby stabilize prices and stimulate exports and recovery.[12]

The structural problems of the global economy also involved leader-ship. Britain was no longer strong enough to act as the hegemon of the global financial system, and America was unwilling to take on that role. Whether any hegemon could have negotiated an alternative to the gold standard remains questionable, but the perceived absence of international financial leadership during the crisis haunted later deliberations about a new financial architecture for the post-World War II order. Finally, pessimists such as European economist Karl Polanyi blamed laissez-faire itself: " ... the origins of the cataclysm lay in the utopian endeavor of economic liberalism to set up a self-regulating market system."[13]

However much analysts disagreed about causes and cures, they agreed that the state responses chosen made a bad situation much worse. Why were efforts at coordinated global action so halfhearted and unproductive? What did the retreat into national solutions for an international crisis mean for transatlantic relations?

Reconfiguring the transatlantic economy

The failure of international cooperation and the focus on narrowly defined national concerns stemmed in large part from conflicts over three transnational issues: reparations and war debts, the gold standard,

---

[12] Barry Eichengreen, *Golden Fetters: The Gold Standard and the Great Depression 1919–1939* (Oxford University Press, 1995), xi, 12–24.
[13] Karl Polanyi, *The Great Transformation: The Political and Economic Origins of Our Time* (Boston: Beacon, 2001), 31.

and protectionism. These Euro-American disputes reshaped the transatlantic and global flows of goods, capital, and people.

The economic crisis worsened disagreements about whether Germany could meet its reparations obligations and whether Allied war debts to the United States were linked to reparations and should be lowered or cancelled. The 1929 Young Plan, named after the key negotiator, Owen D. Young of GE, had rescheduled reparations. As with the Dawes Plan, American banks and business were central, but the United States government was not involved. The Young Plan lowered Germany's total reparations bill to $26.25 billion to be paid until 1988; $500 million a year was due for the next thirty-six years and $375 million a year for the remainder. In conjunction with the Young Plan, a Bank of International Settlements, which the United States did not join, was set up to administer and if possible commercialize the loans necessary to enable Germany to pay reparations and thus France and Britain to repay war debts. The Young Plan assumed that prosperity and vigorous American capital flows to Europe would continue; when they evaporated, Germany's ability to pay was compromised, and the policy of fulfillment and the Atlantic orientation advocated by former Foreign Minister Stresemann were discredited. Disillusioned by the Young Plan, Reichsbank head Hjalmar Schacht "lost any remaining faith in the American solution" to Germany's economic problems.[14]

Despite growing resentment, Europeans initially paid reparations and war debts. By the summer of 1931, however, fears of a German reparations' default escalated, as did European complaints about the intolerable burden of war debts. When the French and British vetoed a proposed German-Austrian customs union, which the United States favored and which might have aided the precarious German economy, United States President Hoover unilaterally proclaimed a one-year moratorium on war debts. This preempted a unilateral German suspension of reparations, but angered the French, who insisted the United States was concerned only with protecting private American loans and had violated Young Plan stipulations. France stood to loose $200 million in reparations, while being forgiven only $115 million in war debts.[15]

As the banking crisis swept across Europe, British, French, and German representatives met at Lausanne in July 1932 and agreed to a moratorium on reparations payments and a dramatic reduction in the total bill, if the United States would cancel war debts. Hoover once again denied any

---

[14] Ahamed, *Lords of Finance*, 396.
[15] Frank Costigliola, *Awkward Dominion: American Political, Economic and Cultural Relations with Europe, 1919–1933* (Ithaca: Cornell University Press, 1984), 236–37.

linkage between reparations and war debts, which he insisted were commercial obligations that must be repaid. American intransigence sabotaged the accord but did not save the entangled transatlantic system of reparations and war debts. In December 1932 France, Italy, Belgium, Poland, Hungary, and Estonia, but not Britain, defaulted on their war debts, and by 1934 every nation but Finland had ceased paying. Reparations ended more abruptly, for immediately after coming to power in January 1933 Hitler declared a unilateral moratorium on all long-term debt. The most contentious interwar economic issue had been settled but through unilateral actions on both sides of the Atlantic that fostered both bitterness and greater willingness to act purely out of national self-interest.

No country wanted to go off the gold standard in 1929 or at any point thereafter. For Britain, France, and Austria, returning to gold had symbolized normalcy; for Germany it was a hedge against inflation; and for smaller nations in East Central Europe it was a requirement of the League of Nations' stabilization programs and aid guarantees. United States Budget Director William L. Douglas histrionically declared leaving gold would be "the end of Western Civilization," while financier Bernard Baruch labeled it "a revolution more drastic than the French Revolution."[16] Yet, by the mid 1930s nearly all nations had abandoned the gold standard, for the alternative to devaluing the currency, namely price deflation and austerity, had failed to stop financial crises or restart production and trade.

The gold standard's demise began in 1931, as gold reserves in Germany, Austria, and Britain dwindled, and Germany and Austria suspended convertibility in order to hoard their reserves. When American and French bank loans failed to bolster sterling, Britain, the linchpin of the prewar global monetary system, did the unthinkable – it went off the gold standard. With yesterday's orthodoxy abandoned by its main defender, countries across Europe and the globe quickly followed suit. Of the forty-seven countries once on gold, only Belgium, France, Italy, Germany, the Netherlands, Poland, Switzerland, and the United States remained on by 1932, but they imposed various forms of exchange controls and monetary restrictions. Many Europeans, fearing the United States would soon devalue, converted their dollars into gold, exacerbating the banking crisis. The once unified global financial order was destroyed.

Going off gold paved the way for national recoveries, based on fiscal stimulus, public works, and deficit spending, but it proved impossible to create a new international financial system. The global economy broke up into currency blocs – the mark dominated in Central, Eastern, and Southern

---

[16] Ahamed, *Lords of Finance*, 462.

Europe, sterling in British Commonwealth countries and Scandinavia, the dollar across North and South America, and the yen in Japan's expanding East Asian empire. France, Belgium, the Netherlands, and Switzerland formed the gold bloc. Trade and investment fragmented along similar lines.

Efforts to restore cooperation in a crisis-ridden global economy proved futile. The World Economic Conference, held in London in June 1933, failed to establish stable exchange rates, raise commodity prices, or restore world trade. President Franklin Delano Roosevelt scathingly rejected European proposals for currency stabilization and a possible return to the gold standard, which the United States had just abandoned. Accusing Europeans of wrongheaded experiments and unjustified efforts to constrain American domestic policy, he insisted that "The sound internal economic situation of a nation is a greater factor in its well being than the price of its currency."[17] American economic nationalism, ascendant in the government and business, undermined prospects for transatlantic cooperation. So too did French, British, and American policymakers' different understanding of the crisis.

Economic nationalism

No issue proved a greater obstacle to transatlantic and global cooperation than protectionism. As prices fell, demand dropped, and world trade shriveled by one-third, state after state sought to isolate home markets from imports and establish preferential trading blocs. With much rhetorical flourish the press, politicians, and in some places labor unions launched "Buy National" campaigns in America, Britain, France, and Germany in the early 1930s. Voluntarism alone, however, could not protect the national economy, and more coercive measures were adopted.

Tariffs were the preferred method for some countries, with the United States leading the way. In the twenties, economic internationalists and economic nationalists or isolationists had been locked in conflict, but neither camp fully controlled American economic policy. As the depression deepened, domestically oriented industry, labor, and Western agriculture, all of which supported protectionism, gained the upper hand. In 1930, over the protests of bankers and economists, Congress passed the Smoot–Hawley tariff, which raised duties on nearly 900 imported manufactured goods and agricultural products to the highest rates in American history. While Smoot–Hawley was by no means solely responsible for the fact that the value of American imports and exports shrank by

---

[17] Charles P. Kindleberger, *The World in Depression, 1929–39* (Berkeley: University of California Press, 1986), 216.

two-thirds between 1929 and 1933, it aroused enormous bitterness abroad. According to one contemporary analyst, nations dependent on exports viewed it as "a declaration of economic war by the strongest economic power against the whole of the civilized world."[18] Spain and France as well as Canada, Mexico, Cuba, Australia, and New Zealand passed retaliatory tariff increases, while Switzerland boycotted United States exports. Each country engaged in beggar-thy-neighbor policies, which sought to alleviate domestic economic problems at the expense of other nations.

With a vast domestic market, America could rely on tariffs alone, but other nations built regional economic blocs with low internal barriers and restrictive external ones. After staunchly defending free trade from the mid-nineteenth century on, even as other states embraced protectionism, Britain gave up laissez-faire and adopted imperial preference. Britain and the Commonwealth nations, such as Canada and Australia, gave one another preferential, often duty-free access to each other's markets while imposing tariffs and quotas on those outside. As a result imperial exports to Britain increased 22 percent and their share of the British market rose from 29 percent to 40 percent, while the British share of exports to the empire grew from 43.5 percent to 50 percent.[19]

Germany adopted economic nationalism of a different sort. If Hitler was its inspiration, Schacht, head of the Reichsbank and minister of economics from 1934–37 was its architect. Despite his cosmopolitan biography in terms of parents, upbringing, and even name – Hjalmar Horace Greeley Schacht – he became a staunch economic nationalist and Nazi sympathizer. He sought to deal with Germany's low foreign currency reserves by tight control of foreign currency allocations for imports. To bolster Germany's uncompetitive exports (for Germany had stayed on gold), he set up clearing arrangements by which Germany bought primary products from depressed southeastern European countries, which, in return, purchased German manufactured exports. Schacht made these bilateral agreements, which were extended to Latin America, along with tight currency controls, the heart of his 1936 New Plan.

By the late 1930s German trade, which was still one-third below pre-depression levels, had been redirected; whereas Germany had previously accounted for only 15 percent of trade with Hungary, Romania, Bulgaria, Yugoslavia, Greece, and Turkey, it now averaged 40 percent and these nations were securely within the mark bloc. German trade with Latin

[18] Emily Rosenberg, *Spreading the American Dream: American Economic and Cultural Expansion, 1890–1945* (New York: Hill and Wang, 1982), 163.
[19] Keith Hutchison, *The Decline and Fall of British Capitalism* (New York: Charles Scribner's Sons, 1950), 218–21.

America returned almost to 1920s levels. This expanded autarky preserved foreign currency, provided markets, and gave Germany access to key raw materials such as oil. It also led Germany to turn away from the United States, and Western Europe. Trade with Western Europe and the British Commonwealth remained at a low level, and between 1928 and 1936 the value of American exports to Germany fell from 2 billion Reichsmark (RM) to 232 million RM, while German exports to America declined from 796 million RM to 150 million RM. Smaller economies also formed exclusionary trading blocs. The Rome Agreement of 1934 brought together Italy, Austria, and Hungary, while the Oslo group included Scandinavia, Belgium, the Netherlands, and Luxemburg. France increased its trade with its colonies, established import quotas, and sought bilateral trade agreements.[20]

In many countries strong domestic coalitions backed economic nationalism, for it helped stabilize fragile economies and revive foreign trade, albeit within limited blocs. A broad spectrum of Conservative, Liberal, and moderate Labour politicians and voters rallied behind the National Government in England. Hitler and leading Nazis deemed economic nationalism an essential prerequisite for remilitarization and expansion. Business and finance grumbled about trade policies and currency regulations but went along because business profitability had been restored, and the suppression of trade unions and political parties prevented any serious opposition.

In the United States, however, there was renewed interest in more open trade and international currency regulation. Some attribute this to a new internationalist outlook in the Northeast and the South, which triumphed over the isolationist West; others to a new coalition of capital-intensive industries, investment banks, and internationally oriented commercial banks. Some claim Roosevelt shifted policy, while others insist he always saw overseas economic expansion as integral to domestic recovery. For whatever reasons, in 1934 Roosevelt pushed through the Reciprocal Trade Agreement Act, which lowered tariffs via bilateral treaties. Twenty-one countries signed such agreements by decade's end; most were Latin American nations or European ones like Finland and Sweden, whose exports did not compete with American manufacturers. Britain was the only major European economy to sign such an agreement. Although American trade doubled, it did not return to pre-depression levels. The United States also negotiated a Tripartite Monetary Agreement with Britain and France in 1936. It produced few concrete results but did signal

---

[20] Frieden, *Global Capitalism*, 205. Adam Tooze, *The Wages of Destruction: The Making and Breaking of the Nazi Economy* (New York: Viking, 2006), 86, 88.

recognition of the need for a global monetary system and United States willingness to participate officially.

While American exports could be redirected and loans quickly curtailed, foreign direct investment was much less flexible, and American multinationals remained a visible presence across Europe and the globe. The value of American direct investment abroad declined from over $7.5 billion in 1929 to just over $6.9 billion in 1936 but was back up to $7 billion in 1940. The major losses were concentrated in Central America and Mexico. In Europe, by contrast, the value of American investments, after declining mid decade, rose above 1929 levels by 1940 and Europe then held 20 percent of American foreign direct investment (fdi). To be sure, some American multinationals cancelled projects and tried to sell off holdings in Britain and elsewhere, and a few like DuPont Chemical and American Radiator pulled out of Europe completely. Overall, however, the number of subsidiaries and affiliates of American multinationals increased from 1,340 to 1,420. American-owned oil refineries enjoyed rapid growth in an effort to circumvent European government restrictions and taxes on imported oil. Britain remained the primary locus of American fdi, with Germany running a strong second place. Indeed, the value of American multinationals' investments in Nazi Germany increased rapidly over the decade because after 1933 the Nazi government prohibited the repatriation of profits. Firms such as International Harvester, General Motors, IBM, and Ford reinvested profits from their German subsidiaries in expanded and modernized plants. While not pleased with such restrictions, American multinationals, like their German corporate counterparts, adjusted to the new order, which brought them prosperity, a lower wage bill, and the elimination of trade unions.[21]

Mobilizing the nation

The depression delegitimized laissez-faire, brought down governments practicing austerity, and challenged states to experiment with unorthodox domestic policies. The new governments that came to power in the early thirties improvised, but did so by drawing on national experiences with economic reorganization and popular mobilization during World War I and on both old social policy debates and new theories about deficit spending, planning, and social welfare. New forms of state intervention

---

[21] United States Department of Commerce, *American Direct Investments in Foreign Countries, 1940* (Washington: United States Government Printing Office, 1930), 4–5. Mira Wilkins, *The Maturing of Multinational Enterprise: American Business Abroad from 1914 to 1970* (Cambridge, MA: Harvard University Press, 1974), 169–88.

came in competing ideological packaging and were supported by quite different national political coalitions, but the resulting policies of democratic, fascist, and communist regimes displayed strong family resemblances. These postliberal experiments narrowed older transatlantic economic and social differences and created new ones.

The magnitude of the depression elicited calls for heroic, militant, and collective responses. From 1933 on Hitler and Roosevelt spoke a language of struggle similar to that which Mussolini had employed since the mid twenties and Stalin throughout the first Five-Year Plan. War metaphors abounded – Mussolini's Battle of the Lira and Battle for Wheat; Stalin's battle against backwardness and struggle to fulfill the plan, and Roosevelt's war against the emergency. As during World War I, the stress was on individual sacrifice and a united popular struggle for the common good, however differently that was defined. Both the New Deal and National Socialism relied on strong leaders and nationalist ideologies and rallied support for government programs through massive propaganda campaigns, such as the New Deal's Blue Eagle Campaign for compliance with industrial codes or the Nazi effort to rally support for the Winter Relief voluntary welfare program. Fascist Italy and Communist Russia displayed similar traits. All promoted and "profited from the illusion of the nation as an egalitarian community whose members looked out for one another's welfare under the watchful eye of a strong leader." All sought to gain popular support for new policies by persuasion and "voluntary compulsion"; Italy, Germany, and Russia by fear and force as well.[22]

New government programs like new political rhetoric shared characteristics but were not identical. Regimes drew on similar World War I experiences and utilized personnel with wartime expertise. They shared a limited repertoire of techniques, ranging from corporatist industrial organization and labor services to public works and military spending. Many projects shared a commitment to productivism and a fascination with technology. To be sure, not every government engaged in mobilizing projects. After going off gold and continuing to pay unemployment insurance, the British National Government let the market direct recovery. In France, the right and left fought bitterly and inconclusively over austerity and social reform, leaving no room for economic innovation or national mobilization. But these were the exceptions.

On both sides of the Atlantic, there were lively discussions about a corporatist reorganization of the relationship between interest

---

[22] Wolfgang Schivelbusch, *Three New Deals: Reflections on Roosevelt's America, Mussolini's Italy and Hitler's Germany, 1933–1939* (New York: Metropolitan Books, 2006), 15, 98.

representation and state power. During World War I governments, especially in Britain and Germany, had negotiated with industry and labor to
coordinate the war economy, and in the 1920s some institutionalized
bargaining between organized interest groups and the state appeared in
liberal Germany and Fascist Italy. The depression encouraged much
more sweeping experiments. Italian Fascism advocated top-down, state-
directed, compulsory corporatism, which organized entire economic sectors into vertical associations that were to replace parliament, but the
Chamber of Corporations was set up late and wielded little power. Nazi
Germany moved toward a weaker form of state corporatism that replaced
private cartels with state-mandated ones but excluded labor. Portugal
moved more tentatively in the same direction. Authoritarian regimes
viewed state corporatism as a substitute for electoral politics and parliamentary democracy and a means of asserting rhetorically the harmonious
interests of the nation over class and party divisions and individual aspirations and rights.

The New Deal's most controversial bill, the 1933 National Recovery
Act (NRA), was another example of corporatism; although encouraged by
the state, it lacked the element of compulsion and the elimination of
democracy characteristic of fascist states. The NRA sought

to provide for the general welfare by promoting the organization of industry for the
purpose of cooperative action among trade groups, to induce and maintain united
action of labor and management under adequate governmental sanctions and
supervision ... [and] to eliminate unfair competitive practices.[23]

Trade groups were urged to adopt self-governing industrial codes, which
the government would review and promote. Some hoped the United States
would move further in the direction of planning. In 1931 Gerard Swope of
GE had proposed compulsory trade associations, supervised by the Federal
Trade Commission; Rexford Tugwell, a leading member of Roosevelt's
Brain Trust and enthusiastic advocate of planning, argued that America
needed the equivalent of scientific management for the economy as a
whole. Middle-class engineers formed Technocracy Inc. to promote their
claim to be the best managers of economy and society. In 1935, however,
the Supreme Court declared the NRA unconstitutional because it regulated intrastate commerce and not just interstate business. Thereafter, the
United States developed more societal forms of corporatist bargaining
between labor and industry with a diminished role for the state.

---

[23] National Recovery Act of 1933, www.civics-online.org/library/formatted/texts/recovery_act.
html.

In other countries such as Sweden, the Netherlands, and Denmark, societal corporatism of a bottom-up, voluntary sort began to emerge. Industry, agriculture, and labor organizations bargained with one another and the state and came to be considered de facto representatives of their class or economic interest group by the state.

Underlying both state and societal corporatism was a shared desire to circumvent the messiness and inefficiency of parliamentary politics; corporatists preferred authoritarian leaders or technocratic planners. Everywhere corporatism benefited organized interests at the expense of less organized ones – labor, industry, and agriculture in the United States and Sweden, but only industry and agriculture in Germany and Italy – and valorized group interests over individual rights. Depression-era corporatism expanded the state's power to adjudicate social conflicts either by fiat or negotiation. It was a distinctly modern phenomenon that sought to stabilize crisis-ridden capitalist economies and polities. After 1945 state corporatism was discredited by its association with National Socialism and Italian Fascism, although it persisted in Portugal and to a lesser extent Spain as well as in non-European countries. Societal corporatism in varied forms would define the post-1945 decades in much of Europe.

Corporatism was not the only transatlantic departure from the principles of the liberal night watchman's state. In the face of unprecedented unemployment, two dozen states on both sides of the Atlantic, including the United States, Germany, Britain, Switzerland, Sweden, and Bulgaria, established labor services. These quintessentially modern institutions focused primarily on men, for states regarded male unemployment as more politically dangerous and destabilizing to the gender order than its female counterpart. Labor services were a substitute for military conscription, a means of social integration, and a way to inculcate loyalty to the state. The two largest and most famous labor services were the Nazi Reich Labor Service (RAD) and the New Deal's Civilian Conservation Corps (CCC).

After coming to power in 1933, the Nazis quickly transformed Weimar's small, voluntary labor service into the RAD, a much more politicized and after 1935 compulsory organization. By 1940, 2.7 million young men had served six-month stints with the RAD. Getting the unemployed off the streets was initially the goal, but after full employment arrived in the mid 1930s, the RAD sought to prepare men physically and mentally for military service and improve the economy for eventual war. Although the RAD taught respect for manual labor, it was less interested in offering vocational training than in inculcating Nazi ideology. Work and life within the confines of a "total camp" were to create the new National Socialist Man, displaying the martial virtues of self-control, courage, and sacrifice and the racist and anti-Semitic attitudes that defined membership in the Nazi *Volksgemeinschaft*

Illustration 8 Reich Labor Service, 1936.

Illustration 9 Civilian Conservation Corps, April 18, 1933. *New York Times.*

or national community. The Nazis followed closely the development of the CCC, but regarded the RAD as superior in both its educational program and its racial purity.[24]

The CCC, one of Roosevelt's first New Deal innovations, stressed work creation, vocational training, and labor productivity more than ideological indoctrination. Voluntary, rather than compulsory, it was explicitly not a paramilitary organization, yet its structure imitated the only available model, the army, and its key institution was the regulated camp. Unlike the RAD, the CCC was not explicitly racially exclusionary, but no blacks served in the South and the relatively few minorities who joined elsewhere lived in segregated facilities. Like the RAD, the CCC exposed the roughly 3 million young men who served in it between 1933 and 1942 to conservative social and gender values (but there was no American counterpart to the housework year required of young German women). The CCC offered a new vision of masculinity centering on strong, healthy bodies, discipline, self-control, commitment, and orderliness. It built on the myth of the frontier and individualism, however, while the RAD glorified the hierarchical camaraderie of World War I trenches. While New Deal officials did not view the RAD as a political model for the CCC, they did study its practical measures and adopted specific programs such as that for training airplane mechanics.[25]

States deployed labor in much more punitive ways as well. In the American South, black chain-gang labor continued to be pervasive. Fascist Italy had no formal labor service but corralled its vast reserves of unemployed as well as political prisoners, and in the late 1930s Jews, to serve as cheap labor on public works projects. The Nazis put political prisoners, mainly Social Democrats and Communists, as well as homosexuals and "asocials" in the first concentration camps, whose initial purpose was not extermination, as it became during World War II, but punishment through labor, isolation, and intimidation.

The Soviet Union mobilized millions through incentives and coercion for vast new building projects, and the forced collectivization of agriculture also pushed millions into construction and industry and into camps, for the Soviets built the largest punitive labor system, the gulag. Begun on a small scale in the 1920s when the judicial system opened labor and reeducation camps, it expanded massively in the 1930s, becoming an integral part of industrialization and forced collectivization. By 1933 roughly 2.5 million were serving sentences in penal labor camps, work colonies, and special

---

[24] Klaus Kiran Patel, *Soldiers of Labor: Labor Service in Nazi Germany and New Deal America, 1933–1945* (Cambridge University Press, 2005), 72, 100–1, 226, 243, 258.
[25] Patel, *Soldiers of Labor*, 162, 171–72, 264–65, 274–79, 285–87, 396–98.

settlements; by 1941 the total had climbed to 3.3 million. The vast majority had been unjustly accused of engaging in industrial sabotage, opposing collectivization, or being political dissidents, or they were members of ethnic minorities. Gulag labor built projects like the White Sea canal, and mined gold in the bitter cold of Kolyma. The aim was not "annihilation through labor," as was the case with Nazi labor camps after 1939, but the result was often much the same.[26]

Across Europe and America governments commissioned monumental infrastructural and industrial projects – the Dnieprostroi dam and the iron and steel city of Magnitogorsk in the Soviet Union, the Tennessee Valley Authority (TVA) in the United States, Italy's Agro Pontino marsh reclamation project, and Germany's autobahns to name the most notable. Some of these gigantic undertakings stressed electrification and industrialization, others agrarian improvement or transportation modernization. All absorbed vast numbers of workers. Each nation sought inspiration in the efforts of others, as technologies and practices circulated and visions were shared. Italy admired Soviet dams and industry, while the Soviet Union modeled its steel mills and tractor factories on American ones, and German autobahns resembled United States highways.

What united the memorable public works projects of the 1930s was "a common striving for technological monumentalism that would modernize and re-form entire landscapes." Communists, fascists and New Dealers alike were seduced by what David Nye has suggestively called the "technological sublime." They lauded unlimited growth, equated bigger and faster with better, and considered instrumental rationality and the exploitation of nature unproblematic. This shared masculinist vision of taming nature valorized work and the factory over consumption and the home. Diverse regimes viewed technology and productivism as tools for building their desired society. Lenin famously quipped that electrification plus Soviets would create Communism. Louis Mumford praised the TVA for marrying technology and political power, and others saw electrification and the New Deal as the basis of the American welfare state. National Socialism attributed less transformative power to technology, emphasizing will and conquest as the keys to economic and social transformation, but it rationalized and modernized its economy nonetheless. Productivism was thus both pervasive and politically promiscuous.[27]

---

[26] Anne Applebaum, *The Gulag: A History* (New York: Anchor, 2003), 3–115. Mark Mazower, *Dark Continent: Europe's Twentieth Century* (New York: Vintage, 1998), 123.

[27] Schivelbusch, *Three New Deals*, 153. David E. Nye, *American Technological Sublime* (Cambridge, MA: MIT, 1996), 131.

Abandoning orthodoxy

After 1945 deficit spending to stimulate effective demand and maintain full employment became the new orthodoxy for achieving capitalist stability and prosperity. During the depression, however, governments adopted an eclectic variety of interventionist measures – backed by expediency and desperation more than economic theory. Most remained wary of running deficits, and in most cases military spending ultimately proved more effective than civilian Keynesianism.

Take the United States. After 1929 President Herbert Hoover understood the need to stimulate aggregate demand, but attempted to do so in self-defeating ways. He insisted on preserving the gold standard, urged business not to cut wages, and relied on the investment initiatives of private capital and state and local governments rather than Washington. Although he did set up the Reconstruction Finance Corporation in 1932 and approved deficit spending, his program had so many restrictions that virtually nothing was funded. Roosevelt, by contrast, pushed through an eclectic mixture of programs that lacked coherence but showed a willingness to experiment. In the First Hundred Days, he tackled the financial crisis with a bank holiday, the Glass–Steagall Act to separate commercial and investment banks, and the establishment of the Federal Deposit Insurance Corporation. The Agricultural Adjustment Act propped up farm prices, the Works Projects Administration (WPA) and the CCC addressed unemployment, and the TVA began restructuring the impoverished and technologically backward South. The NRA sought to coordinate industry, raise prices, and increase labor rights. It also allocated $3.3 billion for public works, but this was counted as extraordinary spending and not as a budget deficit, for Roosevelt had run promising to balance the budget as "the one sound foundation of permanent economic recovery." New Deal measures focused on infrastructure and regional development and targeted individual groups rather than aggregate spending. No wonder Keynes in his December 1933 open letter to the president, published in the *New York Times*, criticized the NRA for only raising prices selectively and failing to increase overall purchasing power by government spending that was financed by borrowing. While New Deal measures improved the economy significantly, critics objected to government intervention, claiming the United States was becoming like a European state. They noted a growing popular tendency "to unconsciously group four names: Hitler, Stalin, Mussolini, and Roosevelt."[28]

---

[28] William J. Barber, *Designs within Disorder: Franklin D. Roosevelt, the Economists and the Shaping of American Economic Policy, 1933–1945* (Cambridge University Press, 1996), 19, 3. Alan Brinkley, *The End of Reform: New Deal Liberalism in Recession and War* (New York: Vintage, 1996), 22.

Although advisors such as the banker Marriner Eccles called for compensatory government spending, Roosevelt remained fiscally conservative. Indeed, in 1937 he began to cut government spending significantly, even though the national income was only three-quarters of its 1929 level and unemployment stood at 16 percent, for he was more concerned about budget deficits and inflation. Only after the economy sank into a steep recession in mid 1937, did Roosevelt and his cabinet come to believe that consumption not investment drove the economy and that fiscal policy and deficit spending, rather than the regulation and restructuring of capitalism, would be the most efficacious and palatable form of state intervention. This homegrown version of Keynesianism came to fruition and stimulated recovery with wartime military spending.

Sweden moved faster and further toward demand stimulus and deficit spending due both to the influence of new economic theories and to corporatist bargaining. The younger members of the Stockholm School of Economics, including Gunnar Myrdal and Dag Hammarskjöld, were preoccupied with Sweden's high unemployment and became staunch proponents of state intervention and countercyclical spending. These Keynesians before Keynes had fully elaborated his theory were active in politics. Ernst Wigforss, the Social Democratic minister of finance, for example, argued as early as 1928 that "State and local government in times of depression ought to commence desirable public works without delay. When private enterprises hesitate to put savings to work, then the public sector must step forward and direct their use."[29] Swedish fiscal policy activism began in 1932 when the Agrarians and Social Democrats negotiated the "cow trade," which committed the government to price supports for agriculture, unemployment insurance, enhanced labor rights, and fiscal stimulus to promote full employment. In 1938 export-oriented business joined the negotiations. The Saltsjöbaden Accord represented corporatist bargaining on a grand scale and committed the organized interest groups and the state to a policy of high wages, full employment, labor rights, agrarian price supports, and extensive state-subsidized social services. In return the Socialist Workers Party and the trade union confederation accepted private ownership and openness to the world market and refrained from striking. While most analysts doubt that deficit spending was responsible for Sweden's recovery, attributing it to improvements in world trade instead, all agree that Sweden had embraced Keynesianism as the legitimate way to preserve capitalism and

[29] Timothy A. Tilton, "A Swedish Road to Socialism: Ernst Wigforss and the Ideological Foundations of Swedish Social Democracy," *American Political Science Review* 73/2 (June 1979): 516.

promote social reform within it. Sweden developed one version of a distinctive European economic and social model that would persist throughout the twentieth century.

The National Socialist government experimented first and most fully with demand stimulus, but after a few years of civilian public works projects officials shifted their attention to military spending. By 1938 the Nazi state spent over half the federal budget, roughly 17–20 percent of GDP, on armaments with the money going both to private firms and the new state sector created by the Four-Year Plan. These substantial sums utilized existing capacity, promoted plant expansion, and restored full employment but did not enhance private consumption, for a policy of low wages, high taxes, and voluntary and compulsory loans to the state curbed demand. According to one estimate, in 1938 the German standard of living was half that of the United States and only two-thirds that of Britain.[30]

Not every nation experimented with Keynesianism. In Belgium, for example, the socialist minister of public works, Hendrik de Man, advocated capitalist planning as a cure for the crisis but failed to win support from either labor or business.[31] In France the Popular Front government attempted to raise wages, support farm prices, and fund some public works, but there was no explicit embrace of fiscal stimulus and the experiment was quickly defeated by capital flight and electoral losses. The British National Government rejected both deficit spending and public works, but a combination of devaluation, tariffs, low interest rates, and a housing boom, funded by private building societies, brought recovery. A more modern and prosperous industrial sector, dominated by new industries, such as automobiles, rayon, and electricity, emerged in the south of England, but the depressed northern areas, home to coal, shipbuilding, and textiles, continued to stagnate.

Social policy

Across the transatlantic world, states expanded social insurance, labor rights and protections, and welfare benefits in an effort to ameliorate the economic consequences of depression, respond to popular pressures, and implement new political projects. Unlike in earlier decades, Europeans were more interested in America than the reverse, and the United States introduced more innovations than did most European states – in part because the social policy backlog was so great. The key architect of the British post-World War II welfare state, William Beveridge, and key

---

[30] Kennedy, *Rise and Fall of the Great Powers*, 304–5. Tooze, *Wages*, 138.
[31] Mazower, *Dark Continent*, 133–36.

shapers of the Swedish one, Alva and Gunnar Myrdal, visited the United States, for example, and French Popular Front leader Leon Blum modeled his rhetoric on that of the New Deal. American New Dealers had fewer European connections than their predecessors and stressed national referents for social thought, even as they drew on policy suggestions that had originated in Europe at an earlier time. Everywhere social policy debates centered around labor rights and unemployment, economic security for the old and young, health, and housing. Did the same problems generate similar solutions and diminish transatlantic differences?

Let's start with labor policies. Before the depression Britain, Ireland, Italy, Austria, Poland, Bulgaria, and Hungary had compulsory national unemployment programs, and another ten European countries, including France, Norway, the Netherlands, and Switzerland gave national government subsidies to voluntary unemployment schemes. In the face of mass unemployment, most countries implemented emergency relief and public works programs, geared overwhelmingly to men. Britain continued to focus on unemployment insurance but standardized and expanded benefits, and Sweden pursued its commitment to full employment by public works and relief work but also gave state subsidies to voluntary unemployment programs. Nazi Germany relied on public works and then rearmament to restore full employment and thus never faced the question of whether or not to restore unemployment insurance to its generous late twenties level. In 1935 America established its first government unemployment program, a decentralized, hybrid federal-state system in which the federal government collected taxes from employers, but states managed the distribution of funds, and this led to substantial differentials in benefits. Agricultural and domestic workers, many of whom were blacks or women or both, were excluded. Unlike the emerging Swedish model, which was centralized and universal, the evolving American social state was decentralized and selective in coverage. These differences were to persist in subsequent decades.

Labor's right to organize and bargain collectively was greatly enhanced in countries such as the United States even as it was completely destroyed in Nazi Germany and Fascist Italy. After outlawing all trade unions and political parties, the German state ordered all white-collar and blue-collar workers into the state-run Labor Front, which claimed to represent workers but did not let them speak for themselves. The Strength Through Joy leisure and travel programs and the Beauty of Work factory improvement schemes in Germany, like the After Work association in Italy, sought to co-opt workers and contain dissatisfaction about low wages and the loss of rights and autonomous organizations. In the United States, which had long lagged behind Europe in labor rights, the Wagner Act of 1935 secured the right to organize and bargain collectively. But the key institution that adjudicated labor rights, the National Labor Relations Board, took a distinctively legal-juridical form, rather than regulating labor disputes via corporatist negotiation, as countries like Sweden did. The United States Fair Labor Standards Act did not follow British precedent and investigate sweated trades sector by sector; rather, it set maximum hours and minimum wages across the board. On the issue of married women's work, the United States was ambivalent and allowed school districts, private businesses, and public utilities to fire or refuse to hire married women but did not push women out of the labor force as the Nazis initially did. Sweden, by contrast, passed legislation forbidding employment discrimination on the basis of marriage or pregnancy.

By decade's end the relative economic and political power of labor was greatest in Sweden, but American workers had acquired substantial influence on both the shop floor and in the political realm, even though there was no class-based social democratic party of a European sort. By comparison, the once-powerful British labor movement was crippled by chronic unemployment and political isolation, while the spectacular gains of the French left during the Popular Front of 1936–37, which included the right to organize and to strike, the forty-hour week and paid vacations, evaporated when the government fell. In terms of labor rights and protections, the United States seemed to be heading in a postliberal direction similar to that of progressive European countries; indeed, along with Sweden it was leading the way.

The United States played catch up with old-age pensions, which had been established in most European countries before World War I. The Social Security Act of 1935 represented both a major step toward assuring economic security and the distinctive and more limited American path toward that goal. Agricultural and domestic workers, who totaled one-quarter of the workforce, were excluded. As in European countries, Social Security was modeled on the male breadwinner and dependent wife and rewarded those, usually men, with stable work careers. In the United States it was assumed that public social insurance would be supplemented by private pension plans. Whereas the German and British pension systems lumped recipients into a few broad categories, America calibrated each individual's contributions and rewarded him or her accordingly. The United States continued to lag in other kinds of state support, such as infant and maternal benefits, which the Swedes had, or family allowances, which the French pioneered and the Nazis introduced for those deemed racially "pure" and politically acceptable. America introduced needs-based aid to dependent children programs, but these were administered by the states, which allowed Southern states to exclude many blacks and to pay those covered less.

In health insurance, the United States failed to move toward state-funded coverage. Many Americans were critical of various European systems, arguing that they focused only on the poor or if they were universal, as most were becoming, were underfunded. While labor and some health reformers lobbied for national health insurance, the American Medical Association and private insurers staunchly opposed it, Roosevelt refused to endorse it, and the National Health Bill died in Congress in 1939. The transatlantic disagreement about whether health insurance was a right or a privilege, a public or a private responsibility intensified.

In terms of social corporatism, Keynesianism, and social policy, America was perhaps more social democratic than at any time before or since, and stood out in the transatlantic context for its innovations. In the 1930s, only Sweden was a model of universalistic reformism, Keynesianism, and grand corporatist bargaining, with Norway, the Netherlands, and Denmark moving in that direction. Germany offered a horrifying racialized version of the modern welfare state, in which eligibility depended on how the state categorized one's race, biological and social worth, and political attitudes. Quiescent "Aryans" and enthusiastic Nazis reaped many benefits, while Jews, Roma and Sinti, Communists, Social Democrats, homosexuals, and the workshy were excluded. After 1939 Germany imposed the Nazi model on occupied Europe.

Postwar Western and Northern European states built on the progressive elements of the thirties to develop social democratic welfare states that were extensive in both programs and coverage. The United States continued to evolve its related but distinctive brand of Keynesianism and social policy that reflected the long-standing opposition to planning, suspicion of big government and centralized programs, and reluctance to offer social benefits on a universal basis. The New Deal was a "halfway revolution,"[32] and the emerging hybrid federal-state, public-private welfare system found no equivalent in Europe.

---

[32] William H. Chafe, *The Rise and Fall of the American Century* (Oxford University Press, 2009), 109–10.

5   Strange affinities, new enemies

European-American relations in the crisis decade were reshaped not only by the depression and responses to it but also by the surprising reception of economic Americanism in the Soviet Union and Nazi Germany. In much of Western Europe, the depression tarnished America's reputation as a nation of unrivaled prosperity, unlimited growth, and unequivocal modernity. Indeed, America seemed to be becoming Europeanized with its poverty, financial crises, class conflicts, and rising labor movement. As many Europeans slyly quipped, America was now "the land of limited opportunities."[1] Yet, for all its problems, America remained a model of economic modernity among regimes highly critical of its political system and cultural values. Nazi Germany, Fascist Italy, and the Soviet Union did not wish to emulate its production methods and consumer culture wholesale, but wanted to appropriate elements of them selectively, as they tried to define distinctive national versions of a rationalized, productive economy, mass consumption, and mass culture.

Italy and Germany sought to harness their transatlantic borrowings to expansionist foreign policies that once again raised the danger of war in Europe. The Soviet Union deployed its borrowings to bolster the communist project about which the United States remained as ambivalent as ever. The actions of all three nations forced the United States to ask who was its friend, who its enemy, questions that proved difficult to answer. Why did communist and fascist countries seek to emulate the American economic model and how did they modify it beyond recognition? Did the exchange of loans, technology, consumer goods, and people bring America closer to Germany, Italy, and the Soviet Union, or did widening political differences drive them further apart? Why did Americans, as well as the British and French, have such difficulty recognizing the threat posed by National Socialism?

---

[1] Philipp Gassert, *Amerika im Dritten Reich: Ideologie, Propaganda und Volksmeinung 1933–1945* (Stuttgart: Franz Steiner Verlag, 1997), 236.

Soviet Americanism

From its inception, as we have seen, the Soviet Union admired Fordism and Taylorism. The two continental powers shared a commitment to productivism, a love of the gigantic, and a belief that new individuals could be forged in and through work in modern factories. But Soviet poverty, the New Economic Policy, and American determination to isolate the Soviet Union politically and economically had minimized exchanges of all sorts. That changed dramatically with Stalin's first Five-Year Plan for rapid industrialization and forced collectivization on the one hand and the acute American depression on the other hand. Stalin wanted American expertise, investment, and equipment, while American businessmen, however anti-communist they might be, wanted orders, and workers needed jobs. It was not just general American economic models that inspired the ambitious and traumatic transformation of the Soviet economy and social structure that occurred between 1929 and 1933; the Soviet Union also borrowed American technology, built American-designed factories, hired American engineers, technicians, and workers, and began revamping consumer venues and products along American lines.

Big industrial and infrastructure projects dominated the first Five-Year Plan, and America was involved in them in a big way. In the early 1930s, the United States provided 25 percent of Soviet imports. Seventy percent of the electrical equipment for the mammoth Dnieprostroi dam, a key part of the Soviet electrification program, came from the United States, with GE providing much of it as well as the expertise to install it. The Albert Kahn architectural firm, which had designed many Ford auto factories, opened a Moscow office in the early 1930s and designed, among other plants, the $40 million tractor plant in Cheliabinsk. Ford built a truck factory in Nizhnii Novgorod, providing the plans, patents, and training for Soviet engineers. It was not an exact replica of River Rouge, but it was distinctly American. United States firms and engineers also had significant input into the new tractor factories in Stalingrad and Kharkov. By the mid thirties the Soviets were producing 100,000 tractors a year, all imitations of American models. Magnitogorsk, the vast iron and steel complex and "Socialist City," constructed from scratch in the Urals, was modeled on Gary, Indiana, and designed by McKee and Co. of Cleveland, Ohio. McKee also supervised the construction phase, but Soviets and Americans fought bitterly over the pace and quality of work and the collaboration ended in 1932. Funding these vast purchases of men and equipment was no easy task. The Soviets sold agricultural products and semi-finished goods such as pulp even as global commodity prices sank. Sales of art, jewelry, and Fabergé eggs from the Hermitage museum also funded the purchase abroad of needed technology. In 1930, for example, United States Treasury Secretary Andrew Mellon bought $7 million worth of paintings from the Soviets – in secret, for the United States did not diplomatically recognize the Soviet Union – and that covered half the Soviet import budget for the year.[2]

American engineers and workers followed American businesses and technology into the USSR. Of the approximately 9,000 foreign experts working there during the first Five-Year Plan, 2,000–3,000 were Americans, while 4,000–6,000 were Germans. Roughly 10,000 foreign workers, many of them American, came as well. Most were sent by their firms as part of technical assistance contracts, some went for adventure, and some from political commitment or simply because they needed a job. Many, such as mining engineer Walter Rukeyser, grew to admire the energy, ambition, and pride of Soviet workers and engineers, even as they remained very critical of the economic and technological shortcomings of what was constructed. Most left after 1932 because their firms departed or they were disillusioned by the famine and repression; others stayed, and some ended up in the gulag.[3]

Although Germany provided more technical experts and workers than the United States did and after 1932 supplied an increasing proportion of Soviet imports, the Soviets looked with admiration to the large-scale, highly mechanized, low-skilled American model that produced masses of standardized goods rather than the German one which emphasized specialized production, smaller firms, quality work, and skilled labor. Economic Americanism seemed better suited to Soviet needs and the Soviet labor force. "America represented youth and invincibility, the triumph of the machine and mass production, the possibility of ending scarcity and inequality." It was a model, to quote the oft-used slogan, "to imitate and surpass."[4]

The Soviets failed to catch up to the United States or Western Europe, but they did experience remarkable growth and transformation while

---

[2] Peter G. Filene, *Americans and the Soviet Experiment, 1917–1933* (Cambridge, MA: Harvard University Press, 1967), 236–37. Alan M. Ball, *Imagining America: Influence and Images in Twentieth-Century Russia* (Lanham, MD: Rowman and Littlefield, 2003), 122–28. Stephen Kotkin, *Magnetic Mountain: Stalinism as a Civilization* (Berkeley: University of California, Press, 1995), 142–50. Susan Buck-Morss, *Dreamworld and Catastrophe: The Passing of Mass Utopia in East and West* (Cambridge, MA: MIT, 2000), 169.

[3] Kendall E. Bailes, "The American Connection: Ideology and the Transfer of American Technology to the Soviet Union, 1917–1941," *Comparative Studies in Society and History* (1981): 433. Filene, *Americans and the Soviet Experiment*, 221–26.

[4] Hans Rogger, "How the Soviets See Us," in Mark Garrison and Abbott Gleason, eds., *Shared Destiny: Fifty Years of Soviet-American Relations* (Boston: Beacon, 1985), 123–24. Ball, *Imagining America*, 32.

Illustration 10   Magnitogorsk.

Western economies wallowed in crisis. According to the lowest Western estimates, the Soviet economy grew at an average rate of 6 percent a year during the 1930s. The rate of investment rose from 12.5 percent in 1928 to 26 percent in 1937. Between 1928 and 1932 the industrial labor force grew from 11.3 million to 22.8 million, as peasants became proletarians and city dwellers. By 1932 when Stalin claimed the first Five-Year Plan had been fulfilled in four, machine-tool, tractor, turbine, and fuel production had increased substantially, but iron and steel production failed to meet projected goals and textile output declined. Some scholars argue that Soviet industrialization was entirely dependent on Western technology; "East Minus West=Zero" was Werner Kerr's succinct conclusion. Yet, buying or copying foreign technology was hardly a Soviet invention; it had been common practice since the early Industrial Revolution. Moreover, borrowed technology always had to be adapted to local circumstances. In the case of the Soviets, this meant that the plan not the profit motive and private property determined what was built and produced. Productivism had a collectivist inflection and a passion bred of the determination to overcome backwardness. Speed and quantity were much more important than quality. Without state direction and the training of hundreds of thousands of new workers and technicians, the new technology would have been useless.[5]

The Soviets attempted to create what Communist leader Karl Radek called "Russian Americans," who would have the energy, technical skill, and work ethic of their United States counterparts. The goal, according to factory worker and poet Aleksei Gastev, was "Soviet Americanism" that would turn the USSR into "a new flowering America." These efforts produced decidedly mixed results.[6] Although Soviet factories had American technology, they did not function along American lines or with American rates of productivity. The sheer pace of construction led to shortages of key machines and materials, inferior products, production breakdowns and accidents. Technicians were rapidly trained or had to learn on the job, engineers lacked the practical experience of their American counterparts, and workers, often fresh from the countryside and illiterate, were unprepared for modern factory work. Industry remained highly labor intensive, and shop-floor relations were much more conflictual than in the United States. Taylorism with its detailed and ostensibly scientific prescription for job performance and piece rates

---

[5] Angus Maddison, *The World Economy in the 20th Century* (Paris: OECD Development Centre, 1989), 62. Mark Mazower, *Dark Continent: Europe's Twentieth Century* (New York: Vintage, 1998), 121. Ball, *Imagining America*, 161–69.
[6] Ball, *Imagining America*, 26, 29.

gave way to Stakhanovism, which exhorted workers to strive for heroic outputs, achieved by whatever means possible. Both approaches to raising productivity encouraged workers to exploit themselves either for individual self-interest or from ideological commitment, and both increased inequality among workers.

The human costs of the Five-Year Plans were as horrendous as their accomplishments were notable. Shock work and ever-escalating plan goals led to waste at best, chaos at worst. Migration, high labor turnover, and inadequate housing in new industrial towns disrupted lives and worsened living standards. If forced industrialization was a mixed success, forced collectivization was an unmitigated disaster. Determined to socialize and mechanize agriculture despite pervasive peasant opposition, Stalin confiscated the property of so-called rich peasants or kulaks, deported millions eastward, and forced those remaining into new collective farms or industrial work. In protest, peasants slaughtered their animals, and grain harvests fell yet again as the government procured ever more grain to support industrialization. The result was a massive and deadly famine from 1931–33. The purges followed in mid decade, when economic sabotage was added to a growing list of political crimes.

As part of total economic transformation, the Soviets were surprisingly open to American mass consumption, and Stalin launched what would be the first of many Soviet initiatives to create a distinctive socialist consumer regime. In the mid thirties, Bolshevik anti-materialism gave way to calls for *kulturnost* or cultured trade and consumption, and inexpensive luxuries replaced the twenties emphasis on rational clothes and household items. The Soviet citizen was recognized as a consumer and not merely a producer. New goods, such as inexpensive champagne, cognac, chocolate, and personal hygiene products, as well as newly mass-produced items like sausage and canned fish and vegetables were available on an expanded scale in new, more attractive retail venues with improved service. Bicycles, watches, gramophones, and cameras were marketed in limited quantities.[7]

Soviet consumption borrowed American ideas and techniques. In 1936 Anastas Mikoyan, minister of the food industry, took a two-month study trip to the United States (after stopping in France to investigate champagne making). He greatly admired the efficiency of American food factories and brought back machines for making hamburgers, ketchup, cornflakes, and ice cream. The Soviets bought German technology for manufacturing paper plates and cups, but only America mass-produced food on the scale the Soviets needed. Soviet engineers, architects, and

---

[7] Julie Hessler, *A Social History of Soviet Trade: Trade Policy, Retail Practices and Consumption, 1917–1933* (Princeton University Press, 2004), 198–213.

store managers studied Western retail models as well, visiting the Printemps department store in France and Selfridge's in England but paying most attention to Piggly Wiggly, Woolworths, and above all Macy's. Soviet magazines reprinted articles from the American publication *Chain Store* to learn how to rationalize all aspects of retail and create a careful and solicitous service worker, preferably female. Model department stores, embodying the lessons learned, opened in Moscow and then in the capitals of each republic. Self-service restaurants and snack bars, revealingly called *amerikanki* opened in urban areas.[8]

The *kulturnost* campaign created "relative abundance in the midst of poverty" for the new urban middle class created by industrialization and the cultural revolution and for Stakhanovite workers, who were to be model consumers as well as exemplary producers. Most Soviets could only fantasize about the new consumer goods and must have found Stalin's slogan "life has become more joyous, comrades" ironic indeed given persistent shortages of all sorts and the escalating purges. Nonetheless, the array of new goods produced and marketed in new retail outlets were part of a serious effort to create a more egalitarian and participatory consumer culture. People often consumed goods in collective settings, associated with work, and the state organized conferences to get feedback on products and service. In the Soviet variant of consumer citizenship, which promoted both public activism and political integration, consumers "positioned themselves as deserving citizens, rather than supplicants or simple purchasers, whose consumer needs and desires, if bettered, would reinforce and further Soviet interests." The emphasis on consumption was both part of a mid-thirties retreat from revolutionary values and a state and party attempt to create a new Soviet person, who would enjoy more material comforts. Consumer goods would introduce people to technology, make everyday life more modern (but not bourgeois), and free women from household chores so they could participate in politics. Whether Soviet consumer culture would make them more committed to socialism remained the unanswered question.[9]

While the Soviet government embraced American technology and tried to modify mass consumption, it rejected American mass culture. The cultural revolution of the late twenties and early thirties made socialist realism the new orthodoxy in art and literature and called for proletarian culture. The regime dismissed jazz as decadent, and Hollywood films

---

[8] Jukka Gronow, *Caviar with Champagne: Common Luxury and the Ideals of the Good Life in Stalin's Russia* (Oxford: Berg, 2003), 108–9.
[9] Gronow, *Caviar with Champagne*, 126. Amy E. Randall, *The Soviet Dream World of Retail Trade and Consumption in the 1930s* (New York: Palgrave Macmillan, 2008), 150.

virtually disappeared from Soviet movie houses, due to both ideological objections and foreign currency shortages. Yet, Soviet cinema continued to be influenced by America. Aleksandrov's 1936 socialist realist classic, *The Circus*, for example, which tells the tale of an American woman who fled discrimination because of her interracial child and found acceptance in the Soviet Union, is filled with Hollywood techniques and mass music and dance numbers, reminiscent of Busby Berkeley films.[10]

The Americanization debate, round three

Official Soviet views of America were complex and shifting. During the first Five-Year Plan, officials and economists readily acknowledged the need to imitate American production methods in order to overtake capitalism. They gave American experts preferential treatment in terms of pay, housing, and food. Socialist realist construction novels often featured an apolitical American engineer who contributed to the building of the Soviet Union and simultaneously grew disillusioned with capitalism. Acknowledging the extent of technological borrowing was trickier. Officials sometimes did so publicly. Yet popular books like *New Russia's Primer*, originally written for school children, opened with a scathing critique of the wasteful boom-and-bust cycles of capitalism and then quickly moved to a sector-by-sector description of what the first Five-Year Plan was and would accomplish. It only vaguely referred to capitalist machinery and nowhere mentioned foreign experts or workers.[11] By the late 1930s, the more confident Soviets no longer spoke of imitating America and minimized their economic and technological debt to the United States. Once the Cold War began, both countries erased their earlier intense economic relationship from public memory.

Popular fascination with America persisted despite shifts in the party line. While people criticized America's social conditions, they admired its economy and technology and were eager to learn about daily life and popular attitudes. They eagerly read the enormously popular *Little Golden America*, the report by Soviet writers Ilf and Petrov on their 1936 road trip across the United States. Ilf and Petrov predictably critiqued economic inequality and exploitation, urban slums, and racism and complained in typical European fashion about unerotic American women and the lack of culture; to their astonishment and dismay, a Chicago audience gave only

---

[10] Buck-Morss, *Dreamworld and Catastrophe*, 154.
[11] Mikhail Il'in, *New Russia's Primer: The Story of the Five-Year Plan* (Boston: Houghton Mifflin, 1931).

tepid applause for a spectacular concert by Rachmaninov. But Ilf and Petrov dwelt in a way few earlier travel reports had on small-town life and the abundance of goods even during the depression. They penned sympathetic portraits of the hospitality and eccentricities of ordinary and famous Americans. Much of what most Soviet people knew about the United States came from this book and the overall impression they got was favorable.[12]

How did Americans view Soviet development and American involvement in it? American observers paid surprisingly little attention to its dark side. Roughly five thousand Westerners a year visited the Soviet Union during the first Five-Year Plan; among them were academics, clergymen, delegates from the Chamber of Commerce, and literary intellectuals, such as Theodore Dreiser, Waldo Frank, and Malcolm Crowley. Reports from the Soviet Union filled American magazines and newspapers, and the Book of the Month Club sold 46,000 copies of *New Russia's Primer*. It was a paean to the wonders of technology, a plea for the transformation of the landscape through dams, machine tools, machinery, and mechanized agriculture, and a confident prediction that the Soviet Union would soon "be independent of the calculations of European and American capitalists," who "are not pleased with our plans." The leader of the National Civic Federation insisted that America "need[ed] ... to meet the cold-blooded communist five-year plan with a warm-blooded ten-year plan of democratic idealism." Thorstein Veblen, who advocated the rule of apolitical technocrats, admired Soviet planning. Louis Fischer of *The Nation* was captivated by the energy and enthusiasm he encountered and sometimes imagined "that nothing is impossible in the Soviet Union."[13]

Focused on Soviet economic accomplishments, all were seduced by what George F. Kennan, who worked in the American embassy in Moscow in the mid thirties, called "the romance of economic development." Many observers argued that industrialization would make Russia more modern and Western. Walter Duranty of the *New York Times*, who won a Pulitzer Prize for his coverage of the Soviet Union, acknowledged the hardship and violence of the Plan, glibly noting that "you can't make an omelet without breaking eggs," but he denied the famine. He and others such as Maurice Hindus blamed peasant passivity and the Russian character for the chaos and costs incurred. Perhaps "American observers found the sacrifices worthy because they considered the people

---

[12] Ilya Ilf and Eugene Petrov, *Little Golden America: Two Famous Soviet Humourists Survey the United States* (London: George Routledge & Sons, 1944). The Soviet original was published in 1936. Rogger, "How the Soviets See Us," 125–26.

[13] Filene, *Americans and the Soviet Experiment*, 193, 217, 241, 255. Il'in, *New Russia's Primer*, 84.

sacrificed so unworthy." The culmination of Soviet development, United States involvement, and favorable American coverage was the diplomatic recognition of the Soviet Union in 1933.[14]

Fascism and Americanism

American attitudes toward Fascist Italy were much less ambivalent but displayed a similar willingness to focus on economic achievements and ignore repressive politics. From Mussolini's rise to power in 1922, American politicians, many public intellectuals, and much of popular opinion viewed fascism as a cure for Italian instability and an alternative to Bolshevism; its politics were more authoritarian than elsewhere in Western Europe, but its social and economic policies were not markedly different. Fascist violence was a way to restore law and order. Although Mussolini dismantled democratic institutions, many felt Italians were not mature enough for them in any case. Throughout the twenties, prominent figures like Hoover and the progressive, muckraking journalists Ida Tarbell and Lincoln Steffens regarded Mussolini as a moderate within the Fascist movement, who would modernize Italy. In the thirties the press contrasted him favorably to Hitler and Stalin. American defenders of fascism claimed it stood for efficiency, discipline, and progress, and hoped it would bring "the Americanization of Italy."[15]

The American economic elite was particularly enthusiastic about the fascist experiment. Bankers, businessmen, such as Judge Elbert Gary of United States Steel, and the president of the Merchants' Association of New York visited Italy in 1923, a year after Mussolini's March on Rome. Italy and America negotiated the cancellation of 80 percent of Italy's war debt, a far greater portion than other Allies received, and bankers like Thomas Lamont of J. P. Morgan and Otto Kahn then brokered much needed loans to Italy. A United States consortium of electrical firms invested heavily in the Italian power system; Standard Oil, City, and Texaco built refineries; Ford and American Radiator opened plants; and Radio Corporation of America (RCA) and International Telephone and Telegraph (ITT) ran the long-distance telephone system. In 1932 *Fortune* magazine wrote that Mussolini's regime "presents ... the virtue of force and centralized government acting without conflict for the whole

---

[14] David Engerman, *Modernization from the Other Shore: American Intellectuals and the Romance of Russian Development* (Cambridge, MA: Harvard University Press, 2003), 157, 215, 243.

[15] John P. Diggins, *Mussolini and Fascism: The View from America* (Princeton University Press, 1972), 21.

nation at once."[16] Only in the mid thirties did business become disillusioned with Italy's weak economy and autarkic policies. Italians, like all aspiring modernizers, continued to look to America. In 1936, for example, Giovanni Agnelli, founder and chief executive of Fiat, sent a company delegation to study Ford and GM plants in Detroit and the Pratt and Whitney engineering firm in Hartford.

The Fascist regime, like the Soviet one, focused on infrastructural development and industrial modernization, not the mass production of consumer goods. Yet, on a much more modest scale than in Britain or Germany, commercial culture and leisure came to interwar Italy. Movie theaters spread, absorbing two-thirds of expenditures for paid leisure, and they overwhelmingly showed Hollywood films. Popular magazines such as *Cinema Illustrazione* displayed images of beauty and fashion based on Hollywood stars like Jean Harlow and Joan Crawford. To be sure, private consumption was unevenly distributed by generation and region, with youth in North and Central Italy enjoying the most. Working-class young women were more exposed to and involved in the mass culture of movies and mass-circulation magazines than their bourgeois counterparts, on whom Fascist and Catholic influences were stronger. Cosmetics, nylons, fashion magazines, and stylish dresses were available to women of all classes. The Fascist regime sought to contain these forms of self-expression and diversion, which challenged the totalizing claims of the nation and were associated with America. It established the Dopolavoro (After Work), a mass organization to discipline the leisure of male workers, promote healthy and productive bodies and good work habits, and create a culture of consent to employers and the state alike. Fascist propaganda sought to combat the dangerous figure of the "crisis woman" – thin, unmaternal, erotic, autonomous – with that of the nubile rural young woman and the mother. Austere styles that were related to one's function and expressed a commitment to the national project were to discipline self-fashioning through makeup, dress and movement.[17] Yet, capitalist Italy had more trouble defining a distinctive Fascist culture of consumption than the Soviets did developing a socialist one.

---

[16] Diggins, *Mussolini and Fascism*, 38.
[17] Victoria de Grazia, "Nationalizing Women: The Competition between Fascist and Commercial Cultural Models in Mussolini's Italy," in Victoria de Grazia and Ellen Furlough, eds., *The Sex of Things* (Berkeley: University of California Press, 1996), 344–51.

Nazism and Fordism

In Germany the Third Reich continued to reference Fordism and American mass culture, but the terms of the debate shifted dramatically. The Nazis vehemently criticized American culture, domesticity, and politics, often in strongly anti-Semitic terms, and debunked American exceptionalism. They regarded the United States as an economic rival and imperialist threat yet sought to Germanize elements of American technology and management practice without, however, acknowledging their transatlantic origins. Through political repression and racial laws, the Nazis successfully silenced the Weimar proponents of Americanism, but it proved more difficult to construct an alternative model that would limit consumerism, eliminate American cinema and jazz, and still win popular support. Hitler's goal was a modernized, racialized, and militarized economy, in which state-sponsored, highly ideological leisure and cultural organizations and commodities would replace commercial mass culture. The reality was much messier.

Although the Nazis criticized much about the United States, Hitler was fascinated by Fordist mass production that enabled mass motorization, and in 1938 he awarded Henry Ford the Grand Cross of the German Iron Eagle in honor of his seventy-fifth birthday. Ford accepted with pleasure. In his *Second Book*, Hitler measured Europe unfavorably against the American standard of living, judged American technology to be superior, and obsessed about the American threat to Europe. He was convinced, however, that the prerequisite for Fordism in Germany was the conquest of *Lebensraum* in Eastern Europe; otherwise the Third Reich would be reduced to the status of Switzerland or the Netherlands. Rearmament, in turn, was essential for war, and from 1933 on German military spending grew exponentially, far exceeding that of the United States or other European states. This military Keynesianism profoundly shaped how economic Americanism was Germanized.[18]

However much Nazi propaganda might indulge in Blood and Soil antimodernist rhetoric, the commitment to war required an expanded and modernized industrial economy. The state promoted investment in iron and steel, airplanes, and machine tools but not consumer durables, and the Four-Year Plan emphasized petroleum, rubber, and iron ore, all vital to the envisioned war effort. Businesses relevant to the military revamped their technology and factory organization, introduced modern management methods, and preached the gospel of productivity and efficiency.

[18] Gassert, *Amerika*, 27. Adam Tooze, *The Wages of Destruction: The Making and Breaking of the Nazi Economy* (New York: Viking, 2006), 10–11.

The giant Siemens electro-technical firm relied heavily on Fordist mass production and semi-skilled women workers. Even the relatively neglected consumer goods industries mechanized extensively in order to cope with labor shortages. The growing German machine-tool industry, by contrast, continued to follow a strategy of flexible specialization that produced quality goods in small batches with universal machines and skilled workers. Wage rates, which had once been determined by broad skill categories, were now determined by Taylorist time and motion studies. Although many practices and techniques resembled those in America, Nazi rhetoric and racialized assumptions about performance (*Leistung*) supplanted references to Americanization.

American firms played a role in modernizing German industry. General Motors, for example, expanded and put new technology in its Opel plant in Rüsselsheim and by 1934 controlled 40 percent of the German car market. Ford transformed its Cologne final assembly plant into a full production facility and advertised its products on the Europahaus in Berlin. Woolworth, Singer, and ITT each invested $20 million in Germany after 1933. IBM was heavily involved in upgrading data processing capabilities. Encouraged by curiosity, long-standing ties to Germany, and a favorable exchange rate, American businessmen, journalists, academics, and students traveled in large numbers to Nazi Germany. Germans tried to maintain ties to their American business colleagues, and until the late 1930s businessmen, filmmakers, engineers, and military personnel traveled to the United States on study tours. In 1937 North German Lloyd ran more than forty trips to the United States, many for specific groups such as artisans and lawyers.[19]

The campaign to build a "people's car" reveals how the Third Reich borrowed from America and created something frighteningly different. For all he admired Ford's Model T, Hitler did not consider it a real people's car that would eliminate class distinctions. Since neither German automakers nor their American counterparts in Germany considered an inexpensive car profitable, Hitler turned to non-market means to develop a distinctive German way of mass motorization. He hired Ferdinand Porsche to design the now famous Volkswagen Beetle and appointed the fascist leisure time organization Strength Through Joy to manage the production and sales of what was initially called the Strength Through Joy car. Workers were to fund production by monthly

---

[19] Gassert, *Amerika*, 152, 157. Hans Dieter Schäfer, "Amerikanismus im Dritten Reich," in Michael Prinz and Rainer Zitelmann, eds., *Nationalsozialismus und Modernisierung* (Darmstadt: Wissenschaftliche Buchgesellschaft, 1991), 203, 205. Tooze, *Wages*, 132–33.

installment payments and receive the car once it was paid in full – a total reversal of Fordist credit purchasing. Porsche studied vertical integration at General Motors before designing the Volkswagen plant and planned to build a modern, integrated production facility, furnished with old Ford machines – a German River Rouge – along with a modern worker city to house the elite German labor force that would be part of a classless society of car owners and drivers. The reality proved quite different. Hard currency shortages prevented the purchase of American machinery, war interrupted plant construction, and pervasive labor shortages meant that most workers were foreign, many were forced laborers, and several hundred came from concentration camps. After turning out a few prototypes of the Volkswagen, this racially ordered factory, modeled on the military and the concentration camp, produced only armaments and even those inefficiently.[20]

Home, like the factory, was to be rationalized and Germanized, but in the interests of traditional gender norms and racial policy, not American-style consumerism. In the 1920s Germany had developed two alternative models of the modern home. Left-wing modern architects, such as Ernst May and Bruno Taut, created modern functional housing complexes in order to engineer efficient, hygienic living, eliminate kitsch, and promote both household and industrial rationalization. The Nazis preferred the austere and traditional variant of domesticity that had prevailed then. Weimar home economists and women's organizations insisted that women could rationalize housework only by Taylorizing their motions, minimally rearranging old furniture, purchasing some standardized utensils and dishes, and perhaps installing a modern linoleum floor. They regarded appliances as too expensive and culturally suspect and canned goods as a bad American habit. They encouraged German women to preserve their own vegetables and fruits and eat only national foods rather than "southern fruits" and other foreign products. The Nazi Women's Organization supported this vision of the efficient but unmechanized home, presided over by a nonworking housewife/mother; they added pronatalism for those deemed racially suitable and motherhood education for Aryan women that would teach racial politics as well as practical skills.[21] The state provided marriage loans to young couples, but the intention was to raise the birthrate, not consumption.

---

[20] Hans Mommsen with Manfred Grieger, *Das Volkswagenwerk und seine Arbeiter im Dritten Reich* (Düsseldorf: ECON, 1996).
[21] Nancy Reagin, *Sweeping the German Nation: Domesticity and National Identity, 1870–1945* (Cambridge University Press, 2008), 112–13, 148–59.

Despite criticism of consumerism and the deferral of mass motorization, consumption did spread in Nazi Germany. To be sure, per capita income was only one-quarter of that in the United States and below that of Britain, Switzerland, the Netherlands, France, and Denmark. In 1938 only half of families had radios, as opposed to 68 percent in Britain and 84 percent in the United States, but by 1941 Germany had caught up to Britain.[22] Poverty was concentrated among the large agrarian population and those in small shops, but many urban dwellers – if they were not Jewish or active leftists – enjoyed steady employment, even if at lower wages, and both old and new forms of consumption. Marriage loans subsidized the purchase of furniture and household goods for newlyweds. As the Aryanization of Jewish property escalated in the mid and late 1930s, goods of all sorts were available at scandalously low prices, and this plundering of Jewish property continued on a massive scale during the war as Jews across Europe were deported and exterminated. The Strength Through Joy organization subsidized an array of leisure activities from sports clubs and theater trips to day hikes and cruises on the North Sea.

The market continued to provide goods and leisure activities much as it had in the 1920s. Women, pushed out of the white-collar and professional labor force in 1933, returned from mid decade on, and magazines featured photos of working women in shops, offices, and labs, all stylishly dressed and well made up. Nightclubs, reviews, and restaurants did a brisk business, but political cabaret was replaced by a Nazi variant, in which naked dancing and precision kick lines persisted. If one met the regime's racial criteria, one could swim at the vast new public beaches, built on the lakes surrounding Berlin. Part of what was widely consumed was distinctly American. Coca-Cola opened two new plants in Berlin and visitors to the Sportpalast, where Hitler's propaganda minister, Joseph Goebbels, frequently spoke, were urged to "Drink ice cold Coca-Cola." Jazz and swing music were officially condemned as primitive "Nigger music," yet they were played not only in private but also at official functions such as the Press Ball. Movie houses screened hundreds of Hollywood films; Greta Garbo, Clark Gable, and Joan Crawford were particularly popular as were Mickey Mouse, Donald Duck, and Goofy. The numbers diminished each year, however, and films produced or directed by Jews or starring Jews were prohibited. This anti-Semitic opposition to Hollywood accounts for part of the decline, but so too did foreign currency shortages and a desire to build a German film industry that would incorporate the best of Hollywood and yet be distinctive. By

[22] Tooze, *Wages*, 136–37, 149.

1940, as German-American relations deteriorated, the Nazis banned all American films; in 1942 they turned UFA-film into a state monopoly and tried to build a German star system. They failed to produce movies that were nationalistic, yet marketable and able to compete with American offerings globally and resorted instead to making escapist adventure films, love stories, and historical epics. Germany was not an affluent society with America's quantity and variety of goods, but many lived comfortable and commodified lives, and this encouraged them to support the regime with enthusiasm or at least to accommodate to it, whatever their qualms.

The long-term weaknesses of both fascist and communist economies and the contradictions of their consumer cultures are evident with hindsight, but it is essential to recall their appeal at the time. While other countries languished in depression, "Fascism, communism, and nationalist developmentalism delivered. They provided jobs, industrial development, modernization, and less tangibly, national pride and cohesion."[23] They were neither liberal nor humane, but they seemed a viable alternative to democratic capitalism.

Hitler wanted not only a fascist alternative to Americanism but also a fascist world order that would challenge American economic superiority and eliminate the political and existential threat he felt America represented. Hitler sought not only to exclude pernicious American cultural elements from Germany but also to reverse the uneven global capitalist development that disadvantaged the Third Reich. Germany, along with Japan and to a lesser extent Italy, offered fascist alternatives to the existing colonial and free trade models of empire and concrete challenges to the British, French, and American positions within them. The growing transatlantic and global foreign policy conflicts, military competition, and racial antagonisms that accompanied economic rivalries pushed the world inexorably toward a war that Germany very much desired and Western Europe and America sought to avoid.

Prelude to war

In the 1930s democracies across Europe collapsed, and a decade and a half of fragile peace gave way to rearmament, annexation, and aggression by Germany, civil wars in Austria and Spain, and an Italian colonial war in Africa. With hindsight, Europe seemed to be marching inexorably toward another war. Yet, democracies on both sides of the Atlantic had great

---

[23] Jeffry A. Frieden, *Global Capitalism: Its Fall and Rise in the Twentieth Century* (New York: Norton, 2006), 228.

difficulty recognizing the fascist threat and were unwilling to defend Ethiopia, Spain, and Czechoslovakia against unprovoked aggression. Germany and Italy implemented their expansionist plans within the spaces provided by transatlantic ambivalence, appeasement, and neutrality.

Troubling signs of danger from the right abounded. Marshall Pilsudski in Poland, King Alexander in Yugoslavia, and General Franco in Spain established traditional conservative and authoritarian regimes. Right-wing corporatist experiments such as the fleeting clerico-fascist regime in Austria and the more enduring corporate state in Portugal were more reactionary in their aims and more expansive in their transformative visions. Finally, mass-based fascist movements emerged. They ranged from the small but violent fascist leagues like the Croix de feu in France to substantial movements like the Hungarian Arrow Cross and the Romanian Iron Guard, and culminated in fascist states of which Italy was the first, but Germany the most important. However diverse their ideologies and methods, these movements all rejected liberalism and parliamentary government, hated socialism and communism, and abhorred modern culture. Many were deeply anti-Semitic. While some rulers, such as Spain's Franco, seized the state in a bloody civil war, most, including Mussolini and Hitler, came to power via a mixture of electoral politics, legality, and widespread violence by fascist paramilitary squads. Mussolini built his fascist regime slowly, while Hitler moved swiftly to construct a radically new state and society.

Within a few months of becoming German chancellor in January 1933, Hitler and the National Socialist German Workers Party outlawed the Communist and Social Democratic parties and all trade unions, suspended parliamentary government, and launched a boycott against Jewish businesses and professionals. Within a year and a half they dissolved all political parties and "coordinated" all non-Nazi organizations, that is, shut them down or merged them into Nazi mass organizations like the Labor Front, the Hitler Youth, and the Nazi Women's Organization. The bureaucracy and universities purged Jews and many women. By mid decade the Nuremberg laws denied Jews full citizenship and forbad sexual relations between "Aryans" and Jews; thereafter "Aryanization" policies deprived them of their property as well. The Third Reich put political dissidents, mainly communists and socialists, into concentration camps and subjected the mentally and physically disabled, the workshy, asocials, and alcoholics to compulsory sterilization. Despite or because of its repressive anti-leftism, militant nationalism, and anti-Semitic and racial policies, the Nazi regime was popular, for to many it brought order, economic recovery, and national self-confidence.

The Nazis intended to transform not only Germany, but also Europe and the global balance of power. Hitler had long preached aggressive nationalism, glorified struggle and militarized masculinity, and promised to revise the hated Versailles order, regain lost territories, and seize the "living space," which, he claimed, Germany needed to dominate a new European order. Rearmament was the first step. In 1930 Germany had spent less on defense than any of the Great Powers; by 1935 it spent over twice as much as the United States or France and over three times as much as Britain. Thereafter, the discrepancies increased still further.[24] In the fall of 1933 Germany, along with Japan, withdrew from the League of Nations. In 1934 Hitler began expanding the German army beyond the 100,000 men allowed by the Treaty of Versailles; the following year he introduced universal military conscription, and by 1938 the *Wehrmacht* had 600,000 soldiers. In 1936 Germany remilitarized the Rhineland in violation of the Versailles and Locarno treaties. Simultaneously it established the Rome–Berlin Axis and allied with Japan in the anti-Comintern Pact. In short, even before the Third Reich moved beyond its borders, it was blatantly militarized, anti-Semitic, racialized, economically mobilized, and disdainful of international agreements. This new Germany was brilliantly and frighteningly celebrated in Leni Riefenstahl's 1935 film *Triumph of the Will*.

Aggression began mid decade with Italy taking the initiative. In pursuit of a new Roman Empire extending beyond the Mediterranean, Mussolini used overpowering force, bombing, and poison gas to invade Ethiopia, which Italy had tried unsuccessfully to conquer in 1896. The League of Nations charged Italy with aggression but proclaimed only ineffectual economic sanctions. Roosevelt condemned fascist autocracy and aggression, and large American oil companies suspended deliveries, but small ones did not, and the public was divided about sanctions. Meanwhile Britain and France secretly tried, in good colonial fashion, to give most of Ethiopia to Mussolini in return for a truce. The Italian conquest of Ethiopia, like the Japanese invasion of Manchuria five years earlier, revealed the bankruptcy of collective security and a transatlantic unwillingness to act forcefully against aggression outside the Euro-American world.

The Spanish Civil War, which broke out in 1936 and ended with the defeat of the Republic in 1939, showed a similar liberal unwillingness to act in defense of democratically elected governments closer to home. The details of this complex conflict, which pitted the legitimate Republican government and its socialist, communist, and anarchist supporters against

---

[24] Paul Kennedy, *The Rise and Fall of the Great Powers* (New York: Vintage, 1987), 296.

an alliance of the military, the Catholic Church, and fascist organizations, are beyond the scope of this study, but three points need to be made. Far from being an obscure conflict, the Spanish Civil War was a distillation of the central questions about fascism and anti-fascism, democracy and authoritarianism, social reform and tradition that preoccupied the entire interwar era. As the Italian author Leonardo Sciascia wrote, "Spain was lit by all the world's hopes and its mistakes."[25] Second, Hitler and Mussolini came to the aid of General Franco, providing troops, munitions, and planes and using the Civil War to experiment with bombing civilians, a tactic first used by Britain and France in the Middle East and North Africa in the 1920s. Guernica, immortalized in Picasso's painting, showed the results. Third, despite fascist intervention, Britain, France, and the United States adopted a policy of nonintervention and strict neutrality. Volunteers joined the International Brigades, but aid to the Republicans came only from the Soviet Union and it was limited.

After Spain, the pace of aggression quickened, as Hitler began to implement his plans for staged expansion, south, east, and then west in preparation for the total war he anticipated occurring between 1943 and 1945. In March 1938, after a campaign of diplomatic pressure, threatened military action, and internal subversion by Austrian Nazis, Hitler annexed Austria. In the fall he threatened to invade the predominantly German areas of Czechoslovakia, to protect, he claimed, an oppressed German minority, which was clamoring for incorporation into the Third Reich. Rather than defending Central Europe's most viable democracy, the British and French heads of state, Neville Chamberlain and Edouard Daladier, rushed to Munich to offer Hitler the territories he desired in return for a promise not to demand more. Chamberlain proudly proclaimed that he had secured "Peace in our Time." Roosevelt sent him a telegram saying "Good man" and assured the United States ambassador to Italy that he was "not a bit upset over the final result."[26] Czechoslovak President Edvard Beneš, who had not been consulted, resigned and went into exile.

Equally disturbing was the radicalization of Nazi anti-Semitism against a background of ongoing discrimination and Aryanization. On November 9, 1938, Nazi storm troopers burned 267 synagogues and looted 7,500 businesses and innumerable homes. At least 90 Jews were killed and 30,000 Jewish men were put in concentration camps. *Kristallnacht* or the Night of Broken Glass provoked widespread shock.

[25] Leonardo Sciascia, *Sicilian Uncles* (Manchester: Carcanet, 1986), 181.
[26] "The Mythology of Munich," *Newsweek* 2008, www.newsweek.com/id/141502.

The British press and clergy expressed outrage, even if many bought the Nazi lie that the attacks were spontaneous. French reaction was cautious on the right and denunciatory on the left. The Soviets responded belatedly, comparing *Kristallnacht* to earlier Russian pogroms. In America Roosevelt condemned Nazi violence and withdrew the American ambassador, religious leaders and the press denounced the pogrom, and protest rallies occurred in several cities. In response the Nazis adopted a more confrontational policy toward America and hurled incessant anti-Semitic propaganda at its leader. The United States was the "headquarters of world Jewry," and Roosevelt was surrounded by Jewish advisors. After 1938 "the 'international Jewish question' came to be understood in the Third Reich as synonymous with America." Yet, neither Roosevelt nor Congress favored a more lenient immigration policy that would have helped Jews seeking to leave Germany.[27]

Misrecognizing fascism

In the face of such aggression and provocation, the Western democracies remained passive for a multitude of reasons, some shared, and others particular to individual nations. It would be comforting but inaccurate to see appeasement and neutrality as part of a considered strategy to buy time while preparing for a war against Nazism that was considered likely and necessary. The overriding fact is that no one besides Hitler wanted war in the late 1930s, not even Italy. Memories of the carnage of World War I were ever present in Britain and France, kept alive by the missing and the maimed, by fiction and films. To risk such horrors again, the danger would have to be imminent, the cause compelling. For most British and French, neither Addis Ababa nor Madrid nor Prague met those criteria. A majority of Americans viewed the intervention in 1917 as a mistake they intended not to repeat; even selling aid to threatened democracies was to be avoided. In 1934 Congress passed the Johnson Act, which forbad nations that had defaulted on their war debts from borrowing in the United States and a year later voted for a strict Neutrality Act.

Americans and Western Europeans saw Italy as a more moderate fascist regime that did not threaten Britain and France militarily and might serve as a counterweight to Hitler's ambitions. Mussolini had blocked Hitler's initial attempt to annex Austria and might be a potential ally; hence the Franco-British effort to placate Italy during the Ethiopian war and the American refusal to endorse economic sanctions. Underlying American

---

[27] Anthony Read and David Fischer, *Kristallnacht: The Nazi Night of Terror* (New York: Random House, 1989), 150–58. Gassert, *Amerika*, 260. Tooze, *Wages*, 282.

caution was not only a vocal Italian-American lobby but also public opinion, which was more critical of war than fascism. When asked in a 1937 poll to choose between fascism and communism, 61 percent of Americans polled selected the former. Among dictators they preferred Mussolini by 53 percent to Stalin 34 percent and Hitler 13 percent.[28]

Most Americans saw Germany as more dangerous than Italy but failed to grasp the radically new and threatening nature of National Socialism, assuming it could be dealt with just as other states. Many in Britain and the United States assumed that Germany's economic demands were legitimate; others sympathized with its territorial claims. Since postwar settlements had protected minority rights by transferring populations in Turkey and the Balkans, doing so by transferring territory might not have seemed a radical or illegal step. Chamberlain and Deladier were not alone in arguing that if "reasonable" concessions were made, Hitler would be satisfied and peace maintained. Finally, some in England actively sympathized with the Nazis and many a right-wing Frenchman in the politically polarized Third Republic embraced the slogan "Better Hitler than Blum," the socialist head of the Popular Front government and a Jew.

Americans were equally confused and ambivalent about what was happening inside Germany. Throughout the thirties government officials, the media, and popular opinion debated whether Nazism was imposed on Germany by a small clique or enjoyed widespread support, whether it was a product of German culture and politics or a reflection of universal problems and propensities, whether it was a bulwark against communism or a danger to democracy. Gangster and disease metaphors abounded in the critical reports of American journalists writing from Europe, such as William Shirer, John Gunther, and Dorothy Thompson. Government officials and the media acknowledged dictatorship and repression but downplayed popular support for Nazism, and the public came to share that view. In the fall of 1939, 66 percent of Americans polled believed that Germans were basically peace-loving but easily misled. Writers for the *Saturday Evening Post* were sympathetic to Hitler's revisionist aims, and mainstream family magazines were more concerned about communism than Nazism.[29]

In both Europe and the United States, the prevalence of anti-Semitism and eugenics limited not only protest against the Third Reich but also an accurate understanding of how its radical racial policies violated the rule of law and the fabric of civilization. Nazi compulsory sterilization, for

---

[28] Diggins, *Mussolini and Fascism*, 292–98, 333.
[29] Michaela Hoenicke Moore, *Know Your Enemy: The American Debate on Nazism, 1933–1945* (New York: Cambridge University Press, 2010), 9, 12, 41–53, 65–68.

example, aroused some criticism in Britain but little comment in America where there was a strong eugenics movement and state sterilization laws that served as models for German ones. Most observers either downplayed, ignored, or misconstrued Nazi persecution of the Jews. The Soviets reduced anti-Semitism to economics and viewed *Kristallnacht* as a Nazi effort to divert the proletariat from its plight. Although Britain and France continued to admit Jewish refugees, as did the Netherlands, government leaders did not speak out against Nazi anti-Semitism even after *Kristallnacht*. American reporters like Dorothy Thompson thought it politically expedient to subsume the persecution of the Jews under the rubric of the repression of religion or the victimization of all Germans. The Non-Sectarian Anti-Nazi League followed suit. This set the pattern for wartime propaganda, which downplayed the fate of the Jews and emphasized the Nazis' attack on religion, understood primarily as Christianity.

Finally, Western anti-communism and Soviet suspicion of capitalism encouraged passivity and ultimately Soviet willingness to ally with Nazi Germany. Although no insurrectionary or revolutionary threats from the left emerged in the 1930s, many in Britain, France, and the United States regarded communism as the main danger. While all the European anti-fascist nations began rearming in the late 1930s, none were close to Germany in the quantity and quality of planes and arms in 1938. Although the Soviets offered to defend Czechoslovakia, neither Britain nor France felt ready to fight and doubted that the Soviets were, given recent purges of the officer corps. In the wake of Munich, about which they were not consulted, the Soviets questioned the seriousness of French and British promises to defend Poland and feared a desire on their part for a German attack on Russia. Abandoning efforts at collective security, Stalin's foreign minister, Vyacheslav Molotov, took the only deal available, a Non-Aggression Pact with Nazi Germany in August 1939.[30] The pact shocked communists everywhere, angered anti-fascists, and led many to apply the label totalitarian, once reserved for fascist regimes, to the Soviet Union as well.

While Hitler repaired his relations with the Soviet Union, those with the Western powers deteriorated. In his January 1939 State of the Union address, Roosevelt warned of "storms from abroad" that threatened American religion and democracy and against which America must defend itself. A few weeks later Hitler delivered a speech to the Reichstag, in which he attacked American intervention in World War I

---

[30] Ronald Grigor Suny, *The Soviet Experiment: Russia, the USSR, and the Successor States* (New York: Oxford University Press, 1998), 301.

and dismissed recent American criticism of Nazi Jewish policy. Viewing Roosevelt as a pawn of Jewish interests, Hitler uttered his infamous threat that "If international finance Jewry inside and outside of Europe again succeeds in precipitating the nations into a world war, the result will not be the Bolshevization of the earth and with it the victory of Jewry, but the annihilation of the Jewish race in Europe." In March Hitler annexed the rest of Czechoslovakia. In response, Britain promised to defend Poland's independence and France did as well. In April Roosevelt demanded that Hitler and Mussolini promise not to invade Poland and over two dozen other countries he named. Hitler countered with a fiery and popular speech, denouncing American intervention in Europe and claiming the equivalent of the Monroe Doctrine for Germany.[31]

Most Americans did not share Roosevelt's growing concerns about fascist aggression. Congress defeated his effort to alter the Neutrality Act so as to aid Britain. Popular attention was focused on the World's Fair, which opened in New York City in April. The theme of that upbeat expo was "Building the World of Tomorrow." The main attraction for Americans just emerging from the depression was General Motors Futurama exhibit, depicting the cities, factories, and farms of the future, connected by an ultra-modern highway system. The world, it promised, was moving inexorably toward ever more consumption and leisure, toward speed, efficiency, and safety. In fact much of the world was heading in a quite different direction. Deeming the time to be strategically and economically opportune, Hitler invaded Poland on September 1, 1939, launching World War II in Europe. It would not end until Germany's unconditional surrender on May 8, 1945.

---

[31] Saul Friedländer, *Nazi Germany and the Jews: The Years of Persecution, 1933–1939* (New York: Harper, 1997), 309–10. Gassert, *Amerika*, 262–66.

6   From world war to Cold War

World War II was both total and global in ways that its predecessor, despite its name, had not been: total in the economic and social mobilization required of the nations involved as well as in the unprecedented death and destruction of soldiers, cities, and civilians across Europe; global in the goals of belligerents and in the scope of the fighting, Europe being only one of several theaters of war. World War II was a war of competing empires and contradictory visions for transforming the global order. It was an ideological contest as well, pitting fascist regimes against an uneasy anti-fascist coalition of liberals, social democrats, and communists. World War II was a war of annihilation in which Nazi Germany and its collaborators committed genocide against Europe's Jews, eliminated millions of others deemed racially inferior, and ruled other Europeans with methods of occupation and exploitation honed and previously deployed only in their colonies.

World War II dramatically transformed the European political, social, and economic landscape and restructured European-American relations more profoundly and permanently than World War I. America's economic strength provided the necessary but not sufficient condition for it to become a superpower; war provided the occasion and created the intention to do so. It also opened the way for challenges to American hegemony from the much weaker Soviet Union. It marked the end of the European global era but not of European nations' efforts to retain their distinctive identities, pursue autonomous domestic policies, and play a role in global affairs. To understand these dramatic postwar changes, we need to explore the origins and nature of the war, for the key events, contributions, and military and civilian costs to different combatants varied greatly as did the meanings assigned to the war at the time and later.

While battles raged across Europe and the globe, both fascist powers and the Allies planned for the postwar era. The Nazi vision of a German-dominated European New Order, geographically vast, racially stratified, and heavily militarized that would serve as a basis for global expansion, was partially realized before being defeated. The Allies strove to design a postwar order that would negate fascism, stabilize capitalism, and foster international cooperation. But how did Britain and the United States imagine the postwar capitalist order, Europe's place in it, and the future of colonial empires? Did the Soviets envision continued cooperation with America and Britain or the construction of an empire of their own?

By war's end, European cities had been reduced to rubble, economies had collapsed, and collaborationist governments had fallen, but the shape of successor regimes was unclear. Millions died, millions more were refugees on the move toward uncertain futures, and few knew how to create the longed for normal life after so much horror. In Europe no revolutionary upheavals shook devastated states and disoriented societies, as they had between 1917 and 1920, but neither could the interwar order be restored. The wartime community of interests among the United States, the Soviet Union, and Great Britain rapidly disintegrated. How and why did this labile situation evolve into the rigidified, confrontational Cold War, which few had anticipated or wanted during the war but which was firmly in place by late 1947?

America holds back

World War II has been the subject of innumerable histories, biographies, memoirs, fiction, and films, yet each nation tells markedly different war stories, centering on different iconic events. Although historians blandly label this titanic struggle World War II, different countries prefer their own terminology, rich in political claims and flattering historical interpretations. For the Americans, World War II is "the good war," in which a nation united behind a politically just cause, fought with moral clarity, and saved Europe and Western civilization. For the British it was the people's war, fought, initially alone, against the Nazi enemy by a people who overcame class differences and were determined to build a more economically secure and socially just society. For the Russians it was "the great patriotic war" in which a united Soviet populace fought heroically for the survival of the Russian motherland and victory over fascism. Neither in victory nor defeat did the Germans have one term for their multifaceted struggle against what they defined as the Judeo-Bolshevik enemy and Jewish-dominated America and for the *Lebensraum* they desired. Given their different investments in and understandings of the total war that began in 1939, how did these diverse combatants negotiate alliances and secure material resources? How central a role did the United States play? Military history tells one part of the story, but it will be touched on only fleetingly because it has been so thoroughly studied. Our primary concern is with the economics of warfare and the complex political relations among Americans, Soviets, and the British.

The war that created the conditions for America's postwar economic, political, and military dominance in much of Europe and globally began without American participation. Nor did the United States abandon neutrality in the face of rapid German victories over Poland in the fall of 1939 and France, Norway, Denmark, Holland, Belgium, and Luxemburg in May and June of 1940. By mid 1940 the Nazi empire extended from Warsaw to Amsterdam, from Oslo to Prague. The Soviets annexed eastern Poland and occupied the Baltic States and part of Romania, while Italy moved into Albania and British-controlled Egypt and prepared to invade Greece. To Hitler's surprise, Britain refused to surrender. It fought alone until Russia joined in after the Nazis invaded the Soviet Union in June 1941 and the United States did so after Japan's attack on Pearl Harbor in December of that year.

As in World War I, American neutrality did not preclude economic involvement. President Roosevelt, like much of the American populace, blamed Germany for aggression but wanted to avoid war while encouraging Britain and France to rearm and serve as a bulwark against Nazi expansion. After the fall of France, those American hopes rested solely on Britain, inaugurating what British Prime Minister Winston Churchill called the "special relationship." Earlier United States government anger about British currency and trade policies and left criticism of British imperialism gave way to celebrations of Anglo-American solidarity and concrete aid offers. A November 1939 modification of the Neutrality Act allowed belligerents to purchase non-military goods for cash and carry them away on their own ships, and Britain did so by depleting its foreign currency reserves. In March 1941 Roosevelt prevailed upon Congress to break with America's World War I policy of aiding Allies only with private loans on commercial terms. It passed Lend-Lease, which enabled the president to authorize aid in return for repayment "in kind or property, or any other direct or indirect benefit which the President deems satisfactory." Under this program $68 billion of equipment, food, resources, and semi-finished goods went to Britain during the war. Churchill proclaimed Lend-Lease "the most unsordid act in the history of any nation," and many Americans have shared this altruistic view of the program and the "special relationship." In fact, both were complex and conflicted; it would be more accurate to speak of "competitive cooperation" or "ambiguous partnership."[1]

---

[1] Stephen Broadberry and Peter Howlett, "The United Kingdom: 'Victory at all costs,'" in Mark Harrison, ed., *The Economics of World War II: Six Great Powers in International*

Lend-Lease was an act of sweeping generosity, but as Keynes, who traveled repeatedly to the United States to negotiate its details for the British government, insisted, it was also passed "for the defense of the United States." Lend-Lease enabled America to avoid military commitments in Europe, even as the president and many others recognized the Nazi danger; Britain would be aided in its own struggle and America's proxy war. Of equal importance, it was a great boon to the American economy, helping to pull it definitively out of the depression. Finally, Lend-Lease gave the American government and internationally oriented business the opportunity to push their economic agenda. The United States Treasury wanted to keep Britain in the war but make it more financially dependent on the United States, while the State Department sought to end imperial preference, which Secretary of State Cordell Hull described as "the greatest injury, in a commercial way" to American interests that he had witnessed. Article VII of Lend-Lease stipulated that Britain would abandon imperial preference at war's end, opening its own and its empire's markets to American goods on equal terms. In addition, Britain was prohibited from exporting any goods that contained Lend-Lease materials, a restriction that worsened its balance of payments deficit and thus its global economic position. The United States insisted Britain was wealthier than it claimed and should enlist its empire to pay more for the war effort; the British thought America wanted to "strip them bare." While some historians claim that there were "no selfish postwar purposes" behind Lend-Lease, British dependence on America was clear to all as were the conflicting visions of the postwar economic order that troubled not only wartime negotiations but also preparations for the postwar order. As Keynes's biographer noted, "The American reluctance to separate the business of business from the business of war was to become Britain's chief grievance against its wartime ally."[2]

Hitler factored the widely publicized Lend-Lease aid into his strategic calculations. His views of American economic and military potential had vacillated wildly in the interwar years. In *Mein Kampf* he depicted America as dominated by Nordic races, enviably capable of managing its vast "living space" and potentially dangerous to German aspirations; after becoming chancellor, he dismissed the United States as a "mongrel society" of mixed and inferior races with little military potential or willingness to fight in Europe. After the American reaction to *Kristallnacht*,

Comparison (Cambridge University Press, 1998), 53. David Reynolds, *From World War to Cold War: Churchill, Roosevelt, and the International History of the 1940s* (Oxford University Press, 2007), 50.
[2] Broadberry and Howlett, "United Kingdom," 53. Robert Skidelsky, *John Maynard Keynes 1883–1946: Economist, Philosopher, Statesman* (New York: Penguin, 2003), 615.

however, the German government and population assumed the United States would eventually join Britain and France. When Hitler invaded Russia, he anticipated a quick victory that would open the way for a vast German colonization of the East. In the fall of 1941 he grandiosely proclaimed: "Here in the East a similar process will repeat itself for a second time as in the conquest of America." The Volga would be Germany's Mississippi and the "inferior" Slavs would be cleared out or killed just as Native Americans had been. In the newly conquered *Lebensraum*, Hitler planned bridges bigger than the Golden Gate and skyscrapers to rival New York's. Although the German army quickly occupied much of the western Soviet Union, took millions of Red Army soldiers prisoner, and began killing Jews by the tens of thousands, it failed to conquer Moscow and Leningrad and became bogged down in the prolonged total war Hitler wanted to avoid. By late 1941 his grandiose imperial plans seemed ever more fantastical, and victory was nowhere in sight.[3]

Why then did Hitler, along with his subordinate allies Italy, Romania, Hungary, and Bulgaria, declare war against the United States in the wake of Pearl Harbor? Strategy, ideology, megalomania, and miscalculation all played a role. Hitler had decided to invade the Soviet Union in June 1941 in part because he expected a quick victory that would isolate and demoralize Britain before America was economically mobilized and militarily engaged. Although Hitler preferred to wait for the inevitable conflict with America until the Soviet Union was defeated, once Japan attacked, he assumed the United States would be preoccupied fighting in the Pacific and have limited ability to aid Britain and the Soviet Union. Of equal importance was the Nazis' growing anti-Semitic paranoia about America. In the spring of 1941 Nazi racial propagandists Joseph Goebbels and Alfred Rosenberg insisted that America supported Britain and contemplated intervention only because Jews influenced Roosevelt; indeed, they claimed, there was a parallel Jewish government alongside the official one. Hitler regarded the August 1941 Atlantic Charter, laying out the rights and freedoms to which Roosevelt and Churchill were committed, as a virtual declaration of war against Nazi Germany. From late 1941 on Nazi propaganda, which labeled Stalin as a "Bolshevik mass murderer" and Churchill as the "gravedigger of empire," placed "most war guilt" on Roosevelt, who was accused of wanting to expand the war because of domestic troubles and being willing to let Jews dominate the world. Increasingly, the Nazis

---

[3] Ian Kershaw, *Hitler 1936–1945: Nemesis* (New York: Norton, 2001), 434–5. Adam Tooze, *The Wages of Destruction: The Making and Breaking of the Nazi Economy* (New York: Viking, 2006), 469–70. Mark Mazower, *Hitler's Empire: How the Nazis Ruled Europe* (New York: Penguin, 2008), 125.

projected their own aims onto their enemies. America was "grasping for world domination," and Roosevelt and the Jews wanted "to exterminate National Socialist Germany." Finally, Hitler underestimated the economic and military capacity of the United States just as he overestimated what Germany could produce and extract from its new empire.[4]

Negotiating alliances

America's entry into the European war brought not only intensified cooperation with Britain, but also a new partnership with the Soviet Union. Because wartime alignments were quickly reversed postwar, Cold War enmities have been read back into a situation that had quite different dynamics; the "special relationship" with Britain is seen as self-evident and easy, the Soviet alliance as counterintuitive and difficult. Although a few historians argue that the USSR was not as committed to the alliance with Britain and the United States as it had been to the Hitler–Stalin pact, most disagree. While debates continue about whether the Soviets ever considered a separate peace with Germany, even those arguing for early overtures claim none were made after the Soviet victory at Kursk in mid 1943. Although American and British diplomats stationed in Moscow complained about a lack of contact with officials and citizens, Roosevelt and Churchill developed a working relationship with Stalin, albeit one lacking the camaraderie the Anglo-American leaders shared.

Economic issues did not divide Soviets and Americans, as they did Britain and the United States, but military strategy persistently did, for Stalin's top priority was a second front in France or in Norway or Finland. American military planners wanted an early invasion of the continent, but the British, who wanted to harbor resources and defend imperial interests, preferred to blockade Germany, attack *Wehrmacht* forces in North Africa, and then invade Italy, all the while hoping Germans might rise up against Hitler. Roosevelt acquiesced to British plans, for he faced an American public, 20–30 percent of whom wanted a negotiated peace with Germany and favored putting all resources into the Pacific War. American troops joined British ones in defeating German General Rommel in North Africa, but Anglo-American forces faced only fourteen Axis divisions there, while the Red Army faced 266 on the Eastern Front. The unequal

[4] Philipp Gassert, *Amerika im Dritten Reich: Ideologie, Propaganda und Volksmeinung 1933–1945* (Stuttgart: Franz Steiner Verlag, 1997), 325–27, 353. Jeffrey Herf, *The Jewish Enemy: Nazi Propaganda during World War II and the Holocaust* (Cambridge, MA: Harvard University Press, 2006), 131.

distribution of military burdens was not substantially altered by the Anglo-American strategic bombing of over one hundred German cities and towns from 1942 to 1945. Controversy persists about the morality of targeting civilians and the bombing's effectiveness in disrupting economic production and the war effort. Churchill and Roosevelt claimed bombing was a substitute for a second front, but the Soviets did not regard it as adequate compensation for the millions of lives lost and cities, factories, and farms destroyed. Moreover, any benefits of the bombing came only after the tide of war had turned.[5]

The Soviets appreciated Lend-Lease aid, even though it did not kick in fully until 1943. The Soviet Union like Britain received extensive food aid, including that quintessential American product Spam. By war's end one-sixth of Soviet combat planes and one-eighth of armored fighting vehicles came from the West. Overall, Lend-Lease amounted to between 4 percent and 20 percent of the value of Soviet public sector output. It helped ease the economic chaos caused by the evacuation of factories and workers beyond the Urals and by the ongoing German occupation. But in the enormously destructive and costly battles between June 1941 and the Soviet victories at Stalingrad in 1942 and Kursk in 1943, Allied aid did not play a significant role. It was, however, much more important in helping the Red Army push the *Wehrmacht* back to Berlin.[6]

Alliances were negotiated not just in the back rooms of power but also in the public imagination, and popular attitudes in both the United States and the Soviet Union toward each other were remarkably positive. In part this came from government propaganda and media coverage, in part from a denser exchange of information and cultural products. Under pressure from his Allies, Stalin allowed greater cultural openness and displayed more tolerance for the once prohibited Russian Orthodox Church. Soviet press coverage of "the great transoceanic republic ... a country to which we are linked by historic friendship," as stilted Soviet prose described the United States, was generous, and American aid was regularly reported. More and more theaters showed Hollywood films; Soviets once again enjoyed playing and listening to jazz; and Russian movies and plays had positive American characters, who were sympathetic to the Soviet Union. There were lectures, travel reports, and books about the United States. Although it is impossible to gauge popular opinion in the wartime Soviet Union, there are indications that many viewed Americans very positively

---

[5] Reynolds, *From World War*, 56–57. John Barber and Mark Harrison, *The Soviet Home Front, 1941–1945: A Social and Economic History of the USSR in World War II* (London: Longman, 1991), 32–34.

[6] Barber and Harrison, *Soviet Home Front*, 190.

and sought contact with them where possible. Stalin reluctantly opened the Soviet Union to more Western journalists, missionaries, and sailors but sought to limit contacts with Russians to formal occasions, for fear of exposing Soviet backwardness. Such restrictions were only partially successful, for prostitutes and so called "good time girls," who were often students, subverted them. And on May 9, 1945, there was a huge and boisterous demonstration outside the American embassy in Moscow to celebrate Germany's surrender. According to George Kennan, then stationed in the embassy, "If any of us ventured out into the street, he was immediately seized, tossed enthusiastically into the air, and passed on friendly hands over the heads of the crowd to be lost, eventually, in a confused orgy of good feeling somewhere on the fringes."[7]

For many Americans it was Russia's military performance that shaped a more positive image. Soviet success in halting the *Wehrmacht* spurred calls for military aid and generated positive press coverage of the Soviet Union, even by *Life* publisher Henry Luce, who was staunchly anti-communist. Later victories seemed to show that the system worked and people were loyal to it. To be sure, American commentators disagreed about whether the Soviet Union was undergoing spiritual regeneration and might be open to democratization. The sociologist Pitirim Sorokin even suggested that Russia and the United States, as highly industrialized nations, shared affinities and might be converging. Mainstream, press coverage of the USSR was "surprisingly charitable," as was *Mission to Moscow*, a movie based on former Ambassador Joseph Davies's enthusiastic and naïve memoir of his wartime stay there. *Fortune* and *Business Week* wrote of possible Russian markets, while Eric Johnston, president of the United States Chamber of Commerce, hoped to both "trade with and uplift Russia." (Foreign Minister Molotov reciprocated, expressing Soviet admiration for American technology but emphasizing an interest in heavy industry, not the consumer goods Johnston and others hoped to sell.) *Time*, which made Stalin its villainous Man of the Year in 1940, bestowed the same title in a positive way in 1943. That same year, *Life* claimed that Russians "look like Americans, dress like Americans and think like Americans," and in 1944 the *New York Times* assured its readers that "Marxian thinking in Soviet Russia is out."[8]

---

[7] Alan M. Ball, *Imagining America: Influence and Images in Twentieth-Century Russia* (Lanham, MD: Rowman and Littlefield, 2003), 178–79.

[8] David S. Foglesong, *The American Mission and the "Evil Empire": The Crusade for a "Free Russia" since 1881* (Cambridge University Press, 2007), 89, 92–97. David Engerman, *Modernization from the other Shore: American Intellectuals and the Romance of Russian Development* (Cambridge, MA: Harvard University Press, 2003), 275. Paul Kennedy, *The Rise and Fall of the Great Powers* (New York: Vintage, 1987), 371.

Wendell Willkie's 1943 bestseller *One World*, which sold 800,000 copies in one month and over 3 million by 1945, presented a more judicious and realistic image of the Soviet Union. In 1942 Roosevelt sent Willkie, who had been the 1940 Republican presidential candidate, to visit key Allied leaders like Stalin and China's Chiang Kai-shek. After two weeks in Moscow and Yakutsk, Willkie concluded that Russia was an "effective society," which was fighting a "people's war" and withstanding Hitler's military challenge "magnificently." He catalogued the death and destruction the *Wehrmacht* had delivered and admired what Soviet defense factories produced, even as he criticized their poor organization and low productivity. In conversations with journalists, military officers, and factory directors, he came away with a sense of their patriotism and pride but also of their inflexible commitment to Marxism and the Soviet state. Knowing that Americans both admired and feared the Soviet Union, Willkie urged the United States to cooperate with Russia in order to secure peace and economic stability. Like the May 9 demonstration in Moscow, the enthusiastic reception of Willkie's book suggests a moment of possibility.[9]

The special relationship

In certain ways relations between the United States and Britain were more strained. They shared intelligence and collaborated on efforts to develop nuclear weapons, which neither did with the Soviet Union, yet Americans saw Britain as the junior partner in these areas as well as economically. Feeling simultaneously inferior and superior, some British leaders worried about their exclusive dependence on America, yet believed themselves more knowledgeable and experienced. During the joint Anglo-American campaign in North Africa in 1942, Harold Macmillan, a Conservative politician and future prime minister, perfectly captured this ambivalence by comparing the British to Greek slaves and the Americans to imperial Romans. He found

the Americans much as the Greeks found the Romans – great big, vulgar, bustling people, more vigorous than we are and also more idle, with more unspoiled virtues but also more corrupt. We must run the Allied Force Headquarters as the Greek slaves ran the operations of Emperor Claudius.[10]

Tensions at the government and military levels were compounded by the American "occupation" of Britain. Between 1942 and 1945 over 3 million

[9] Wendell Willkie, *One World* (New York: Simon and Schuster, 1943), 53–80, 100–2.
[10] Reynolds, *From World War*, 65.

American soldiers and airmen passed through England; prior to the landing at Normandy in June 1944, over 1.5 million were stationed there. As
many Brits quipped then and afterward, the problem was that American
military personnel were "oversexed, overpaid, overfed and over here."
These young men, and they were overwhelmingly men, were paid,
clothed, and fed better than British soldiers and civilians, indeed, better
than they had been at home before the war. These "rich relations" made
themselves and American popular culture an everyday presence in
Britain.[11] To young women, they represented an exciting alternative to
the drabness of wartime, to young men, social and sexual competition, to
still others a frightening or refreshing breakdown of traditional class
barriers and sexual mores. Conflicts abounded about sex, crime, and
race. American officials wanted the British to regulate prostitutes, while
the British military and civilian leaders insisted soldiers be controlled. The
American Army refused to allow British courts to try GIs charged with
civil or criminal offenses; the British reluctantly granted extraterritoriality,
the traditional sign of colonial subservience. While the Americans rigidly
segregated their soldiers, the British criticized the color bar and welcomed
black GIs, even as they sought to limit interracial sexual relations. The
American occupation and subsequent joint military campaign left the
British with both a clear picture of American wealth, consumer power,
and military might and a belief that they were more like Americans than
were the French, Germans, or Soviets. The Americans, for their part,
came away feeling superior; only black GIs were more ambivalent about
the relative virtues of America and Britain. This first American occupation
and the reactions to it foreshadowed what would happen postwar in Italy,
Germany, and other Western European countries as well as in Japan and
Korea.

There was one issue that caused remarkably little dissension among the
Allies – how to respond – or not respond – to the news of the extermination of Europe's Jews. Throughout 1942 many reports of the murder of up
to 1 million Jews in Poland and the Soviet Union circulated through
diplomatic channels, Jewish networks, and the British and American
press. In August, Gerhard Riegner, the representative of the World
Jewish Congress in Geneva, relayed to London and Washington a report
from inside Germany that Hitler planned to exterminate all European
Jews. Although there were protest meetings in New York and London,
much of the public, including Jewish leaders, did not understand or did
not want to understand what was happening. Allied leaders persistently

---

[11] David Reynolds, *Rich Relations: The American Occupation of Britain, 1942–1945* (New
York: Random House, 1995).

gave priority to winning the war over rescuing Jews, seeing the two goals as conflicting. The United States refused to alter immigration laws; Britain restricted Jewish entry into Palestine, and both rejected Jewish pleas to bomb Auschwitz. All three Allied governments sought to limit publicity about the Holocaust and condemned Nazi barbarism without noting the singularly horrific persecution of the Jews.

Popular anti-Semitism on the one hand and political priorities on the other explain such reticence and passivity in the face of genocide. The British Ministry of Information and the American Office of War Information did not publicize reports of extermination for fear of increasing popular anti-Semitism. They, like the Soviets, feared German policies would not be unpopular. In addition, after the false atrocity stories of World War I, officials believed the public would dismiss stories of murder on such an unprecedented scale. Some argue that bureaucratic politics explain Roosevelt's failure to act; others insist it was impossible for the Allies to intervene effectively. While there was little that could have been done in 1941–42, thereafter Allied bombing of railroad lines to extermination camps, pressure on German allies and satellites, and publicity to warn Jews and urge others to help might well have significantly limited the death toll. For Roosevelt, as for Churchill, however, saving Jews was a low priority and a politically inexpedient one at that. Both leaders argued for a policy of rescue through victory, but at war's end few were alive to be saved.

Mobilized economies

World War II with its epic tank battles and pervasive bombing saw a vastly enhanced mechanization of warfare, even as the fighting "underwent a radical process of demodernization,"[12] especially on the Eastern Front. For the Allies, waging total war entailed constantly negotiating military plans and economic aid; for the Germans dictating strategy to their allies and extracting economic resources from conquered territories. For both sides, total war required a massive mobilization of the home front that reordered production, redeployed labor, and restructured the state. As in World War I, all belligerents faced shortages of manpower, munitions, finances, and food. In different states economic mobilization displayed both general similarities in means and striking differences in magnitude, and once again the toll taken on European societies was much greater than on America. The Allies were able to outproduce the Axis and this was a

---

[12] Omer Bartov, *Hitler's Army: Soldiers, Nazis and War in the Third Reich* (Oxford University Press, 1992), 12.

key to victory, but the respective contributions of the United States, the Soviet Union, and Britain to victory were more complex than myth and memory on all sides would have it.

States and societies underwent unprecedented militarization. By the late 1930s Germany and the Soviet Union had Europe's largest militaries, but Britain's army increased from 400,000 in 1938 to 5 million in 1944–45, while the United States went from 190,000 in 1939 to 8.5 million in 1944–45. Britain, the United States, and the Soviet Union vastly expanded their air forces, as did Germany, but only the United States pushed ahead to construct a two-ocean navy. Germany's large state, party, and SS bureaucracies sought to coordinate the use of public and private resources and exploit the sprawling Nazi empire. Britain and the United States expanded and militarized their national governments. American presidential powers increased greatly as Dr. Win the War replaced Dr. New Deal. Programs such as the WPA and the CCC were closed, but the number of federal employees ballooned from 1 million in 1940 to nearly 4 million in 1945 and the federal budget grew from $10.1 billion to $106.9 billion in the same period. The American state had ceased to be distinctive in terms of the size of its bureaucracy and military. In 1943 and 1944 the Germans devoted over 70 percent of their GDP to the war effort, compared to roughly 60 percent for the USSR, 55 percent for Britain but only about 45 percent for the better endowed United States.[13]

Most states funded their skyrocketing military expenditures by forced savings, rationing, and moving money and labor out of agriculture and consumer goods. In Britain consumption decreased by 21 percent, in the Soviet Union by much more and wages dropped precipitously as well. German consumption declined after 1942, but Germans were spared the extreme hardships, severe rationing, hunger, and malnutrition so many other Europeans suffered because they exploited the conquered territories of Hitler's New Order so severely. There is little agreement about exactly how much Germans gained from their empire and whether such benefits explain their tenacious support for the Third Reich. It is clear that while Britain and the Soviet Union relied heavily on taxes to finance the war, Germany imposed occupation payments that provided over one-third of state income and covered nearly half of war expenses. France, Belgium, and the Netherlands were the most lucrative sources of revenues as well as

---

[13] Peter Clarke, *Hope and Glory: Britain 1900–2000* (London: Penguin, 2004), 200. Stanley Buder, *Capitalizing on Change: A Social History of American Business* (Chapel Hill: University of North Carolina Press, 2009), 219, www.usgovernmentspending. com/year1945_0.html#usgs302. Mark Harrison, "The Economics of World War II: An Overview," in Harrison, ed., *The Economics of World War II*, 21.

of goods to buy, while the conquered territories in the east, where fighting continued, failed to provide the anticipated food, oil, and iron ore. The American experience was distinctive. Tax increases were modest, rationing limited, and although consumer durables were in short supply, overall consumption increased. In comparison to the depression, "Americans never had it so good."[14]

The United States also had an easier time mobilizing labor. The millions of unemployed flocked to war industries; hundreds of thousands of rural Southern blacks moved north and west, and "Rosie the Riveter," the iconic woman war worker, built airplanes and tanks. In Britain women and the unemployed staffed war industries; in the Soviet Union, millions of men moved into the military, while women replaced them in industry, and agriculture became the preserve of women, children, and the elderly. This massive reallocation, occurring as thousands of factories and millions of workers were evacuated east of the Urals, created chaos in production, food supplies, and individual and family lives that was only partially resolved after 1942. Germany, which had full employment before 1939 as well as a higher percentage of women employed than Britain or the United States, deployed over 11 million foreign laborers in the course of the war; by 1944 they made up half the agricultural labor force and one-third of those in key war industries. Some were recruited from Italy and the occupied countries of Western Europe; most were forced laborers, conscripted from the east, Soviet POWs, and slave laborers from the concentration camps. Despite the magnitude of labor mobilization on both sides of the Atlantic, there were few of the gender and labor conflicts that had marked World War I. The enormity of the conflict, the prior bitter experience of total war, and the blurred line between home front and battlefront (except in America) meant that production for survival and victory took precedence.

Allied and Axis home fronts committed themselves to the war effort with determination and tenacity but unequal success. Although industrial superiority does not assure victory in every kind of war, the Allied ability to outproduce the Axis in all kinds of munitions contributed significantly to victory. In 1944, for example, the Germans manufactured 17,800 tanks, the Allies 51,500; between 1941 and 1945 the Germans built 18,606 aircraft, the Allies 84,806.[15] The German war economy suffered from a lack of oil, a shortage of coalminers, the failure of economies in occupied Western Europe to grow, and a preference for producing fewer

---

[14] Alan Milward, *War, Economy and Society, 1939–41* (Berkeley: University of California Press, 1979), 90, 93, 107, 137–38. Hugh Rockoff, "The United States: From Ploughshares to Swords," in Harrison, ed., *The Economics of World War II*, 84–93.

[15] Kennedy, *Rise and Fall of the Great Powers*, 354.

high-quality weapons rather than a larger number of simpler ones. Failure to defeat the Soviet Union and the disruptions from bombing strained the war economy long before the Anglo-American invasion.

Allied economic success is often attributed solely to the United States. After his defeat in North Africa, German General Rommel said that "since the entry of America into the war, there has been little prospect of our achieving ultimate victory." America had the world's largest economy, the most unused capacity, and the highest GDP per capita; by 1944 it produced 40 percent of the world's armaments and 60 percent of Allied war *matériel*. The Soviet Union, however, was "the exceptional performer." By specializing in a few simple weapons and relying on Lend-Lease for trucks, the Soviets were able to produce more tanks, planes, and arms than the Germans or the British. Despite a GDP per capita that was only 29 percent of America's and the dislocations of the German invasion and occupation, the Soviets ultimately produced half as much war *matériel* as America.[16]

Neither the Americans nor the Soviets could have won economically or militarily without the other. Reflecting both national self-absorption and Cold War paradigms, however, Soviet public memory focused on the horrors and heroism of the Eastern Front and the march to Berlin, while American war narratives scarcely mention the Eastern Front. Russians memorialize Stalingrad and the deadly 900-day siege of Leningrad, Americans Pearl Harbor, D-Day, and the Battle of the Bulge. Americans attribute victory to aid and the invasions of Italy and France, ignoring both earlier Soviet victories and the vast quantities of munitions and men supplied. From the 1950s onward, Americans expunged the Soviet-American alliance from the public memory, demonized the "Asiatic" Bolsheviks, and mythologized the intentions of the *Wehrmacht* so as to exonerate it from its proven involvement in the Holocaust.[17] Only the British, who remember holding out alone against Nazi Germany, recognized their dependence on both American money and Russian troops.

Suffering societies

Just as Americans have forgotten what the Soviets contributed to the war, they have ignored the price paid by Europeans, victors and vanquished

[16] Richard Evans, *The Third Reich at War* (New York: Penguin, 2009), 468. David Reynolds, "Power and Superpower: The Impact of Two World Wars on America's International Role," in Warren F. Kimball, ed., *America Unbound: World War II and the Making of a Superpower* (New York: St. Martins, 1992), 21. Tooze, *Wages*, 588. Barber and Harrison, *Soviet Home Front*, 180.

[17] Ronald D. Smelser and Edward J. Davies II, *The Myth of the Eastern Front: The Nazi-Soviet War in American Popular Culture* (Cambridge University Press, 2008).

alike. Death tolls illustrate this starkly. The Soviet Union lost 27 million of whom over 8 million were soldiers. This astonishing figure, which was not initially admitted publicly by Soviet leaders, meant that one in eight Soviets did not survive the war. More Soviets died in the siege of Leningrad than Americans and British combined in the entire war. Five to five-and-half million Germans, mostly soldiers, died. Poland lost over 6 million, the vast majority civilians, most of whom died in camps and ghettos. At least 1.5 million Yugoslavs perished. The Germans murdered 6 million Jews in and outside of the camps and singled out 3 million other Slavs and Gypsies/ Roma for extermination on racial grounds. France lost roughly 600,000, Hungary nearly 500,000, and the Netherlands, 200,000; in all cases the majority were civilians. Britain lost roughly 400,000 and Italy around 300,000, with soldiers predominating among the dead in both countries. Estimates of American war dead range from just under 300,000 to just over 400,000 military deaths in both theaters of war.[18]

The war in the East was particularly brutal toward all civilians, but the liberation of Western Europe in 1944–45 also involved bombing, fighting, military occupation, and for civilians shortages, hunger, malnutrition, and deaths. As a result of German and Allied bombing and fighting, cities lay in rubble from Stalingrad to London, from Hamburg to Naples. At war's end roughly 30 million refugees and displaced persons – civilians, forced laborers, prisoners of war, Germans expelled from Eastern Europe, and in much smaller numbers, concentration camp survivors – were on the move, returning to former homes or seeking new ones.[19] As Europe was liberated from the east and the west, wartime collaborationist regimes fell and countries such as Greece descended into civil war. The United States was spared the massive civilian death tolls that were the hallmark of World War II.

Economies barely functioned in much of Europe, as factories closed, hunger mounted, and governments imposed extreme rationing. By war's end the GDP of Europe, excluding the Soviet Union, had declined by 25 percent. The Soviet losses were greater still. Seventeen thousand cities and 70,000 villages and hamlets had been destroyed, as were 31,000 factories, 3,000 oil wells, and over 1,000 coal mines. Agriculture was devastated by the death of 17 million cattle, 20 million pigs, 27 million sheep and goats. The loss of 15,800 locomotives and 65,000 km of railroad

---

[18] Twentieth Century Atlas. National Death Tolls for the Second World War, http://users. erols.com/mwhite28/ww2stats.htm. Estimates of war dead vary greatly. I have used either the widely accepted figure or the range of estimated dead.

[19] Dirk Hoerder, *Cultures in Contact: World Migrations in the Second Millennium* (Durham: Duke University Press, 2002), 478–79.

Illustration 11 Destruction of Warsaw, 1945.

track crippled transportation. Economically, the Soviet Union was indeed "the defeated victor." Poland, Yugoslavia, and Hungary lost half their railroad capacity; Poland three-fourths of its bridges, and Yugoslavia half its deep-sea ships and 40 percent of its peasant carts. Whereas the Soviet Union lost one-quarter of its capital stock, Germany lost only 13 percent. Despite its willingness to collaborate with the Nazis, France's national income was only half its 1938 level, and all currency reserves had flowed east to Germany. Britain suffered less physical damage but had exhausted its gold and currency reserves; it exported only one-third as much as prewar and was increasingly dependent on American aid.[20]

---

[20] Melvyn Leffler, "The Cold War: What Do We Now Know," *American Historical Review* 104/2 (April 1999): 513. Mark Harrison, "The Soviet Union: The Defeated Victory," in Harrison, ed., *The Economics of World War II*, 268. Ivan T. Berend, *Central and Eastern Europe 1944–1993: Detour from the Periphery to the Periphery* (Cambridge University Press, 1996), 6. Milward, *War, Economy and Society*, 333. Kennedy, *Rise and Fall of the Great Powers*, 366–67.

Common to all European experiences and memories was the cost of war – in lives lost, families torn apart, hopes crushed, morality tarnished, politics discredited, economies devastated, and societies destabilized. The price paid by victors and vanquished alike left Europeans with a deep and abiding mistrust of military solutions and unilateral aggression on their continent (even if they still resorted to them in the non-European world).

America's war experience was utterly different. Despite deaths and harsh battles, military losses were tolerable, civilians were spared, the depression ended, and the United States emerged triumphant. The American economy grew by 50 percent; its citizens earned more and consumed more at war's end than when it began. As the American economist John Kenneth Galbraith noted, "Never in the history of human conflict has there been so much talk of sacrifice and so little sacrifice." By 1945 the United States was producing one-half of the world's goods and held one-half of the world's currency reserves. There was no fighting on American soil, no bombing, no mass civilian deaths, and no occupation with all the temptations of collaboration. Americans could see themselves as liberators, untarnished by Europe's racism – as long as they overlooked the internment of Japanese-Americans and segregation at home and in the military. They emerged from World War II with no understanding of the gulf that separated their experience from that of Europeans or Asians. The loss of one member of a family or neighborhood, a school or a workplace is tragic. Losses seventeen times greater, which Poland and Germany suffered, or sixty-five times greater, which the Soviets did, left deep and lasting scars not only on individuals but on entire societies. They disrupted gender and generational relations, created massive labor shortages, and feminized the workforce. They left a longing for normal family lives, homes, and jobs, even as the obstacles to realizing them were nearly insurmountable.[21]

Death was but one aspect of the trauma that afflicted Europe at war's end. Collaboration and indifference to the persecution of Jews and others had discredited many political ideologies and movements and left many people morally compromised. At the individual and societal level, Europeans faced political and economic uncertainty, cultural dislocation, and a loss of clearly defined identities. World War II profoundly shaped Europeans' attitudes toward war and peace, international law and

---

[21] Kennedy, *Rise and Fall of the Great Powers*, 368. Melvyn P. Leffler, *For the Soul of Mankind: The United States, The Soviet Union, and the Cold War* (New York: Hill and Wang, 2007), 40. Reynolds, "Power and Superpower," 30. William I. Hitchcock, *The Bitter Road to Freedom: The Human Cost of Allied Victory in World War II Europe* (New York: Free Press, 2008), 132.

national security in ways Americans seldom understood and all too readily dismissed in subsequent decades.

World War II marked the passing of the European age globally. The simultaneous rise of American hegemony, as David Reynolds aptly noted, was not simply a result of remarkable economic growth: "America's transformation from power to superpower was very much the consequence of World War II."[22] It resulted not only from Europe's destructive civil war and the price America's allies paid for defeating Nazism; it came as well from America's pursuit of both self-interest and a new global vision that began as the Allies planned for peace long before victory was assured.

Preparing for peace

Visions for the postwar order were global in scope, but designing them was an Anglo-American project. Both states were determined to avoid a repetition of Versailles, a renewal of the depression, and a continuation of its legacies of diminished foreign trade, economic and social insecurity, and a world economy segmented into closed currency and trading blocs. America's ongoing involvement in European economic and political affairs had to be assured and barriers to renewed aggression constructed. From 1941 on politicians, intellectuals, and the press in Britain and America called for strengthening international law, expanding rights and freedom, building multilateral institutions, and modifying laissez-faire. Many insisted that economic prosperity was integral to collective security. Yet, shared commitments to these sweeping goals hid a multitude of disagreements that emerged as the United States and Britain laid out the principles of the postwar order in the Atlantic Charter, established the United Nations, and developed a new architecture for the global financial system at Bretton Woods.

The Atlantic Charter, drafted by Roosevelt and Churchill in August 1941, marked a first effort to define what Britain was fighting for, why neutral America supported her, and what a postwar order should look like. Neither country wanted to annex territory or alter borders; both were committed "to the right of all peoples to choose the form of government under which they will live." The defeat of Nazi tyranny was the immediate goal; disarmament and "a wider and permanent system of general security" the more long-term ones. The Charter called for free trade, an open global economy, and equal access for all to natural resources and trade so as to assure economic prosperity. It notably said that rights pertained to individuals as well as to nations and enumerated economic and social as well as

[22] Reynolds, "Power and Superpower," 30.

political ones. It advocated improved labor standards, social welfare, and employment security. This was necessary to assure that "all the men in all the lands may live out their lives in freedom from fear and want."[23]

The Atlantic Charter was an ambitious and expansive statement of a possible liberal democratic, capitalist postwar order. Elizabeth Borgwardt argues that its combination of Wilsonian idealism, Roosevelt's Four Freedoms, and free trade marked the first step in America's effort to develop a "New Deal for the World." Yet authorship was not solely American, for Churchill added some of the most potentially radical passages about freedom from want and rights for all. Whether these reflected European calls for postwar social reform or were Churchillian rhetorical flourishes remains unclear. In either case, their inclusion gave the document an unintended radical potential, while highlighting its ambiguities. Were colonial subjects to enjoy self-determination? Would Britain and the United States really assure equal access to trade and resources or only, as the document suggested, "with due respect for their existing obligations"? Could economic rights and social security be reconciled with free trade? These issues were debated not only during the war but also long after. In the interim, the Atlantic Charter remained, in Churchill's phrase, "not a law" but "a star."[24] The Axis did not issue any counterstatement, even though Mussolini urged Hitler to clarify that he was not waging a colonial war but rather building a New Order in Europe.[25] The United States and Britain, however, followed up by building multilateral institutions that gave substance to some of these principles and were equivocal about others. These institutions both committed the United States to international involvement and served its national interests.

The best known is the United Nations, which was the successor to the defunct and ineffectual League of Nations and took shape in wartime declarations and meetings. In January 1942 the Declaration by the United Nations endorsed the Atlantic Charter and committed signatories to pursue the war with all possible resources. The United States, the Soviet Union, Britain, and China signed, as did five British Commonwealth nations, including India, nine Central American states, all long subject to American influence, and eight European governments in exile, ranging from Belgium to Yugoslavia. South America, the Middle East, and Africa were absent, although Iran, Peru, Turkey, and Venezuela endorsed the document later. In August 1944 the Big Four – the United States, Britain,

[23] Atlantic Charter, www.internet-esq.com/ussaugusta/atlantic1.htm.
[24] Elizabeth Borgwardt, *A New Deal for the World: America's Vision for Human Rights* (Cambridge, MA: Harvard University Press, 2005), 45.
[25] Mazower, *Hitler's Empire*, 316.

the USSR, and China – drafted the UN Charter at the Dumbarton Oaks conference in Washington. The proposed organization looked remarkably like the much-criticized League, contained no explicit human rights language, and made no commitment to decolonization. References to human rights were reinserted at the founding conference of the United Nations, held in San Francisco in June 1945, but only after the prerogatives of national sovereignty and veto power for the permanent members of the Security Council had been guaranteed.

The shortcomings of the UN were multiple. Roosevelt, who asserted that he was not a Wilsonian idealist, wanted both a new global organization and a world in which the Four Policemen, the United States, Britain, the Soviet Union, and China, would dominate and keep the peace. Churchill preferred regional councils and a focus on Europe to a global organization. The UN lacked effective enforcement mechanisms to secure peace or protect individual human rights because no nation was willing to see its sovereignty curtailed. Although the dominant powers spoke glowingly of their commitment to economic and social rights, they considered them secondary to political and legal ones. Moreover, the fledgling UN had no resources to lessen poverty. Staunchly anti-imperialist, Roosevelt wanted to turn all colonies into trusteeships, which the great powers would guide gradually toward independence. Churchill opposed decolonization across the board, as did many who looked to the Commonwealth as a model for the UN. The UN had its roots not only in American ideas but equally in those of such British imperial thinkers and statesmen as Alfred Zimmern and Jan Smuts, who wanted an international organization that would preserve British influence, cement American global leadership, and reconcile freedom and empire.

The United States and Britain saw economic stability as a prerequisite for collective security, and the thirties had taught that multinational cooperation was essential in order to replace the discredited gold standard. America and Britain thus gathered delegates from forty-six countries in Bretton Woods, New Hampshire, in July 1944 to discuss a new set of institutions to regulate global currency exchanges and capital flows. But the Bretton Woods system, as it came to be known, was effectively the work of two men, Keynes and American Treasury official Harry Dexter White. They were a study in contrasting personalities and competing but equally grand visions. Keynes was an elite-educated, prominent public intellectual and economic theorist, who moved easily among the academy, government, and artistic circles. White, the Harvard-educated son of immigrants, was a New Deal economist, who both mastered complex economic problems and popularized them but had none of Keynes's charisma. Both were committed to multilateral solutions to currency issues and hoped that

Illustration 12 Harry Dexter White (left) and John Maynard Keynes, 1946.

substantial sums would be made available for reconstruction, the stabilization of commodity prices, and countercyclical spending.

They approached these systemic economic questions from very different perspectives, reflecting the diametrically opposed positions of their countries. Keynes, representing a weakened and defensive Britain, wanted to protect the sterling area; White, speaking for a confident and prosperous United States, wanted "to project American power and responsibility beyond the two Americas." White was eager to secure Soviet participation, Keynes was indifferent. Keynes favored an International Clearing Union, funded to the tune of $26 billion, which would have its own banking money, the Bancor, from which members could draw generously. White favored an International Monetary Fund (IMF), at one-fifth the size and with restrictive borrowing rights. White, envisioning permanent American dominance in decision-making, favored a strong and interventionist directorate for the IMF; Keynes preferred a weaker directorate and more leeway for national discretion. The State Department and internationally oriented business, eager to move toward an open global economy, wanted currencies to be convertible immediately and opposed restrictions on capital flows; the British, anticipating postwar problems, favored restrictions in both areas. The Americans believed free trade was the prerequisite for full employment, the British saw full employment as a precondition for trade liberalization. White and the Americans negotiated the new system with a phalanx of lawyers and "business habits of mind." Keynes and the British government believed that "Britain had made much greater sacrifices for the common cause than the United States and that this asymmetry should be rectified as a *matter of justice.*" America flatly rejected the idea of "moral debt" and had the economic and political power to impose its view.[26]

The key Bretton Woods institution was the IMF, designed essentially as White envisioned it. Every member set the value of their currency in terms of gold or dollars and promised to keep it within 1 percent of that value. This gold exchange standard made the dollar the linchpin of the global financial system, occupying the position once held by sterling. Britain did win some concessions regarding the control of capital flows, a key issue for countries wanting to stabilize employment and fund social welfare. A Bank for Reconstruction and Development, later renamed the World Bank, was established but remained relatively inactive in its first decade or more. The contentious issue of fully free trade remained unresolved.

Bretton Woods, argued Henry Clay of the Bank of England, was "the greatest blow to Britain next to the war."[27] Some later analysts saw it as key to securing the postwar triumph of the American version of open international capitalism over European ideas of national capitalism. Certainly both the symbolism of holding all key meetings on American soil and the substance of the institutions created showed that financial power had shifted across the Atlantic and that the United States had assumed the hegemonic role it had rejected in the 1920s. As we shall see, however, it proved easier for America to design the system it wanted than to enforce the rules in the troubled economic reality of the postwar decades. Although the Soviets did attend the Bretton Woods conference, perhaps because they hoped for a postwar loan, by December of 1945 Stalin decided not to join the new

---

[26] Skidelsky, *John Maynard Keynes*, 695–96, 756 italics in original.
[27] Skidelsky, *John Maynard Keynes*, 767.

system, arguing that since America had refused credits, Soviet membership might be seen as weakness.

Designing postwar Europe

America dominated the global aspects of preparing for peace, but it had to contend with the Soviet Union and Britain in planning the postwar order in Europe. At issue were questions of national sovereignty and self-determination, territorial borders and constitutions, war guilt and indemnities, and the legitimacy of spheres of influence. Bilateral meetings and the Big Three conferences debated these thorny issues. At Tehran in late 1943, for example, Stalin argued strongly for a second front and raised concerns about postwar security. The Big Three agreed that the Soviet border could be pushed west, incorporating the Baltic States, Bessarabia, and parts of Poland. No regimes or confederations threatening to Soviet security interests were to be allowed in Central Europe and the Balkans. As is usually the case, the definition of national security was capacious and vague, and the permissible internal constitutions of states bordering the USSR were left unspecified. In October 1944 Churchill and Stalin, both of whom saw a value in traditional spheres of influence as opposed to Roosevelt's preference for vaguely defined, open ones, met in Moscow and hammered out the (in)famous percentage agreement. Russia was to have 90 percent influence in Romania, Great Britain 90 percent influence in Greece; Russia would have 75 percent influence in Bulgaria, while Hungary and Yugoslavia would be split 50–50. Churchill saw this as a way to defend British interests in the Mediterranean and get a free hand against growing communist influence in Greece. If Roosevelt was critical about such horse-trading involving Southeastern Europe, he had fewer qualms violating the self-determination thrust of the Atlantic Charter and UN Declaration in regard to colonies. At Yalta in February 1945, the United States agreed to a "strategic trust system" according to which America and other nations could claim some colonial trustee areas as strategically vital, station military there, and rule them with no UN supervision. In addition, Roosevelt and Stalin finalized details about Russia's entry into the Pacific War once Hitler was defeated and settled their differences on the structure of the UN.

At Yalta, all three leaders signed the Declaration of Liberated Europe, promising to foster representative governments in newly freed states, but, like other wartime proclamations of moral purpose and liberal principles, it had no enforcement mechanisms. Simultaneously, the Polish question was being resolved by facts on the ground rather than negotiation. Throughout the war Poland was highly visible and contentious in part because the Soviets, after being attacked by Germany twice in twenty-five years, regarded a strong and friendly Poland as vital to their security. For Americans Poland symbolized Wilsonian self-determination, for Britain the occasion of war in 1939. During the war the conservative London Poles, running the government in exile, and the Lublin Poles, backed by the Soviet Union, competed for recognition as the legitimate government of a yet-to-be reconstituted state. No resolution was reached among the Big Three before the Red Army occupied Poland and installed the Lublin Poles in power in late 1944. At Yalta Churchill and Roosevelt agreed to move both the Soviet and Polish borders westward and recognized the provisional Lublin government while urging it to include some London Poles.

On the most vital and intractable issue, the fate of postwar Germany, little progress was made. Roosevelt, Churchill, and Stalin had agreed to fight until Germany surrendered unconditionally, but frequent discussions of the desirability of politically dismembering Germany produced no concrete plans. Nor were they clear on how to prevent future German military aggression. Stalin demanded reparations from Germany, while Churchill was staunchly opposed, and there was no agreement among the leaders or within each national government about whether to dismantle the mines and heavy industries of the Ruhr and Saar, as United States Secretary of the Treasury Morgenthau proposed, or to keep Germany economically unified. They did agree to a three-power occupation of Germany at war's end, and expanded that to include France after it had had been liberated and de Gaulle took power.

Many have condemned Yalta as a betrayal of Poland and of Anglo-American principles, as a tragic result of either Roosevelt's illusions about Stalin or his rapidly declining health. That assumes Stalin's intentions were fixed, maximally expansive, and knowable, rather than evolving, flexible, and opaque – a subject about which historians remain deeply divided. Moreover, Yalta essentially confirmed what had been agreed upon earlier, and with the Red Army occupying Poland and moving west, Roosevelt had no leverage to extract concessions. Most importantly, at Yalta as earlier, defeating Germany and then Japan was the overriding priority. To achieve it, Roosevelt and Churchill made concessions to one another and to Stalin, as he did to them, despite mutual suspicions, different expectations about postwar cooperation, and serious substantive disagreements about self-determination in Eastern Europe and the colonies. After Germany surrendered, the unresolved questions about Germany and Eastern Europe would play out in a new context of growing Soviet and American suspicion and conflict and with a new cast of characters. How did their resolution push Europe and America into a Cold War?

The alliance unravels

The wartime Allies, who triumphantly celebrated the defeat of fascism on May 8, 1945, became Cold War enemies within a few tumultuous years. Liberated Europe and conquered Germany were divided into rigidly separated Soviet and American spheres of influence, and the stage was set for multifaceted political, economic, and cultural competition and conflict. The Cold War, a term coined by Bernard Baruch and popularized by the American journalist Walter Lippmann, provided the defining context and central drama of transatlantic and intra-European history for the next four decades.

Was the Cold War that took shape in the late 1940s an inevitable outcome or a contingent development? American historian John Gaddis is convinced that *"as long as Stalin was running the Soviet Union a cold war was unavoidable."* It was a struggle of good and evil and Stalin was an ideological romantic. Yet, the Soviet move from Entente through détente to Cold War and the American shift from cooperation to containment were not inevitable, even if the ambitions, actions, and reactions of each superpower made confrontation increasingly likely. Norman Naimark believes that Stalin "had no firm plan for postwar Europe, not even what we would call today a 'road map'"; he was both too opportunistic and too tactically inclined. European historians Csaba Bekes and Geoffrey Roberts argue that Stalin wanted to make East Central Europe socialist by peaceful means and hoped to continue to cooperate with the United States and Britain. Nor can responsibility be put exclusively on the intentions and interventions of either one or the other superpower. The Cold War was a joint production, whose origins lay in misperceptions and missed opportunities, conflicting global visions and expansive definitions of national security, competing social systems and diametrically opposed postwar economic situations. According to Melvyn Leffler, the postwar situations "created risks that Truman and Stalin could not accept and opportunities they could not resist ... [Neither] was in control of events."[28]

Although the Cold War did not begin definitively until 1947, the relationship among the Big Three began to fray in mid to late 1945. The wartime alliance was built on personalities as well as political and military calculation, but Roosevelt, who was most committed to postwar cooperation with the Soviets, died in April. In mid May Churchill, always more ambivalent

---

[28] John Lewis Gaddis, *We Now Know: Rethinking Cold War History* (Oxford University Press, 1997), 292. Italics in original. Norman Naimark, "Stalin and Europe in the Postwar Period, 1945–1953: Issues and Problems," cited in Leffler, *For the Soul*, 53. Leffler, *For the Soul*, 57–58.

about Russia, instructed British military planners to consider "Operation Unthinkable," an Anglo-American military attack against Russia to get a better Polish settlement. His generals dismissed the plan as "fantastic and ... impossible." Churchill was defeated in July elections, but the new Labour government under Clement Attlee was anti-communist and wary of the Soviets. Of greater importance, America's new president, Harry Truman, was inexperienced in foreign policy, less committed to cooperation, and immediately adopted a harder line. In April he shocked Soviet Foreign Minister Molotov by his confrontational tone and reprimand to "carry out your agreements." (Or so Truman claimed in his memoirs; Molotov's minutes from the meeting describe it as cordial despite disagreements over Poland.) By year's end Truman asserted, "I'm tired of babying the Soviets." At this stage, Truman did not want a Cold War, but his stance reflected a "belief in American purity" and "an expanded notion of American security." And the American public once again turned against the Soviet Union. Whereas a *Fortune* magazine poll from January 1945 showed that Americans were most worried about unemployment and a future depression, by late summer Russia ranked second only to unemployment as a source of concern. In late 1945 Stalin did not want to end cooperation with the United States and Britain and partition Europe, yet, as Lloyd Gardner noted, neither he nor Western leaders "could square their pretensions about international cooperation with a policy of 'control.'"[29]

Control took varied forms and created resentments and conflicts. Postwar aid was one. On May 9 the United States terminated Lend-Lease to Britain and Russia, turning ships around mid-ocean. Both nations protested vigorously but were only able to secure an extension until Japan surrendered in August. Neither got the aid they felt they deserved for their wartime sacrifices, and only Britain was able to negotiate a postwar loan. America and Britain refused to let the Soviets take reparations from the British-controlled Ruhr. The United States developed, tested, and used the atomic bomb without consulting its Soviet ally. Whether the United States used nuclear weapons at Hiroshima and Nagasaki to hasten the end of the war and avoid an invasion of Japan or to keep the Soviets out of the Pacific War or both, the Soviets felt threatened and blackmailed. America's nuclear arsenal foreshadowed a new kind of war, diminished relative Soviet power, and suggested the United

[29] Reynolds, *From World War*, 250. Geoffrey Roberts, *Stalin's Wars: From World War to Cold War, 1939–1952* (New Haven: Yale University Press, 2006), 268. William Taubman, *Stalin's American Policy from Entente to Détente to Cold War* (New York: W. W. Norton, 1982), 127. Lloyd Gardner, *Architects of Illusion: Men and Ideas in American Foreign Policy, 1941–1949* (Chicago: Quadrangle, 1970), 58. Lloyd Gardner, *Spheres of Influence: The Great Powers Partition Europe from Munich to Yalta* (Chicago: Ivan R. Dee, 1993), 261.

States would not retreat into isolation. In 1945–46 America rejected far-reaching proposals for international control of weapons, offering only the Baruch Plan, which the Soviets regarded as "a veiled monopoly for the United States." In response the Soviet Union accelerated work on its own bomb and championed arms control and disarmament.[30]

Control was imagined and contested in territorial terms. Trouble began in areas long part of Britain's sphere of influence and long of interest to both Imperial and Soviet Russia. The Soviet Union pressured Turkey to establish joint Russian-Turkish control of the Black Sea Straits, thereby assuring Soviet access to the Mediterranean. Simultaneously the Soviets kept troops in northern Iran, even though they and the British had promised to end their occupation of Iran within six months of war's end. The Soviets sought oil concessions similar to those that the British had and that the Americans were negotiating; they also considered the possible incorporation of Iranian territory into Soviet Azerbaijan. In both cases the Soviets pressured, the United States protested, and the Soviets backed down. In May 1946 Soviet troops left Iran and talk of restructuring control of the Straits petered out. Stalin's actions suggest that cooperation with the West took priority over expansion into the Middle East. Yet, both contemporary Anglo-American leaders and many later historians saw the Soviets' provocative behavior on the periphery of Europe as an indication of their aggressive intentions in Europe's core.

Throughout 1945 both Soviet actions and United States reactions in Eastern Europe presented a mixed picture. Developments in Poland, Bulgaria, and Romania gave weight to more sinister interpretations of Soviet plans. Although Stalin slightly modified the composition of the Communist-dominated Polish government, no free elections were held. The same was true in Romania and Bulgaria that had allied or cooperated with Nazi Germany. Czechoslovakia and Hungary had genuine coalition governments, with strong but minority Communist representation, and they were committed to anti-fascism, more democratic rule, and social reform, especially land reform. Finland successfully resisted Moscow's pressure to become both communist and an ally and remained neutral. American responses were ambivalent. By late 1945 the United States had lost interest in Poland and, after protesting the Bulgarian situation, recognized the Communist government at year's end. Truman and others might plead for the universal application of principles articulated in the Atlantic Charter and Declaration on Liberated Europe, but Secretary of State James

---

[30] Michael D. Gordin, *Red Cloud at Dawn: Truman, Stalin, and the End of the Atomic Monopoly* (New York: Farrar, Straus, and Giroux, 2009), 53.

Byrnes was willing to recognize the Soviets' control of its sphere, if they did the same for areas America considered vital.

As Stalin told the Yugoslav Communists, he regarded World War II as different because the victors would impose their social system as far as their armies reached.[31] If this was harsh realpolitik, it was hardly unique to the Soviets. The Americans and British had excluded Stalin from any say in the management of occupied Italy, despite his request for a role, and the Italian precedent was then applied to liberated France. The United States administered occupied Japan on its own. And Stalin did honor the militarized spheres of influence within Europe. He stayed out of the Greek Civil War, despite pleas from Greek Communists for aid against the superior British and Greek royalist forces. He discouraged both the French and Italian Communist parties from making a bid for power even though they had legitimacy from their leading anti-fascist role, were supported by one-fifth of the electorate, and controlled large union movements.

In short, developments on the ground were contradictory. Soviet and American statements and actions vacillated, motives and intentions were opaque, and cooperation and conflict seemed by turns likely and impossible. Could the Soviets maintain the wartime alliance while increasing control of Eastern Europe? Would the United States assertively push its version of liberal democracy and free market capitalism and expand its definition of national security? Over the course of 1946 and 1947 these questions would be answered in ways that solidified a Cold War.

Polarization

The United States, Britain, and the Soviet Union all hardened their positions in 1946 as Kennan's Long Telegram, Churchill's Iron Curtain speech, and the Novikov Telegram vividly illustrate. George Kennan, a career diplomat and Soviet specialist, who served in the American embassy in Moscow in the mid thirties and again in 1945–46, was deeply conservative and critical not only of the Soviet Union but also of the United States. In February 1946 he sent his famous 8,000-word assessment of the Soviet threat to his State Department superiors in Washington, and it was published in *Foreign Affairs* in July 1947.

According to Kennan, Soviet leaders dominated the masses, believed in capitalist encirclement, and saw no possibility of permanent peaceful coexistence with capitalist democracies. They foresaw conflicts among capitalist nations and attacks on the Soviet Union. Nothing in their

---

[31] Lloyd Gardner's "'Long Essay' on Cold War History," www.h-net.org/~diplo/essays/PDF/Gardner_LongEssay.pdf.

understanding of the world was objective or based on experience. "At the bottom of Kremlin's neurotic view of world affairs is traditional and instinctive Russian sense of insecurity." Xenophobia, inferiority, and insecurity were timeless cultural attributes; nowhere did Kennan mention the experience of World War II. The Soviets' distorted worldview made them fear foreign penetration and seek to advance Soviet power by a promiscuous array of tactics. They wanted to expand into Iran and Turkey and exploit unrest, especially in colonies. They preferred economic autarky and were engaged in "intensive military-industrialization." They sought to subvert the United States and Western European nations not only by deploying communist organizations but also by infiltrating labor unions, youth groups, women's clubs, and even churches. They believed "that it is desirable and necessary that the internal harmony of our society be disrupted, our traditional way of life be destroyed, the international authority of our state be broken, if Soviet power is to be secure."

Despite this dire analysis, Kennan advocated neither war nor atomic diplomacy. Rather, because the Soviets understood the logic of force, the United States should amass sufficient military and economic power to contain Soviet expansion and subversion. If America showed a willingness to deploy force, it would rarely have to do so, for the Soviet Union was weaker than the United States. Containment should be complemented by American self-improvement. American experts should study the Soviet Union with the detachment of a medical doctor and educate the public accordingly. Of equal importance, Americans had "to solve internal problems of our own society, to improve self-confidence, discipline, morale and community spirit." Finally, the United States had to avoid becoming "like those with whom we are coping."[32]

The Long Telegram's conceptualization of the Soviet Union as an expansionist threat and rival imperial hegemon with whom one could not compromise was enormously influential. Kennan articulated the new policy of containment that the United States would implement in Europe. By late 1946 Truman's advisors Clark Clifford and George Elsey depicted the Soviet pursuit of world domination in much more frightening terms and urged the United States to fight them on all fronts. Truman did not publicize the report, but its views of the Soviet Union were widely accepted in his administration.

A month after the Long Telegram, Churchill, no longer prime minister, gave his Iron Curtain Speech in Fulton, Missouri, Truman's hometown, with Truman present. Its most often quoted lines lamented that

---

[32] George Kennan, Long Telegram, www.gwu.edu/~nsarchiv/coldwar/documents/episode-1/kennan.htm.

From Stettin in the Baltic to Trieste in the Adriatic, an iron curtain has descended across the Continent. Behind that line lie all the capitals of the ancient states of Central and Eastern Europe. Warsaw, Berlin, Prague, Vienna, Budapest, Belgrade, Bucharest and Sofia, all these famous cities and the populations around them lie in what I must call the Soviet sphere, and all are subject in one form or another, not only to Soviet influence but to a very high and, in many cases, increasing measure of control from Moscow.

The Soviet Union wanted to divide Germany and expand west, south, and into the Far East. It wanted not war, but "the fruits of war." Across Europe, "Communist parties or fifth columns constitute a growing challenge and peril to Christian civilization." Western democracies had to stand together against Soviet designs abroad and communist machinations at home. Churchill was equally concerned to strengthen "a special relationship between the British Commonwealth and Empire and the United States." Both peace and the success of the UN depended on this. "Sinews of Peace" was the speech's now forgotten title. Although the speech subsequently became famous, it aroused relatively little attention at the time, except from the Soviet Union. Stalin called Churchill a warmonger; *Izvestia* reminded Soviet readers that the term "iron curtain" had first been used by Nazi Propaganda Minister Goebbels; and Western correspondents said ordinary Russians were terrified that war was possible.[33]

The Soviets also took a more critical look at relations with Britain and America. The press talked of growing divisions within both nations between realist and democratic forces that were willing to compromise and hard-line ones that sought world domination for Anglo-American forces. The Soviet ambassador in Washington, Nikolai Novikov, was much more pessimistic. In September 1946 he sent a telegram to Foreign Minister Molotov to help brief delegates who were to attend a four-power meeting about the contentious issues of Iran, Turkey, and Eastern Europe. Novikov's analysis focused on America's foreign policy and military, rather than culture and psychology, but his conclusions mirrored Kennan's in seeing the other side as intransigent and committed to global expansion. "The foreign policy of the United States, which reflects the imperialist tendencies of American monopolistic capital, is characterized ... by a striving for world supremacy." Its leaders believe they have "a right to lead the world." The United States seeks "a system of naval and air bases stretching far beyond the boundaries of the United States," and its enhanced naval presence in the Eastern Mediterranean and Black Sea Straits "constitute a political and military demonstration against the

---

[33] Winston Churchill's Iron Curtain Speech, http://history1900s.about.com/library/weekly/aa082400a.htm. Roberts, *Stalin's Wars*, 307–8.

Soviet Union." The United States was challenging British imperial interests, especially in the Middle East, but it was unclear if this would cause a
permanent rift between the two capitalist powers. America had adopted
a hard line toward the USSR; Novikov took talk of a "third war" against the
Soviet Union seriously. He did not offer any policy recommendations,
and it is not clear how widely his views were shared. In late 1946, however,
Stalin ordered Molotov to compromise to maintain cooperation with the
United States.[34]

These public and private assessments are full of simplistic and fallacious
claims, and plausible but often-incorrect interpretations, yet they accu-
rately reflect pervasive transatlantic anxieties, insecurities, and pessimism.
The misperceptions and exaggerations were fueled by Soviet and
American actions in 1945–46 and in turn fueled the dramatic polarization
that occurred over the course of 1947, as the Truman Doctrine, the
Marshall Plan, and the Cominform led to the consolidation of a Cold
War order.

The Cold War begins

In March 1947 Truman present his eponymous doctrine to Congress; it
charted an expansive and interventionist new foreign policy for America
in response to ongoing turmoil in the contentious Eastern Mediterranean.
In February 1947 Britain, financially weakened by the cost of war and
postwar loans, announced it would cease aid to Greece and Turkey in six
weeks. The United States must step into that vacuum, Truman argued,
for in Greece "a militant minority, exploiting human want and misery,
was able to create political chaos" and prevent economic recovery. The
Greek government asked for financial and other assistance as well as
United States help in using it effectively. Turkey, although not suffering
from civil war, "deserves our attention" and "financial assistance ... for
the purpose of effecting that modernization necessary for the maintenance
of its national integrity." Neither the Soviet Union nor communism were
specifically mentioned, but their presence was felt in the doctrine's invo-
cation of totalitarianism. Truman did not accuse the Soviets of interven-
ing economically, politically, or militarily in Greece, for they were not so
doing; nor had they invaded Turkey, as some Americans feared they
might. American intervention was preemptive, not reactive; it was also
unilateral, for although Truman's speech invoked the principles of the
UN Charter, he did not call for UN action.

---

[34] For the telegram and commentary on it, see "The Soviet Side of the Cold War: A
Symposium," *Diplomatic History* 15/4 (Oct. 1991): 523–63.

The Truman Doctrine articulated the rhetoric and policies of liberal interventionism that would be the hallmark of United States foreign policy throughout the Cold War. It gave a sweeping ideological defense of "free nations" against "totalitarian regimes," even as it offered a capacious definition of free and democratic. As Truman admitted, the Greek regime had made "mistakes," and he condemned "extremist measures of the right" as well as the left. He "advised tolerance," presumably as both a policy for the Greek government to follow and an attitude for the United States to adopt toward the repressive and undemocratic Greek regime. Articulating the domino theory, Truman argued that if Greece fell "to an armed minority . . . Confusion and disorder might well spread throughout the entire Middle East." Any reference to oil was omitted. The Truman Doctrine showed American willingness to take over Britain's neocolonial role, even as the United States criticized European imperialism. The Truman Doctrine, a name resonant of the Monroe Doctrine, indicated an expansion of America's claimed sphere of influence far beyond the Western Hemisphere. As Truman put it, "The free peoples of the world look to us for support" and "it must be the policy of the United States to support free peoples who are resisting attempted subjugation by armed minorities or by outside pressure." The Truman Doctrine provided the rhetoric and arguments that the United States deployed as it projected power globally after 1945.[35]

The Soviet response to Truman's speech was "surprisingly muted." The press saw it as an indication of American expansionism, but Stalin himself did not speak out. Kremlin leaders may have been reluctant to speak out because they saw Truman's proclamation as payback for Stalin's earlier "Turkish probe." The reaction to America's next policy initiative, the Marshall Plan, was quite different.[36]

Two years after war's end, European trade remained disrupted, black markets flourished, currencies were unstable, factories were idle, and goods of all sorts in short supply. Thus, on June 5, 1947 United States Secretary of State George Marshall unveiled a proposal for massive American economic aid to Europe. As he argued,

It is logical that the United States should do whatever it is able to do to assist in the return of normal economic health in the world, without which there can be no

---

[35] Truman Doctrine, www.yale.edu/lawweb/avalon/trudoc.htm. Lloyd Gardner, *Three Kings: The Rise of an American Empire in the Middle East after World War II* (New York: New Press, 2009), 3.

[36] Roberts, *Stalin's Wars*, 313. Valdislav Zubok and Constantine Pleshakov, *Inside the Kremlin's Cold War: From Stalin to Khrushchev* (Cambridge, MA: Harvard University Press, 1996), 93.

political stability and no assured peace. Our policy is directed not against any country or doctrine but hunger, poverty, desperation and chaos. Its purpose should be the revival of a working economy in the world so as to permit the emergence of political and social conditions in which free institutions can exist.[37]

Marshall invited all European countries to cooperate in drawing up plans for aid that would promote recovery, open national markets to trade and investment, and encourage European economic integration. The United States first discussed the proposal with Britain and France, but not the Soviet Union, and then held a meeting in Paris with representatives of over two dozen countries. The Soviets attended with a hundred-person delegation but walked out before the meetings ended. The Czechs, Poles, and Yugoslavs remained for the next round but then acceded to Moscow's pressure to withdraw.

Why did the Soviets refuse to join? Traditional interpretations argue that ideology and paranoia led Stalin to view the Marshall Plan from the beginning as a strategy of rollback, which would weaken Soviet control in Eastern Europe, either by persuading some states to join or by offering aid on unacceptable terms. More recent works insist that the Soviets did seriously consider participation. The Soviet press, for example, initially interpreted the Marshall Plan as a response to economic problems within the United States. According to leading Soviet economist Eugen Varga, the United States needed markets abroad for American products and could create them only by offering Europeans credits. By midsummer, however, the Soviets became convinced that the Marshall Plan was an extension of the Truman Doctrine that would lead to interference in the domestic affairs of Eastern European countries if they joined and confront them with a bloc directed against them if they did not. "For Stalin the Marshall Plan was the breaking point ... It indicated that co-operation with the Americans was no longer possible without putting in jeopardy the Soviet sphere of influence in Eastern Europe."[38]

Marshall denied that his program was directed against the Soviet Union. Yet, with France and Italy in mind, he did insist that economic crisis and poverty were a "breeding ground for communism." From conviction or necessity, he sold the unpopular aid program to Congress and the American public less on humanitarian grounds than on those of American economic self-interest and national security, and he feared that Congress would kill the plan if the Soviets accepted. The British and French prime ministers opposed Soviet participation, as did leading American advisors. According

---

[37] "The 'Marshall Plan' Speech at Harvard University, June 5, 1947," www.oecd.org/document/10/0,3343,en_2649_201185_1876938_1_1_1_1,00.html.

[38] Roberts, *Stalin's Wars*, 317.

to Kennan, "The Marshall Plan was offered to the Soviet Union with the intention that it would be turned down." Although the United States hoped to use the Marshall Plan to lessen Soviet influence in Eastern Europe, two British historians argue, "in working so conspicuously to achieve this goal, the United States actually made the Sovietization of the region more or less inevitable."[39]

For their part, the Soviets embraced confrontational rhetoric and exacerbated the growing divisions within Europe. In September 1947 they established the Communist Information Bureau or Cominform, which was a revival of the interwar Communist International and included not only the Communist parties of Eastern Europe but also those throughout the world. Its head was Andrei Zhdanov, whose fiercely ideological approach to the world was summarized in his two camps theory. The world was divided into the imperialist and anti-democratic camp and the anti-imperialist and democratic one; cooperation between them was impossible, neutrality unviable. At the founding meeting, Zhdanov severely chastised the French and Italian Communist parties for reformism, and the Soviets subsequently worked to tighten the communist grip on governments in Poland, Bulgaria, and Romania. Both the United States and the Soviet Union gave up on negotiation and compromise.

Throughout the first two postwar years, the inability of the four powers to resolve the German question created ongoing tensions that exacerbated and were exacerbated by other conflicts. Both the Soviets and the Americans oscillated between desiring economic unification and a cooperative political settlement and wondering if division would best serve their interests. At Potsdam they created clear spheres of influence for each occupying power; thereafter the United States advocated a united Germany because it worried about Soviet expansion westward, while the Soviets did so because they still hoped for reparations from the Western-controlled Ruhr. The Soviets favored first reconstructing a centralized German state and then unifying it economically, while the British and Americans gave priority to economic unification and preferred a federal state. All agreed to demilitarize Germany but were unsure how far to push de-Nazification beyond the Nuremberg trials and a spate of smaller ones. Economic questions proved most intractable. The Russians took reparations from the east and continually demanded them from the western zones, while the British and Americans viewed reparations as detrimental to economic recovery and democratization. The British and Americans abandoned the Morgenthau Plan, but were divided about how to curb cartels and whether to punish the industries

---

[39] Michael Cox and Caroline Kennedy-Pipe, "The Tragedy of American Diplomacy: Rethinking the Marshall Plan," *Journal of Cold War Studies* 7/1 (Winter 2005): 110, 131.

most involved in the war and Holocaust. As a result they left the German economy in their zones largely intact, while the Soviets expropriated and collectivized large Junker agrarian estates, socialized some industries, and dismantled and shipped thousands of factories to Russia. While the Soviets sought to enhance the power of the Communist Party from above, the Western powers slowly built democracy from the bottom up.

As conflicts and suspicions between the United States and the Soviet Union intensified and the European economic crisis deepened, the Americans and British pushed for a division of Germany. Some American policymakers favored this in order to contain perceived Soviet aggression, others to avoid giving the Soviets reparations or to promote German economic recovery and expand free trade in Europe. On January 1, 1947, Britain and America merged their occupied territories into Bizonia, thereby transgressing the Yalta prohibition against dividing Germany, and incorporated the French zone in April 1948. Two months later they introduced a much-needed currency reform in the now unified western zone, and announced plans to introduce the new D Mark into their sectors of four-power occupied Berlin. This violated the Potsdam agreement and threatened Soviet power in its part of the city.

The Soviets responded in July 1948 by blockading Berlin, which was entirely within their zone. They wanted to force negotiations, not risk war, but the blockade increased the dangers of conflict. General Clay, the American military governor in Germany, favored going into Berlin via land and the United States National Security Council debated using atomic bombs. Fortunately, an American airlift supplied Berlin with food and coal month after month in round-the-clock flights that kept the city alive (along with West Berliners' ability to buy food from the Soviet Zone). In May 1949 the Soviets lifted the blockade. The Berlin airlift was an enormous political and symbolic victory for the Americans; the blockade a fiasco for the Soviets, for it solidified the division of Germany and assured a permanent American military presence in the heart of Europe. By the end of 1949 the Federal Republic (FRG) and the German Democratic Republic (GDR) had been established and divided Berlin was becoming the iconic Cold War city. Twelve nations, led by the United States and Britain and including France, Canada, Belgium, and Norway, established the North Atlantic Treaty Organization (NATO). The Soviets initially saw it as a political more than a military threat. As many quipped, NATO's purpose was to keep the Americans in, the Soviets out, and the Germans down.

As Cold War divisions solidified, each superpower intervened more forcefully in its sphere of influence. In 1947 the Soviets rigged elections and repressed non-communist parties in Hungary; in February 1948 they

Illustration 13 Superpowers playing chess: Truman and Stalin, L. G. Illingworth. *Daily Mail*, February 1949

staged a Communist coup in Czechoslovakia; and from 1949 on they helped make the GDR the most Stalinist state in Eastern Europe. In 1948 the United States pumped money into Italy and France to help defeat the communists in elections, while the CIA ran special operations in Italy. As Communists were forcibly installed in the East, they were politically and economically marginalized and in some cases outlawed in the West. The stabilized, conservative capitalist regimes that emerged in the West were a product not only of American action, but also of Soviet non-interference.

The American move from cooperation to conflict and containment was a response to real and imagined Soviet intentions and actions, while the Soviets acted from vulnerability and ideology more than from strength. The Soviets, as Odd Arne Westad has argued, wanted to have their cake and eat it too; they wanted to cooperate with and receive aid from the United States and Britain, but also control Eastern Europe, preferably by peaceful means. This created a foreign policy that was "not as much inexplicable in its parts as incoherent in its whole."[40] United States policy was more coherent, for it was not only reactive; it reflected America's new global vision of national security and confident assumption that its interests and values should triumph. In the wake of Pearl Harbor, the air war, and the A-bomb, the United States came to define its national interests not in terms of protecting the Western Hemisphere but in terms of a new "air age globalism."[41] For the president, Congress, the National Security Council, and the media, Western Europe and the Mediterranean as well as the Middle East and East Asia were as central to United States security as Central and South America. They felt America was entitled to bases as well as political influence and an economic presence in new areas because of wartime sacrifices, postwar insecurities, and a new sense of global mission. Nowhere did they acknowledge that the Soviets had similar security concerns, had made far greater sacrifices, and faced far greater reconstruction needs. The United States proclaimed a commitment to self-determination for all but perceived a need and desire to step into the power vacuum left by Britain. Americans assumed that their value system and liberal capitalism, which was integral to it, could and should become universal. Europe, transatlantic relations, and much of the rest of the world would live with the Cold War that resulted for the next four decades.

---

[40] Cited in Leffler, *For the Soul*, 53.
[41] Alan K. Hendrickson, "The Map as an 'Idea': The Role of Cartographic Imagery during the Second World War," *The American Cartographer* 2/1 (1975): 19–53.

7   Cooperation, competition, containment

From the late 1940s on, the Cold War provided the geopolitical context and discursive framework for European-American relations; it shaped and warped transatlantic economic, political, and cultural interactions; it became a way of life. The Cold War was not synonymous with everything that happened, but virtually everything from the arms race and economic development at home and abroad to political debates and cultural exchanges was inflected by it. Europe was not the only arena in which Americans and Soviets confronted one another, but they did so there most directly and with the greatest ideological, military, and economic investment. The European Cold War was part of a Euro-American civil war that began with the Russian Revolution but had deeper roots in long-standing conflicts about political and social rights and competing visions of equality and justice.

The Cold War in Europe was a joint American and Soviet project, even though the United States was unquestionably the dominant power economically and militarily. Both states – or, more accurately, empires – promoted their ideologies, defended their real and imagined security interests, and pursued their economic goals. European states also shaped the Cold War as they pursued their own interests and criticized the actions and ideologies of the superpowers. And the Third World offered the United States, the USSR, and Western Europe a further arena for conflict and competition that also influenced transatlantic relations.

In the first Cold War decades, Europe was rigidly divided between the capitalist West and the communist East, but the character and intentions of each bloc were initially unclear. Would Western European states be America's partners or subordinates and would they emulate the American economic model or continue to develop their own varieties of capitalism? Were the Soviets bent on expansion and confrontation and would the United States contain or rollback communism? Although German and Japanese empires had collapsed and European ones were unraveling, the shape of the new global order remained open.

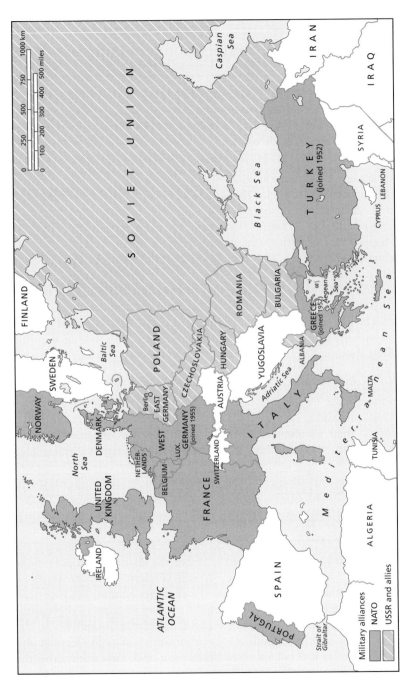

Map 2 Cold War Europe

Economic Americanism

America's postwar hegemony rested on its economic prowess, military predominance, and an ideology that linked free institutions, freedom of thought, and free markets. America's "visionary globalism" strove to construct a democratic capitalist bloc stretching from Western Europe across North America to Northeast Asia that was bolstered by Western control of Middle East oil and by French and British colonial resources. Western Europe was at the heart of what Americans labeled the "free world" and seemed a particularly promising region for American influence, due to economic ties, cultural affinities, and shared anti-communism. The American military was present not only in West Germany, Austria, and Italy but also in Britain, France, and the Netherlands; the United States dominated the IMF and NATO and boasted the world's only prosperous economy. According to John Foster Dulles, secretary of state under Eisenhower, America's wartime contributions and its postwar aid gave it "both moral rights and political power" in Western Europe.[1] Yet Western Europe was also a problematic base from which to secure American power, for its economies were prostrate, its societies demoralized, and its politics unstable. War had eroded European economic power and weakened states without, however, destroying desires for national autonomy or British and French great-power aspirations.

American interventions to reshape Western Europe focused first and foremost around economic reconstruction and modernization. The sheer size of the United States economy imbued Americans with a sense of entitlement and made them fearful. It had grown by 50 percent during the war and was larger than all other economies combined in 1945. The United States stood at the center of the new global financial order, manufactured the vast majority of the world's consumer durables, and shipped over half of the world's trade. But who would consume all that it could produce if Western Europe did not recover and open its borders? Americans also viewed economic recovery as the prerequisite for containing communism in France and Italy, legitimizing democracy in West Germany and Italy, and stabilizing polities and economies across Western Europe. Finally, American businessmen, engineers, politicians, and labor leaders believed, as they had since the 1920s, that American

[1] James Peck, *Washington's China: The National Security World, the Cold War, and the Origins of Globalism* (Amherst: University of Massachusetts, 2006), 1. David Ellwood, "America as a European Power: Four Dimensions of the Transatlantic Relationship, 1945 to the Late 1990s," in Carl Levy and Mark Roseman, eds., *Three Postwar Eras in Comparison: 1919–1945–1989* (New York: Palgrave, 2002), 69.

productivity, technology, corporate organization, and labor relations were the most advanced and efficient; they could and should be emulated.

American policymakers and businessmen promoted more than Fordist assembly lines or Taylorist time and motion studies; they offered a comprehensive vision of the interrelationship of economics and politics in a revamped transatlantic order. If the private sector increased output through economic rationalization and technological modernization, Europeans could enjoy sustained growth, just as Americans did. By improving infrastructure, transportation, communications, and energy, Western Europeans would become competitive and eventually enjoy American-style mass consumption. If they imitated American-style business management, established multidivisional corporations, outlawed cartels, and imported American business unionism, growth would be further enhanced. The "politics of productivity" would enable Europeans to escape from the zero-sum distributional struggles and ideological battles of earlier decades and build sound democratic institutions. If all this were done, according to Marshall Plan head Paul Hoffman, "the American assembly line" would replace "the Communist Party line."[2]

American policymakers also advocated Western European economic integration in order to both create a large, American-style market and contain the potential dangers of a revived German economy. Finally, Europeans should apply the Bretton Woods principles of free trade, convertible currencies, and free capital flows. This would strengthen transatlantic economic ties, provide a sound economic footing for the NATO military partnership, and foster the idea of an Atlantic community, whose geographic contours were admittedly vague but whose identity was equated with freedom and Western civilization.[3]

These ideas arrived in Western Europe through many channels, some private but most public, for unlike after World War I, the American government was massively involved in European recovery efforts. An army of American Marshall Plan administrators distributed aid of all sorts, advised individual nations, and staffed the European Cooperation Agency in the late forties and the United States Technical Assistance and Productivity Program (USTA&P) in the fifties. Businessmen crossed the Atlantic first to

---

[2] Charles Maier, "The Politics of Productivity: Foundations of American International Economic Policy after World War II," in Charles Maier, *In Search of Stability: Explorations in Historical Political Economy* (Cambridge University Press, 1987), 121–52. Marie-Laure Djelic, *Exporting the American Model: The Postwar Transformation of European Business* (Oxford University Press, 1998), 78.

[3] William I. Hitchcock, "The Marshall Plan and the Creation of the West," in Melvyn P. Leffler and Odd Arne Westad, eds., *Cambridge History of the Cold War*, vol. I: *Origins* (Cambridge University Press, 2010), 154.

advise governments and industrialists and then to expand American corporate investments while labor leaders counseled their social democratic and Catholic counterparts. Europeans traveled in the other direction to learn first hand about the American model. Five thousand West German businessmen, engineers, and trade unionists, 4,500 French ones, and 1,500 Italians participated in study tours of America, organized and subsidized by the United States government. Many others came on privately funded tours or scholarships. Europeans who had previously studied or visited America, like French businessman and architect of European economic integration Jean Monnet, preached the gospel of economic Americanism. Eager to spread the message of productivity beyond elites, the American government sent a train filled with pedagogical exhibits and consumer goods across Scandinavia, France, Belgium, Italy, and West Germany. Over 6 million Europeans saw it.[4] Millions more viewed the many Marshall Plan films, translated into multiple languages, which documented the massive influx of American raw materials and food, celebrated hydro-electric dams and oil refineries funded by the Marshall Plan, and depicted the dangers of communist subversion if growth and modernization failed. "You can be like us" was their promise and their plea.

Marshall Plan and multinationals

Aid on an unprecedented scale accompanied all this propaganda to Americanize. The Marshall Plan spent $14 billion in sixteen countries between 1948 and 1952; Britain received one-quarter of the funds and France one-fifth, while smaller countries received proportionally more per capita. Thirty-nine percent of the aid was food, feed, and fertilizer, 26 percent semi-finished goods and raw materials, and 16 percent fuel. Everything was boldly marked "For European Recovery. Supplied by the United States." European governments sold these goods and put the revenues in counterpart funds and used them, at American urging, to increase capital investment, balance budgets, and promote a more open economic environment. From 1948 to 1952 the presence of the unilateral Marshall Plan, which deliberately circumvented both UN agencies and the International Bank for Reconstruction and Development, was visible from Turkey to the Netherlands, from Norway to Italy.[5]

---

[4] Harm G. Schröter, *Americanization in the European Economy: A Compact Survey of American Economic Influences in Europe since the 1880s* (Dordrecht: Springer, 2005), 49–51.
[5] Schröter, *Americanization*, 47–48. Nicolaus Mills, *Winning the Peace: The Marshall Plan and America's Coming of Age as a Superpower* (Hoboken: Wiley, 2008), 172–75.

Illustration 14   Marshall Plan "America helps with Europe's reconstruction."

Since the 1950s Americans have held up the Marshall Plan as a shining example of altruism and effective aid, and there have been recurring but unheeded calls for Marshall Plans for other areas of the globe. Historians are much more divided in their assessment. Western European economies did grow spectacularly during what the French call *le trente glorieuses* and the West Germans the *Wirtschaftswunder*. By the sixties Western Europe was enjoying an age of affluence, built on growth rates in real national product that averaged over 4 percent for both decades. The Federal Republic grew an astonishing 7.8 percent per annum in the 1950s, Austria and Italy 5.8 percent, while France grew by 4.6 percent in the 1950s and 5.6 percent in the following decade. Belgium and Ireland limped through the 1950s, but met or surpassed European averages thereafter. The chronically troubled British economy, however, grew at only 2.7 percent in the 1950s and just 3.1 percent in the 1960s.[6]

While some attribute recovery to the Marshall Plan, others insist that Western European economies were fundamentally sound in 1947–48 but

---

[6] Gerold Ambrosius and William H. Hubbard, *A Social and Economic History of Twentieth-Century Europe* (Cambridge, MA: Harvard University Press, 1989), 145.

suffered from a dollar gap that limited their ability to import. American aid only speeded up a recovery that was already in progress. Those seeking a middle ground claim the Marshall Plan provided "a crucial margin of help" and stress its psychological benefits and political payoff.[7] The vastly different outcomes in the Federal Republic, France, and Britain suggest that American aid was mediated and relatively modest. All three were major recipients of goods, funds, and technical and policy recommendations, but it was the interaction of aid and advice with the varied economic infrastructures, state policies, and business and labor organizations that determined success or failure. Countries whose economies were relatively intact and technologically modern, like West Germany, or which had activist, modernizing governments that oversaw recovery and restructuring, like France, did much better than Britain, which was saddled with outmoded facilities, colonial obligations, and a weak currency.

With the outbreak of war in Korea in 1950, the United States gave priority to national security and rearmament over European reconstruction. The Marshall Plan slogan "For European Recovery" was replaced by the Mutual Security Agency motto "Strength for the Free World. From the USA." Western European states hoped to balance recovery and rearmament; the United States pressed only for the latter, wanting "the Organization for European Economic Cooperation to function as the economic arm of NATO."[8] This created inflationary pressures, shortages, shrinking dollar reserves, and disputes over social versus military spending. Many Western Europeans criticized America's Korean policy as politically and militarily reckless and economically detrimental. These controversies marked the beginning of ongoing transatlantic disagreements about who should pay the cost not only of defending Western Europe but also of supporting America's global commitments. In the Korean case, Britain and France grumbled but provided troops.

Private investment accompanied government aid. As American multinationals expanded factories and purchased subsidiaries, they occupied a more prominent place in Western Europe than prewar. In 1950 one-seventh of United States fdi or $1.7 billion went to Europe; by 1970 one-third or $24.5 billion did. Yet, this was equivalent to just over 7 percent of GDP in the mid 1960s, the same level as after World War I. Americans initially invested in order to circumvent Europe's dollar shortages and

---

[7] Mills, *Winning the Peace*, xi. Alan Milward downplays it: *The Reconstruction of Western Europe, 1945–51* (Berkeley: University of California Press, 1984).
[8] Michael J. Hogan, *The Marshall Plan: America, Britain, and the Reconstruction of Western Europe, 1947–52* (Cambridge University Press, 1987) 344.

restrictions on remittances and later to gain access to the Common Market in Europe and the British Commonwealth.[9]

The biggest United States manufacturing and banking firms continued to dominate. By the late 1960s 85 percent of Fortune 500 companies and a total of 3,350 firms had invested abroad. Most of the leading chemical, machinery, and electrical goods firms had European branches, and United States automobile companies controlled one-quarter of the European car market. As oil supplanted coal as Europe's chief energy source, Standard Oil, Socony-Vacuum, and Caltex expanded older refineries and built new ones across Germany, Italy, Holland, France, and Spain. As Jean-Jacques Servan-Schreiber lamented in his widely read 1967 book *The American Challenge*, United States multinationals controlled the cutting-edge computer industry in Europe, and they ran their firms exactly like American businesses. IBM alone produced over 60 percent of all Western European computers. American banks and supermarket chains expanded much more slowly, however, and the steel industry had no investments abroad. Britain remained the favorite location, and American firms owned one-fifth of fixed manufacturing capital and accounted for one-quarter of British exports. On the continent Germany received the most, followed by Belgium, which offered tax incentives and subsidized loans, while France neither welcomed nor received much American investment.[10]

Varieties of capitalism

Did American business and Marshall Plan aid Americanize Western Europe? American multinationals certainly provided their European employees as well as governments and business communities with highly visible models of American technology, organization, and management. Neither contemporary observers nor subsequent analysts, however, agree about whether European firms and economies followed these examples or the advice of Marshall Plan officials. Those positing Americanization look at the most advanced industrial sectors like steel or autos, emphasize the growing production of consumer durables, and note the adoption of American corporate organization, advertising, and management practices. Others see the persistence of varieties of capitalism and emphasize the diversity of firms,

---

[9] Geir Lundestad, "'Empire by Invitation' in the American Century," *Diplomatic History* 23/ 2 (Spring 1999): 200.

[10] Stanley Buder, *Capitalizing on Change: A Social History of American Business* (Chapel Hill: University of North Carolina Press, 2009), 310. J.-J. Servan-Schreiber, *The American Challenge* (New York: Atheneum, 1968). Mira Wilkins, *The Maturing of Multinational Enterprise: American Business Abroad from 1914 to 1970* (Cambridge, MA: Harvard University Press, 1974), 301–45, 374–404.

production processes, and technologies in Western Europe. They point to distinctive labor relations, worker training, and firm financing, and note the prevalence of corporatist bargaining among labor, capital, and the state in countries such as Sweden, the Netherlands, Belgium, Austria, and Britain.

"Selective adaptation, creative modification and innovative hybridization" most accurately capture European developments, for although Western European economies were significantly modified postwar, distinctive varieties of capitalism nonetheless persisted. Europeans negotiated with American products, processes, and practices, but they also drew on their own traditions and visions of the future. The concept of Americanization cannot be dispensed with entirely, however, for it highlights the ideas and practices that the United States sought to export and the criteria by which it judged Western Europe. It captures the postwar power relations that made America the model against which Western Europeans defined their economic practices. This was particularly true in the early postwar period when the United States dominated global production and had exemplary productivity. By the late 1960s, however, America accounted for only 35 percent of global manufacturing and was failing to improve productivity, while European nations had regained competitiveness, enjoyed unprecedented prosperity, and no longer felt impelled to look to America.[11]

Western Europeans accorded the state a much greater economic role than did Americans. Postwar Britain, for example, nationalized the Bank of England, aviation, coal mines, railroads, and public utilities; the French government took over banks, coal, insurance, and collaborationist firms like Renault and deployed indicative planning to promote modernization through influence, subsidies, grants, and taxes. Italy had inherited a large state sector from the Fascist era, and the state-funded *Casa per il Mezzogiorno* sought to revamp agriculture and encourage industry in the perennially underdeveloped south. USTA&P programs advised Europeans to standardize and rationalize along American lines, but government officials, industrialists, and trade unionists generally ignored their nations' productivity boards. Americanization was an ideology that did not readily translate into practice. In most of Europe cartels remained legal, even if legislation sought to limit their abuses, for governments and business encouraged firms to cooperate and believed markets should be organized.

Although European growth rates were higher than in the United States, the overall level of consumption was much lower, especially in the 1950s.

---

[11] Jonathan Zeitlin, "Introduction," in Jonathan Zeitlin and Gary Herrigal, eds., *Americanization and Its Limits: Reworking US Technology and Management in Post-war Europe and Japan* (Oxford University Press, 2000), 15. Schröter, *Americanization*, 123.

European economies were driven primarily by civilian production and consumption, while in America the government generously funded defense industries, which were an increasingly important source of profits, innovation, and employment. From the Korean War on, the United States had the largest defense spending not only in absolute terms but also as a percentage of GDP. No European country except the Soviet Union developed a comparable military-industrial complex.

Labor relations looked different on the two sides of the Atlantic. German, Swedish, and British trade unions wielded more power on the shop floor and in the state than their American counterparts, but the Italian and French labor movements were marginalized in factories and parliament. Across Europe unions retained their ties to socialist and Communist parties rather than adopting American business unionism. And nowhere were benefits like health insurance and pensions tied to the workplace rather than to the state.

The gap between European and American social policies, which had narrowed during the depression, widened once again. During the war policymakers on both sides of the Atlantic debated far-reaching reforms to enhance social security, stabilize employment, and improve health and welfare. There was the Beveridge Plan in England, Alva Myrdal's *Nation and Family* in Sweden, and the reports of the American National Resources Planning Board. But only Europeans, suffering from the ravages of depression, fascism, and war, built multifaceted, universalist welfare states. America's federal state and distinctive political coalitions blocked extensive reforms, as did Cold War anti-communism that led many to equate European universal social programs with socialism and dismiss them accordingly.

The differences among postwar welfare states are worth enumerating for they would persist into the twenty-first century. After 1945 Britain established the National Health Service, centralized an array of social programs, and guaranteed a "national minimum" of protection for everyone. Sweden augmented its generous insurance programs and social policies, combining them with Keynesian macroeconomic management and corporatist bargaining. Indeed, Sweden became the model social democratic welfare state. In France, West Germany, Italy, and Austria, programs were also universalistic, but less egalitarian and redistributive; in areas like health they combined universal insurance with private provision. Governments aided the unemployed with insurance programs and sought to create jobs by public spending, targeted interventions in particular industries and regions, and provided extensive job training and worker relocation programs. Despite their variations, all European welfare states, from social democratic Sweden through corporatist Austria to social market West Germany believed that the state must play a role in creating and maintaining social security and spent a larger proportion of GDP on social provision than the United States. Eligibility for employment programs, old-age pensions, healthcare, education, housing, and family support was in most cases universal, not means-tested, for social rights were seen as necessary adjuncts to legal and political ones.

The United States, by contrast, failed to expand the universalist programs initiated during the New Deal to areas like health. The GI Bill, for example, accorded education benefits, housing loans, and health insurance only to veterans and their families, and even there, white male veterans benefited more than African-American male veterans and all women. Except for social security, assistance was means-tested, entitlement rules strict, and benefits meager. Aid to Families with Dependent Children, for example, assisted those below the poverty line as did food stamps beginning in the sixties, but there were no universal family allowances of a European sort. Health insurance came with a job – or with some jobs – or had to be purchased privately. President Lyndon Johnson's Great Society programs did create Medicare and Medicaid in 1965, which provided state-funded but not state-provided healthcare for those over sixty-five or with low incomes. Both universal and means-tested programs were decentralized, allowing states to offer differential benefits and engage in discriminatory practices. In short, the mixed public-private welfare system of the prewar era persisted. Americans defined social rights more narrowly, gave maximum room for the market and a minimal role for the state. Individual responsibility was stressed, social reciprocity downplayed. As long as the market, aided by tax policies and some business subsidies, delivered abundance, stability, and security, a majority of Americans were content with programs that seemed to Europeans to be both ungenerous and unjust. For political and economic reasons, postwar European states could not afford to emulate the American social policy model – and did not wish to.

A new transatlantic economy

The United States wanted the liberalization of transatlantic economic relations laid out in Bretton Woods to accompany national economic restructuring. This occurred only partially and generated both benefits and conflicts. The United States prevented Western European states from rebuilding the forms of closed national capitalism that had existed in the interwar years but was unable to construct a fully open transatlantic economic order in which currencies were convertible, capital flowed freely, and tariffs were eliminated. Instead, a compromise, "embedded liberalism," emerged.[12] The postwar United States push for currency convertibility, which was necessary for the free movement of capital, floundered on European political and financial realities. Governments needed to protect their new interventionist welfare states, so crucial to their political legitimacy, from currency speculation, disruptive international capital flows, and capital flight. Domestic needs took priority over American wishes. The American government nonetheless insisted that Britain make the pound convertible (and open colonial markets to American goods) as the prerequisite for a desperately needed loan. Britain did so in 1947 with disastrous results; the pound collapsed and after six weeks the government reimposed tight controls. Inflation and deficits precluded similar experiments elsewhere, and full convertibility of Western European currencies did not come until 1958.

Trade did become freer as tariffs were reduced by roughly half in the first postwar decade, but both the American Congress and Western European parliaments insisted on protecting agriculture and vulnerable national industries. Europeans initially lacked dollars for purchasing American exports and then the European Payments Union, established in 1950, facilitated trade among Western European countries more than across the Atlantic. Increasingly, Europeans preferred to build dollar reserves and purchase goods at home or elsewhere in Europe. All European countries except Germany imported more than they exported, but none had as large a balance of payments deficit as the United States. It stood at $6.38 billion in 1966 as compared to $1.2 billion for Britain, the largest in Europe. America's balance of payments problems were due not only to importing more than it exported; American investments abroad, tourism, and above all the cost of maintaining troops in Europe and elsewhere also contributed to the outflow of dollars.[13]

The dollar drain, in turn, threatened America's gold reserves, for under the Bretton Woods system, dollars could be exchanged for gold. America, which had the world's largest reserves, lost $3.4 billion in gold to Europe in 1958 alone. This seemingly esoteric aspect of transatlantic finance became a major Euro-American political issue. President Eisenhower feared the balance of payments deficit and gold drain would force America to pull troops out of Europe, thereby strengthening the Soviet Union, and President Kennedy claimed, "the two things which scared

---

[12] John Gerard Ruggie, "International Regimes, Transactions, and Change: Embedded Liberalism in the Postwar Economic Order," *International Organization* 36/2 (Spring 1982): 379–415.

[13] Diane B. Kunz, *Butter and Guns: America's Cold War Economic Diplomacy* (New York: Free Press, 1997), 151.

him most were nuclear weapons and the payments deficit."[14] Popular culture even picked up on the obsession with gold. In the 1964 James Bond thriller *Goldfinger*, the eponymous villain, aided by Pussy Galore and the Communist Chinese, plotted to detonate a nuclear bomb at Fort Knox, thereby irradiating America's gold supply and undermining its global economic power. The fantasy threat was thwarted more readily than the real one posed by Europe's growing dollar reserves, which were increasingly converted to gold. The United States insisted Europeans should either pay more for defense or defend themselves; the Europeans countered that America was profligate and produced too few non-military goods Europeans wanted to buy.

As acrimony and the gold drain increased in the 1960s, the United States closed the private gold market and pressured West Germany to purchase American goods, above all military hardware, to compensate for the cost of keeping United States troops there. West Germany initially made these offset payments, but by 1966, the economy was in crisis and more arms unnecessary. When Chancellor Erhard nonetheless succumbed to United States pressure, he was thrown out of office, ending the hegemony of the Christian Democrats, America's most loyal ally in Western Europe. Pressure on the French to ante up fed into their decision to leave the integrated NATO command in 1966. The Germans and French did agree, however, not to cash in their dollars for gold.

Bretton Woods was basic to America's postwar economic hegemony and did make European and American economies more interdependent. Some key provisions of the agreement were suspended, however, and others were only partially implemented; Bretton Woods did not always work to America's advantage. For Bretton Woods to function optimally, the United States would have had to withdraw troops from Europe, but that was politically unfeasible. Cold War rivalries, domestic anti-communism, and imperial aspirations trumped costs.

European integration

The second pillar of the new transatlantic architecture was European integration. After World War II Europeans like the Belgian Paul-Henri Spaak and the Frenchmen Robert Schuman and Jean Monnet advocated economic integration; Churchill spoke out for a United States of Europe, although he was vague on Britain's place in it; and West German Chancellor Konrad Adenauer favored greater cooperation. United States

---

[14] Francis J. Gavin, *Gold, Dollars, & Power: The Politics of International Monetary Relations, 1958–1971* (Chapel Hill: University of North Carolina Press, 2004), 59.

officials were even more vociferous in urging Western Europeans to create transnational institutions to regulate economic and military affairs and, perhaps eventually, political ones. Americans saw European integration as a means to contain West Germany and thereby mitigate French fears, strengthen Western Europe against the Soviet bloc, reduce America's economic and military burdens in Europe, and create an efficient market on the American model. Europeans would have to take the initiative, but American politicians and officials always assumed that integration would occur within an Atlantic framework and that a unified Europe would continue to show deference to American leadership, rather than become an independent third force. The United States was pursuing "hegemony, or even 'empire' by integration."[15]

Truman and United States Secretary of State Dean Acheson initially hoped that Britain would lead the way, but Britain was ambivalent about linking up with the continent and thereby diluting its "special relationship" with America and diverting attention from the Commonwealth. Instead, France was the driving force in creating first the European Coal and Steel Community in 1950 and then the European Economic Community/ Common Market (EEC) in 1957. These institutions knitted the economies of France, West Germany, Italy, and the Benelux countries closer together, promoted trade among them, and coordinated their policies toward the rest of Western Europe, the United States, and the Third World. American business was initially divided about the EEC, for it threatened American exports but would aid American investments in Europe; government officials stressed the political benefits and were publicly optimistic about the economic effects. In the short run America negotiated somewhat lower tariffs with the EEC, and United States multinationals circumvented restrictions by producing in Europe. French President de Gaulle, however, thwarted America's desire to see Britain join the Common Market, for he viewed Britain as an "American Trojan horse," which would make the EEC into an Atlantic rather than a European institution.[16] The basis for a potentially powerful and more autonomous Europe that could rival the United States was laid, although it would only come to fruition later in the century.

European military integration also played out in contradictory ways. It began under American auspices with the establishment of NATO, but in 1950 French Defense Minister René Pleven proposed the European Defense Community (EDC), a 100,000-man army, drawing its forces from across Western Europe, including West Germany. The United

---

[15] Geir Lundestad, *"Empire" by Integration: The United States and European Integration, 1945–1997* (Oxford University Press, 1998), 4.
[16] Lundestad, *"Empire" by Integration*, 67.

States initially opposed the EDC, but eventually supported it as compatible with the Atlantic-oriented NATO, only to have the French parliament reject it. This ended the possibility of an autonomous, integrated European military, solidified NATO under American leadership, and paved the way for West German rearmament under the umbrella of NATO. It did not, however, curb French desires for a more independent military and foreign policy, either in conjunction with other European countries or alone. In 1963, for example, de Gaulle signed a treaty of cooperation with West Germany, much to the annoyance of United States officials who felt Adenauer was being shockingly disloyal to his American patron. De Gaulle launched a French nuclear weapons program against American wishes, and when he took the French military out of NATO, 26,000 American military personnel had to leave Paris for Brussels.

European integration illustrates both the success and the limits of American influence. Militarily, the Americans choreographed European rearmament and dominated NATO, yet they failed to pressure Europeans to pay a significantly increased share of defense costs. Economically, the United States contributed to the revival and restructuring of European economies, but these failed to Americanize in the ways prescribed and came to compete with as well as complement the United States. Politically, America achieved the most, for it encouraged and supported democratic regimes, which were dominated by center or right-wing parties and marginalized communists. A democratic, economically prosperous, and rearmed West Germany was securely embedded in European and transatlantic institutions. There was a shared community of values, deemed specifically Western, ranging from democracy and freedom to the rule of law and human rights. Capitalism came in varied forms but no alternatives to it were considered. America was hegemonic, but Western Europe consented; it was, to borrow Geir Lundestad's phrase, "an empire by invitation,"[17] or perhaps more accurately, by invitations from national elites that were accepted by the population with varying degrees of enthusiasm.

Consent did not eliminate conflict, however, and harmony should not be nostalgically romanticized. The most important Western European states resented American tutelage and did not always do America's bidding. The British retained great-power aspirations and clung to the special relationship; the French challenged American economic and military leadership in Europe, and the Germans, it was feared, would flirt with neutralism. And when gentler means of persuasion did not yield compliance, the United States used economic pressure and threats of military

---

[17] Geir Lundestad, "Empire by Invitation? The United States and Western Europe, 1945–1952," *Journal of Peace Research* 23/3 (Sept. 1986): 263–77.

withdrawal. American officials, the media, and the population at large frequently treated their European allies like obstreperous adolescents or ungrateful adults who forgot how much they owed their American liberators and benefactors. The French were effeminate or hysterical or willfully wrongheaded, while the Germans were alternately neurotic, irrational, insecure, or childlike. They lacked the robust masculinity of Americans or the dangerous hypermasculinity of the Soviets.[18]

Hegemony had to be constantly renegotiated; invitations to leadership and intervention could be withdrawn. European dependence was conditional, for Europeans had their own interests and plans; they wanted to be dominated on their own terms.[19] Increasingly they got their way. Both sides could live with this mixture of collaboration, compromise, and conflict, for the mutual benefits each received on the one hand and the Cold War fears they shared on the other made alternatives seem undesirable, indeed unimaginable. The Soviet Union, present in the heart of Europe, did more than anything else to cement the Western alliance. But what was the nature of the Soviet-American rivalry and did the United States and Europe want to deal with the Soviets and communist Eastern Europe in the same way?

Defining the Soviet enemy

Churchill famously described Russia as "a riddle, wrapped in a mystery, inside an enigma," and Western observers and historians agreed, for until the 1990s access to Soviet government documents was impossible. The limited opening of archives since then has generated a wealth of new material but little consensus. Some historians view Stalin as an ideological romantic, others as operating within a revolutionary-imperial paradigm, and still others as motivated by national security concerns. All acknowledge Stalin's growing intransigence from 1947 on but stress as well his desire to avoid war, at least in the short run, in order to solidify control of Central Europe, which he accomplished, and to maintain cooperation with the West, which he failed to do. Stalin aggressively pushed the Soviet nuclear program, which tested an atomic bomb in 1949 and a hydrogen bomb four years later. Stalin installed pliable Communist rulers in Eastern Europe,

---

[18] Frank Costigliola, "The Nuclear Family: Tropes of Gender and Pathology in the Western Alliance," *Diplomatic History* 21/2 (Spring 1997): 167, 170, 178–79.

[19] Ellwood, "America as a European Power," 76. John Lewis Gaddis, *We Now Know: Rethinking Cold War History* (Oxford University Press, 1997), 227. Michael Geyer, "Cold War Angst: The Case of West-German Opposition to Rearmament and Nuclear Weapons," in Hanna Schissler, ed., *The Miracle Years: A Cultural History of West Germany, 1949–1968* (Princeton University Press, 2001), 378ff., 392–99.

Sovietized states and societies there, and eliminated oppositional elements in notorious purge trials. But he did not support any communist challenges to the American-backed capitalist order in Western Europe.

Nikita Khrushchev, who emerged victorious from the power struggles following Stalin's death in 1953, was complicated in different ways. He exposed many of the crimes of Stalinism in his famous 1956 secret speech, initiated a period of greater intellectual and political freedom known as the Thaw, and devoted increased resources to domestic economic development. He proclaimed "peaceful coexistence" with the West, arguing that competition should be economic and political, not military. Simultaneously he rearmed massively, provoked crises around Berlin, involved the Soviet Union in Third World struggles, and engaged in dangerous nuclear diplomacy. He helped broker an end to the Korean War and the first Indochina conflict and withdrew from Austria and bases in Finland, but he also took an uncompromising line on the German question and brought the world to the brink of nuclear war by stationing nuclear missiles in Cuba. Khrushchev was by turns a clever strategist and a pragmatic gambler, sometimes guided by ideology, at other times operating from ignorance. He was often reckless and acted impulsively and emotionally, displaying by turns insecurity and overconfidence.

United States leaders saw only Khrushchev's negative side, viewing him as unpredictable, at times incomprehensible, and often intransigent; they dismissed conciliatory gestures as propaganda ploys. United States leaders did not acknowledge Soviet hegemony in Eastern Europe and saw no role for traditional diplomacy. They regarded the USSR, like Nazi Germany, as a totalitarian state and a slave society that represented the antithesis of and a grave danger to American freedom. Negotiation and compromise were equated with appeasement. As President Eisenhower stated in his 1958 State of the Union speech, America was fighting a total cold war.[20] America's bellicose, moralistic, at times apocalyptic anti-communism undergirded this policy of non-recognition and non-negotiation that made the conflict a Cold *War*.

Belief in a communist world conspiracy and crusading anti-communism were popular and politically effective within America but were less central to Western European domestic politics. For Europeans diplomacy was the natural recourse. "I do not hold that we should rearm in order to fight," argued Churchill. "I hold that we should rearm in order to parlay."[21]

---

[20] Kenneth Osgood, *Total Cold War: Eisenhower's Secret Propaganda Battle at Home and Abroad* (Lawrence: University Press of Kansas, 2006), 11.

[21] Fredrik Logevall, "A Critique of Containment," *Diplomatic History* 28/4 (Sept. 2004): 475–91.

French, British, and West German leaders might disagree on when to talk and on which issues to compromise, but they never dismissed negotiations a priori. They regarded political dialogue and economic trade as compatible with containment. American policy, however, moved in quite different directions.

Psychological warfare

From the late forties on, the United States State Department and the CIA waged psychological warfare, an umbrella term for a variety of overt and covert initiatives, ranging from cultural diplomacy and educational exchanges to support for anti-communist émigré groups, economic boycotts, and sabotage. While some programs were directed at the non-communist countries, the National Security Council (NSC) and the CIA's Office of Policy Coordination (OPC) focused their efforts on subverting communist regimes. The United States sought to bombard Eastern Europe with propaganda of all sorts. The OPC funded a film of George Orwell's *Animal Farm*, for example, and toyed with the idea of dropping extra-large condoms, labeled "Made in USA. Medium," over the Soviet Union. While balloon drops of leaflets to "captive peoples" were common, radio was the preferred means of spreading an anti-communist message. The ostensibly private, but secretly state-funded, Radio Free Europe (RFE), spread a much more provocative message than the official Voice of America. RFE's self-described mission was "to contribute to the liberation of nations imprisoned behind the Iron Curtain by sustaining their morale and stimulating in them a spirit of non-cooperation with the Soviet-dominated regimes." The National Committee for a Free Europe (NCFE), a private institution with close ties to the government – it counted Lucius Clay, the former American commander in Berlin, and Eisenhower among its board members – supported these efforts. Established in 1949, the NCFE also subsidized a Free European University in Exile in Strasbourg.[22] While it is difficult to gauge the effectiveness of such propaganda efforts, the impact of the United States-led economic embargo of Eastern Europe is clearer.

In 1948 the United States stipulated that any country receiving aid had to follow United States trade and embargo policies, which prohibited the sale of a capacious list of military and civilian "strategic goods" to

---

[22] Scott Lucas, *Freedom's War: The American Crusade against the Soviet Union* (New York University Press, 1999), 67, 101–3.

communist countries. In addition, any Western European products made with Marshall Plan aid materials could not be sold to non-participating nations, and the Battle Act of 1951 further tightened trade restrictions. The so-called Cocom (Coordinating Committee for Multilateral Export Controls) list of prohibited goods covered 30–50 percent of all commodities in international trade. While American government, business, and media leaders supported a sweeping embargo, Western Europeans were highly critical, for they disliked being coerced, stood to suffer economically, doubted the policy would harm the Soviet Union, and resented American hypocrisy. As British philosopher and social critic Bertrand Russell noted, "It is ironic that the curtailment of freedom in the west has been chiefly due to the belief that the West is fighting for freedom." An embargo of military goods was acceptable, but as the French paper *Le Monde* protested: "The economies of Eastern and Western Europe needed one another … Only America is hindering the solution." German industrialists complained vociferously, and the British parliament criticized both particular embargoed items like rubber and the overall policy. Yet, economically needy Western European governments cooperated; they "sold out their trade principles for good American cash," according to one resentful French official.[23]

By the mid 1950s, as Western Europeans had predicted, the embargo had not substantially hurt the Soviet or Eastern European economies. Although it may have slowed growth somewhat, it did not prevent the Soviets from developing nuclear weapons. It limited East-West trade in Europe but did not lessen Western European dependence on some key Soviet exports. In 1961, for example, the Soviet Union provided 80 percent of Iceland's oil, 35 percent of Finland's, and between 19–22 percent of oil for Greece, Italy, Austria, and Sweden.[24] The embargo enabled the Soviet Union to integrate Eastern European economies more closely into its own, and it strengthened the Council for Mutual Economic Assistance (CMEA or Comecon), which had been established in 1949 to coordinate European communist economies. The embargo worsened East-West political relations and caused friction between the United States and Western Europe. Yet it continued because for the United States political motives outweighed economic ones and the socialist economies of Eastern Europe seemed utterly antithetical to the American model. For Western Europeans economic considerations predominated; moreover, they may well have seen

---

[23] Gunnar Adler-Karlsson, *Western Economic Warfare 1947–67: A Case Study in Foreign Economic Policy* (Stockholm: Almqvist & Wiksell, 1968), 5–11, 24–27, 37–38, 47.
[24] David S. Painter, "Oil, Resources, and the Cold War," in Leffler and Westad, eds., *Cambridge History of the Cold War*, I, 505.

similarities between themselves and Eastern Europeans, for economies across Europe were trying to recover from a devastating war, industrialize and modernize, and were doing so with a high degree of state involvement. These differing attitudes toward the economics and politics of trade with European communist states were to persist throughout the Cold War.

Rollback

The United States endorsed much more aggressive actions than propaganda and embargoes and these "measures short of war" blurred the line between containment and rollback. Indeed, Kennan himself, who had called for "the adroit and vigilant application of counter-force at a series of constantly shifting geographical and political points," did so when he helped write NSC 10/2, the 1948 National Security Council directive, which laid out plans for militant, covert measures.[25] From 1949–51 the United States and Britain infiltrated insurgent groups into Albania, strategically located between Greece and the dissident communist state of Yugoslavia, in the hope of sparking an uprising. They parachuted émigré Russians, Romanians, Hungarians, Czechs, and Poles behind the Iron Curtain with similar intent. In virtually all cases, these paramilitaries were quickly captured, tried, and sentenced. Rather than undermining the regimes, such covert operations simply fed communist paranoia about American intentions and served as a pretext for conspiracy trials and increased military spending. The OPC and its successor the Psychological Strategy Board (PSB) also contacted anti-communist groups in Eastern Europe and the Soviet Union, encouraged defections, and resettled refugees. Some highly visible defectors, such as Victor Kravchenko, author of *I Choose Freedom*, aided the American cause, but few Eastern European refugees joined the United States Army, and plans to build a fifty-division Volunteer Freedom Corps had to be shelved, due to a lack of refugee support and opposition from Western Europe.

While psychological warriors devised schemes to subvert communism, Paul Nitze and his State Department staff crafted NSC 68, a 1950 policy recommendation, which depicted the Soviet threat in extreme, indeed apocalyptic, terms.

The Soviet Union, unlike previous aspirants to hegemony, is animated by a new fanatic faith, antithetical to our own, and seeks to impose absolute authority over the rest of the world ... The issues that face us are momentous, involving the fulfillment or destruction not only of this Republic but of civilization itself.

---

[25] X [George Kennan], "The Sources of Soviet Conduct," *Foreign Affairs* (July 1947): 566–82.

The United States must not only defend the free world but also "foster a fundamental change in the nature of the Soviet system." The Soviet Union was "inescapably militant because it possesses and is possessed by a worldwide revolutionary movement, because it is the inheritor of Russian imperialism, and because it is a totalitarian dictatorship." While acknowledging that the United States economy was four times as large as the Soviet one, NSC 68 claimed that the Soviets were capable of overrunning Western Europe, conquering parts of the Middle East, and damaging key North American targets. NSC 68 greatly overestimated the Soviet stockpile of nuclear weapons, claimed the Soviet Union devoted vastly more resources to the military than the United States and Western Europe, but correctly noted that it had much larger conventional forces.[26]

NSC 68 insisted that new methods and vastly expanded resources were required to deter the Soviet Union. Isolationism was politically undesirable and economically self-defeating, while a preemptive attack on the Soviet Union would bring prolonged, destructive war to Western Europe. Instead, the United States must rapidly stockpile atomic weapons and build up its military strength in order to defend its global interests. NATO allies must do their part militarily and economically if they wished to eliminate the danger of Soviet occupation in any future war. A rapid military buildup might divert United States resources from consumption and domestic programs, but it was imperative to strengthen the free world.

Kennan and Charles Bohlen, the former ambassador to Russia, judged NSC 68 to be alarmist and provocative; Truman was reluctant to increase defense spending massively; and the document itself was kept secret until 1975. Nonetheless, its rhetoric and worldview pervaded the popular media and it profoundly shaped American policy. When North Korea invaded South Korea in June 1950, and the United States joined in what they insisted was a Soviet-inspired venture, the way was clear to triple the American defense budget and generously fund not only the Korean War but also the nuclear arms race and an expansive military-industrial complex. As more than one proponent of aggressive containment noted, "Korea saved us."

NSC 68 envisioned extensive Western European rearmament and help with America's balance of payments problem; Korea made that imperative. But Western Europeans were less enthusiastic, for they prioritized social over military spending. Of equal importance, they feared that United States involvement in Korea, an area of little concern to them, might encourage the Soviets to act aggressively in Western Europe. These criticisms, in turn,

---

[26] NSC 68, in Ernest R. May, ed., *American Cold War Strategy: Interpreting NSC 68* (Boston: Bedford/St. Martins, 1993), 25–26, 29, 34.

fueled United States fears that Western Europe was not sufficiently anti-communist and supportive of American foreign policy and might succumb to emotional neutralism. When Eisenhower became president in June 1953, Western European concerns increased, for Eisenhower and his secretary of state, John Foster Dulles, laid out a new foreign policy that emphasized "strategic superiority, deterrence, containment and a calculated, prudent rollback" and advocated "massive retaliation" against any Soviet aggression. Dulles soon criticized containment as a weak and immoral policy that abandoned 500 million Eastern Europeans. Calling for a "Policy of Boldness," he threatened massive retaliation if the Soviets threatened Western Europe and promised a political offensive to liberate Eastern Europe.[27]

Fiery rhetoric, however, did not translate into action. The aim of propaganda, embargoes, and covert operations was to spark revolt in Eastern Europe, but when revolt occurred, the United States offered only verbal support. In June of 1953 workers across the German Democratic Republic took to the streets to protest the regime's harsh economic policies and soon disgruntled East Germans called for the removal of the Communist leadership. Although West Berliners rallied in support, neither the Americans nor the French and British, all of whom had troops in West Berlin, took action, for all feared fighting might then spread to the West. Soviet tanks quickly suppressed the rebellion. As United States High Commissioner in Germany James Conant rather cynically remarked, the United States wanted "to keep the pot of communist unrest simmering, but not bring it to a boil."[28]

The American response to the much more massive Hungarian Revolution of 1956 was similar. As economic and political protest escalated, students, workers, and intellectuals, whether Catholic, nationalist, or reformist socialist, coalesced behind demands for democratization, a multiparty system, withdrawal from the Warsaw Pact, and nonalignment. The United States government and media praised Hungarian "freedom fighters," and Radio Free Europe offered encouragement and tactical advice, but the United States did not intervene overtly or covertly, and Soviet troops brutally repressed the revolt. The United States had not developed plans for "liberating the captive nations of Eastern Europe," and it was preoccupied with the Suez crisis. After

[27] Melvyn P. Leffler, *For the Soul of Mankind: The United States, the Soviet Union and the Cold War* (New York: Hill and Wang, 2007), 133. Gregory Mitrovich, *Undermining the Kremlin: America's Strategy to Subvert the Soviet Bloc, 1947–1956* (Ithaca: Cornell University Press, 2000), 105, 108–9.

[28] Hope M. Harrison, *Driving the Soviets up the Wall: Soviet-East German Relations, 1953–1961* (Princeton University Press, 2003), 38.

Hungary, rollback and liberation were dead, but two other issues continued to trouble relations among Soviets, Americans, and Western Europeans – Germany and nuclear weapons.

The German question

The unresolved German question lay at the troubled heart of the Cold War in Europe. Neither the Potsdam conference nor the division of Germany had resulted in a peace treaty, and German reunification and rearmament remained unresolved, as did the status of four-power occupied Berlin. The Soviets put the German question on the table repeatedly between 1952 and 1955 and again from 1958 to 1962, but were they ever serious about giving up communist East Germany for a unified state? For all their rhetorical commitment to reunification, did the Americans and the West Germans ever envision anything but a Federal Republic securely integrated into Western Europe and NATO?

In March 1952 Stalin proposed talks for a German peace treaty that would result in a reunified but neutral and disarmed Germany. Written in a last-ditch effort to keep West Germany out of the proposed EDC, the Soviet proposal may have been simply a propaganda ploy. It was, however, taken up again after Stalin's death, reiterated after the June 1953 uprising in East Germany, and put forth once more during the 1955 Geneva summit and foreign ministers' conference. The Kremlin, however, remained divided, with Khrushchev and Foreign Minister Molotov arguing that a unified bourgeois Germany would revive the danger of militarism and that the GDR must be defended, while Lavrenty Beria and Georgy Malenkov, who ruled jointly with Khrushchev, were more open to trading the socialist GDR for a neutral unified Germany that might serve as the centerpiece of European collective security. All agreed that any way forward had to begin with peace negotiations, rather than free elections.

Churchill favored a summit on the German question and the French were eager to explore ways to limit West German remilitarization. Eisenhower and Dulles, however, wanted West Germany integrated militarily and economically into the Atlantic alliance, as did Chancellor Adenauer, and opposed such negotiations. They insisted that free elections precede peace talks and that a unified Germany be allowed to rearm and choose its allies. Unburdened by traumatic memories of World War II, the Americans regarded French and British concerns about a resurgent Germany as unfounded. The United States had moved on to a new enemy in a new war, while for Europeans the memories and material and social effects of the previous conflict were palpably present.

Ideology, memory, Kremlin infighting, and America's confrontational New Look defense policy thus all prevented any serious negotiations, and all parties settled for an outcome that none had initially wanted – a divided Germany, a divided, four-power occupied Berlin, and the economic and military integration of each Germany into its respective bloc. In November 1958, however, Khrushchev provocatively raised the German question once again. His Berlin ultimatum demanded that the United States, Britain, and France sign a peace treaty with the GDR and turn West Berlin into a demilitarized free city within six months. If not, the Soviets would turn over control of the access to Berlin to the East Germans. Khrushchev's motives were multiple and their relative significance unclear. On the one hand, he was boastfully confident because the USSR had launched Sputnik, the world's first satellite, in 1957. On the other hand, he felt insecure because the Soviet nuclear arsenal was far smaller than that of the United States and frustrated because his conciliatory gestures had not elicited the desired reciprocal overtures from the United States. Provocation might produce a response or even a summit. Of equal importance, Khrushchev, always wary of West German military might, feared the FRG would acquire the nuclear weapons it had asked for in 1957. Finally, the GDR leadership, suffering economically from thousands of East Germans fleeing to the West, pressured incessantly for the diplomatic recognition and enhanced power that a peace treaty would provide. This confusion of goals was pursued through erratic, contradictory, and counterproductive tactics that kept the Berlin crisis at the center of the European Cold War for four years.

The United States firmly rejected the ultimatum and threatened war if the Soviets unilaterally abrogated Western rights in Berlin. Britain and France insisted Berlin was not worth a conventional conflict and certainly not a nuclear one and favored pursuing negotiations; even Adenauer, who opposed any recognition of the GDR, wanted to avoid war. Yet, efforts to lower tension and reach a settlement proved futile. Both Vice President Richard Nixon's trip to Moscow and Khrushchev's tour of America in 1959 were marked by inconclusive private conversations among the leaders and Khrushchev's confrontational public outbursts. To be sure, Khrushchev dropped his deadline and a summit was held in Paris in May 1960, but the Soviets walked out in angry protest. A month before, an American U-2 spy plane had been downed over the Soviet Union and the pilot Gary Powers unexpectedly survived. After first denying the incident, Eisenhower took responsibility, and while he promised to curb future flights, would not apologize, as Khrushchev demanded.

In 1961 Khrushchev reissued the ultimatum. He knew he was risking nuclear war but believed "there is more than a 95% probability that there will be no war." The United States would still not accede to demands for a peace treaty and a free city. Unable to win concessions, Khrushchev solved the East German problem by allowing the GDR president, Walter Ulbricht, to build the wall he desired to stem the flow of population into West Berlin. Since no country could unify Germany on terms it found acceptable, everyone was content to see it stay divided, especially since the United States stopped threatening to withdraw troops from Europe and West Germany agreed to remain a non-nuclear state. The British, French, and Americans continued to occupy West Berlin; Berlin remained the iconic Cold War city, but ceased to be a flashpoint for Soviet-American tensions. No peace treaty would be signed for another thirty years. As Kennedy remarked, "It's not a very nice solution but a wall is a hell of a lot better than a war."[29]

The nuclear question

If fundamentally incompatible American and Soviet views prevented resolution of the German question, their remarkably similar attitudes toward nuclear weapons thwarted efforts at arms control and disarmament and encouraged dangerous atomic diplomacy. Once the Soviets broke the American nuclear monopoly in 1949 and then followed up America's vastly more powerful hydrogen bomb with their own, the nuclear arms race was well underway. During the fifties both states regarded nuclear weapons as necessary, usable, and economical. Eisenhower and Dulles built America's New Look defense strategy around the conviction that any local war would escalate into a general, that is, nuclear one and prepared only for that. By expanding America's nuclear arsenal, they hoped to deter the Soviets from launching local probes in Europe or a general attack, but they were prepared to counter Soviet actions and to act preemptively, using nuclear weapons, if an attack was believed imminent. The New Look promised to cut American defense spending by limiting conventional forces and weapons and forcing European states to increase their armies and military budgets. Although the Soviets relied much more heavily on conventional forces in Europe, Khrushchev also advocated nuclear weapons as a deterrent, a bargaining chip, and a way to cut military costs and redirect money to the ailing civilian economy.

The arms race began unequally and proceeded asymmetrically. The United States went from 369 nuclear weapons in 1950 to 27,000 in 1962

---

[29] Aleksandr Fursenko and Timothy Naphtali, *Khrushchev's Cold War: The Inside Story of an American Adversary* (New York: Norton, 2006), 356. Gaddis, *We Now Know*, 149.

Illustration 15 Berlin Wall and Brandenburg Gate.

and developed elaborate air, land, and sea delivery systems, while the Soviets went from a handful of weapons to 3,000 but had no aircraft carriers or bases close to the United States.[30] Each side tried to guess how much the other was spending and ramped up its own military budget accordingly, but the burden was much greater on the smaller and weaker Soviet economy. Once the superpowers became so heavily invested in nuclear arms, Western European countries wanted to share in American nuclear decision-making or develop their own national programs. France and Britain saw nuclear weapons as the new symbol of great-power status, West Germany as the mark of its full rehabilitation and equality. The United States considered nuclear-sharing arrangements in the fifties, but thereafter sought unilateral control. Both politicians and the press criticized French efforts to build a national nuclear force, deeming it anti-American to prefer a national or European orientation to an Atlantic one.

Military planners in both the USSR and the United States initially insisted that nuclear war would be survivable and winnable. Governments across the Atlantic world developed vast public and private civil defense schemes. Hermann Kahn of the Rand Institute laid out a scenario for fighting and surviving thermonuclear war, and NATO and the Soviets did the same. All envisioned millions of deaths and casualties and massive property destruction in the best case; in the worst one, the entire Northern Hemisphere might be destroyed. Such nuclear war planning, as Dulles noted, sent "a wave of hysteria" through Western European leaders, who were not sure if America's nuclear plans provided an umbrella of protection or made them a lightning rod for Soviet attack. Popular opinion was even more hostile to nuclear weapons. In Britain the annual Easter marches from London to the secret atomic weapons plant at Aldermaston began in 1958, drawing tens of thousands who demanded nuclear disarmament. Late 1950s polls showed that between half and three-quarters of West Germans opposed all nuclear weapons. They feared Europe would be the battleground in a nuclear conflict that would bring collective death on a scale surpassing World War II. Opposition was strongest among blue-collar workers and active Church members, while intellectuals and the educated classes had a faith in technology and American nuclear leadership.[31]

Eisenhower and Khrushchev recognized the horrifying destructiveness of nuclear weapons and the risk that any military conflict might quickly escalate out of control. Yet, neither would acknowledge that these

---

[30] David Holloway, "Nuclear Weapons and the Escalation of the Cold War, 1945–62," in Leffler and Westad, eds., *Cambridge History of the Cold War*, I, 387.
[31] Gaddis, *We Now Know*, 227.

powerful and expensive weapons might be utterly useless; neither trusted the other to disarm; and neither was willing to abandon nuclear diplomacy. Each alternated threats to use atomic weapons with proposals for their limitation or elimination, albeit ones hedged with reservations that made them unacceptable to the other side. In 1953, for example, the United States threatened to use nuclear weapons against China and North Korea if they failed to sign an armistice and repatriate American POWs. In 1956 Khrushchev threatened to attack French and British cities, thereby risking nuclear war, if they did not cease fighting Egypt over Suez. Both nations were convinced that their nuclear threats had produced the desired effect; in fact, it was Stalin's death and American and Chinese concessions on POWs that paved the way for the Korean War settlement and American economic pressure that forced the British to stop fighting. The illusion that brinkmanship and bluff worked, however, perpetuated reckless behavior; threats were seen as proof of Soviet and American credibility.

There were, to be sure, gestures toward arms limitation. The Soviets took the first initiatives, for with a much smaller nuclear arsenal and enormous economic problems, they stood to gain the most. But the Soviets were not willing to allow the open-skies or on-site inspections that Americans considered essential, for they feared exposing their many economic and military weaknesses. The Geneva summit in 1955 failed to reach any arms agreement, but the Soviets came away convinced that both sides understood the nuclear danger and Europe was not in a prewar situation. The 1957 London disarmament talks collapsed because the Soviets would not reduce their conventional forces, and the Americans insisted that the stockpiling of fissionable material be frozen before any test ban treaty. The West also rejected Polish Foreign Minister Adam Rapacki's proposal for a nuclear-free Central Europe. The 1960 Paris summit similarly collapsed, due not only to the U-2 affair and ongoing disagreements about inspections, but also to United States fears of a missile gap.

The Soviets tested the first intercontinental ballistic missile (ICBM) in 1957, and the United States responded by offering intermediate-range ballistic missiles with nuclear warheads to its NATO allies. Italy, Britain, and Turkey, right on the Soviet border, accepted the Jupiter missiles. Khrushchev boasted that the USSR could mass produce precision ICBMs, but these claims were utterly unfounded, as United States intelligence knew. Nonetheless, in 1960 American politicians, journalists, and presidential candidate John Kennedy decried the dangerous missile gap and insisted it be rectified through massive military spending and a militant stance. The stage was set for the Cuban Missile Crisis.

Illustration 16 Fidel Castro and Nikita Khrushchev at the UN 1960.

The outlines of the 1962 Cuban Missile Crisis, which brought the United States and the Soviet Union to the brink of nuclear war, are clear. The Soviets secretly sent over forty medium-range ballistic missiles to Cuba, where Fidel Castro had staged a successful revolution in 1959. The United States, which had embargoed and tried unsuccessfully to invade Cuba and continued to plan covert operations against it, discovered the missiles and publicly demanded their immediate withdrawal. After several days of provocative public statements, tense secret negotiations, and military mobilizations on all sides, Khrushchev backed down, the missiles left, and an American invasion was averted. As a quid pro quo, Kennedy secretly agreed to remove the Jupiter missiles from Turkey. But why did Khrushchev precipitate this crisis? And how was Armageddon averted?

Khrushchev's motives mixed revolutionary romanticism, realpolitik, and unreflective brinkmanship. As part of his increasing attention to the Third World, Khrushchev was committed to the Cuban Revolution. He wanted to keep Castro in the Soviet camp, thwart Chinese influence there, and project an image of communism moving forward. Using Cuba as leverage for a Berlin settlement does not seem to have been a primary concern. Khrushchev hoped a bold move would gain American respect, and he viewed Soviet missiles in Cuba as analogous to those the United States had in Western Europe and Turkey. The United States, however, regarded Soviet missiles in an already unacceptable communist state 90 miles off America's shore as an egregious violation of the Monroe Doctrine and an existential threat to American security. United States generals pushed for a military response; Kennedy settled on a naval embargo and diplomacy, backed by threats of invasion or airstrikes. Historians still debate whether nuclear war was averted due to Kennedy's brilliant crisis management, Khrushchev's unilateral decision to end the crisis, a joint realization that nuclear weapons should not be used and a deal had to struck, or just dumb luck.

The crisis did clearly show that atomic diplomacy was exceedingly dangerous and nuclear weapons could not be rationally deployed. Neither side was willing to renounce them, but they took the first tentative steps toward arms control. This time the Americans, feeling they were operating from strength and pressured by an antinuclear movement at home, took the initiative. In a 1963 commencement speech at American University, Kennedy emphasized that communism was "profoundly repugnant" but acknowledged the Soviets' unprecedented suffering during World War II and called for "relaxing tensions without relaxing our guard." A nuclear hotline was set up between the Kremlin and the White House, and a Limited Test Ban Treaty, prohibiting above-ground detonations, was signed. A 1966 treaty prohibited nuclear weapons in outer space, and the 1968 Nuclear Nonproliferation Treaty sought to limit their spread to non-nuclear countries. Kennedy and Secretary of Defense Robert McNamara replaced "massive retaliation" with "flexible response" in order to give the United States more military options short of total war. These treaties and policy changes reduced tension within Europe and reinforced acceptance of the geopolitical status quo.[32] Nuclear issues would not seriously trouble Soviet-American or Western European-American relations again until the late 1970s – even though the arms race continued under the reigning doctrine of mutually assured

---

[32] Leffler, *For the Soul*, 183–85.

destruction (MAD), which ostensibly discouraged both from risking a first strike.

The Cold War did not end in the wake of the Berlin and Cuban Missile crises, but its most acute phase was over. The most dangerous confrontations shifted to Southeast Asia, decolonizing Africa, Latin America, and the Middle East. These areas had troubled European-American relations ever since World War II ended.

Decolonization and a new American empire

World War II defeated German and Japanese efforts to create a new global order but also severely weakened European colonialism and increased America's global aspirations. In 1945 it was unclear whether the British, French, Dutch, Belgian, and Portuguese empires could be rebuilt or whether decolonization would begin. The non-Euro-American world posed a shifting set of challenges for European-American relations. Should the United States push for decolonization or support the imperial aspirations of European allies? How would the United States and the Soviet Union, both of which claimed to be anti-colonial, try to shape political and economic development in Asia, the Middle East, Africa, and Latin America? Competing Western European and American global visions dominated the first Cold War decade; thereafter Soviet-American rivalries came to the fore, as both states waged war, ran covert operations, and launched development projects in Asia, the Middle East, and from the late 1950s on in sub-Saharan Africa and Latin America.

Decolonization was the first source of contention. As we saw, the Atlantic Charter of 1941 proclaimed a universal right to self-determination. In 1941 Roosevelt dismissed colonies as morally unacceptable remnants of a bygone era and insisted that Algeria, Indochina, and Dakar not be returned to France, that the Netherlands leave Indonesia, and Britain prepare to divest itself of its vast empire. This ringing anti-colonial rhetoric drew on American values and Wilsonian principles as well as on the American vision of an open, liberal, and integrated global economy, unhindered by colonial protectionism. Roosevelt, however, quickly toned down his sweeping proclamations in favor of the more modest goal of postwar trusteeships that would prepare colonial areas for eventual self-government and then independence. And at the UN founding conference in 1944, trusteeships were further restricted to only former League of Nations mandates. The wartime need to retain the cooperation of Europe's colonial powers pushed United States policy in a conservative direction as did the postwar belief, in the words of Senator Henry Cabot Lodge, Jr., that "we need . . . these countries to be strong and they cannot be strong without their colonies."[33] Policy reflected the competing claims of an American belief in freedom, fear of revolution, and racism. American policymakers imagined a middle road between immediate decolonization and the indefinite perpetuation of European colonialism, holding up the fifty-year American rule of the Philippines as a model.

In practice, this middle way proved elusive. Statements supporting colonialism in the short run while relegating decolonization to a distant future antagonized national liberation movements in Asia and the Middle East. But American anti-colonial rhetoric alienated European allies and that worried the United States more. De Gaulle was determined to regain France's Indochinese and North African territories and retain his sub-Saharan African ones. Churchill, who had immediately exempted Britain from the anti-colonial clauses of the Atlantic Charter, declared in 1942 he had not become prime minister "to preside over the liquidation of the British Empire." A popular Dutch slogan insisted, "If the Indies are lost, ruin will follow."[34]

America's contradictory attitudes produced inconsistent policies, which, however, had an underlying logic or rather competing logics. Allow decolonization if the threat of communism was deemed slight; thwart it if the economic costs to Europe and the goal of a free market global capitalist economy seemed large. Never deny the long-run desirability of colonial independence, but defer it wherever possible in order to keep Western European states a crucial part of America's anti-communist coalition. Thus, the United States refused to support Dutch efforts to regain Indonesia, where a nationalist but non-communist government under Sukarno had come to power, and threatened to withdraw Marshall Plan aid until the Dutch capitulated. It supported Indian independence in 1947 but also endorsed British efforts to retain tin- and rubber-rich Malaya for another decade by means of a brutal counterinsurgency campaign against Communists there. The United States helped prop up its influence in North Africa by taking over Britain's sphere of influence in Greece and Turkey with the Truman Doctrine. The United States posed no obstacles to France's reassertion of colonial claims. Throughout the late 1940s and 1950s, the United States supported European colonial rule in sub-Saharan Africa, urging colonial powers to promote economic and social development. This alienated Africans, but American policymakers' desire to win hearts and minds was outweighed by their belief that Africans were

---

[33] Wm. Roger Louis and Ronald Robinson, "The Imperialism of Decolonization," *Journal of Imperial and Commonwealth History* 23/2 (1994): 468.
[34] John Darwin, *After Tamerlane: The Rise and Fall of Global Empires, 1400–2000* (New York: Bloomsbury, 2008), 435, 439.

incapable of running an economy and state and the fear that "premature independence" would make nations easy prey for communist subversion.

There were limits, however, to how far the United States would go in support of European colonialism, as the 1956 Suez crisis showed. Both contemporaries and historians disagree about whether the Suez crisis was precipitated by Eisenhower and Dulles's refusal to fund Egypt's Aswan High Dam, by Egypt's President Nasser's nationalization of the Suez canal, by French and British determination to hang onto their colonial influence in the region, or by Israeli willingness to cooperate with them to gain greater security. In pursuit of their far-reaching ambitions and confident that Egypt could not run the canal alone, Britain, France, and Israel attacked Egypt, determined to teach Nasser a lesson and perhaps overthrow him. The Americans had not been consulted, however, and strongly opposed the war. When diplomatic pressure on its allies failed, the United States played the economic card, refusing to help Britain with its dollar drain and falling pound until it ceased fighting.

The crisis reshaped Euro-American relations in key ways. Far from restoring British and French influence in the Middle East, Suez marked the end of British imperialism there, although the French would continue their costly war against the Algerian National Liberation Front for another six years before withdrawing. The Suez debacle forced Britain to acknowledge that it lacked the economic and military might to pursue an independent foreign policy against American wishes. France drew a different lesson, becoming more distrustful of the United States and determined to build up its own military and nuclear might. Suez was no clear-cut victory for the United States, however. Occurring at the same time as the Hungarian Revolution, it limited America's ability to gain a propaganda victory from Soviet repression, for the British and French were engaging in the same kind of illegal military intervention. Of longer-term importance, it drew the United States ever more deeply into the Middle East: in 1957 it proclaimed the Eisenhower Doctrine, which promised to support democratic and freedom-loving states in the region (of which there were few); in 1958 it sent marines into Lebanon, and it increased support for Israel.

The Middle East was only one of the areas into which the United States moved to fill what it perceived as the vacuums left by declining European influence. After the Communist victory in China, the United States, as the sole occupying power in Japan, became the dominant Western power in East Asia. With the Truman Doctrine and the establishment of the United States naval command in the Mediterranean, the United States took over the former British role there. Determined to avoid another Pearl Harbor, the United States got special trusteeship over Pacific Islands, which the

Japanese had held or to which Britain and New Zealand laid claim. The United States also strengthened its interests in Latin America via the 1947 Rio Treaty. In 1955 the South East Asian Treaty Organization (SEATO) and the Baghdad Pact attempted to build counterparts to NATO in areas considered crucial to United States interests. The United States both reasserted the informal empire of free trade, which it had long promoted, and constructed a new "empire of bases." United States military power was anchored at both ends of the Eurasian continent, spanned the Americas, and spread across key islands in the Pacific and Atlantic. By 1955 the United States had 450 military installations in thirty-six countries.[35]

The growing dominance of the United States in what has aptly been called "the imperialism of decolonization" became further evident in the 1950s, as it intervened in Third World nations and inherited the European colonial mantle in the Middle East and Indochina.[36] Sometimes the United States cooperated with its Western European allies, at other times it acted alone. In 1953, for example, the United States and Britain collaborated to overthrow the prime minister of Iran, Mohammed Mossadeq, who had nationalized the oil industry. This joint venture put Iran securely within the Western orbit, gave the United States a significant stake in its lucrative oil holdings, and moved it one step closer to supplanting Britain as the major power in the region. A year later it worked alone to oust Jacobo Arbenz, the president of Guatemala, who had implemented land reform. In both coups, Americans touted the danger of communist subversion as the justification for deposing democratically elected rulers, who were not communists, but whose economic policies were deemed a threat to both specific Western economic interests and the goal of an open capitalist global economy. As the returning French found themselves embroiled in a prolonged struggle with Viet Minh forces led by Ho Chi Minh, the United States provided extensive military and economic aid. After the French defeat at Dien Bien Phu in 1954, the United States took over the French role of promoting conservative alternatives to the victorious nationalist Communist forces.

As was America's wont, in Vietnam as elsewhere, it did not rule directly, but rather sent advisors, provided aid, engaged in covert actions, and sought local rulers who would be competent, honest, anti-communist, and popular – no easy task. Nonetheless, the United States inherited the problems and pitfalls of previous colonial rulers and exacerbated them by seeing countries exclusively in Cold War terms and being insensitive to

---

[35] Darwin, *After Tamerlane*, 471. Chalmers Johnson, *Sorrows of Empire: Militarism, Secrecy and the End of the Republic* (New York: Metropolitan, 2004), 5.

[36] Louis and Robinson. "Imperialism of Decolonization."

nationalism and desires for neutralism. That tendency was exacerbated by growing Soviet interest in the Third World.

The Soviet Union and the Third World

Stalin had paid as little attention to the non-European world after 1945 as he had in the interwar years. Building Soviet socialism and creating a ring of friendly or at least subordinate states in Central Europe and the Balkans remained his top priority. Despite his ideological commitment to anti-colonialism, Stalin did not engage in revolutionary adventurism. Although he pushed into Turkey and Iran when the war ended, he quickly withdrew in the face of Western opposition. He did not encourage Mao to seize power in China but did offer large loans and much technical aid once the revolution succeeded. Nor was he the driving force behind the Korean War; it was Kim Il Sung, the ruler of the Democratic People's Republic of Korea, who secured the support of Stalin and Mao. Although the Soviets supplied aid, they refused to send ground troops.

Khrushchev took much more interest in the Third World. Buoyed by the wave of decolonization and encouraged by the emergence of leaders like India's Nehru, Ghana's Nkrumah, and Indonesia's Sukarno, Khrushchev courted newly independent nations. In 1955 he toured India, Afghanistan, and Burma and offered loans to Egypt and India. Afghanistan got $3.5 million in credits and the Soviets built two grain elevators, a flour mill, and a bread factory. Irrigation systems, roads, oil storage tanks, and a technical institute in Kabul followed later. Khrushchev offered Nasser arms and funds for the Aswan High Dam, threatened to attack Britain and France if the war continued, and sought to maintain a foothold in the Middle East thereafter. In 1960 the Peoples' Friendship University, whose mission was to educate Asian, African, and Latin American students, opened in Moscow, as did new institutes to study Africa and Latin America.

Khrushchev's initiatives created enormous anxiety in the Eisenhower administration and brought Soviets and Americans into competition for influence over the non-communist Asian and African nations that came together at the 1955 Bandung Conference and sought to promote South–South trade and cooperation and find an independent position between the two blocs. Washington was as staunchly opposed to neutralism in the Third World as it was in Europe, believing that it opened countries to Soviet political influence and was morally reprehensible. While the Soviets worried about the independence of the nonaligned movement, they welcomed it as a break with the imperialist West.

More direct confrontations occurred in Africa, where the Americans continued to back colonial powers and from the mid 1950s warned of the dangers of Soviet colonialism. The Congo, which gained its independence from Belgium in 1960 but quickly descended into civil war, was the first battleground. The Americans, like the Belgians, opposed the new prime minister, Patrice Lumumba, viewing him as the African equivalent of Castro. The United States blocked UN intervention to stabilize the new government and prevent mineral-rich Katanga from seceding and discussed plans to poison Lumumba; the Soviets sent economic and military aid to support Lumumba. Neither superpower controlled the situation, however, and Lumumba was assassinated by the forces of Mobuto, who would rule the Congo, renamed Zaire, dictatorially from 1965 to 1990. Deftly exploiting anti-communism, he had the full support of the United States, France, and Belgium. For the remainder of the Cold War, Soviet and American conflicts in and about the Third World would eclipse those in relatively stable Europe.

Development

These conflicts involved economics as much as politics. From the 1950s on development was a favorite slogan of Americans, Soviets, Western Europeans, and Third World leaders and economists, but it meant quite different things to different groups. All proponents of development promised to transform rather than exploit Third World economies; they spoke glowingly of growth, technology, and modernization. But these concrete markers of progress were to be achieved by quite different means and to serve incompatible social and political ends. Americans and Soviets offered the same models of development to the Third World that they followed at home and promoted in the areas of Europe they controlled. They shared a determination to master nature, an unbounded faith in technology, a reliance on expert over local knowledge, and a love of gigantic projects. Both Soviets and Americans funded big hydroelectric dams, vast steel mills, sweeping infrastructure projects, and mechanized, chemically fertilized agriculture. Both promised rapid economic growth and social transformation to be achieved through social engineering on a grand scale.

The United States insisted that development could best be promoted by Third World self-help and private sector investment. For American policy planners and development economists like Walt Rostow and Max Millikan, modernization, their preferred term, would prove the virtues of the United States model by transforming economies through private capital rather than state direction. Modernization, as Rostow outlined in *The Stages of Economic Growth: A Non-Communist Manifesto* in 1960, would enable the Third World to move through the disruptive transition to industrial capitalism without falling prey to communism.[37]

European colonial powers had begun modernization projects in the thirties and forties to provide ideological legitimation for colonial rule and continued them in Africa until it became too expensive. After decolonization Western Europeans were primarily concerned that developing economies retain ties to their former colonial rulers and granted bilateral aid accordingly. Used to state planning and intervention at home, they did not share the American objections to mixed economies abroad. But until the mid 1960s, Western European countries were too focused on reconstruction and modernization at home to invest heavily in development projects in the Third World.

The Soviets insisted that their state-run, highly centralized development model was more suited for export to the Third World than either American capitalism or China's more agrarian and decentralized socialism. It had rapidly industrialized backward Russia, was transforming the virgin lands of Kazakhstan into an agricultural paradise – or so Khrushchev fantasized – and created the world's most advanced space program. Elements of the Soviet model of planning and collectivism could be embraced by mixed economies, and the Soviets were willing to fund not only Communist China but also countries like India, Egypt, and Afghanistan to keep them at least partially out of the capitalist orbit.

Many Third World politicians and economists, such as Raul Prebisch, ascribed their problems not to backwardness, as both Soviets and Americans did, but to dependency on the capitalist world, which kept them underdeveloped. While they subscribed to the same high-tech, large-scale, expert-directed model of transformation that Europeans and Americans advocated, they insisted it could be achieved only through import substitution industrialization. They strove to represent Third World interests through the United Nations Conference on Trade and Development (UNCTAD) out of which the Group of 77 (G-77) grew. They lobbied not only against the American push for free trade and access to resources but also against the European Economic Community's exclusion of Third World agrarian imports and efforts to find synthetics to replace colonial raw materials.

Throughout the 1950s and early 1960s, there was very little aid given by the World Bank or the UN and very little multilateral development coordination. Each nation targeted strategic states and ran its own

---

[37] W. W. Rostow, *The Stages of Economic Growth: A Non-Communist Manifesto* (Cambridge University Press, 1960).

programs. The United States focused its military and economic aid on what it regarded as front-line Cold War states like Pakistan, Turkey, Iran, South Vietnam, and South Korea but provided little to Latin America until the Soviets began furnishing aid. The Soviets, who had many fewer resources to dispense, first focused on China, but after the Sino-Soviet split, made loans and provided technical aid to an array of countries in Asia, Africa, and Latin America. Under Khrushchev, the Soviets gave nearly twice as much economic assistance as military aid, but Brezhnev and his successors reversed that. India, Egypt, and Afghanistan were the primary recipients. Nehru, for example, who looked to the Soviet Union as an economic model, welcomed Soviet aid for state sector projects. By the late 1960s the Soviets had given over $1 billion dollars to vast undertakings, such as the Bhilai Steel complex, which produced one-fifth of India's steel. But India took United States aid money for agriculture and rural community development. The Soviets ran development projects in northern Afghanistan in the 1950s and 1960s, while the Americans ran them in the southern part of the country.

Neither donors nor recipients got the results they anticipated. Aid failed to produce the economic development both superpowers desired, for both underestimated the obstacles to growth and modernization. Nor did aid produce the hoped-for increase in trade and political loyalty. The Third World tried to gather resources from Soviets, Americans, and Western Europeans alike, while developing their own mixed economies and often pursuing nonalignment. But that became increasingly hard. In return for aid the United States demanded access to markets, the right to repatriate profits, and the exclusion of communists from government. West Germany enforced the Hallstein Doctrine that prohibited aid to any country, such as Egypt, that recognized East Germany. The Soviets imposed fewer restrictions but of necessity aid came in the form of loans or credits from which Soviet goods, often of an inferior sort, were to be purchased. Despite these limitations, Soviets, Americans, and Europeans, locked in Cold War competition, continued to increase bilateral development spending.

By the mid 1960s the shape of the new global order was clear. European colonialism was finished, except for the Portuguese colonies in Africa and Macau and the British outpost of Hong Kong. The Soviets solidified their power in Europe, but the myth of worldwide monolithic communism was shattered by the Sino-Soviet split and competing claims to global revolutionary leadership. The United States empire of free trade, financial hegemony, and military bases was secure. Parts of the world, such as Europe, were ruled by persuasion and consent; other parts, like Japan, adjusted to the economic and political order imposed by America, while still other areas, such as Latin America and Iran, required subversion and force in addition to economic and military aid. The American empire did not look like its European predecessors, for it eschewed territorial control and direct rule. It stressed mutual economic benefits, even if it often failed to deliver those to the Third World. American hegemony was couched in the language of anti-colonialism, even if those claims rang hollow to many outside the United States and Europe. What American journalist Walter Lippmann wrote in 1927 was even more accurate in the postwar decades:

The rest of the world will continue to think of us as an empire. Foreigners pay attention to what we say. They observe what we do. We on the other hand think of what we feel. And the result is that we go on creating what mankind calls an empire while we continue to believe quite sincerely that it is not an empire because it does not feel to us the way we imagine an empire ought to feel.[38]

---

[38] Walter Lippmann, *Men of Destiny*, cited in David Ryan, "By Way of Introduction: The United States, Decolonization and the World System," in David Ryan and Victor Pungong, eds., *The United States and Decolonization: Power and Freedom* (Basingstoke: Palgrave Macmillan, 2000), 18–19.

8   Culture wars

Cultural conflicts abounded in the postwar transatlantic world. Many involved the Americanization – actual or imagined – of Western European high culture, popular entertainment, and everyday life. Americanization was hardly new but was greatly intensified by United States postwar prosperity, business and government determination to export cultural products and the American way of life, and the pervasive crisis on the other side of the Atlantic. While some Western Europeans welcomed Americanization, many others, east and west, viewed culture as a terrain on which to fight to preserve their national patrimony and identities. And Eastern European communists felt almost as threatened by the soft power of American movies and music as by American troops and nukes.

Other cultural conflicts were an integral part of the Cold War, for the superpowers and their allies and satellites took culture seriously and viewed it as political. Soviets and Americans saw culture as a vehicle to assert the superiority of their own system, arouse envy and discontent in the enemy camp, and win adherents for communism or capitalist democracy. At home it was a means to manufacture consent and create new men and women. Culture was defined capaciously and fought over in multiple arenas ranging from elite art exhibits and operas through urban design and academic exchanges to movies and sports. It included consumer culture and domesticity as well. Cultural competition spanned the public and private, involved business and states, and targeted everyone from intellectuals and artists to youth and housewives.

Sometimes Americanization and Cold War cultural competition ran on separate tracks but often they intersected. Earlier in the twentieth century, Americanization was associated with private sector initiatives; after 1945 the state often launched or subsidized Americanization efforts, making them an integral part of Cold War struggles. This emerged clearly in American and Soviet cultural diplomacy, the official state-sponsored or -encouraged cultural programs of the first Cold War decades. Americanization of an earlier sort persisted in the dramatic penetration of American mass culture into Western and to some extent Eastern Europe. (There was no Soviet counterpart to export.) In these arenas the United States promoted its ideas and products more successfully than the Soviets or Western Europeans but never as fully as they wished. Americanization was least successful in the three-way competition among Soviets, Europeans, and the United States over how to rebuild war-ravaged European cities and reshape homes and the new consumer culture built around them. Behind conflicts over what should be seen and heard, built and bought, lay disagreements about what cultural products and practices were desirable and what forms of everyday life and gender relations should be encouraged.

Ideas, goods, and individuals moved in multiple directions: from the now hegemonic United States to a declining Europe, from the Soviet Union to its reluctant satellites, and within Europe along multiple east–west and north–south trajectories. Some cultural exports were easily identifiable as American or Soviet or European, but many had compli-cated biographies and changed shape and meaning in different settings. Did this complex circulation of cultural norms, models, goods, and personnel across national borders, the Atlantic, and the Iron Curtain create hybrid cultures in Europe? Or did becoming modern – and European cultures and lifestyles became emphatically more modern in the decades after 1945 – necessarily mean becoming Americanized?

Cultural diplomacy

Cultural diplomacy was the overt and legal part of psychological warfare; rather than destabilizing enemy regimes, it sought to win hearts and minds. (Although the line between the two was often thin, for they shared ideological beliefs and often personnel.) Both Soviets and Americans directed some cultural diplomacy programs at one another, but the main cultural battlegrounds lay initially in Europe and later in the Third World. The Soviets sought to reshape Eastern European cultures and instill positive attitudes toward the Soviet Union. Americans, according to the United States Information Agency (USIA),

are in competition with Soviet Communism primarily for the opinion of the free world. We are (especially) concerned with the uncommitted, the wavering, the confused, the apathetic, or the doubtful within the free world.[1]

---

[1] Kenneth A. Osgood, "Hearts and Minds: The Unconventional Cold War," *Journal of Cold War Studies* 4/2 (Spring 2002): 99.

Cultural diplomacy was also a potential means by which the United States and the Soviet Union could each make their claim to be a *Kulturnation* on a par with France or Germany or Italy.

Soviets and Americans invested heavily in cultural diplomacy, but at differential rates. The Soviets pioneered cultural diplomacy in the interwar years through programs arranged for Western visitors to the USSR and in the anti-fascist Popular Front. The United States developed information and propaganda organizations during World War II, only to shut them down in 1945. It revived them when it intervened in the 1948 Italian elections by channeling money to the Vatican, non-communist parties, and probably even organized crime, mobilizing Americans to write letters to their Italian relatives, and threatening economic reprisals if the Communists won. Determined to combat communism globally, Congress passed the Smith–Mundt Act, which established informational and educational exchange programs, which soon operated in ninety-three countries. The Soviets spent lavishly on the Society for Cultural Relations with Foreign Countries (VOKS), its successor the State Committee for Cultural Ties, and the Soviet Information Bureau as well as the Cominform and front organizations like the World Peace Council (WPC). One widely quoted estimate is $2 billion dollars by 1960, but Soviet statistics are notoriously unreliable. By contrast, the USIA got only $88 million in 1955, but it was not the only agency fighting on the culture front.[2] The State Department, the White House, the CIA, and the Department of Defense were involved, and the United States developed more voluntarist state-private networks that included the Ford Foundation, the Advertising Council, and the Congress for Cultural Freedom.

These state agencies, front organizations, and quasi-civil society associations collaborated on overarching propaganda efforts, such as the Soviet Peace Campaign, Truman's Campaign for Truth, and Eisenhower's People's Capitalism initiative. The rhetoric they produced remained remarkably consistent. The Soviets championed peace and disarmament, contrasted socialist egalitarianism to capitalist exploitation, national liberation to American imperialism, and criticized United States race relations. The United States, according to USIA deputy directory Abbott Washburn, should emphasize its essential values, foremost among which were "Belief in God. Belief in the right to ownership of property and better living for each individual. Belief in the family as sacred." American democratic capitalism

---

[2] Laura A. Belmonte, *Selling the American Way: United States Propaganda and the Cold War* (Philadelphia: University of Pennsylvania Press, 2008), 67. Philip M. Taylor, *Munitions of the Mind: A History of Propaganda* (Manchester University Press, 2003), 256.

was superior not only to communism but also to Europe's "cartel-like or feudalistic capitalism," for it provided high wages, abundant consumer goods, social welfare, and opportunities for African-Americans. Yet Americans were not materialistic, for religion shaped all aspects of society in contrast to atheistic Russia.[3]

Each insisted that their society was classless and their economy superior, but Soviets measured success in terms of science and technology, especially after Sputnik, while Americans stressed consumption. Each praised its own literature, art, and music and argued that Western and Central European claims of cultural superiority were unjustified. Each purported to have achieved equality for women, but Americans defined that in terms of home, family, and volunteer community work, not paid employment and collective childcare as the Soviets did. Soviet propaganda portrayed American women as lazy, promiscuous, materialistic, and distinctly unequal. The Soviets presented their message in stilted language, often misjudged their audiences, and lacked access to the Western press. Americans drew on a long tradition of advertising, but snappy style did not necessarily guarantee acceptance of the message.

Radio was a principle tool for cultural diplomacy. The United States-sponsored VOA and RFE initially criticized communism and called for liberation, but by the late fifties devoted more time to music, cultural discussions, and descriptions of the American way of life. The Soviets, who had provided most households with radios, either jammed these stations or tried to counter their political messages and cultural offerings. They were less successful in doing that in Eastern Europe and had no access to American radio, let alone television audiences.

Magazines played a limited propaganda role between the United States and the Soviet Union, for the foreign press could be readily excluded, and the nonpolitical, picture magazines, exchanged by official agreement, circulated to very restricted audiences. *Amerika*, focused on consumer goods, science and technology, and inspirational biographies, *Soviet Life* on high culture, science, education, healthcare, and national minorities. In Western Europe, however, magazines played a central role in United States efforts to build bridges between American and European anti-communist intellectuals.

Soviets and Americans worked assiduously to woe the broad educated public in their spheres of influence. In Berlin, for example, the Soviets revived opera and theater immediately after 1945 and opened a House of Culture. Throughout the Cold War they sent translated books, plays, and

---

[3] Belmonte, *Selling the American Way*, 58, 121.

movies to all Eastern European countries and opened libraries and reading rooms as well. The Americans were most active in Germany, where by 1951 they had established twenty-seven America Houses in cities and 135 reading rooms in smaller towns to encourage Germans to learn about and emulate the United States. The America Houses held lectures on topics ranging from "What We Can Learn from America" to "The Meaning of Kant for American Culture," and in Munich sponsored regular talks and fashion shows for women. Germans flocked to these libraries with their broad array of older and contemporary American authors. In 1953, however, under pressure from Senator McCarthy and to the dismay of West Germans, the America House libraries purged all books by Communists and suspected fellow travelers, including works by the mystery writer Dashiell Hammett, the black poet Langston Hughes, and journalist and novelist Agnes Smedley. The United States government attacked state-controlled culture, even as it produced a version of it.[4]

Peace versus freedom

Competition was most intense for the allegiance of intellectuals. The Soviets began mobilizing artists, scholars, and scientists at the 1948 World Congress of Intellectuals for Peace in Wroclav, Poland, attended by delegates from forty-six countries, including such luminaries as Pablo Picasso. Peace was the central organizing theme, and the French and Polish Communists set up Partisans for Peace. A second Cultural and Scientific Conference for World Peace was held at the Waldorf Astoria hotel in New York City in 1949. Whether Moscow totally controlled this conference and the National Committee of Arts, Sciences, and Professions, which planned it, and how free debate was among the politically diverse audience are still intensely disputed. What is clear is that the State Department refused visas to many Communists and a counter group, Americans for Intellectual Freedom, disrupted the proceedings and planned a counter organization. Peace became a contested political term over which the Communists asserted ownership.

In 1949 over two thousand delegates attended the Paris conference that established the WPC. Heavily funded by the Soviet Union, the WPC drew political support from Communist parties around the globe, atomic scientists, increasingly worried about nuclear proliferation, and members of

---

[4] Axel Schildt, "Die USA als 'Kulturnation': Zur Bedeutung der Amerikahäuser in den 1950er Jahren," in Alf Lüdtke, Inge Marssolek, and Adelheid von Saldern, eds., *Amerikanisierung: Traum oder Alpentraum in Deutschland des 20. Jahrhunderts* (Stuttgart: Franz Steiner, 1996), 262–67.

the wartime French resistance. French scientist and Nobel laureate Frédéric Joliot-Curie, a former resistance activist, was elected president. Its founding manifesto, which avoided attacks on America and NATO, called for peace and international regulation of atomic energy. In 1950 the WPC launched the Stockholm Peace Petition, calling for the abolition of nuclear weapons, and by 1950 100 million people from fifty countries had signed, a reflection of pervasive fears of renewed war and nuclear weapons.[5] The United States government and media condemned the Peace Petition as a cynical propaganda ploy, claimed that the numerous Eastern European signatures were coerced, and insisted national security was the prerequisite for peace. They actively discouraged Americans and Western Europeans from signing.

To counter the Soviet peace campaign, Americans raised the banner of freedom. Enthusiastic cold warriors, backed by anti-communist intellectuals such as the philosopher Sidney Hook, the writer Mary McCarthy, the critic Dwight McDonald, and the historian Arthur Schlesinger, set up the Congress for Cultural Freedom (CCF). It sought to rally Western Europe's disillusioned ex-Communists and non-communist leftists to combat totalitarianism, defend Western freedom in an Atlanticist community, and eschew neutralism. George Orwell, Arthur Koestler, Ignazio Silone, and Raymond Aron were among the most prominent figures who joined.

The CCF devoted most of its attention to Europe, for in America McCarthyism had solidified a Cold War consensus, while the commitments of European intellectuals were less clear. Even those disliking communism were not necessarily enthusiastic about America. To woo them, the CCF published hundreds of histories, memoirs, and novels, many by the anti-communist left, such as Koestler's *The God that Failed* and Schlesinger's *The Vital Center*. Conferences like the 1949 International Day of Resistance to Dictatorship and War in Paris brought together European and American intellectuals and artists to warn of the twin dangers of communism and neutralism. Most importantly, the CCF founded and funded high-quality, anti-communist magazines of cultural and political analysis. Britain got *Encounter*, France *Preuves*, Italy *Tempo Presente*, and Germany *Der Monat*.

The CCF claimed to promote free intellectual exchange and a robust civil society from a position of political and financial independence. In fact, it was secretly funded by the CIA's International Organizations Division, which in turn drew on Marshall Plan counterpart funds and

[5] Scott Lucas, *Freedom's War: The American Crusade against the Soviet Union* (New York University Press, 1999), 97.

periodic supplementary monies from the Ford Foundation. The CIA intervened in day-to-day operations only sporadically, as, for example, when it pushed out Koestler because his passionate anti-communism threatened to alienate European intellectuals. But extensive coordination was not necessary, for the CIA and the CCF shared a political worldview and collaboration was voluntary. Many leading CCF figures knew about CIA funding, but others as well as the general public were left in the dark. When CIA funding was exposed in 1967, a public uproar ensued and the CCF lost much credibility on both sides of the Atlantic. Some leading figures like Stephen Spender and Isaiah Berlin resigned, but many CCF activists justified distasteful means by the ends served.

The CCF successfully encouraged many centrist and moderate left intellectuals to condemn communism as totalitarianism and abandon any aspirations for a third way in favor of rapprochement with America. It was less effective in making European intellectuals into enthusiastic proponents of Americanization. Aron, for example, shared the CCF's anti-communism, but viewed American capitalism as "a model neither for humanity nor for the West."[6]

Women and youth

Soviets and Americans also competed to influence social groups viewed as politically important but ideologically susceptible to the overtures of the enemy, such as women. In December 1948 the Women's International Democratic Federation (WIDF) was established to work against a recurrence of war and fascism and for the interests of women and children. While a wide range of European women initially joined, it soon came to be considered a Soviet front organization. The United States State Department and Bureau of Labor tried to counter Soviet initiatives, especially in occupied Germany, by running democracy education programs for women. Across Western Europe American women's organizations, ranging from the League of Women Voters and the American Association of University Women to the Young Women's Christian Association, the National Council of Negro Women, and the National Federation of Business and Professional Women's Clubs joined in these efforts. They emphasized democracy but not feminism, rejected women's associations affiliated with political parties, and promoted American-style voluntary organizations. As the Cold War escalated, they focused on anti-communism and abandoned their internationalism for Cold War

---

[6] Volker Berghahn, *America and the Intellectual Cold Wars in Europe* (Princeton University Press, 2001), 94–95.

nationalism. They denounced the WIDF, rejected any criticism of American labor or race relations in the UN Commission on Women, and condemned the Stockholm Peace Petition. Like male cold warriors, they feared that women's emotional nature and maternal instincts made them susceptible to pleas for peace. American women activists then formed the Committee of Correspondence (CoC) to influence leaders of women's organizations in Europe and Asia, but its strident anti-communism alienated many Europeans. The CoC claimed to be an independent civil society initiative, but it too was funded by the CIA.[7]

Youth were another prime target of competitive organizing. The Soviets took the initiative, establishing the World Federation of Democratic Youth and the International Union of Students and sponsoring world festivals of youth every few years from 1947 on in Prague, Berlin, Bucharest, and Warsaw. The festivals brought communist youth together under the slogans of peace and international friendship, drew in non-communists, and increasingly reached out to the Third World. They had the unintended effect of bringing the world into the closed societies of Eastern Europe, as Moscow learned, when it hosted the largest festival in 1957. Americans and Western Europeans worked with mixed success to keep their youth away. Britain formed its own World Association of Youth and National Students Union, while the CIA covertly funded groups like the United States National Student Association and its work in Europe. The United States never attempted to hold mass counter festivals, relying instead on the power of American popular culture to win over youth.

Cultural exchanges

Educational and cultural exchanges were a vital part of cultural diplomacy. Until the late 1950s, however, American exchange programs focused exclusively on Western Europe. The Marshall Plan sponsored trips for innumerable European businessmen, trade unionists, and engineers to study the United States economy and for academics, journalists, and politicians to learn about democracy, civil society, and the American way of life. The Fulbright Program, begun in 1946, sent American students and professors abroad and brought foreign ones to the United States in order to promote mutual understanding. The Salzburg Seminar in American Studies, established in 1947 by Harvard students and subsequently funded by American foundations, gathered young European and American students together to foster American Studies in Europe. Much

---

[7] Helen Laville, *Cold War Women: The International Activities of American Women's Organizations* (Manchester University Press, 2002).

less is known about Soviet exchanges with Eastern European states, but Eastern Europeans did study in Russia and their governments mandated Russian as the primary foreign language. Soviet-American exchanges were nonexistent, for after the relative openness of World War II, the Soviet Union retreated into isolation. Citizens were forbidden to marry foreigners and admonished not to "grovel before the West," and Stalin launched a strongly anti-Semitic campaign against cosmopolitanism. At the same time the McCarran Acts severely restricted the entry of Soviets and East Europeans into the United States.

After Stalin's death the Soviets pushed for more cultural openness, hoping educational and cultural exchanges would enhance security, expand trade, and provide access to Western science and technology. The United States was initially reluctant, but came to view exchanges as a way to encourage consumer desires in communist countries and thereby promote regime change. In 1958 the United States and the Soviet Union signed the Lacy–Zarubin Agreement on Exchanges in Cultural, Technical, and Educational Fields. The Soviets sent scientists and technicians to America, while the United States sent humanists eastward, and sports teams traveled in both directions. A few privileged and loyal Soviets visited America, and twelve thousand Americans toured the Soviet Union in 1959. The most popular exchanges involved musicians and dancers, including the cellist Mstislav Rostropovich and the Bolshoi Ballet from the Soviet Union and the Boston Symphony and Dizzy Gillespie from America. Hoping to improve Russian as well as Western European views of American racism, the government sent African-American artists such as Louis Armstrong and Marian Anderson.

Painting presented more problems for both sides. In 1946 the United States sent the Advancing American Art exhibit, containing impressionist, expressionist, and abstract works, to Paris and Prague; the Soviets countered with a display of socialist realism in Prague. The lines seemed clearly drawn and many have concluded that America "stole the idea of modern Art" and co-opted the avant-garde for Cold War liberalism.[8] The story is much messier. Although the CIA and USIA, encouraged by the Museum of Modern Art (MoMA), promoted abstract expressionism, government officials and congressmen condemned it as communist art and insisted that more representational painting replace or supplement it. Although many Soviet artists and young members of the Thaw generation embraced modern art, many others condemned it as bourgeois and decadent. There was no consensus in either the United States or the Soviet Union about

---

[8] Serge Guilbaut, *How New York Stole the Idea of Modern Art: Abstract Expressionism, Freedom, and the Cold War* (University of Chicago Press, 1983).

what sort of painting should properly represent their respective high cultures and political ideologies.

These varied ventures in cultural diplomacy were part of a European and transatlantic civil war, fought at times ferociously over the Enlightenment heritage. The United States came closer to promoting anti-communism and marginalizing neutralism in Western Europe than the Soviets did in manufacturing consent in Eastern Europe. Yet, cultural diplomacy did not convince most Western Europeans that America was a cultural leader on a par with Europe. In a 1950 public opinion poll, 62 percent of West Germans said Americans could learn from Germany in the cultural sphere and the number increased thereafter. Fewer than 10 percent of Western Europeans in a 1956 survey thought the United States was doing enough to improve race relations.[9] Some observers claim that cultural diplomacy was instrumental in shaping those Soviets who became reformers, but historians of the Soviet Union are skeptical, arguing that dissidents did not embrace American culture and politics or initially give up hope of reforming communism. Nor, as 1968 and its aftermath were to show, did either Americans or Soviets secure the allegiance of the younger generation.

By the late 1960s cultural diplomacy had petered out. The Soviet invasion of Czechoslovakia discredited its peace campaign, while the exposure of CIA funding delegitimized the CCF and many other organizations. Educational and cultural exchanges had become routine. Was the export of American mass culture more successful?

Coca-Cola, rock 'n' roll, and Hollywood

Although American policymakers and intellectuals offered Europeans abstract expressionism and serious literature as alternatives, Hollywood films and rock 'n' roll were more popular. As we have seen, elements of American popular culture had crossed the Atlantic from the late nineteenth century on, receiving both praise and condemnation. In his 1941 "American Century" essay, Luce claimed that "American jazz, Hollywood movies, American slang" along with "American machines and patented products" had already created "an immense American internationalism." They were "the only things that every community in the world, from Zanzibar to Hamburg, recognizes in common."[10] After 1945 American movies, music, and blue jeans spread across Europe due

---

[9] Belmonte, *Selling the American Way*, 133, 170. Schildt, "Die USA," 268.
[10] Henry Luce, "The American Century," *Life*, February 1941.

to aggressive American marketing, United States government support, and the presence of hundreds of thousands of GIs. They filled the cultural vacuum created by the collapse of fascism and the discrediting of intellectual elites who had collaborated with it. And on the terrain of popular culture, the Soviets offered no competition.

The new music, movies, dances, dress styles, and foods appealed above all to younger Europeans, creating a transatlantic youth culture in which America was a central referent. Older generations, however, were deeply ambivalent when not outright hostile, believing that American mass culture contributed to social and cultural modernization, created moral danger and gender disorder, and seduced Europeans away from their national values and cultural heritage. In Western as well as Eastern Europe, governments and elites alternated between repressing American music and movies, reluctantly tolerating them, and dismissing them as harmless diversions.

Take Coca-Cola, that quintessentially American beverage. The Coca-Cola Company opened its first European bottling plant in Germany in 1929 and dozens more followed, while the Nazis tried to recode the popular drink as German. Britain had a much smaller Coca-Cola operation, but expansion into the rest of Europe began only when American troops arrived. After Pearl Harbor, Coca-Cola president Robert Woodruff promised "every man in uniform gets a bottle of Coca-Cola for five cents, wherever he is and whatever it costs our company." It was a brilliant marketing ploy, which the government and military supported by exempting the company from sugar rations and facilitating the transport of bottling plants to American troops fighting in North Africa and Italy as well as the Pacific. At war's end, the company opened permanent bottling plants in the Netherlands, Belgium, Luxemburg, Switzerland, Italy, and France and resumed production in West Germany.[11]

Coke occupied a central place in the American beverage market but met a decidedly ambivalent response in Western Europe. Manufacturers of wine, beer, fruit juices, and mineral water rallied against the new drink, asserting it contained dangerous amounts of caffeine and failed to disclose all ingredients as local laws required. Italian Communists claimed Coke turned children's hair white, while their French comrades insisted its distribution system might serve as a spy network. According to *Le Monde*, Coke was attacking France's "most vulnerable point . . . the

---

[11] Mark Pendergrast, *For God, Country and Coca-Cola: The Unauthorized History of the Great American Soft Drink and the Company that Makes It* (New York: Charles Scribner, 1993), 199–202, 225–28. Richard Kuisel, *Seducing the French: The Dilemma of Americanization* (Berkeley: University of California, 1993), 52.

national beverage." The French Ministry of Finance worried about Coke's effects on the nation's balance of payments, while the Catholic press saw it as the "avant-garde of an offensive aimed at economic colonization." French government efforts to limit Coca-Cola's expansion failed, however, less because of the drink's popularity than because United States Ambassador David Bruce warned of "possible serious repercussions," if restrictions were enacted. The American press reminded the French that they were obligated to allow American business in because the United States had saved France in two world wars. Moreover, one editorial asserted, "You can't spread the doctrines of Marx among people who drink Coca-Cola."[12]

While Coca-Cola was conquering new European markets after 1945, Hollywood tried to regain those lost to fascist protectionism and Nazi conquests. It was well positioned to do so, for it had money, talented writers and directors from America and Europe, and stars of international renown, as well as a vast backlog of films never shown in Europe that promised to deliver to eager audiences the quality entertainment for which Hollywood was famous. Recognizing the political usefulness of movies, the State Department and American occupation officials worked closely with leading industry figures to secure unrestricted access to European markets and recognition of film as a commodity like any other, not a cultural object deserving of special treatment.

They disagreed, however, on how to achieve their shared goals. Hollywood claimed its films would promote democracy, anti-communism, and goodwill toward America, but government officials worried that gangster movies, tales of corruption, and depictions of divorce and sexual scandal conveyed precisely the wrong image. While American audiences could separate fantasy from reality, European ones might not be able to do so. American movie producers were eager to shut down or take over the German film industry, their only serious European competitor, but the State Department insisted on rebuilding a German cinema. Hollywood retaliated by holding first-run movies off the German market. While Hollywood agreed not to show some films, such as the *Grapes of Wrath*, which might spur leftist criticism of the United States, it did produce *Desert Fox* about German General Rommel, ignoring State Department fears that the film might seem to whitewash Nazism and endorse German remilitarization. Hollywood put profits over politics, while the government juggled competing priorities.

---

[12] Kuisel, *Seducing the French*, 54–64.

Although Hollywood did regain much of its earlier influence across Western Europe, it was unable to achieve the total dominance it desired due to European poverty and dollar shortages and determination to rebuild national film industries. Hollywood was not able to secure free trade in films, but neither were Western European countries able to enforce quotas on American movies. When Britain placed a high tariff on American films, Hollywood imposed a total boycott on Britain, and in the face of popular unhappiness and a need for American loans, the Attlee government capitulated. France successfully bargained for more modest concessions regarding screening rights – American films could be shown eight out of every thirteen weeks. Italy, which imported the most American films in the immediate postwar years – 600 in 1945–46 alone – passed legislation requiring that revenues from American film showings remain in Italy.[13] This encouraged Hollywood to produce jointly with European studios or film in Italy rather than export movies made in America.

As a result of unequal power relations, American films penetrated Western Europe as never before, but some national film industries nonetheless flourished. By the 1960s Italian cinema did well by imitating American costume dramas and historical spectacles, producing spaghetti westerns, promoting its own international stars, like Sophia Loren, and exporting its movies. France developed the New Wave in the sixties, and West Germany produced distinctive national genres such as the *Heimatfilme*. Throughout the 1950s and 1960s, domestic films overwhelmingly dominated the list of top ten movies there.

American films were undoubtedly very popular, but did they Americanize Europeans or promote pro-American attitudes? Some European observers regard American movies as part of a "colonization of the European subconscious" and a key means by which "the American Dream of the pursuit of happiness and mass consumption became the European Dream."[14] Yet, like any widely distributed cultural product, films had ambiguous meanings, reception varied by class, gender, generation, and education, and different identities were constructed around

[13] Jean-Pierre Jeancolas, "From the Blum-Byrnes Agreement to the GATT Affair," in Geoffrey Nowell-Smith and Steven Ricci, eds., *Hollywood and Europe: Economics, Culture, National Identity, 1945–9* (Los Angeles: BFI Publishing, 1998), 50–51. Giuliana Muscio, "Invasion and Counterattack: Italian and American Film Relations in the Postwar Period," in Reinhold Wagnleitner and Elaine Tyler May, eds., *Here, There and Everywhere: The Foreign Politics of American Popular Culture* (Hanover: University Press of New England, 2000), 120.
[14] Reinhold Wagnleitner, "American Cultural Diplomacy, the Cinema, and the Cold War in Central Europe," in David W. Ellwood and Rob Kroes, eds., *Hollywood in Europe: Experiences of a Cultural Hegemony* (Amsterdam: VU University Press, 1994), 197–98.

and against them. Some Germans, for example, enthusiastically embraced films like *Rebel without a Cause*, *Rock around the Clock*, and *Blackboard Jungle*, while other educated youth distanced themselves, and the older generation vociferously condemned both the films and the *Halbstarken* or punks who imitated them. These teen rebel films did become part of an emerging transatlantic youth culture that was shaped even more strongly by music.

American rock 'n' roll hit Europe in the mid fifties and the music scene was forever changed. Promoted by the VOA, Radio Luxembourg, and armed forces stations, as well as by records, concerts, and European imitations of American stars and songs, rock not only spread across Western and Northern Europe but also moved beyond the Iron Curtain in a way that movies and Coke could not. Bill Haley and his Comets, Chubby Checker, and above all Elvis Presley brought not only new sounds but new modes of self-presentation that were greeted with often wild enthusiasm by teenagers and students. Rock's appeals were many; there was the sheer pleasure of listening to the new vibrant and provocative music, which was seen as thoroughly American and daringly modern but not necessarily as black. There were new dance styles, in which one jumped, gyrated, flung ones arms and legs, and swiveled one's hips in imitation of Elvis's famous pelvis. Girls and boys alike shed the proper dance attire of dresses, jackets, and ties and moved apart from one another. Music, dance, and dress offered youth new ways to act out generational conflict, experiment with sexual expressiveness, and put off entry into the postwar adult world obsessed with reconstruction and productivity. For young, working-class West German men, wearing blue jeans and James Dean hairstyles, riding motorbikes, and listening to American rock were simultaneously an exaggeration of traditional prole-tarian behavior, an embrace of new American models, and a protest about their relative exclusion from Germany's economic miracle. For East Germans it was an alternative to the regime's serious, thoroughly politi-cized youth activities. Everywhere the pleasures of listening and dancing were enhanced by the horrified reactions of older generations.

American music carried different political and cultural connotations in different countries. Christian Democrats felt it threatened social restabi-lization in West Germany, while Communists in the GDR claimed it undermined socialist reconstruction, political discipline, and anti-Americanism. Italian Catholics saw rock as a moral danger, the Communists as a political one. The French worried about rock's impact on the national language, while Soviets believed it was incompatible with their more serious alternative modernity. Throughout the 1950s commu-nist countries preferred outright prohibition, except for Yugoslavia, which practiced toleration, and Hungary, which eased restrictions after 1956, seeing rock as a possible diversion from politics and infinitely preferable to revolution. Western European governments required radio stations and dance clubs to play a specified percentage of national as opposed to American songs. Record labels and music magazines promoted less threatening national role models, such as Conny Froboess and Peter Kraus in Germany and Gianni Morandi and Rita Pavone in Italy, who were hip but not sexualized, into music and media but not rebellious, and part of a teen culture that reinforced dominant values and national identity. As rock and teen rebel movies spread and the initial shock wore off, elites in West Germany and elsewhere reinterpreted them as apolitical and psychologically normal, even if offensive. American rock seemed to have found a prominent, secure, and unthreatening place in Western Europe, even if it remained much more controversial in the East.

That changed in the mid sixties, as first the Beatles and then the Rolling Stones invaded the United States and became the dominant popular musical force on the continent. Rock became European or international rather than exclusively American.[15] States became more tolerant, even in Eastern Europe. The Stones, for example, performed in Warsaw in 1967, and a vibrant if partially underground rock scene developed in Moscow. France promoted its enormously popular Elvis-like rock star Johnny Hallyday, while in the 1970s the Soviet Union did the same with the American-born Dean Reed.

As rock became more accepted, however, the youth culture of which it was an integral part took on an increasingly political edge. In the fifties rock fans had applauded American consumerism and global power, whereas the small number of more educated jazz fans criticized American racism and consumerism. By the late sixties American or American-inspired rock no longer generated support for American policies in Europe or globally, and youth on both sides of the Atlantic and Iron Curtain criticized domestic institutions and policies and rejected Cold War binaries.

International modernism versus socialist realism

Cultural competition around architecture, urban planning, and housing was also intense in the first two decades of the Cold War because the stakes were high, the needs great, the audience large, and the expectations

---

[15] Laura E. Cooper and B. Lee Cooper, "The Pendulum of Cultural Imperialism: Popular Music and Interchanges between the United States and Britain, 1943–1967," in Sabrina P. Ramet and Gordana Crnkovic, eds., *Kazaam! Splat! Poof!: The American Impact on European Popular Culture, since 1945* (Lanham, MD: Rowman and Littlefield, 2002), 74–77.

invested in reshaping the built environment inflated. Opportunities for urban redesign and housing construction abounded, for bombing and ground warfare had damaged virtually all European cities and nearly completely destroyed places like Warsaw, Dresden, and Rotterdam. War exacerbated an already acute housing deficit, for crisis-ridden interwar European economies had built little, and the Soviets gave priority to factories. From Magnitogorsk to Manchester, overcrowded homes, lacking such basic amenities as central heating and indoor plumbing, let along appliances, were the norm. Architects, urban planners, politicians, and advocates of the postwar welfare state viewed housing as a means to create economic security and stability, improve living standards, and enhance the state's popularity. They believed that transformed dwellings would reform everyday life, above all for the working classes, who were the main targets of this social engineering zeal. The built environment was expected to make political as well as aesthetic statements, reflecting and promoting socialism or democratic capitalism.

From the mid 1940s to the mid 1950s, American international modernism faced off against Soviet socialist realism, the former claiming to be the architecture of freedom and choice, the latter of socialism and popular welfare. Both architectural theories originated in the interwar period. Modernism, a transatlantic movement par excellence, developed in twenties Europe as architects from France, Germany, Holland, Sweden, and the Soviet Union elaborated new ideas about form and function, technology and materials. The European pioneers of modernism engaged with one another and traveled to America, whose skyscrapers, city planning, functional zoning, sleek grain elevators, and rationally designed factories spurred debate about what could and should be emulated.[16] But Europeans occupied center stage. The enormously prolific Frenchman Le Corbusier imagined houses as machines for living; the Dutchman J. J. P. Oud built his social housing in Rotterdam, while the Germans Martin Wagner, Ernst May, and Bruno Taut built vast social housing projects in Frankfurt and Berlin and designed in the Soviet Union during the first Five-Year Plan. In 1928 architects from across Europe and the United States established the International Congress of Modern Architecture (CIAM) to develop the principles of modernism and the functional city. In 1933 it met in Moscow, where the modernism of Soviet architects like El Lissitzky and Moise Ginzburg was still politically acceptable.

The Bauhaus was central to interwar modernism. A school of art and design, it was founded in Weimar in 1919 by Walter Gropius, operated in

---

[16] Jean-Louis Cohen, *Scenes of the World to Come: European Architecture and the American Challenge, 1893–1960* (Paris: Flammarion, 1995), 63–65.

Dessau in the late 1920s under Hannes Meyer, and moved to Berlin under Ludwig Mies van der Rohe before being closed by the Nazis in 1933. It gathered leading figures in painting, design, and architecture, from Paul Klee and Wassily Kandinsky to Marcel Breuer and Piet Mondrian. The Bauhaus theorized, experimented, designed, and more rarely actually built exteriors and interiors that broke radically with tradition. Many in the Bauhaus, like the broader German modernist movement, were sympathetic to social democracy or communism and committed to designing social housing.

Bauhaus modernism began its transatlantic migration in 1932, when MoMA staged an exhibition of European and American Modern Architecture, for which MoMA director Alfred H. Barr coined the term International Style. Bauhaus aesthetics but not its politics were embraced by Philip Johnson, who later became America's leading modern architect, but most Americans found European modernism foreign and unappealing.[17] Despite this, architects like Gropius and Mies van der Rohe soon came to America, fleeing the inhospitable anti-modernist climate of Nazi Germany.

During and after World War II, American architects and popular opinion came to embrace modernism as the architecture of democracy. *McCalls* magazine insisted that modernism would promote "our demand for a brand new life in a brand new world." Edgar Kaufmann, director of MoMA's industrial design department, insisted that "Modern design is intended to implement the lives of free individuals." According to *House and Garden* magazine, it was "the unmistakable product of democracy." The USIA and the museum community transmitted American modernism to postwar Europe via exhibits, such as the Frank Lloyd Wright shows in Zurich, Paris, Munich, and Rotterdam. The government brought European architects to America and sent European architects like Gropius back home to publicize American modernism. Marshall Plan advisors regarded "international modernism as the Esperanto of continental consumer culture," from which American and European business could benefit. Housing exhibitions, such as the American-sponsored 1952 Berlin show "We Build a Better Life," spoke of a transatlantic architecture, claiming that the housing displayed showed "how rationally designed products from different countries in the Atlantic community can be combined harmoniously." Europeans, however, regarded the generously proportioned and appliance-filled display homes as distinctly

---

[17] Cordula Grewe and Dietrich Neumann "From Manhattan to Mainhattan: Reconsidering the Transatlantic Architectural Dialogue," *Bauhaus in America and Europe, GHI Bulletin Supplement* 2 (2005): 3–4, 6.

American. In claiming modernism as its own, Americans harnessed it to Cold War anti-communism. They eliminated modernism's commitment to social housing, for even in its social democratic form, social housing was confused with socialism.[18]

Socialist realism, a prescription for style and a political program, had a more parochial history. It emerged in the 1930s as part of a broader reorientation of society in which Soviet leaders abandoned cultural experimentation and social egalitarianism in favor of gender conservatism, social hierarchy, and embourgeoisement among elites. In 1932 Stalin called for painting and literature about Soviet life that would "point out what is leading it toward socialism."[19] Socialist realism's mixture of representation and romanticism was very different from the experimental, constructivist art of the 1920s, but its pedagogical aim of projecting a new reality and educating the masses was identical.

Socialist realism rejected modernism, but what it prescribed varied; in painting representation, preferably of brawny factory workers, smiling collective farmers, or Stalin himself, became the norm; in literature didactic depictions of work and workers. Architecture was to be "socialist in content but national in form," a slogan that translated into more traditional designs, ornamental facades, and apartments of varied size and quality to reflect and reward differential status. Public buildings were monumental, statues heroic, and decoration abundant. Grandiosity, symmetry, and neoclassicism would, it was hoped, buttress the state and link Soviet culture to the timeless traditions of classical Rome.

Arriving in Eastern Europe as "the architecture of victory," socialist realism was part of Sovietization. It claimed to be the architecture of peace and an alternative to the decadent modernism associated with cosmopolitanism and American imperialism. Similar to American modernism, socialist realism was spread by study trips to the Soviet Union, exhibits, magazine articles, and Soviet advisors. Eastern Europeans returning from years in the Soviet Union like Polish architects Helena Syrkus and Edmund Goldzamt dismissed interwar modernism as inadequate to the task of transforming society. According to the East German architect Kurt Liebknecht, who had worked with Mies van der Rohe before spending the thirties in Moscow, "We are against the Bauhaus because Functionalism is the height

---

[18] George H. Marcus, *Design in the Fifties: When Everyone Went Modern* (Munich/ New York: Prestel, 1998), 56–57. David Crowley, "Europe Reconstructed, Europe Divided," in David Crowley and Jane Pavitt, eds., *Cold War Modern: Design 1945–1970* (London: V and A Publishing, 2008), 54. Greg Castillo, "Marshall Plan Modernism in Divided Germany," in Crowley and Pavitt, eds., *Cold War Modern*, 66–67, 71.

[19] Ronald Grigor Suny, *The Soviet Experiment: Russia, the USSR, and the Successor States* (New York: Oxford, 1998), 270.

of imperialist Cosmopolitanism, the height of decadence and decay." Another East German lamented that modernism "disassociate[d] the people from their native land, from their language and their culture, so that they adopt the 'American lifestyle.'"[20]

Rebuilding Europe

Neither Americans nor Soviets were able to impose their politicized style of choice fully. In Western Europe American influences were much more visible in public buildings and construction methods than in housing. In Eastern Europe, the insistence on national forms for socialist content encouraged eclecticism, while economic constraints limited construction. Only Berlin became a showcase for full-blown architectural competition.

The United States military was one crucial conduit of American modernism, for bases with modern offices, tract housing, and supermarkets dotted Germany and Italy. American multinationals were another. Bechtel and Knudsen, for example, built European oil refineries, power plants, and chemical factories, sometimes operating alone, as in Greece, at other times partnering with European firms, as in France. United States businesses and technical advisors urged Europeans to purchase American construction machines and adopt American building methods. The impact of the military and multinationals was significant where American troops and long-standing economic relations were numerous but much less significant in Sweden, the Benelux countries, Spain, and Portugal.

Destroyed cities like Hamburg and Hanover rebuilt along American lines and postwar Frankfurt am Main was nicknamed Mainhattan, but they were exceptions. Many cities preserved historical buildings in old city centers, while adding individual iconic glass curtain wall skyscrapers. In West Germany eclecticism prevailed except in official architecture, where Bauhaus modern dominated in buildings like the glass-walled parliament in Bonn or the West German pavilion at the 1958 Brussels World's Fair. In other countries with less compromised political pasts, official architecture did not need to be so dramatically revamped.

The Hilton hotels, built in the fifties in major European and Middle Eastern capitals, were pure Americana. They used modern design, "dazzling standardization," and the requisite glass, steel, and concrete

---

[20] Anders Åman, *Architecture and Ideology in Eastern Europe during the Stalin Era: An Aspect of Cold War History* (Cambridge, MA: MIT, 1992), 56, 63. David Crowley, "Paris or Moscow? Warsaw Architects and the Image of the Modern City in the 1950s," *Kritika* 9/ 4 (Fall 2008): 775, 780, and 782. Greg Castillo, "Blueprint for a Cultural Revolution: Hermann Henselmann and the Architecture of German Socialist Realism," *Slavonica* 11/4 (April 2005): 42.

materials, had air conditioning and ice water in every room, and were surrounded by suburban-style lawns and accessible only by car. They had American cocktail lounges and served American fast food as well as haute cuisine. According to the chain's owner, the devout Catholic, Conrad Hilton, these hotels would allow Europeans and Middle Easterners to "inspect America and its ways at their leisure." In addition, they delivered a strong political message. The Istanbul Hilton, he claimed, represented "a challenge ... to the way of life preached by the Communist world," whose Soviet border, he mistakenly claimed, lay a mere 30 miles away, instead of 300. When the Berlin Hilton opened in 1958, he proudly announced that "we have hit upon a new weapon with which to fight Communism, a new team made up of owner, manager and labor with which to confront the class conscious Mr. Marx." Although a symbol of American entrepreneurship, the Berlin Hilton was largely funded by the city government, which in turn was heavily subsidized by the United States government. While Hilton hotels were welcomed in Istanbul and Athens, they met more opposition in Berlin, Rome, and London and were prohibited in Florence.[21]

American influence on Western European housing was limited, for national and European models carried more weight, the state played a major role in the housing market, and suburbanization was limited. To be sure, Europeans saw American housing at exhibits, such as the 1949 How America Lives show in Stuttgart, the American pavilion at the 1958 Brussels World's Fair, and numerous smaller trade shows. When European architects visited America, Levittown was an essential stop. The response of French architects was typical; they admired American rationalization, standardization, use of prefabrication and streamlined management systems and adopted many of these practices, but not to build the iconic postwar wood frame American suburban tract houses.

The French Ministry of Reconstruction and Urbanism, which built nearly a quarter of a million housing units a year, looked to mass production and prefabrication, embraced a theory of universal needs, and designed similar housing for the working and middle classes. Its first experimental project at Noisy-le-Sec in Paris contained models from France, Finland, Sweden, Canada, Switzerland, Britain, and the United States. There and elsewhere functionally designed interiors drew on interwar French and German influences more than American ones, and although some single-family homes were built, *grand ensembles*, vast apartment blocks with 800 to 3,500 units, were preferred. Le Corbusier's Unite

---

[21] Annabel Jane Wharton, *Building the Cold War: Hilton International Hotels and Modern Architecture* (University of Chicago Press, 2001), 6, 35, 87.

Illustration 17 Levittown, Pennsylvania, c. 1959.

d'Habitation in Marseilles had extensive communal facilities as well. Like many Frenchmen, he rejected suburbs, calling them "The Great American Waste."[22]

The British criticized American housing as chaotic and sprawling, preferring denser new towns. The 1951 Festival of Britain exhibition built modern housing in London's bombed out East End that drew on models displayed at the 1930 Stockholm Exhibition. Postwar reconstruction in Sweden and the Netherlands drew on national and European interwar traditions of an austere modernism. The much-praised Lijnbaan project in Rotterdam, for example, reflected Dutch modernism, pioneered Europe's first pedestrian zone, and combined housing density with mixed-use zoning in distinctively European ways. In West Germany many conservatives criticized American housing as too high-tech and expensive, and although many single-family homes were built, their layout and appearance remained traditional.[23]

Western Europeans preferred to rent rather than buy their homes, and American efforts to promote ownership, such as in the housing built in the Ruhr by the United States Economic Construction Administration, met with opposition from miners. In Belgium, which did have high rates of private ownership, little else about homes resembled American ones. Due both to the severity of the housing crisis and the social democratic commitments of countries like Sweden, France, the Netherlands, and Britain, housing was regarded as a social right, and broad sectors of the population lived in subsidized apartments. In the United States, housing was thoroughly commodified and the very limited public housing carried the stigma of need.

Postwar European housing also had a distinctive pedagogical function. In Britain many hoped modern housing would reform the everyday practices of family life and leisure to both reflect and reinforce the social democratic vision of modernity; in Germany it was to promote rational, disciplined consumption, vital to national recovery; in France it strove to modernize working-class everyday life and encourage families to have more children. Americans, by contrast, described homes in terms of

---

[22] Nicole Rudolph, "Domestic Politics: The Cité Expérimentale at Noisy-le-Sec in Greater Paris," *Modern and Contemporary France* 12/4 (2004): 483–95. Crowley, "Europe Reconstructed," 54.

[23] Cohen, *Scenes of the World to Come*, 197. Marcus, *Design in the Fifties*, 74–77. David Crowley and Jane Pavitt, "Introduction," in Crowley and Pavitt, eds., *Cold War Modern*, 17. Werner Durth, "Architecture as a Political Medium," in Detlef Junker, ed., *The United States and Germany in the Era of the Cold War, 1945–1968: A Handbook* (New York: GHI and Cambridge University Press, 2004), 482.

Illustration 18 Stalinallee, International Peace March, May 11, 1955.

affluence and changing expectations, desires not needs. They were sites of individual choice and mobility, not societal transformation.

The Soviets tried to exert greater control over architecture. In Moscow they built six monumental skyscrapers that borrowed prewar American methods of high-rise construction and an ornamental style, reminiscent of New York's Woolworth building. Plans to place similar wedding cake skyscrapers in East European capitals did not come to fruition except in Riga with the Academy of Sciences and in Warsaw's monumental and ornate Palace of Culture, which the Soviets built and paid for, hoping to promote Soviet-Polish friendship. Poles resented it as a symbol of Soviet domination.[24]

The Soviets pressured Eastern European countries to undertake projects with "socialist content," such as dams, iron and steel complexes, factories with ornate entry gates, housing projects, and high rises for government offices. But these were to be "national in form" and the results were eclectic. Monumental buildings such as the Bucharest Casa Scînteii, headquarters for all publishing in Romania, adopted Byzantine motifs, while Czechs deployed Hussite themes. Everywhere there was an abundance of oversized statues of Stalin, Lenin, and Marx as well as memorials to the Soviet liberators and war dead, such as the vast Treptow cemetery in East Berlin. Overall, however, the impact of Soviet socialist realism was minimal, for it arrived late and was short-lived. While East Germany and Bulgaria embraced it enthusiastically, Poland and Romania saw it as a threat to national cultural traditions, and Hungary and Czechoslovakia built little in that style.

Only in Berlin did Soviets and Americans as well as East and West Germans make an architectural showcase of their respective ideologies. East Berlin launched the competition in 1952 by building vast, ornate neoclassical apartment buildings along the bombed out Stalinallee, a wide boulevard in the city center. Although it deployed a distinctly nineteenth-century bourgeois style, this symbol of socialism claimed to serve popular needs, recognize popular taste, and provide "dwelling palaces" for the population (or at least those with important government and party positions). Stalinallee also contained the new monumental neoclassical German Sport Hall, built for the 1951 World Youth Festival.[25]

[24] Cohen, *Scenes of the World to Come*, 177–78. Crowley, "Europe Reconstructed," 49.
[25] Åman, *Architecture and Ideology*, 185. Francesca Rogier, "The Monumentality of Rhetoric: The Will to "Rebuild in Postwar Berlin," in Sarah Williams Goldhagen and Réjean Legault, eds., *Anxious Modernisms: Experimentation in Postwar Architectural Culture* (Cambridge, MA: MIT, 2000), 172–76. Crowley, "Europe Reconstructed," 51–52.

Illustration 19 Congress Hall Berlin, 1957.

West Berlin responded in 1957 with the Interbau housing complex in the devastated Hansaviertel. Architects from several nations, including Gropius, Oscar Niemeyer, and Alvar Aalto, built distinctive modern apartment buildings, situated on curved streets, surrounded by green space, and separated from commerce and manufacturing. Interbau was "an exercise in ideology." The United States contribution, the Congress Hall with its sweeping inverted curved roof, described itself as "a beacon toward the East" and an "expression of today." Like Stalinallee the Hansaviertel was full of contradictions. It claimed to embody freedom, but drew on 1944 Nazi plans for "the ordered and dispersed city." Its planners extolled the virtues of the market, but it was government subsidized. It presented itself as an alternative to the proletarian "rental barracks," but only the upper-middle class could afford to live there. In the early 1960s the glass curtain wall Europa Center joined Interbau as a symbol of West Berlin's effort to adopt American modernism and lifestyles and claim the status of a world city.[26]

A European modernism

No sooner were the architectural and ideological lines sharply drawn than they began to dissolve, for after Stalin's death, the Soviets abandoned socialist realism for modernism – but of a distinctly European sort. This architectural about-face was part of political de-Stalinization, a broader cultural thaw, and an anxious legitimation of consumption. It was also a response to an acute housing shortage, which forced many families to share communal apartments. Finally, it was a reaction to the popular uprisings in the GDR in 1953 and in Poland and Hungary in 1956, which protested the lack of housing and basic consumer goods as much as the absence of democracy.

In 1954 Khrushchev announced that "An architect ... must know the new progressive materials, reinforced concrete sections and parts, and most of all, must have an excellent understanding of construction economy." Launching a major housing program under the slogan "better, faster and more economical," the government called for form to follow function in the production of modern mass-produced dwellings both by state-run programs and by "people's construction" of their own homes and apartments. In 1957 Khrushchev sent study trips to Scandinavia and West Germany and made the single-family apartment with its own kitchen the goal. Between 1956 and 1970 the Soviet Union built 34 million

---

[26] Crowley, "Europe Reconstructed," 59, 61. Åman, *Architecture and Ideology*, 235.

housing units into which more than half the population moved; another 25 million units were constructed in the ensuing two decades. Most were apartment buildings made with prefabricated concrete panels and modern construction techniques and having functional interiors.[27]

Eastern Europe eagerly abandoned socialist realism. Polish architects once again looked west. Poland, Romania, and Bulgaria followed the Soviet model of industrialized panel construction of high-rise blocks, for this was the cheapest and fastest way to build mass housing. East Germany's rationalized apartment blocks with plain prefab exteriors and functional interiors became the norm for mass housing, including on those parts of Stalinallee, renamed Karl-Marx-Allee, built up from the late 1950s on. To compete with West Berlin on modernist terms, East Berlin initiated an ambitious reconstruction of Alexanderplatz whose centerpiece, the House of Teachers, tried to imitate the Seagram building in New York and the Mannesmann headquarters in Düsseldorf. The Sporthalle was torn down to make way for modern buildings and a modernist TV tower, the tallest structure in both Berlins, became East Berlin's centerpiece.[28]

The massive construction of functional single-family apartments with modern furniture was intended to improve material conditions and encourage modern everyday practices. In the Soviet Union designers and state officials argued it would help de-Stalinize people, for ornamentation, overstuffed furniture, and lampshades with a fringe, the hallmarks of the Stalin era, were said to promote petty bourgeois attitudes. Communist modernism did "impose disciplining Modernist norms in the domestic realm," but such attention to everyday life was not unique.[29]

---

[27] Crowley, "Paris or Moscow," 786. Steven E. Harris, "In Search of 'Ordinary' Russia: Everyday Life in the NEP, the Thaw and the Communal Apartment," *Kritika* 6/3 (Summer 2005): 596–97, 607–8. Christine Varga-Harris, "Homemaking and the Aesthetic and Moral Perimeters of the Soviet Home during the Khrushchev Era," *Journal of Social History* (Spring 2008): 565. Mark B. Smith, "Khrushchev's Promise to Eliminate the Urban Housing Shortage: Rights, Rationality and the Communist Future," in Melanie Ilic and Jeremy Smith, *Soviet State and Society under Nikita Khrushchev* (London: Routledge, 2009), 26, 31. Henry W. Morton, "What Have Soviet Leaders Done about the Housing Crisis?" in Henry W. Morton and Rudolf L. Tökés, eds., *Soviet Politics and Society in the 1970s* (New York: Free Press, 1974), 163. Blair A. Ruble, "From *khrushcheby* to *korobki*," in William Craft Brumfield and Blair A. Ruble, eds., *Russian Housing in the Modern Age: Design and Social History* (Cambridge University Press, 1993), 233, 238–40.

[28] Peter Müller, "Counter-Architecture and Building Race: Cold War Politics and the Two Berlins," *Bauhaus in Europe and America*, 107, 109. Crowley, "Europe Reconstructed," 59–63.

[29] Victor Buchli, "Khrushchev, Modernism, and the Fight against 'Petit-bourgeois' Consciousness in the Soviet Home," *Journal of Design History* 10/2 (1997): 168, 175. Susan E. Reid, "Destalinization and Taste, 1953–1963," *Journal of Design History* 10/2 (1997): 178.

Europeans east and west believed functional dwellings would rationalize domesticity and transform nuclear families. They differed only about the social and political goals that such modern living would promote. The modern dwelling proved as compatible with communism as with social democracy, Christian democracy, and American democratic capitalism.

When the Soviets abandoned socialist realism for modernism, they severed the links posited between style and ideology. Architecture was no longer a useful Cold War weapon, and, according to Anders Åman, the gap between East and West closed. But which West? Some Polish supermarkets and the Soviet pavilion at the Brussels World's Fair borrowed heavily from American models and materials, but socialist prefab housing looked more like its counterparts in Western and Northern Europe than like American suburban housing. And communist Eastern Europe employed American methods of industrial construction much more fully than Americans ever did. By the 1960s, architecture and urban planning across Europe had become stylistically similar, but the result was not Americanization so much as a distinctive European modernism. Much the same happened with the modern kitchen and the new consumer culture in which it was so thoroughly implicated

Kitchen debates

At the 1959 American exhibition in Sokolniki Park, Moscow, Khrushchev and Vice President Richard Nixon held their famous "kitchen debate." Surrounded by the wonders of American home technology, they argued about the virtues and vices of consumer choice and planned obsolescence; they professed their desire to help "the ladies" but disputed the proper roles for women in family and society. Far from being an amusing but idiosyncratic event, the kitchen debate was emblematic of an early Cold War obsession with kitchens and household consumer durables as an expression of national identity and political ideology and a measure of a nation's progress. According to American historians, Nixon emerged victorious, for the three display kitchens and a plethora of other consumer goods, stylish clothes, and cosmetics captivated the over 2.7 million Russians who visited the exhibition.[30]

Who would not want such spacious kitchens, well equipped with technologically sophisticated appliances, gadgets, and the latest in plastic goods including Tupperware? Many Europeans, as it turned out, for Khrushchev was not alone in having reservations about American

[30] Walter L. Hixson, *Parting the Curtain: Propaganda, Culture and the Cold War, 1945–1961* (New York: St. Martins, 1998), 201.

consumer culture. The modern American kitchen was certainly the point of reference for postwar European kitchen debates, for exhibits and magazines publicized its size and extensive mechanization, along with images of cheerful, affluent housewives. In the transatlantic imaginary, kitchens became the iconic symbol of American modernity and prosperity, just as cars had been in the interwar years. When debating how to build kitchens and restructure domesticity, however, Western Europeans drew on their own design traditions and understandings of gender, family, and housewifery more than on American influences in order to shape distinctive European households and consumer cultures. Eastern Europeans, in turn, looked to Western and Northern Europe for inspiration when the single-family kitchen replaced any talk of collectivizing housework.

Kitchens were the locus of hopes and anxieties about economics and politics, family and gender. As war economies converted to peacetime and Europeans sought a path to recovery, household consumer durables – radios and televisions but above all kitchen appliances and washing machines – stimulated demand and promoted growth, albeit later and more slowly in Europe than in the United States. They were thus essential for social stability and political legitimacy, and economists, politicians, women's groups, and social commentators abandoned their interwar qualms about the desirability and economic feasibility of filling homes with consumer durables.

There was a transatlantic discursive retreat into the home in the 1950s and 1960s that reflected shared anxieties, such as fear of nuclear weapons, but also nationally specific concerns. In the United States modern homes and the idealized American family – patriotic, prosperous, and religious, with breadwinner husband, a stay-at-home mother, and obedient children – were both a refuge from the Cold War and the home front of that multifaceted struggle. For West Germans, the retreat into the home and the restoration of traditional gender relations offered a possible way to repair the material and emotional damage of fascism and war without confronting the Nazi past personally or politically. The consuming housewife was a key agent in the construction of both the social market economy and a new postnational identity. In France the transformation of domestic spaces and practices was part of a sweeping modernization of postwar society. The modern kitchen displayed at the 1951 Festival of Britain offered a diversion from both austerity and the loss of empire and directed attention away from the drabness of the war and postwar years onto the promise of a bright new future. In Eastern Europe, modern kitchens and a socialist form of mass consumption were integral to communist efforts to improve material conditions, quell social unrest and achieve legitimacy. To some home came to symbolize the accomplishments of socialism, to others its economic failings. For many it was an apolitical refuge from the demands of the state.[31]

The modern home, with its new kitchen, functional layout, and simple furniture, represented a space in which family life, disrupted by depression and war, could be both restabilized and reconfigured. On both sides of the Atlantic, families of all classes were smaller and children became the focus of intensified parental emotional investment. In Britain and West Germany as in the United States, there was a renewed emphasis on the importance of improved mothering for children's development and societal well-being. The family became a unit of consumption; indeed, it was precisely the shared project of consuming goods, television programs, leisure activities, and vacations that was to unite families and create a modern lifestyle.

Finally, in Western Europe and America efforts to redefine the housewife as an important, indeed glamorous, new woman were integral to "normalizing" gender relations after the enormous disruptions of World War II. War had given women a taste of economic and emotional independence, weakened male power, and presented conservative politicians with the challenge of simultaneously democratizing politics, restructuring the economy, and restabilizing the male-headed family while granting women expanded political and social citizenship. Many hoped the modern home would entice women to resume more traditional roles within the family, even if they worked outside it. American government programs and businesses exported the image of white, middle-class women embracing gender traditionalism within a well-appointed modern home – even though this did not reflect the varied conditions found in the United States. Western Europeans found this a much less threatening new woman than the twenties one had been. But from economic necessity, political ideology, or cultural preference, she was not embraced as a model. In Eastern Europe the working mother, juggling the triple burden of waged work, housework, and political activity, became normative.

American image, Western European reality

After 1945, Western Europeans were bombarded with images of heavily commodified domesticity. State Department exhibits in West Germany first featured photos of American homes and then complete houses,

---

[31] Elaine Tyler May, *Homeward Bound: American Families in the Cold War Era* (New York: Basic, 1988), 10–15. Erica Carter, *How German Is She? Postwar German Reconstruction and the Consuming Woman* (Ann Arbor: University of Michigan Press, 1996). Becky E. Conekin, *"The Autobiography of a Nation": The 1951 Festival of Britain* (University of Manchester Press, 2003). Kristin Ross, *Fast Cars, Clean Bodies: Decolonization and Reordering of French Culture* (Cambridge, MA: MIT, 1996), 4–10, 71–78.

containing American-built kitchens with actors to illustrate the proper use of new technology. Marshall Plan and later USIA exhibits of kitchens and home furnishings as well as the Caravan of Modern Food Service, containing a model supermarket, toured Western Europe. The American pavilion at the 1958 Brussels World's Fair and the Sokolniki Park exhibition featured yet more lavish and futuristic presentations of American domestic abundance, such as the $250,000 RCA Miracle Kitchen, complete with robotic floor cleaners and a high-tech dishwasher that came to the table to collect dishes.[32] Officials and the media claimed the average worker enjoyed the full array of modern household amenities. While this ignored rural and black poverty, Americans consumed three-quarters of the world's appliances in the early fifties and produced most of them. No European country had anything comparable to the commoditized prosperity enjoyed by white Americans of all classes.

Americans imagined the modern kitchen as a distinctly American invention that embodied the essence of what the USIA called "People's Capitalism" – choice, abundance, and free enterprise. However, the American modern kitchen, like modern architecture, was only partially American, for United States designers drew on Dutch, French, and German interwar designs. These were recoded as American when they were re-exported back to Europe. United States observers predicted that Western Europe would move toward what West German critics called the American "fat kitchen," but Dutch, French, and Finnish architects and planners found them too costly, ostentatious, and style-conscious for European conditions. National design councils in every country sought to develop recognizably modern but distinctively national domestic cultures. Women's organizations in Belgium and the Netherlands judged America's large, gadget-filled kitchens to be excessive, even decadent, and preferred more austere forms of modernism. In 1944 British women's organizations polled their members about what kind of kitchen they hoped for postwar and found desires were modest: a rational layout and built-in cabinets, a stove and hot running water; a refrigerator that would supplement the traditional larder, not replace it, and a good copper pot for clothes washing with a wringer rather than a washing machine.[33]

---

[32] Cristina Carbone, 'Staging the Kitchen Debate: How Splitnik Got Normalized in the United States," in Ruth Oldenziel and Karin Zachmann, eds., *Cold War Kitchen: Americanization, Technology, and European Users* (Cambridge, MA: MIT, 2009), 63–75.

[33] Hixson, *Parting the Curtain*, 133–34. Greg Castillo, "The American 'Fat Kitchen' in Europe: Postwar Domestic Modernity and Marshall Plan Strategies of Enhancement," in Oldenziel and Zachmann, eds., *Cold War Kitchen*, 33–57. Kirsi Saarikangas, "What's New? Women Pioneers and the Finnish State Meet the American Kitchen," in Oldenziel and Zachmann, eds., *Cold War Kitchen*, 285–311. Oldenziel and Zachmann, "Kitchens as

As Europeans rebuilt their housing stock, consumerist domesticity was realized at uneven rates across Europe. By the late 1950s electric stoves and vacuums were ceasing to be luxury items in West Germany, and many households had purchased new furniture, but only one in twenty had a refrigerator as opposed to one in two in the United States and Switzerland. By 1963 nearly two-thirds of Dutch and Belgium households had washing machines, while nearly half of Swiss and British households and roughly one-third of West German, French, and Austrian ones did. Only a scant 8 percent of Italian households had one, indicating the delayed onset of consumer society there. Scarcely any Finnish homes had washing machines in the early 1950s but over half did by the mid 1960s, and refrigerators followed a similar trajectory. The Dutch had the highest percentage of vacuums, exceeding the 79 percent United States level, while West Germany and Britain came close to it. West Germany led in refrigerators, with 58 percent of households owning one. This was a marked increase from the previous decade and put West Germany well ahead of France, Britain, and Italy in the competition for that much-coveted item. Televisions, however, spread even faster and by the mid sixties nearly half of Italian homes, two-thirds of West German ones, and over four-fifths of British ones had this centerpiece of family leisure. (Less than one-third of West German homes had phones, however.) By the late 1960s "for the first time in history, ease and comfort were now within the reach of most people in [Western] Europe."[34]

Household technology, once seen as the preserve of privileged America, came to be associated with national or other European models. West German publications, for example, discussed Swedish as well as American kitchen designs and carried ads for a wide array of appliances, cabinets, tables and chairs, and flooring that were manufactured by German firms like Bosch, Siemens, AEG, and smaller furniture manu-facturers.[35] Germany and the Netherlands exported appliances to Western Europe, Scandinavian designs circulated widely, and Italian

Technology and Politics: An Introduction," in Oldenziel and Zachmann, eds., *Cold War Kitchen*, 20. Pleydell-Bouverie, *Daily Mail Book of Post-War Homes* (London: Daily Mail, 1944), 48–54.
[34] Sue Bowden and Avner Offer, "Household Appliances and the Use of Time: The United States and Britain since the 1920s," *Economic History Review* 47/4 (November 1994): 725–48. Jennifer A. Loehlin, *From Rugs to Riches: Housework, Consumption and Modernity in Germany* (Oxford: Berg, 1999): 70. Saarikangas, "What's New," 303. Paul Ginsborg, *A History of Contemporary Italy: Society and Politics, 1943–1988* (London: Penguin, 1990), 240. Arne Andersen, "Das 50er-Jahre-Syndrom: Umweltfragen in der Demokratisierung des Technikkonsums," *Technikgeschichte* 65/4 (1998): 334. Tony Judt, *Postwar: A History of Europe since 1945* (New York: Penguin, 2005), 353.
[35] *Der ideale Haushalt: Ein Sonderheft der Constanze-Verlag* (Hamburg: Constanze-Verlag, 1958), 188, 198.

low-cost refrigerators were sold all over Western Europe and in more limited quantities in the East. Even in Sweden, "labeled the most Americanized nation in Europe ... visiting Americans found that the American styles, goods and rituals mostly had been Swedified beyond recognition." Everyday modernity was national and European more than Americanized.[36]

The same was true for other types of consumer durables. American modern designs were exhibited in Europe and some like the Eames chair were widely imitated, just as Italian and Scandinavian designs were sold in America in limited quantities. In general, however, American products were often too large, streamlined, and expensive for Europeans, whereas Vespa scooters, Olivetti typewriters, German appliances, and Scandinavian furniture were popular and widely exported. Intra-European circuits were more important than transatlantic ones.

Socialist domesticity

Communist Eastern Europe, usually presented as the antithesis of Western capitalist consumerism, developed forms of domestic consumption that bore a family resemblance to those in Western Europe, even though these were understood as part of an emerging socialist consumer culture. The Soviets built single-family apartments with modern kitchens with plumbing, electricity, a stove, and refrigerator, and the percentage of the population having televisions expanded rapidly from the 1960s on. (The family car, however, was nowhere on the horizon.) Khrushchev saw domestic consumption as integral to efforts to "catch up and overtake" the United States. He both feared it would erode commitments to socialism and hoped that a modern, rationalized home would introduce women to the "technological-scientific revolution" and make them model citizens.[37]

Soviet officials and some visitors to Sokolniki Park did not want to emulate the American model of affluence and planned obsolescence, however, favoring instead kitchens that were lean, less gadget-filled, and closer to the Nordic modernism popular in Western Europe. Most Soviets assumed the new styles were indigenous, but those in the design community looked for inspiration to the Baltic States, their internal "other," which had long-standing contacts with Scandinavia, and to

---

[36] Orvar Löfgren, "Materializing the Nation in Sweden and America," *Ethnos* 58/3–4 (1993): 190.

[37] Susan E. Reid, "The Khrushchev Kitchen: Domesticating the Scientific-Technological Revolution," *Journal of Contemporary History* 40/2 (2005): 289–316.

Czechoslovakia, Poland, and the GDR, for they, not America, represented the West for Soviets.[38] Scandinavians and the Ulm Institute for
Design in West Germany influenced Eastern bloc modernists just as they
did those in Western Europe.

The GDR privileged production as the site of social transformation,
but the 1953 uprising, competition from West Germany, and constant
pressure from women forced the regime to expand consumer durables
as well as "the 1000 little things" from sewing needles to shoe laces that
were essential to a minimally functional everyday life. The GDR looked
abroad to Sweden, Czechoslovakia, Denmark, the United States, and
the USSR for model household goods, and over the course of the 1960s
consumer durables came into East German homes. Whereas in 1960
only 6 percent of homes had washing machines and refrigerators, by
1970 over half did and two-thirds had TVs. From the 1970s, head of
state Erich Honecker expanded domestic consumption further by shifting resources away from heavy industry and borrowing extensively from
the West.[39] Under communism as under capitalism, the consumption
of consumer durables was to enable women to master rationalized
modern domesticity without disrupting the traditional domestic division of labor.

Across Europe there was a shared vision of individual families, surrounded by the commodified accoutrements of modern life – refrigerators
and washing machines, electric mixers and vacuums, Tupperware and
televisions. In different ways and with varied degrees of success,
Communists tried to distribute these highly individualized goods more
equitably and surround them with forms of collective solidarity. But the
basic unit, the consumerist domestic space and the modern woman as
consuming housewife responsible for all domestic labor remained the
same. The ideologically promiscuous modern kitchen could be instrumentalized by different regimes for competing political projects.

From the 1950s to the 1970s the socialist East like the European
capitalist West developed hybrid forms of domestic modernity, inspired
by the American model, yet diverging significantly from it. Initially
from necessity, later from choice, Europeans had less stuff in their
homes, kept what they had longer, and moved much less frequently.

---

[38] David Crowley, "Thaw Modern: Design in Eastern Europe after 1956," in Crowley and
Pavitt, eds., Cold War Modern, 148–49.

[39] Donna Harsch, Revenge of the Domestic: Women, the Family, and Communism in the German
Democratic Republic (Princeton University Press, 2007), 165–97. Judt, Postwar, 445.
Karin Zachmann, "Managing Choice: Constructing the Socialist Consumption
Junction in the German Democratic Republic," in Oldenziel and Zachmann, eds., Cold
War Kitchen, 261–67.

A modern home, such as the French grand ensembles apartments of the late 1950s, had heating, indoor plumbing, and electricity, but did not come equipped with appliances, which had to be acquired over time. Every apartment in the 1960s upper-middle-class Barbican housing development in London had the same prefab, small functional kitchen, with basic appliances and few outlets for electrical gadgets. The kitchen was not an arena for displaying and constantly updating affluence. Spacious American kitchens with large, streamlined appliances were suited for suburbs, which, in turn, required cars; but suburbanization came only partially to Europe and widespread car ownership belatedly. As household technology spread in Europe, appliances did not become larger and more energy consuming, as was the case in the United States. Furthermore, Europeans did not buy two of the items that featured so prominently in American homes from the 1950s on, air conditioners and clothes dryers. The obsessive, never satisfied, wasteful quality of American consumerist domesticity, criticized so strongly by thinkers like John Kenneth Galbraith, Betty Friedan, and Vance Packard, was less evident in Europe. Both Europeans and Americans were committed to making housework more efficient but did so by different means. Europeans preferred a more austere form of modernism, emphasizing functionality, rationality, ergonomics, and basic durable appliances rather than the American model stressing technological abundance, space, and constant change. The ultimate winner of the kitchen debate was Sweden, widely admired on both sides of the Iron Curtain, or the Netherlands, Germany, and Italy, and not the United States.[40]

Home and society

European homes were embedded in a different sociopolitical context than their American counterparts. Even in the heyday of American Keynesianism and progressive social policy from the 1940s to the mid 1970s, Americans prioritized the individual, the private, and the market. The American goal was a "consumers' republic" in which family-centered mass consumption and consumer choice would produce optimal economic outcomes and individual happiness and would simultaneously be the criteria according to which the state would be judged.[41] By comparison, across Europe more homes were publicly built or state funded; social

---

[40] David Heathcote, *Barbican Penthouse over the City* (Chichester: Wiley Academy, 2004), 138–46. Oldenziel and Zachmann, "Kitchens as Technology," 8.

[41] Lisabeth Cohen, *A Consumers' Republic: The Politics of Mass Consumption in Postwar America* (New York: Vintage, 2003).

programs were more generous and were universal rather than means-tested. There were more public goods and services, and the modern home and family were less isolated from the public sphere. Western Europeans did not embrace the distinctive American conception of consumer citizenship that defined the individual purchaser as citizen, exercising her or his free choice in the market. European ideas of consumer citizenship involved not only choice but state regulation and extensive state social benefits.

Eastern Europeans attempted to construct socialist consumer cultures, in which commodified domesticity was embedded in state-run, often factory-based, distribution networks. The GDR, for example, strove to distribute goods more equitably and to find non-market mechanisms to regulate supply and demand. It appropriated capitalist market research and advertising but with the exclusive aim of teaching consumers what they should need, not to find out what they wanted. Hungary developed a form of market socialism or "goulash communism." In the Soviet Union housing became a social right, even if apartments and appliances were in short supply and often of poor quality. There, as elsewhere in Eastern Europe, the private ownership of consumer durables coexisted with the public consumption of collective goods such as childcare, education, and healthcare. While this certainly distinguished communist societies from American capitalism, it made them resemble the European social democratic variety. But, as we shall see, the pursuit of domestic consumption, which was the key to the success of Western capitalist economies, would contribute significantly to the failure of socialist ones.[42]

Cultural competition hardly fits a simple model of America came, Western Europe succumbed, and Eastern Europe envied. America did indeed send people, ideas, and products across the Atlantic in abundance, hoping to win over Western Europeans and vanquish communism. Europeans negotiated with these models and goods; it was impossible not to, given the power of the United States and the prominence of its images and products. Yet rather than wholeheartedly emulating American cities, homes, and consumer cultures or even wanting to do so, Europeans both observed America and drew on their own national traditions and modernist heritages. There were complex circuits along which ideas, goods, consumer practices, architectural forms, and visions of domesticity circulated. The United States initially dominated transatlantic movements, although by the late 1960s European products were increasingly heading west. Within Europe products and models moved

---

[42] Katherine Pence and Paul Betts, eds., *Socialist Modern: East German Everyday Culture and Politics* (Ann Arbor: University of Michigan Press, 2008).

among Western, Northern, and Southern European countries, within the Eastern bloc, and across the Iron Curtain. Europeans developed distinctive varieties of modernity, consumer culture, and ways of living that were, to be sure, influenced by America but should not be understood as successful or failed imitations of it. The early Cold War culture wars and fears about Americanization subsided from the 1970s on, but distinctive European models of modernity persisted, as economic crises and foreign policy conflicts widened the Atlantic.

9   The American Century erodes, 1968–1979

Student protests and massive strikes, Soviet troops moving into Prague and American ones leaving Saigon, rising oil prices and endless gas lines, soaring inflation and collapsing economic growth, arms control and renewed missile crises, détente in Europe and hot Cold War conflicts in Africa and Asia. These contradictory events from the tumultuous late sixties and seventies threw transatlantic relations into turmoil. The postwar economic order descended into crisis due to the collapse of Bretton Woods, the exhaustion of Fordism, and the ineffectuality of Keynesianism. The Cold War political consensus frayed, creating stormy domestic politics and opening the way for a renegotiation of East–West relations in Europe as well as for new social movements and transnational alliances. A weakened and less confident United States sought to reassert leadership in Europe and globally, while Western Europeans strove for more autonomy. American hegemony – economic, cultural, military, and political – faced a serious challenge for the first time.

The American Century in Europe rested on five pillars. The first was American economic prowess, embodied in Fordist mass production, technological innovation, unmatched productivity, and high wages that enabled the mass consumption of cars, consumer durables, and mass culture. The second was America's unchallenged military might, conventional and nuclear, and the presence of American weapons and military personnel across Western Europe. The third was the transatlantic consensus about anti-communism and containment but also about Keynesianism and generous social policies. The fourth pillar was widespread Western European admiration for America's political values, global presence, and popular culture. Finally, Western Europe accepted, if at times grudgingly, its role as the junior partner in an American empire built largely by invitation but supplemented by American pressure, threats, and covert intervention when necessary. How did the challenges and crises of these years erode the hard and soft power on which America's postwar dominance had been built?

1968: Common themes and national variations

Nineteen sixty-eight was a year of massive, and for the postwar period unprecedented, protests across Europe, the United States, and areas of the Third World ranging from Japan and Mexico to Turkey and Ethiopia. Students occupied universities in such cities as Paris, Naples, and New York; they demonstrated and clashed with police in the streets of Berlin, Prague, Rome, London, Chicago, and Warsaw. In Europe workers staged gigantic strikes – 5 million walked off the job in France alone in May; they occupied factories in Italy and France and organized clandestine unions in Spain. In India radical peasant insurgencies erupted, and in Mexico hundreds of student protesters were slaughtered by police and the military. In America there were race riots and the assassinations of Martin Luther King and Robert Kennedy; in China Mao's destructive Cultural Revolution continued. Across the capitalist and communist worlds, protesters challenged entrenched political regimes and established political categories.

Nineteen sixty-eight is also shorthand for the more extended wave of protests, new political movements, and youth cultures that emerged from the early sixties through the early seventies – the civil rights, black power, and antiwar movements in the United States, the ongoing labor unrest that began in Italy's Hot Autumn of 1969 and continued for another two years, the waves of student protests and proliferation of alternative institutions that swept over West Germany and West Berlin from the mid sixties on, and the less well-known but sustained development of new cultural norms and political protests in places like the Netherlands, Switzerland, Belgium, and Yugoslavia. These were all part of a decade of unrest, upheaval, and uncertainty that some found exhilarating, and many others anxiety provoking or abhorrent. These movements were rooted in particular national contexts but created other transnational alliances than those the United States and the Soviet Union had arduously constructed. Americans and Western Europeans condemned the United States war in Vietnam; Eastern Europeans denounced the 1968 Soviet invasion of Czechoslovakia, and everywhere newly mobilized students, workers, and intellectuals criticized their governments as undemocratic, illiberal, and unjust.

Some historians draw a sharp distinction between the protest movements of the sixties in Western and Eastern Europe, arguing that the French, Italians, and West Germans were naïve, utopian, and self-referential, concerned only with culture and lifestyles, while Czechs and Poles were mature, realistic, and pursued serious political goals.[1] Such a

---

[1] Tony Judt, *Postwar: A History of Europe since 1945* (New York: Penguin, 2005), 407–12. Paulina Bren, *The Greengrocer and His TV: The Culture of Communism after the 1968 Prague Spring* (Ithaca: Cornell University Press, 2010), 26–27.

dichotomized assessment misreads the diverse goals of complex movements and ignores their entanglements with one another. Across Europe
and in the United States, a younger generation pioneered new political
and cultural practices. Neither the depression, nor World War II nor
postwar austerity was their formative experience; rather, it was the postwar boom that spread consumption and varied levels of prosperity across
Europe. Relative affluence, along with democratization in Western
Europe and the post-Stalinist thaw in the East opened spaces for youth
to develop distinctive identities and interests and for students, workers,
and intellectuals alike to articulate sharp critiques of both communism
and capitalist democracies.

Sixties protesters attacked not only ruling elites but also the very structure
of politics. In the words of one May '68 graffiti in France, "No replastering.
The structure is rotten." Soviet Premier Leonid Brezhnev, Polish head of
state Władysław Gomułka, French President Charles de Gaulle, Spanish
dictator General Franco, and United States President Lyndon Johnson,
among others, were dismissed as old, conservative, out of touch, interventionist abroad and authoritarian at home. The New Left was equally critical
of hierarchical and cautious old left Social Democrats and Communists.
Protesters across Europe and America shared an anti-authoritarian outlook, demanding genuine democracy, however differently they defined it,
and rejecting hierarchies at work, in school, and in society. They criticized
the increasing bureaucratization of mass societies, both communist and
capitalist, and challenged the claims of experts to order economy and
politics. In the words of a provocative French slogan, "Humanity won't
be happy till the last capitalist is hung with the guts of the last bureaucrat."
They lamented pervasive alienation more than economic exploitation.
According to the Port Huron Statement of the American Students for a
Democratic Society, "Loneliness, estrangement, isolation describe the vast
distance between man and man today." Whether they saw themselves as
substitutes for the working class, as in West Germany and the United
States, as allies of them, as in Italy, or both, as in France, the students of
1968 imagined themselves to be crucial agents of social change. Although
very much a part of the transatlantic mass culture of music, movies, and
distinctive clothing styles, the sixties generation nonetheless criticized both
the boredom and wastefulness of consumer capitalism and the failure of
socialist consumer cultures to provide meaningful alternatives to it.
Students, workers, and intellectuals condemned the United States for
violating its proclaimed freedom, democracy, and anti-colonialism, and
the Soviet Union for not realizing its promise of abundance and egalitarianism. The younger generation took governments, elites, and older generations to task for not dealing with the legacies of slavery and racism in

Illustration 20 May 1968, Paris.

America, of fascism, genocide, and colonialism in Western Europe, and of
Stalinism in Eastern Europe.[2]

Western governments continued to warn of the communist menace,
while communist ones sounded the alarm about capitalist infiltration, but

[2] For graffiti, www.bopsecrets.org/CF/graffiti.htm.

youth no longer heeded these admonitions. Nor did they support the arms race, deeming nuclear deterrence wasteful and dangerous. Neither Soviet Marxism nor American democratic capitalism offered coherent ideologies or promising policies, and many sought a third way, be it more participatory and decentralized democracy or market socialism or new lifestyles or a combination of these. They insisted that people needed to change themselves in order to change society and experimented with various forms of prefigurative politics that sought to implement in the present the values and institutions of the desired future. There was a willingness to make expansive, to some utterly outrageous, demands on state and society. "Be realistic. Demand the impossible," chanted French students, while workers at the vast Fiat Mirafiori plant insisted "We want everything" – higher and more equal wages, democratization of the unions, and worker control of the shop floor. German, French, and American students called for an end to the Vietnam War, far-reaching university reform, and greatly expanded personal and sexual freedom. Czechs and Slovaks demanded freedom of speech, a democratization of the state and Communist party, and economic reforms, while Polish students defended their right to criticize the political system and celebrate their national cultural heritage. Everyone impatiently wanted to achieve all of their demands immediately. Across Europe and the United States, protesters shared the heady experience of intense communication, debate, and cooperation, of solidarity with protesters at home and abroad. There was a pervasive optimism, however naïve in retrospect, that politics, culture, and everyday life could be dramatically transformed in ways that would benefit both society and the individual. One could change the world and have a good time.[3]

There were, of course, significant differences across national protest movements, some of which fell along the East–West divide. Protesters in Prague and Warsaw called for multiparty parliamentary democracy and the rule of law, while those in Paris, Berlin, Rome, and Washington detailed the shortcomings of liberal institutions, demanding more participatory and decentralized forms that would give people a greater voice in politics, work, and education. *Autogestion* or self-management was a popular slogan across Western and Southern Europe, but in Eastern Europe criticizing Western liberalism seemed objectionable and counterproductive. When Rudi Dutschke, leader of the Socialist German Student

---

[3] Gerd-Rainer Horn, *The Spirit of '68: Rebellion in Western Europe and North America, 1956–1976* (Oxford University Press, 2007), 216, www.bopsecrets.org/CF/graffiti.htm. Arthur Marwick, "Youth Culture and the Cultural Revolution of the Long Sixties," in Axel Schildt and Detlef Siegfried, eds., *Between Marx and Coca-Cola: Youth Culture in Changing European Societies, 1960–1980* (New York: Berghahn, 2006), 47.

League (SDS), and Czech students met in 1968, they were interested in developments in each other's country but unable to forge a common program because distinctive Cold War experiences had created very different political problems and aspirations. Freedom of expression stood at the forefront of demands from Warsaw to Paris, but Eastern Europeans gave it a traditional political definition, Western Europeans a more cultural and personal one. Eastern European protesters faced censorship and imprisonment when speaking out, while Western Europeans and Americans encountered the more elusive restrictions of what in a famous 1965 essay the German-American philosopher Herbert Marcuse called "repressive tolerance." Protest and a free press were allowed, but as American poet and peace activist Grace Paley lamented, "The elected or appointed leaders of our country have often applauded our enactment of these freedoms. They were then able (with clear conscience) to undertake and sustain the awful wars we spoke and assembled against for 10 years."[4]

The Vietnam War played a central role in the sixties. Protest movements in the United States and Western Europe viewed it not as a vital battle between communism and democracy but rather as a struggle between national liberation and American imperialism, pitting countries of astonishingly unequal wealth and arms against one another. The war did not play a comparable role in Eastern Europe, however, for Soviet expansionism was the problem and anti-imperialism a discredited official slogan. Some Western European protesters regarded the Third World as a challenge to the first world and a substitute for the second. This third worldism ranged from a romantic and ill-informed infatuation with Maoism to ongoing engagement with African and Asian students in the first world to a sober insistence that North–South issues should decenter Cold War East–West ones. In West Germany and West Berlin, for example, students in the early and mid 1960s interacted with Iranian, Congolese, and South African students, who educated Germans about their struggles for democracy and civil rights and involved them in protests with new tactics around these issues. By decade's end, however, a more distant and romantic identification with China and Cuba emerged.[5]

Other differences evolved along national lines. In France, Italy, Spain, and Portugal, workers played a prominent role in the protests, while in West Germany and elsewhere in Northern Europe they at most staged

[4] Herbert Marcuse, "Repressive Tolerance," in Robert Paul Wolff, Barrington Moore, Jr., and Herbert Marcuse, *A Critique of Pure Tolerance* (Boston: Beacon Press, 1969), 95–137. Grace Paley, *Just as I Thought* (New York: Farrar, Straus, and Giroux, 1998), 87.
[5] Quinn Slobodian, *Foreign Front: Third World Politics in Sixties West Germany* (Durham: Duke University Press, 2012).

modest strikes. Czech workers took to the streets in large numbers only after the Russians invaded in August 1968, while Polish ones were quiescent both when students demonstrated and when their protests were crushed. In the United States the labor movement and the New Left disagreed vehemently about the war and civil rights. Race and racism were central to the American sixties, but Western European societies remained relatively homogeneous; they envisioned that their "guest workers" from the Middle East, Asia, and Africa would return home and were not yet grappling with multiculturalism. Polish and Slovak protesters were proudly nationalistic, while those in Western Europe, burdened by a bitter half-century of wars and their aftermath, questioned nationalism, and many in America rejected calls for a patriotic crusade against the purported dangers of Asian communism. Western and Eastern Europeans were haunted by the memories of the fascist and Stalinist past; Spaniards and Portuguese by a dictatorial, quasi-fascist (and in Portugal still colonial) present. Americans, ever ready to forget the past, focused on the future of race relations, anti-poverty campaigns, and foreign policy.

Dissent and protest frequently became violent, sometimes because of provocations from students and workers, sometimes because of repressive, even deadly, policing from the state, sometimes from a vicious cycle of protest and suppression. Repression was worst in Czechoslovakia, where the Soviets killed some, arrested many, and rolled back all reforms, and in Poland, where thousands were forced into exile. In Western Europe, new forms of direct action expanded the repertoire of protest, but new laws and policing methods intensified surveillance and state violence. If most of Europe was embroiled in 1968, there were exceptions. In the Soviet Union Brezhnev had curbed intellectual dissent, and after the state brutally squashed the protest of workers and students in Novocherkassk in 1962, the streets were quiet. Although an intellectual New Left emerged in Britain and Britain and Sweden saw some modest university and anti-Vietnam War demonstrations, both remained relatively quiet. Sweden, however, did open its doors to American GIs who deserted the military. In Greece the junta of colonels ruled with an iron fist.

Transatlantic connections

What do these similarities and differences tell us about transatlantic connections? Opinions are divided. Some argue that the parallel development of abundance, consumerism, mass universities, and youth culture produced similar cultural and political radicalism in different countries. Others give greater causal force to the circulation of ideas, information,

Illustration 21 Burning Russian tank in front of the building of Radio
Prague, August 1968.

and individuals but differ about the role of the United States. In one view,
America led and Europe learned – from the Berkeley Free Speech
Movement, the Mississippi Freedom Summer of 1964, the civil rights
movement's use of direct action and civil disobedience, and the American
antiwar movement. The German student movement displayed the closest
ties and the most borrowings. Many Germans had studied in the United
States; many more were exposed to the large American military presence,
strong political influence, and abundant cultural products. Dutschke
regarded American protest as a key reference point, and many, like
journalist and later terrorist Ulrike Meinhof, adopted the American slogan
"From Protest to Resistance." Some argued that just as blacks were an
internal American colony, so West Germany was an external one, com-
plicit in American imperialism. K. D. Wolff established the German Black
Panther Solidarity Committee, which engaged in "education ... about
the fascist terror of the ruling class in the USA" and "agitation and
propaganda among GIs stationed in Germany." Belgian student activists
named their 1966 protest march from Ostend to Leuven "the James
Meredith March," after the first African American to attend the
University of Mississippi. Italian sociology students, who were influenced
by the theories of C. Wright Mills and Herbert Marcuse, led student

strikes and sit-ins at the University of Trento, and in 1967 and 1968 Marcuse spoke to enthusiastic student audiences across West Germany.[6] There were some Europeans active in United States protest movements, such as German SDS's Michael Vester, who helped draft the Port Huron statement, the founding manifesto of the American New Left. Overall, however, the American SDS or Students for a Democratic Society was more self-contained and was torn about whether to stress only domestic issues or attend to international ones as well. It was encouraged by global protest against the Vietnam War but felt it should lead the antiwar movement. Americans who attended the 1968 Ljubljana meeting of New Left leaders from Switzerland, Spain, West Germany, France, Finland, and Canada complained that debates were too ideological and abstract.[7] All too often the American New Left, like the country it critiqued, imagined itself the center of global protest from whom others could and should learn.

Europeans, by contrast, were more knowledgeable about and willing to borrow from countercultures and protests in other European countries; indeed, influences closer to home were often more important than distant American ones and mediated the latter. West Germans or Belgians or Italians could easily follow developments in neighboring countries. Many knew more than one language, and books and articles by Europeans as well as Americans circulated widely. The media had strong European coverage that both publicized and encouraged the flamboyant performativity of the counterculture and protest movements. Student exchanges increased moderately during the 1960s, and European youth tourism grew exponentially. By the mid 1970s three-quarters of German youth, two-thirds of French ones and over half of British had been to a foreign country, usually within Europe. While travel to the West remained restricted for most within the Soviet bloc, Czechs, if they had funds, could do so from 1965 on and many visited Austria and West Germany. Yugoslavia was a popular destination for Western European vacationers and a meeting place for Eastern and Western European Marxist theorists such as Agnes Heller, Ernest Mandel, and Leszek Kolakowski. For those involved in the counterculture, Amsterdam was the favorite pilgrimage site in 1966–67. Belgian demonstrators active since 1966 immediately traveled to Paris when students took over the Sorbonne, and throughout

---

[6] Maria Höhn and Martin Klimke, *A Breadth of Freedom: The Civil Rights Struggle, African American GIs, and Germany* (New York: Palgrave Macmillan, 2010), 114. Horn, *Spirit of '68*, 72, 75–80.
[7] Martin Klimke, *The Other Alliance: Student Protest in West Germany and the United States in the Global Sixties* (Princeton University Press, 2010), 46–48, 101.

1968 French and German protesters collaborated. Western Europeans visited Prague in 1967–68 but so too did 2.6 million East Germans. The British, however, were relatively isolated from developments on the continent.[8]

Information and theoretical debates about imperialism and *autogestion* circulated via personal contacts and political networks as did tactics. For example, French Trotskyists learned about pushing the boundaries of legality at demonstrations from West German demonstrators, who in turn, had earlier learned it from Guy Dubord and the Situationists, who protested the impoverishment of everyday life and the society of spectacle through artistic interventions and disruptive happenings.[9] While Europeans listened to Bob Dylan and other American musicians, many of their cultural products and practices were now shaped more by Britain than the United States.

Protesters across Western and parts of Eastern Europe demanded open frontiers and questioned nationality as the basic identification. When the French Communist Party denounced French protest leader Daniel Cohn-Bendit as a German Jew and the government barred him from reentering France, protesters and posters proclaimed "We are all Germans and Jews." There was growing talk of European citizenship and the possibility of a European culture and identity. As the philosopher Ivan Sviták succinctly put it in his "Ten Commandments for a young Czech Intellectual": "Think like a European. You live in Europe not America or the Soviet Union."[10]

American anxiety

Nineteen sixty-eight shocked the transatlantic world but achieved few of its goals and those only belatedly. In France 5 million workers struck, paralyzing the country, universities shut down, and de Gaulle fled only to return and remain in power. Although Johnson decided not to run for president again, the United States remained in Vietnam. The Soviet Union lost any remaining legitimacy by invading Czechoslovakia, but it did crush the Prague Spring. Workers gained some important material benefits, although these were eroded over the course of the seventies and

---

[8] Axel Schildt and Detlef Siegfried, "Youth, Consumption, and Politics in the Age of Radical Change," in Schildt and Siegfried, eds., *Between Marx and Coca-Cola,* 26–27. Richard Ivan Jobs, "Youth Movements: Travel, Protest, and Europe in 1968," *American Historical Review* 114/2 (April 2009): 383. Timothy S. Brown, "East Germany," in Martin Klimke and Joachim Scharloth, eds., *1968 in Europe: A History of Protest and Activism, 1956–1977* (New York: Palgrave Macmillan, 2008), 194.
[9] Ingrid Gilcher-Holtey, "France," in Klimke and Scharloth, eds., *1968 in Europe,* 120.
[10] Jobs, "Youth Movements," 391, 400.

eighties. Universities were partially reformed but never became the egalitarian and culturally innovative collectivities students imagined. The protests of 1968 failed due to the movements' weaknesses, the strength of states across Europe, and the majority's commitment to the existing order, despite criticisms of it. The New Left emphasized direct action, not party building, decentralized control and not seizing state power, and no political parties or European or transatlantic organizations emerged.

Despite these failures, American officials worried nearly as much about what was happening in Europe and the Third World as they did about Detroit, Chicago, or Kent State. Secretary of State Dean Rusk called May 1968 in France "a sobering lesson." The State Department's Interagency Youth Committee was particularly concerned about losing the loyalty of future European leaders. German youth were skeptical about America's global role and the Atlantic partnership, and neither they nor many of their elders believed that the United States was defending Berlin in Saigon, as Americans asserted. United States officials were encouraged when the Berlin city government held a pro American Peace and Freedom Rally in 1968 to which 150,000 came, but for many Berliners such a state-sponsored political demonstration for which public sector employees were given the day off seemed reminiscent of the Nazi era.[11]

Presidential advisor and modernization theorist Walt Rostow attributed the global protests to a multitude of factors ranging from new technology and mass education to entrenched old oligarchies. The CIA insisted that communists were not behind the troubles, but Johnson and Vice President Hubert Humphrey, who had had balloons filled with pudding thrown at him by West Berlin demonstrators in 1967, were convinced otherwise. A 1968 State Department Student Unrest Study Group argued that protests could be ignored – unless they contested "the objectives of United States foreign policy, our relations with the country concerned or the worldwide functioning of our business interests and our free enterprise economic system" or disrupted the Atlantic alliance.[12] Protesters certainly tried to do all of the above.

In the first postwar decades Western European youth had been enamored of America, admiring its ideals and wealth, enjoying its music and movies, and sharing vicariously in the American dream. The real and imagined affinities were shattered by the Vietnam War, opening the way for a new kind of anti-Americanism. Unlike the European right, the European New Left did not reject modernity, even as it criticized the American model of it; unlike cultural elites, youth did not reject

---

[11] Klimke, *The Other Alliance*, 175–77, 195.   [12] Klimke, *The Other Alliance*, 196.

American mass culture, even as they attacked the excesses of consumerism. Conservative and Christian Democratic forces had supported American anti-communism and military presence in Europe, while distancing themselves from American materialism; the New Left rejected anti-communism without becoming pro Soviet and opposed the presence of American forces in Europe and elsewhere around the globe. While prewar conservative and fascist anti-Americanism had hoped to modify capitalism with corporatist institutions, new left anti-capitalism conjured vague visions of a democratic and decentralized socialism. For United States officials and businessmen, this new anti-Americanism was perhaps more disturbing than the old, for it grew out of the democratization and modernization of Western Europe, and it targeted America's global role. It was a product of and response to the American Century.

Fear went beyond youth, for there was growing concern that governments, political parties, and elites no longer wholeheartedly supported the United States. A 1968 USIA report on public opinion found a sharp decline in Western Europeans' conviction that they shared basic interests with the United States. In West Germany the drop was from 77 percent in early 1965 to a mere 11 percent at the end of 1967, and older Germans were more critical of America's Vietnam policy than those under 25. Such criticism did not make American leaders more self-reflective. As Humphrey angrily lashed out in 1967:

Europeans have rejected the world after the loss of their colonies. They resent United States power ... The Europeans are selfish. We should challenge them to participate in the world outside their borders. We must keep pounding at them on this problem.[13]

This American anti-Europeanism, inklings of which had first been heard during the Korean War and around the disputes over offset payments, was to resurface repeatedly in subsequent decades.

Protests in Eastern Europe offered ideological solace but few practical political benefits to American cold warriors. The United States long since abandoned talk of liberating Eastern Europe, and politicians and the public alike were reeling from antiwar protests, political assassinations, and uprisings in black ghettos. And they were still bitterly divided about the brutal and costly war in Vietnam. Immediately after the Soviet Army invaded Prague in August 1968, pictures of police and National Guardsmen battling demonstrators outside the Democratic National Convention in Chicago filled television and newspapers at home and

[13] Jeremy Suri, *Power and Protest: Global Revolution and the Rise of Détente* (Cambridge, MA: Harvard University Press, 2003), 176.

abroad. As during the 1956 Hungarian and Suez crises, neither side could easily claim the moral high ground.

A new political landscape

The short-term victories for established regimes could not reverse the cultural and social changes underway since the early sixties; nor could they restore the political status quo ante. Countercultural institutions such as communal housing, food co-ops, health clinics, experimental kindergartens, and new journals and publishing houses proliferated across Western Europe. Sometimes this alternative scene produced new forms of left politics; sometimes it served as the basis from which to launch the "long march through the institutions" that Dutschke had called for; and sometimes it was an apolitical escape. As new political movements and ideologies emerged, the appeal of established ones diminished.

The most publicized new political phenomenon was terrorism, embraced by a small minority of leftists who abandoned mass organizing for brutal demonstrative acts in the hope of sparking urban guerilla warfare. Throughout the 1970s the West German Red Army Faction or Baader-Meinhof Gang attacked American military bases, robbed banks, and kidnapped and killed German politicians and businessmen. In Italy the left terrorism of the Red Brigades, which included the kidnapping and murder of Christian Democratic leader Aldo Moro in 1978, was matched by neofascist violence that indiscriminately murdered civilians. To protest conditions in Northern Ireland, the Irish Republican Army carried its terrorism campaign to England. By contrast, the American Weather Underground, an offshoot of SDS, was short-lived and did minimal damage except to itself. Although these terrorist movements achieved none of their goals and increasingly subordinated politics to survival underground, they contributed to an atmosphere of political crisis and cultural pessimism. They provoked massive state surveillance and repression against themselves and in West Germany against the entire alternative scene.

Of more lasting importance were new social movements that fit uneasily into older political party divisions between Republicans and Democrats in the United States, Conservatives and Labour in Britain, or Christian Democrats and Social Democrats on the continent and disrupted the transatlantic cooperation built on them. By the mid 1970s the utopianism and radicalism of 1968 had evaporated, but feminists, environmentalists, and peace activists on both sides of the Atlantic challenged ideologies of unlimited growth, the embrace of nuclear power and weapons, and gendered understandings of public and private. In Italy there was mass agitation for better housing and sustained protests by the unemployed.

Human rights movements emerged as well, especially in France and the United States, but their concerns were directed at the Soviet Union and the Third World rather than their own nations.

The antinuclear and green movements were larger, more visible, and more radical in Europe, especially Germany, than in the United States and had a significant impact on nuclear power development. By the 1980s the German Green Party had gained significant parliamentary representation. Women's movements focusing on issues of empowerment, autonomy, sexuality, and reproductive rights emerged across the Atlantic world, but liberal, rights-oriented feminism dominated in the United States, while socialist feminist movements had greater weight in several European countries. Whether demanding the right to abortion, equal pay, wages for housework, or women's studies programs, feminists challenged misogynist attitudes and male-dominated hierarchies and material privileges. They asserted the primacy of gender over categories like class and made the personal political in entirely new ways.

To complicate the post 1968 order even more, communism changed on both sides of the Iron Curtain. After crushing the Prague Spring, Brezhnev proclaimed that

Each communist party is free to apply the principles of Marxism-Leninism and socialism in its own country but it is not free to deviate from these principles ... The weakening of any of the links in the world system of socialism directly affects all the socialist countries, which cannot look indifferently upon this.[14]

The Soviet Army and the Brezhnev Doctrine ended any hope of achieving "socialism with a human face," but could not generate ideological commitment or enthusiasm for "real existing socialism," as the status quo was called. Dissidents continued to write and speak in the Soviet Union; workers protested in the Gdansk shipyards in Poland. The Czechoslovak regime of "normalization" offered privatized citizenship in return for political quiescence. People were promised self-realization through a modicum of consumer goods, a relaxed work life, and a country cottage. Leading dissident Václav Havel dismissed normalization as a post-totalitarian "coming together of a dictatorship and a consumer society," but it was effectively sold to Czechs and Slovaks as a lifestyle qualitatively superior to that of the West. Czech returnees from Austria or America publicly complained that the West was too materialistic, the work pace too intense, culture and entertainment too expensive. Czechoslovakia was, many claimed in an

---

[14] www.fordham.edu/halsall/mod/1968brezhnev.html. *Pravda*, September 25, 1968.

echo of a long-standing European view, "a more spiritually mature nation than America."[15]

In the mid and late 1970s, Communist parties in Italy, Spain, Portugal, and France reoriented their programs and tactics in a reformist and Europeanist direction. The Italian Communist Party (PCI) led the way toward Eurocommunism, for it was critical of the Soviet suppression of dissent in Eastern Europe, weakened by the defection of young workers and students, fearful of the resurgent right within Italy, and worried by the 1973 American-backed coup against the democratically elected president of Chile, Salvador Allende. In the early 1970s PCI head Enrico Berlinguer proposed an "historic compromise" among Communists, Catholics, and Socialists. While Communists initially envisioned it as a means to defend democracy and keep the middle classes from moving right, many later hoped it would foster a transition to democratic socialism. The PCI accepted the European Economic Community and agreed to keep Italy in NATO. In Portugal and Spain the formerly illegal Communist parties promoted the transition from dictatorship to democracy. Eurocommunism disappointed its architects and supporters, however, for the PCI never joined a coalition government, even though it had one-third of the popular vote, and was unable to push through substantial political and social reforms in the face of Christian Democratic opposition. In both Portugal and Spain, Socialists quickly outflanked Communists once elections were held. By decade's end Eurocommunism was dead.

Despite its brevity and failure, the effort to create a genuinely autonomous European communism was greeted with extreme hostility by United States officials. American Ambassador John Volpe told the Italian press that the United States staunchly opposed PCI participation in the government. Secretary of State Henry Kissinger was more comfortable with the authoritarian regimes of Salazar and Caetano in Portugal than with their moderate revolutionary successor. For the United States government, Eurocommunism did not represent a third way but rather communism in a new and equally dangerous guise. Many, like Kissinger, preferred the clear-cut divisions of the classic Cold War to flexibility and openness to compromise. The flexibility and compromise that might promote a European pole in a bipolar world, a space between the blocs, and increased autonomy were as unwelcome in Washington as in Moscow.[16]

---

[15] Bren, *Greengrocer and His TV*, 186, 197.
[16] Geoff Eley, *Forging Democracy: The History of the Left in Europe, 1850–2000* (Oxford University Press, 2002), 409–15. Paul Ginsborg, *A History of Contemporary Italy: Society and Politics, 1943–1988* (London: Penguin, 1990), 356–57, 373–74, 400–1.

The protests of 1968 and the new social movements spurred a conservative backlash and resurgence of fundamentalist Christianity in the United States. Europe also had heated debates about university reform, divorce and abortion, and changing sexual mores and gender relations. Yet, these controversies never took on the breadth, acrimony, and longevity of the American culture wars. European secularization continued, despite the existence of established churches in many countries, and attitudes toward sexuality were more relaxed. Moreover, Western Europeans were publicly and intensively grappling with their fascist and collaborationist pasts, for which they could not hold rebellious youth or liberated women responsible. Many Americans bitterly resented their country's loss in Vietnam and blamed the war's opponents.

Gold, oil, and economic crisis

Western Europe's increasingly independent and critical stance toward America came not only from politics and culture but also from economics. During the seventies the postwar era of unprecedented growth and qualitatively new prosperity came to a grinding halt. Fluctuating exchange rates, escalating oil prices, stagflation, and debts destabilized economies across the Atlantic world, and traditional Keynesian methods of steering the economy failed. Fordist models of mass production were in crisis, and sixties talk of meaningful work gave way to fears about unemployment. While neither Europe nor the United States experienced anything like the depression of the thirties, the Golden Age ended and with it confident expectations about a future of full employment, expanding consumption, and generous social programs.

The time of economic troubles began in August 1971 when President Richard Nixon and his advisors decided unilaterally to abandon the Bretton Woods monetary system in which the dollar and its exchangeability with gold were central. The United States had long been running a balance of payments deficit due to the costs of maintaining military forces around the globe, United States investments abroad, and growing European and Japanese competition in export markets. In 1971 imports exceeded exports and America ran its first balance of trade deficit. For over a decade foreign countries, worried about the value of the dollar, had turned in their dollars for gold, substantially depleting United States gold reserves. Instead of responding to these problems with domestically unpopular measures like raising interest rates, Nixon declared that dollars could no longer be exchanged for gold and floated the dollar's exchange rate. Simultaneously, he imposed a 10 percent tax on imports and a ninety-day wage and price freeze. America's European allies were neither consulted nor informed in advance. American officials rebuffed European requests to cooperate in constructing a new international financial order, putting their faith in free trade and the free movement of capital.

The United States government's actions reflected its growing dislike of such European Community (EC) policies as the exclusion of agricultural imports and special trade arrangements with countries like Spain and Israel. While some officials worried about foreign reactions, Secretary of the Treasury John Connally remarked "So the other countries don't like it. So what?" United States officials told Europeans that they were expected to capitulate to America in monetary policy. In 1972 Nixon told his advisors that Europeans "enjoy kicking the United States around … European leaders want to 'screw' us and we want to 'screw' them in the economic arena." Western Europe had to choose between constructive competition and economic confrontation with America. A year later the new Treasury Secretary, Georg Schultz, was more diplomatic but equally insistent that United States policy would be determined solely by domestic interests.[17]

The decision to jettison Bretton Woods was a sign of both American economic weakness and American willingness to act boldly and unilaterally. A year later the United States lifted controls on the movement of capital, opening the way for unfettered financial markets of the sort that had existed in the interwar years. America's New Economic Policy (as Nixon called it, without presumably knowing that Lenin had used the term in the 1920s) represented a clear repudiation of postwar embedded liberalism. The United States benefited in the short run, for it could run large deficits without having to adjust its currency or fear a gold drain. Europe suffered, for the value of currencies like the German mark rose and exports were more expensive; this was America's intention. But the United States could not force Western Europeans to absorb substantially more American goods, and the United States ran a balance of trade deficit every subsequent year of the century, except 1975.

Transatlantic economic tensions exacerbated long-standing American concerns that the Atlantic partnership was fraying and led Kissinger to announce the Year of Europe in April 1973. Asserting the benevolent intentions of the United States, he called for "a new Atlantic Charter" and urged Western Europeans to articulate "a clear set of common objectives" shared with Americans. He noted that "the European Community has

---

[17] Diane B. Kunz, *Butter and Guns: America's Cold War Economic Diplomacy* (New York: Free Press, 1997), 204. Herbert Zimmermann, "Unraveling the Ties that Really Bind: The Dissolution of the Transatlantic Monetary Order and the European Monetary Cooperation, 1965–1973," in Matthias Schulz and Thomas A. Schwartz, eds., *The Strained Alliance: United States-European Relations from Nixon to Carter* (Cambridge University Press, 2010), 139, 141.

increasingly stressed its regional personality," while the United States was responsible for the global trading and financial system. "We must reconcile these two perspectives." This proclamation was not well received on the other side of the Atlantic. The EC, which was absorbed with integrating its new members – Britain, Ireland, and Denmark – found Kissinger's call premature. The French deemed the speech "imperious" and directed against a French-led Europe. German Chancellor Willy Brandt criticized America for dealing with Western European nations bilaterally and ignoring the EC. He objected to the term new Atlantic Charter since the original had targeted Germany. British Prime Minister Edward Heath claimed that "for Henry Kissinger to announce a Year of Europe without consulting any of us was rather like my standing between the lions of Trafalgar Square and announcing that we were embarking on a year to save America."[18]

Rather than revivifying the Atlantic alliance, the Year of Europe encouraged further European integration and led to a European Declaration of Identity. The 1969 EC Hague Summit had recognized the need for more economic integration but took no concrete action. In the wake of Washington's 1971 decision, however, EC countries tried to float their currencies jointly within a narrow band of exchange rates in order to limit uncertainty and facilitate intra-EC trade. The "snake," as the joint float was called, worked poorly, but its very failure, combined with American monetary unilateralism, encouraged the EC countries to establish the European Monetary System in 1978. This was a key step along the road that would eventually lead to the European Union and the euro and was hardly the capitulation that the United States had envisioned.

The oil shock of 1973 proved equally divisive for transatlantic relations, even as it disturbed intra-European cooperation as well. The changing structure of the oil industry, growing worldwide demand, and the politics of the Middle East interacted to cause the oil crisis. Since World War II, United States oil consumption had increased markedly and the United States had to import up to a third of its oil. Europe shifted steadily away from coal to oil for industry, heating, and transportation, and that oil came overwhelmingly from the Middle East. As demand rose, the Organization of Petroleum Exporting Countries (OPEC), founded in 1961, grew more assertive in securing "participation" in the multinational oil companies and a promise of eventual majority ownership. It was the Yom Kippur

---

[18] Henry Kissinger, "Year of Europe Address," April 23, 1973, www.ena.lu/address_given_henry-kissinger-new-york-23-april-1973-2-9561. Daniel Möckli, "Asserting Europe's Distinct Identity: The EC Nine and Kissinger's Year of Europe," in Schulz and Schwartz, eds., *Strained Alliance*, 199–202.

Illustration 22 Oil crisis, November 1973, horses replace cars in the Netherlands.

War between Egypt and Israel, however, and America's decision to aid Israel without consulting its NATO allies that sent prices spiraling from $3 a barrel to $11 by January 1974 and led OPEC to impose an embargo on the United States, the Netherlands, Portugal, and South Africa.

Americans responded to rising gas prices, long gas lines, and shortages with a volatile mixture of anger, anxiety, and pessimism about the future of their car-dependent country. But the government developed no new energy policy either in 1973 or after the second oil shock in 1979, when oil prices shot up to $40 a barrel in the wake of the Iranian Revolution. Across Western Europe prices rose steeply, governments mandated carless Sundays, and although supplies remained relatively stable, anxiety spread. Finding a common transatlantic response proved exceedingly difficult. The United States and the Netherlands advocated a more confrontational stance toward OPEC, but most Western European states wanted Israel to withdraw from Egypt and the UN to broker a peace treaty. They also supported Palestinian rights. France pushed for a common EC response to the crisis, but other European states jockeyed to protect their national interests, and the United States feared Western European states would sign bilateral treaties with OPEC countries like Iran or Saudi Arabia. As the United States tried to impose its policies and Western European states oscillated between autonomy and Atlanticism, relations within the EC and with the United States deteriorated.

The oil shocks further disturbed the international order by redistributing wealth globally. Between 1973 and 1977 OPEC oil profits increased 600 times to $140 billion, shifting wealth away from oil-consuming Western Europe, Japan, the Third World, and to a lesser extent the United States. OPEC deposited over half of those profits back in Western European and above all American banks.[19] Awash in these petro dollars, banks lent increasingly large amounts to Eastern Europe and Third World countries, above all in Latin America. It was very lucrative in the short run but unviable by the 1980s, as we will see. The influx of petro dollars also encouraged the United States to eliminate any restrictions on capital flows and pressure its reluctant allies to do the same. The growing importance of the financial sector, above all in the United States, was also driven by the structural crises affecting all European and American economies.

Stagflation and the decline of Fordism

As growth rates slowed in the late sixties and then dropped precipitously after 1973, Europeans and Americans alike viewed the decline as temporary; by decade's end it was clear that the postwar boom had definitively ended. Per capita growth in GDP declined worldwide from 3.5 percent in the 1960s to 1.8 percent in the 1970s. Across Western Europe and in the United States, the average annual growth in GDP slowed from between 4.4 percent and 5.8 percent to more modest rates in the 3 percent range in the same period, while Britain dropped to 2.3 percent. Equally troubling was the simultaneous rise in unemployment and inflation, which was fueled by rising prices for oil, commodities like copper and rubber, and food. In France and Italy the consumer price index, which had risen 3.8 percent per year in the sixties, increased to 8.8 percent and 12.2 percent respectively in the seventies. In the United States, the rise was from 2.4 percent to 7 percent. Only West Germany kept its inflation in check and its unemployment rose only from 1 percent in the early 1970s to 3.2 percent after 1974. Matters were worse elsewhere: French unemployment averaged 4.8 percent after 1974, British 5.6 percent and Italian and American 6.7 percent. Manufacturing profitability in the wealthiest countries declined by a quarter between 1968 and 1973; the New York

---

[19] Judith Stein, *Pivotal Decade: How the United States Traded Factories for Finance in the Seventies* (New Haven: Yale University Press, 2010), 74. Kunz, *Butter and Guns*, 254.

Stock Exchange lost half its value between 1972 and 1974/75; and New York City, the center of the global economy, went bankrupt.[20]

Stagflation was the term used to describe this unprecedented combination of slow growth, rising prices, and high unemployment that had multiple causes. American economic hegemony, productivity, technological innovations and consumption had helped sustain the postwar boom, but all were eroding by the seventies. The United States accounted for over one-third of the world's GDP in 1950 but just under one-quarter in 1976, and the American share of world trade declined by 23 percent in the 1970s. Western Europe was catching up; its productivity had risen from 50 percent to 70 percent of that of America, and its trade was growing more rapidly, as was Japan's. Take cars, for example. Throughout the twentieth century, America had dominated the global car industry, but in 1968 it imported more cars than it exported, and Western Europe and Japan were manufacturing them. After the EC expanded to include the UK, Ireland, and Denmark in 1973, its population and trade were larger than America's and its GDP almost as big. The EC had become, in Connally's words 'a rival economic block." To be sure, the United States still invested more in Western European countries than vice versa, but the latter were growing faster than the former. Although still the world's largest economy, America did not accept its diminished status gracefully. According to Peter Peterson, United States special envoy to the EC, "For 25 years we have helped these European bastards getting back on their feet and now they take us for a ride." Although Western Europe caused trouble for the United States, it had problems of its own. Reconstruction, modernization, urbanization, and the provisioning of populations with new housing and the first generation of consumer durables had created the long boom. As these one-time processes came to an end, so did extraordinary growth rates and the need for foreign workers.[21]

Postwar growth and prosperity had been built around large-scale heavy industry, mass-produced consumer durables, and mass, fairly uniform consumption, but by the seventies Fordism was in crisis across the Atlantic world. The classic industries of the second industrial revolution

[20] Niall Ferguson, "Crisis, What Crisis?" in Niall Ferguson, Charles S. Maier, Erez Manela, and Daniel J. Sargent, eds., *The Shock of the Global* (Cambridge, MA: Harvard University Press, 2010), 9. Charles S. Maier, "Malaise,' in Ferguson et al., eds., *Shock of the Global*, 28. Ivan T. Berend, *Europe since the 1980s* (Cambridge University Press, 2010), 21. Jeffry A. Frieden, *Global Capitalism: Its Fall and Rise in the Twentieth Century* (New York: Norton, 2006), 366.

[21] Stein, *Pivotal Decade*, 200. Frieden, *Global Capitalism*, 340. Edward M. Graham, "Transatlantic Investment by Multinational Firms: A Rivalistic Phenomenon?" *Journal of Post Keynesian Economics* 1/1 (1978): 95. Zimmermann, "Unravelling the Ties that Really Bind," 136.

from iron and steel to cars and kitchen appliances were no longer sources of growth and innovation. Japan and newly industrialized countries like Korea and Taiwan had become the major producers of iron and steel, televisions, and washing machines. In some areas they employed Fordist methods at lower labor costs; in others they pioneered new lean and flexible just-in-time production techniques. On both sides of the Atlantic, the manufacturing sector shrank and with that the high-paying, mostly male, unionized jobs that were central to postwar prosperity. In Amsterdam in the 1950s, for example, 40 percent of the workforce was in industry; by the mid 1970s only 14 percent was. The industrial region of Lorraine in northern France lost 28 percent of its manufacturing jobs. The Fiat automobile plant fired 65,000 of its 165,000 workers by introducing robots.[22] Across the Ruhr mines and mills shut down. British mining, Detroit car manufacturing, Pittsburgh steel all suffered from deindustrialization, and "rust belt" entered the vocabulary. The shape of the postindustrial or post-Fordist economy, however, was not yet clear.

Western Europe weathered the crisis relatively better than the United States, for the state intervened to support manufacturing, productivity held up, trade and investment within Europe by Europeans increased, and growth was stronger than it was to be in the eighties. In West Germany there was optimism about *Modell Deutschland*. This 1978 electoral slogan of the Social Democrat Helmut Schmidt reflected German pride in its strong exports, quality work, and rising standard of living but also in its particular balance of market and state, economic success and social equalization. In France and Italy business was more anxious and labor relations more contested. The British economy continued to flounder, inflation spiraled, and strikes multiplied, culminating in the Winter of Discontent in 1978–79. Neither Labour nor Conservatives could bring social peace or economic recovery. In the United States middle-class and working-class anger about the economy, conflicts between labor and business, and the realization that Western Europe and Japan were serious economic competitors generated a pervasive sense of crisis and loss of confidence that was exacerbated by America's defeat in the Vietnam War and the Watergate scandal. As the United States dropped from first to fifth in standard-of-living rankings, once-optimistic Americans came to believe that subsequent years would be even worse.[23]

Only Eastern Europe seemed exempt from the crises. Growth remained strong until the end of the decade and consumption increased as regimes

---

[22] Judt, *Postwar*, 459.
[23] Kunz, *Butter and Guns*, 188. William H. Chafe, *The Rise and Fall of the American Century* (Oxford University Press, 2009), 229.

sought to enhance their legitimacy through material improvements rather than political mobilization. The Soviet Union benefited greatly from being an oil and natural gas producer, and trade between CMEA countries and Western Europe increased. Communist states remained wedded to the Fordist model of heavy industry and mass production and supported employment in them. Beneath the veneer of prosperity, however, problems were looming. While the Soviets profited from rising oil prices and sales to Western Europe, their allies in Eastern Europe suffered from having to pay market prices for once subsidized Soviet oil. During the 1960s the Soviet Union and the GDR tried to modernize technology, and countries like Czechoslovakia and Hungary introduced market reforms. By the 1970s internal reforms stalled and socialist states sought to buy technology from the West. Unable to produce manufactured goods that capitalist societies would buy, the Soviet Union exported raw materials, but most Eastern European countries had to borrow from Western European banks and governments. Unable to produce enough of the consumer goods their populations demanded, countries like the GDR and Poland imported them from the West. This required still more borrowing of convertible currencies (which socialist currencies like the zloty and the ruble were not). As socialist states purchased more goods from capitalist ones, they had to pay higher prices due to inflation and rising energy costs. Again, more borrowing was the temporary solution. Over the course of the seventies, Eastern European hard currency debts increased from $6 billion to $79 billion and no end to continued borrowing was in sight.[24] Socialist borrowers, like their capitalist lenders, preferred to focus on the short-term benefits rather than the long-term dangers of such debts. The United States and Western Europe could not paper over their undeniable cyclical and structural problems with loans. How then did they respond?

Keynesianism, neoliberalism, and the "crisis of democracy"

The economic crisis of the seventies reactivated earlier battles between those who believed in classical economic liberalism and those advocating state regulation of the economy. This time, however, neoliberalism and not Keynesianism was in the ascendency. As the crises persisted, politicians, economists, and pundits on both sides of the Atlantic lamented the inability of traditional Keynesian deficit spending to stimulate demand,

---

[24] Ivan T. Berend, *Central and Eastern Europe, 1944–1993: Detour from the Periphery to the Periphery* (Cambridge University Press, 1996), 223–30.

employment, and growth. They debated the pros and cons of monetarism, free trade, and unregulated capital flows. In 1975 the heads of state of France, West Germany, Italy, Japan, Britain, and the United States met in Rambouillet, France, to discuss the global economy. Their concluding Declaration announced their commitment to combating unemployment, inflation, and energy problems, while restoring growth. They promised "to achieve the maximum possible level of trade liberalization," increase trade with socialist countries, and "counter disorderly market conditions, or erratic fluctuations, in exchange rates." Developing countries would receive help in financing their deficits. The Declaration pledged both "to secure for our economies the energy sources needed for their growth," and to reduce dependency on foreign oil by conservation and alternative sources.[25] The leading economies plus Canada formed the G7 in 1976, in order to discuss pressing economic problems regularly.

Common policies were harder to develop. The United States emphatically rejected the 1974 call by the G-77 developing countries at the UN for a New International Economic Order that would regulate commodity prices and foreign investments in the Third World and give the global South a greater voice in the IMF and World Bank. Western Europeans, such as Brandt, Swedish Prime Minister Olaf Palme, and Austrian Chancellor Bruno Kreisky, were more open to these demands and more committed to North–South dialogue and development aid. The G7 could not agree about whether countries with a trade surplus like Germany and Japan should accept more imports or whose tariffs should be lowered. There was no consensus about whether energy conservation was feasible and which alternative sources were desirable. Most importantly, nations differed on the relative roles the market and the state should play in economic recovery. By the 1980s the United States and Britain were embracing neoliberalism enthusiastically while Western Europeans sought to retain key elements of their more coordinated market economies.

The United States was the first to turn away from Keynesianism. Economists rejected demand stimulation in favor of monetarist adjustments of the money supply and focused on microeconomic assessments of individual choice rather than macroeconomic regulation. The government did not try to stimulate investment, subsidize research, embark on energy conservation, or develop jobs programs. Instead, it put its faith in the market, advocating free trade, unregulated capital flows, and tax policies favorable to the wealthy. Inflation was seen as the main economic problem, not unemployment. After a decade of unsuccessful measures to

[25] 1975 Rambouillet Summit Declaration, www.g8.utoronto.ca/summit/1975rambouillet/communique.htm.

curb inflation, Paul Volker, head of the American Federal Reserve Bank, raised interest rates from near zero to 10 percent. While this curbed inflation, unemployment shot up to 11 percent, real wages dropped 15 percent in the following three years, and median family income declined 10 percent.[26] This marked the beginning of America's neoliberal order, which would shift power from labor to business, increase income inequality, and shrink the welfare state. When Margaret Thatcher became prime minister in 1979, she steered Britain in a similar direction. Proclaiming her belief in individuals and markets and insisting that the state could not stem national decline, she privatized industries, transportation, and communication, promoted finance over manufacturing, attacked trade unions and local government autonomy, and supported deregulation. Keynesianism was dead in Keynes's native land.

Other European countries did not follow suit however. The EC, for example, increasingly cooperated on monetary policy and in 1975 established the European Regional Development Fund to aid its poorer areas. Germany and Sweden both retained substantial elements of their postwar compromises, which entailed balancing the interests of labor and capital and according the state a significant role in job creation, demand management, job training, and regional development. In the early 1970s the Swedish Social Democrats even sought to radicalize the corporatist model with the Meidner Plan, which proposed to use a percentage of profits to purchase shares that a union-managed fund would own. To be sure, all continental countries liberalized capital markets somewhat and encountered problems managing inflation and unemployment, but they did not turn against labor unions or try to diminish workers' rights. They did not rhetorically dismiss the state, as American and British leaders did; nor did they see the unfettered market as a panacea for all economic ills. These disagreements about economic policy were paralleled by ones about social rights.

In 1975 the Trilateral Commission, composed of government officials, businessmen, and social scientists from America, Western Europe, and Japan, published an alarmist assessment of social rights and social spending in the wealthiest nations. According to its widely read report, *The Crisis of Democracy*, the United States, Western Europe, and Japan were becoming "ungovernable" because too many demands were being made by too many social actors. There was too much democracy and too little social discipline. Assessing conditions in Europe, Michel Crozier argued that "the European political systems were overloaded with participants and

---

[26] Frieden, *Global Capitalism*, 372–73. Stein, *Pivotal Decade*, 206.

demands." Governments were unable to master the complexity resulting from economic growth, more social participation, less social control, and the decline of traditional institutions like churches, universities, and the military. Moreover, there were "too many intellectuals, would-be-intellectuals and para intellectuals" who failed to create cohesive values and provide moral leadership. Despite these serious problems, Crozier argued, many things in Europe did function, and there was less protest and crime than in the United States.

Samuel Huntington's view from the United States was considerably more pessimistic. More Americans made more demands on the government but had less and less confidence in it. Increased government spending led to deficits and inflation. The power of the presidency was eroding and an "excess of democracy" meant that expertise and seniority were ignored or overridden. Ever mindful of America's global role, Huntington argued that the government lacked the authority to impose the sacrifices on the population that were necessary for the United States to meet its foreign policy and military needs. "A decline in the governability of democracy at home," he concluded, "means a decline in the influence of democracy abroad."[27]

The discourse of ungovernability showed how far the transatlantic world had moved from the sixties' calls for participatory democracy or Brandt's early seventies' plea to "dare more democracy." Politicians and academics now talked about security more than equality and urged people to be realistic and focus on essentials. But these shared concerns turned out to mean very different things in different national contexts.

On the EC and national levels, Western Europe continued to defend the postwar social project. In 1973 the nine EC members pledged their determination "to defend the principles of representative democracy, of the rule of law, of social justice – which is the ultimate goal of economic progress – and of respect for human rights." Western European states continued to spend a large proportion of GDP on social programs ranging from universal health insurance, pensions, and free higher education to social housing and family allowances. In West Germany, for example, social spending rose from 26 percent of GDP in 1966 to 33 percent in 1974. Between the early 1970s and early 1980s, social spending in the Netherlands increased from 49 percent of GDP to 66 percent; in Sweden from 45 percent to 66 percent. While United States expenditures on social security, education, welfare, and health payments for Medicare and Medicaid increased over the 1970s, social spending remained a much

---

[27] Michel Crozier, Samuel P. Huntington, and Joji Watanuki, *The Crisis of Democracy* (New York University Press, 1975), 12, 31, 113, 106.

smaller percentage of GDP than in Europe. The United States continued to spend much more on defense than Western Europe did; its social programs were much less universalistic and its social rights less numerous. Why did the transatlantic social policy gap, which had narrowed in the first two postwar decades, widen once again?[28]

The profound crisis of confidence and growing economic conflict that shook the United States in the wake of Vietnam, the Watergate scandal, and Nixon's resignation found no counterpart across the Atlantic. In Western European countries like Sweden and West Germany the seventies were a social democratic decade; in Italy social reform continued till mid decade, and Spain, Portugal, and Greece all reestablished democratic governments. However critical of particular state policies and institutions they might be, established political parties and the new social movements in Western Europe still regarded the state as central to social progress, whereas the United States and Britain were moving in an anti-statist neo-liberal direction. In the wake of 1968 and the economic problems of the 1970s, Western Europe and the United States were developing increasingly distinctive versions of modern society and economy. Finding agreement among the Atlantic allies on foreign policy proved no easier.

Détente and *Ostpolitik*

The superpowers, individual European states, and the European Community undertook multiple initiatives to improve diplomatic relations, enhance security, and increase economic and cultural exchanges across the increasingly permeable Iron Curtain. While steps to ease Cold War tensions and limit nuclear testing began after the Cuban Missile Crisis, there were no sustained, multifaceted, and multiparty negotiations during the sixties, as the arms race and the Vietnam War escalated, and unrest at home and abroad preoccupied the superpowers. By the seventies, however, there were multiple if contradictory pressures for détente. The superpowers wanted more security at lower costs, while the smaller states desired greater autonomy from the United States and the Soviet Union; the former wanted to stabilize the Cold War order, the latter to transform it. Economics, culture, and human rights mixed uneasily with nuclear diplomacy and the ongoing Berlin question in the multidirectional negotiations that began in the late 1960s and culminated with the Helsinki Final Act in 1975.

---

[28] Document on the European Identity published by the Nine Foreign Ministers on December 14, 1973 in Copenhagen, www.ena.lu. *Das Ende der Zuversicht? Die siebziger Jahre als Geschichte*, ed. by Konrad H. Jarausch (Göttingen: Vandenhoeck & Ruprecht, 2008), 120. Frieden, *Global Capitalism*, 368.

Despite a shared commitment to improving relations, many issues created conflict within each bloc and across them. The superpowers felt entitled to control détente, but the smaller states also wanted to play a major role. In his Year of Europe speech, Kissinger insisted that "The United States has global interests and responsibilities. Our European Allies have regional interests." In its subsequent Declaration of European Identity, however, the EC insisted:

> International developments and the growing concentration of power and responsibility in the hands of a very small number of great powers mean that Europe must unite and speak increasingly with one voice if it wants to make itself heard and play its proper role in the world.

Was détente a transatlantic as well as a superpower project, or did it contribute to the erosion of American power in Western Europe?[29]

Soviet and American leaders pursued détente for both shared and distinctive reasons and from strength as well as weakness. Kissinger and Brezhnev, the principal architects of superpower détente, envisioned it as a conservative policy that would stabilize the existing bipolar European order and be designed and implemented solely by the United States and the Soviet Union. For American leaders détente was less an abandonment of containment than the pursuit of it by other means. Since the Soviet Union had reached near parity in nuclear weapons, the arms race and mutually assured destruction no longer seemed to guarantee American primacy. Kissinger, impatient with the moralism and exceptionalism of American Cold war politics, insisted that the United States was a nation like other nations, which had to recognize its limits, prioritize its interests, and act from realism rather than idealism.[30] If the United States could not dominate as it previously had, it could nonetheless stabilize, in cooperation with the Soviet Union, a Cold War order in which it remained the most powerful state.

Security and the economy were the Soviets' top priority. Although not involved in a draining and divisive war, the Soviets found it even more difficult than the Americans to fund both guns and butter. The rising cost of the arms race and a large military impinged on growing social entitlements and ongoing efforts to provide adequate consumer goods and buy technology abroad to jump-start the economy. In addition, détente might offer a compensation for the repression of dissent at home and refurbish the Soviet image that the invasion of Czechoslovakia had so badly

---

[29] Kissinger, "Year of Europe Address." Document on the European Identity.
[30] Mario Del Pero, *The Eccentric Realist: Henry Kissinger and the Shaping of American Foreign Policy* (Ithaca: Cornell University Press, 2010).

tarnished. Most importantly, détente promised to give formal recognition to the post-1945 settlement of borders and regimes. Many Soviet leaders saw détente as an indication that history was moving in favor of communism. Brezhnev, a member of the war generation, however, sought a deal with the United States principally in order to avoid a repetition of the experience of World War II from which the Soviets had emerged victorious but at horrific cost.[31]

In early 1972 the United States took the initiative on détente with Nixon's surprise visit to China, which it had not recognized since the 1949 revolution. Soviet leaders were stunned. Realizing that the Sino-Soviet split could not be repaired and fearing potential attacks from its former ally, they were most receptive to the idea of a summit in Moscow in May. That produced an Agreement on the Basic Principles of Relations between the two nations in which they pledged to "refrain from the threat or use of force against the other Party," and "to remove the danger of nuclear war." This was followed by the signing of the Strategic Arms Limitation Treaty (SALT I) and the Anti-Ballistic Missile (ABM) Treaty, which outlawed the building of missile defense systems. While this was a substantial step forward in regulating nuclear weapons, it nonetheless left the Soviets with roughly 2,400 missile launchers and the Americans with 1,700. There were no restrictions on American strategic bombers or on multiple independently targeted reentry vehicles (MIRVs), the most potentially deadly missiles. The Soviets continued to develop nuclear submarines and strategic bombers, spending nearly 18 percent of their GDP on the military. While American military spending declined from 8.1 percent of its much larger GDP to 4.6 percent over the decade, it retained a preponderance of power.[32]

Despite these shortcomings, the Moscow Summit seemed to have achieved the conservative, stabilizing aims of détente Soviet-American style. To the annoyance of Nixon and Kissinger and the mixed assessment of Brezhnev, however, other players were pursuing their own détente agendas. The GDR wanted diplomatic recognition from the West, and the governments of Hungary, Romania, and Poland wanted more autonomy from the Soviet Union. Western European nations sought improved political and cultural relations with the Soviet Union and other Eastern European states. De Gaulle, for example, had long envisioned a "Europe

---

[31] Vladislav Zubok, "The Soviet Union and Détente of the 1970s," *Cold War History* 8/4 (Nov. 2008): 427–47.

[32] www1.umn.edu/humanrts/peace/docs/preventwar1973.html. Vladislav M. Zubok, *A Failed Empire: The Soviet Union in the Cold War from Stalin to Gorbachev* (Chapel Hill: University of North Carolina Press, 2007), 205, www.truthandpolitics.org/military-relative-size.php#gdp-graph.

from the Atlantic to the Urals," in which France would, of course, play the dominant role and Europe alone would settle the German question. In the 1960s and 1970s British prime ministers paid visits to Moscow to improve relations. All Western European countries wanted to circumvent the Cocom restrictions and increase trade with Eastern Europe, and the Italians negotiated an agreement with the USSR for Fiat to build a huge automobile factory in Togliattigrad. Of equal importance the nine EC members sought to coordinate their foreign policies and gain recognition for the European Community as an international political actor.

Most importantly, West Germany embarked on a new *Ostpolitik*. Under Adenauer and the Christian Democrats, the FRG had been a major obstacle to any easing of tensions with Eastern Europe, for it refused to recognize the GDR or to have diplomatic relations with any country that did. It denied that the Oder-Neisse line was the permanent border with Poland and continued to claim territories to the east of it. These hard-line policies began to ease when a Grand Coalition of Christian Democrats and Social Democrats ruled from 1966–69, and *Ostpolitik* took off after the SPD came to power in alliance with the Free Democrats in 1969. Chancellor Willy Brandt, who came from a working-class background, had been active in the SPD in his youth, and fled Germany during the Third Reich, was shaped by his anti-Nazi past. He was convinced that West Germany had to acknowledge what Germany had done in World War II, accept the results of history, and reconcile with Eastern European nations. He also wanted to forge a more autonomous German foreign policy after his experience as West Berlin's mayor when the Wall went up and America stood by passively. For Kennedy, "a wall was better than a war." For Brandt, as he wrote in his memoirs, "in August 1961 a curtain was drawn aside to reveal an empty state. . . . we lost certain illusions . . . and it was against this background that my so-called Ostpolitik . . . took shape."[33]

Aided by his special ambassador and fellow Social Democrat Egon Bahr, Brandt pursued a broad policy of "change through rapprochement." By recognizing existing borders and establishing relations with East European states, Brandt sought to improve material conditions for citizens there and liberalize regimes. The long-term goal of *Ostpolitik* was German reunification, but the immediate aims included recognition of the GDR, regulation of the status of Berlin, and acceptance of "one nation, two states." Brand and Bahr knew they needed to work with the Soviet Union and avoid obstruction by the United States, but their goal

---

[33] Timothy Garton Ash, *In Europe's Name: Germany and the Divided Continent* (New York: Vintage, 1993), 60.

was to delink German-German relations from Soviet-American ones. Bahr asserted that the FRG would have to be "more self-reliant and not always compliant" to United States wishes.[34]

Brandt pursued *Ostpolitik* through bold rhetoric, demonstrative gestures of apology for German war crimes, and a willingness to push German and European interests in the face of American ambivalence and occasional hostility. He and Bahr successfully concluded a series of treaties that reshaped European relations and provided a solution to the Berlin and German questions that would last until 1989. In August 1970 West Germany signed a treaty of nonaggression and cooperation with the Soviet Union that recognized existing borders. In December 1970 a treaty with Poland acknowledged the Oder-Neisse line as the official Polish-GDR border. In September 1971 the four occupying powers signed the Quadripartite Treaty guaranteeing free access to Berlin. In December 1972 the German-German Treaty recognized the GDR and regulated interactions with and financial flows from the FRG. Treaties with Hungary, Czechoslovakia, Romania, and Bulgaria followed.

Ostpolitik was controversial among German Christian Democrats and aroused equally negative reactions in the United States. Although the State Department's European Bureau look favorably on *Ostpolitik*, Kissinger, who disliked Brandt and Bahr, feared that it would weaken NATO, lead the Soviets to be lenient toward Europe and intransigent toward America, and edge Germany toward neutrality or Finlandization as it was called at the time. In 1970 Nixon told British Prime Minister Heath that American officials believed "*Ostpolitik* was a dangerous affair and they would do nothing to encourage it."[35] They did not encourage, but neither did they obstruct. They took a similar attitude toward the Conference on Security and Cooperation in Europe (CSCE).

Helsinki

The idea of a European security conference had been broached several times before the CSCE finally convened in the early 1970s. In 1954 the Soviets proposed an exclusively European meeting, and the 1966 Bucharest

---

[34] Thomas A. Schwartz, "Legacies of Détente: A Three-Way Discussion," *Cold War History* 8/4 (Nov. 2008): 516.

[35] Stephan Kieninger, "Transformation or Status Quo: The Conflict of Stratagems in Washington over the Meaning and Purpose of CSCE and MBFR, 1969–1973," in Oliver Bange and Gottfried Niedhart, eds., *Helsinki 1975 and the Transformation of Europe* (New York: Berghahn, 2008), 69–70. Mary Elise Sarotte, "The Frailties of Grand Strategies: A Comparison of Détente and Ostpolitik," in Fredrik Logevall and Andrew Preston, eds., *Nixon in the World* (New York: Oxford University Press, 2008), 151.

Declaration of Warsaw Pact nations reiterated that suggestion. A year later NATO pushed for a security conference that would include its members plus Warsaw Pact ones, and in 1969 the Budapest Appeal repeated that proposal. After much deliberation, European states, the USSR, the EC, and the United States conducted multiparty talks from 1972–75 that concluded with the signing of the Helsinki Final Act in 1975.

The Soviets pushed hardest for the CSCE in part to secure recognition of existing borders and in part to promote scientific, technological, and economic exchanges. They also hoped that such an initiative might weaken the cohesion of the EC and NATO and slow the process of European integration. Eastern European states, especially Romania, hoped the CSCE would give them more autonomy from the Soviet Union and open the way for more economic and cultural exchanges with Western Europe. Western European states were divided, with the FRG and Italy showing the most enthusiasm, while Britain was lukewarm, France preferred bilateral talks, and the Netherlands opposed the entire project. As talks progressed, however, they came to see the CSCE as a promising opportunity. The EC eagerly embraced this new initiative and used it as an occasion to test the European Political Cooperation (EPC), which had been set up at the 1969 Hague Summit "to prepare the way for a united Europe capable of assuming its responsibilities in the world of tomorrow."[36] The EC wanted to increase the exchange of goods and ideas and the movement of people, but it also sought official Warsaw Pact recognition of the EC and greater European autonomy in international affairs, especially regarding détente. The EC alone pushed for the inclusion of human rights clauses in the final agreement.

The United States was uninterested in raising the right to emigrate and freedom of religion and speech, for Kissinger saw these as marginal to the key issues of missiles and borders and potentially disruptive of superpower détente. He opposed the Jackson–Vanik Amendment, passed by the American Congress, which denied most-favored-nation trading benefits to the Soviets unless they guaranteed free exit for Soviet Jews. Indeed, American officials displayed remarkably little interest in the entire CSCE process, seeing it as at best a bargaining chip but never as an opportunity for change. Nixon and Kissinger kept the negotiations for Mutual Balanced Force Reductions off the CSCE agenda and exclusively in Soviet and American hands. And as the Final Act was being drawn up, Kissinger dismissively told his staff, "They can write it in Swahili for all I care."[37]

---

[36] Angela Romano, *From Détente in Europe to European Détente* (Brussels: Peter Lang, 2009), 79.

[37] Jussi Hanhimaki, "'They Can Write it in Swahili': Kissinger, the Soviets, and the Helsinki Accords, 1973–75," *Journal of Transatlantic Studies* 1/1 (2003): 37.

The Helsinki Final Act was, in the view of a British jurist, "a new kind of animal. It had the body of a treaty, the legs of a resolution and the head of a declaration of intention." It imposed no juridical obligations on the thirty-five signatories, but the hope was they would feel ethically and politically responsible for adhering to it. Basket I, as the first part was called, recognized the territorial settlement that had been de facto accepted in previous decades and de jure in various *Ostpolitik* treaties, but it also stated that "frontiers can be changed, in accordance with international law, by peaceful means and by agreement." Other clauses defended both nonintervention in the internal affairs of states and the equal rights and self-determination of all peoples as well as "respect for human rights and fundamental freedoms, including freedom of thought, conscience, religion or belief." Basket II discussed ways to improve commerce, promote scientific and technical exchanges, cooperate on industrial projects, and address environmental issues. This opened the way for many more bilateral European treaties on these issues. The now famous Basket III contained human rights language affirming freer human contacts, family reunification, and educational and cultural exchanges.[38]

The Soviets reacted positively to the Final Act, and Brezhnev insisted that "Those who belong to the generation which experienced the horrors of World War II most clearly perceive the historic significance" of the CSCE. Reactions in Western Europe were mainly positive, for the CSCE embodied the Western European conception of détente and gave recognition to the EC. The Final Act contained the desired language on the peaceful change of borders and enhanced human contacts. The United States, which had had a much less traumatic experience of war, reacted in a much more hostile manner. Although President Gerald Ford, who had succeeded Nixon when he was forced to resign, endorsed the Final Act at Helsinki, the American media was uniformly hostile. According to the *New York Times*, the CSCE "should never have been convened." When Ford foolishly claimed that "There is no Soviet domination of Eastern Europe," presidential candidate Jimmy Carter countered that Helsinki "ratified the Russian takeover of Eastern Europe." Soviet dissident Alexander Solzhenitsyn shared this view, arguing that "the countries of Western Europe will confirm the slavery of their brother countries of the East, all the while believing they are strengthening the prospects for peace." Ford quickly forbade use of the term détente. When President Carter gave his inauguration speech, however, he did pick up on the

---

[38] Romano, *From Détente in Europe*, 29. Helsinki Final Act, full text, www.osce.org/mc/39501.

theme of human rights, which had first been prominently raised in the Helsinki Final Act.[39]

The demise of détente and persistence of *Ostpolitik*

The differential judgments of Helsinki were one factor leading to the rapid collapse of détente in the late seventies, but many others proved of greater importance. Both American and Soviet actions eroded détente. Carter, for example, wrote a letter in support of prominent Soviet physicist and dissident Andrei Sakharov, which Brezhnev regarded as interference in internal Soviet affairs and a violation of the Final Act. The Soviets were disappointed that they were not granted economic aid and most-favored-nation status and grew increasingly worried that many in communist countries and outside took the human rights clauses of the accord seriously. Americans criticized the Soviets for deploying SS-20 missiles that could hit Western European targets, while the Soviets (and many Western Europeans) objected to American plans to develop a neutron bomb that would kill people but do minimal damage to property.

In the face of disappointment and criticism at home, Brezhnev succumbed to the temptation to intervene in the Third World, above all in the Horn of Africa. Carter took a hard line about growing Soviet involvement in the region and in the 1977–78 war fought in the Ogaden desert between Ethiopia, which had been allied with the United States but now sided with the Soviet Union and Cuba, and Somalia, which had shifted allegiances in the opposite direction. The Soviets did not realize how determined the United States was to keep them out of a region which they saw as strategically marginal, but the Americans regarded as vital. The Soviet leadership had no desire to endanger détente with its African adventures, but the United States responded by building up its forces in the Middle East and Indian Ocean and giving up on better relations with the Soviets. Carter's national security advisor, Zbigniew Brzezinski, later claimed that "détente lies buried in the sands of the Ogaden."[40]

It was in 1979, however, that the fate of détente was sealed. The United States extended formal diplomatic recognition to China, surprising and upsetting the Soviets. NATO took its two-track decision to deploy

---

[39] Melvyn P. Leffler, *For the Soul of Mankind: The United States, the Soviet Union and the Cold War* (New York: Hill and Wang, 2007), 251. *New York Times*, July 21, 1975. Michael Cotey Morgan, "The United States and the Making of the Helsinki Final Act," in Logevall and Preston, eds., *Nixon in the World*, 166. Romano, *From Détente in Europe*, 34.

[40] Odd Arne Westad, *The Global Cold War: Third World Interventions and the Making of Our Times* (Cambridge University Press, 2005), 282.

new medium-range nuclear missiles in Western Europe and to discuss arms reduction with the Soviets. The Iranian Revolution, which brought Ayatollah Khomeini and the Islamic Republic to power, challenged Cold War political categories and frightened both superpowers. When United States embassy officials were taken hostage for 444 days, America became involved in Iran and the larger Middle East in ways neither Western Europe nor the Soviets were. Finally, in December 1979 the Soviet Union invaded Afghanistan in support of a tottering communist regime. Although the Soviets saw their action as defensive and limited, Americans feared it marked a push toward the oil-rich Gulf. Carter proclaimed that "An attempt by any outside force to gain control of the Persian Gulf region will be regarded as an assault on the vital interests of the United States of America and such an assault will be repelled by any means necessary, including military force."[41] Carter then boycotted the Moscow Olympics, suspended the SALT II talks, expanded the military budget, advocated pursuit of nuclear superiority rather than parity, and established a military central command, CENTCOM, in the region. Like the Truman Doctrine, the Carter Doctrine staked out an expanded American sphere of interest, and it marked the beginning of sustained American involvement in the Gulf and diminished attention to Europe.

Although détente collapsed and Soviet-American relations worsened, *Ostpolitik* continued. Having lost their former colonies, Western European states were much less interested in Africa and the Middle East than was the United States and less concerned about Soviet involvement. They were not happy about the Iranian Revolution and the Soviet invasion of Afghanistan but were also not eager for a confrontational response. Indeed, several European countries, including Britain, France, Belgium, and Italy refused to heed the American call to boycott the Moscow Olympics. In the late 1970s and beyond, Western European states continued to negotiate economic treaties with Eastern European countries, extend loans, and participate in gas pipeline projects with the Soviet Union. Economic détente remained the preserve of Western Europe due to its proximity and interests and to United States domestic policy, which refused to countenance trade, aid, and loans. The continuation of *Ostpolitik* benefited individual Western European countries and showed the EC the value of cooperative policies and enhanced integration. It bolstered repressive regimes in Eastern Europe but also contributed to their long-term demise by encouraging dissent and deepening economic dependence on the West. But in the late seventies, no one anticipated that communism would soon collapse.

[41] Leffler, *For the Soul*, 335–36.

The 1970s did not witness the abrupt end to the American Century but rather its slow erosion; only American military might survived relatively unscathed. The end of the American Century was hardly possible while the Cold War persisted, but that order and America's role in it were subject to increasing challenges – from economic crises and America's loss of confidence, from European desires for greater national and EC autonomy, and from popular criticisms of American nuclear policy, interventions, and neoliberalism. The erosion of American political, economic, and cultural influence was not steady, for both the EC and individual Western European states oscillated between autonomy and Atlanticism. But henceforth the pressures and desires for autonomy increased, while commitments to Atlanticism waned.

Although Western European states did not achieve unified policies on all issues, they did cooperate on currency questions and the Common Agricultural Policy, and Helsinki showed the value of coordinating policy via the EPC. The first direct elections to the European Parliament in Strasbourg were held in 1979. There was a proliferation of Europe-wide initiatives ranging from the European University Institute to increased scientific collaboration.

For all that the United States claimed to favor European integration, it continued to envision a more united Europe as an adjunct to an American-led Atlantic community. The United States oscillated between ignoring Europe and patronizing and pressuring it to toe the American line. By the end of his Year of Europe, a resentful Kissinger remarked that "talking with Europeans was becoming worse than negotiating with the Soviets."[42] America viewed itself as the entitled leader of the Atlantic community, whose values and policies should be emulated, even as these changed from the Keynesianism, welfare statism, and multilateralism of the postwar years to neoliberalism, structural adjustment, unilateralism, and growing ambivalence toward international institutions and laws.

In 1973 Berndt von Staden, the German ambassador to Washington, wrote that Kissinger's Year of Europe speech reflected "the yearning for the situation of the 1950s and 1960s . . . when the United States possessed undisputed supremacy, when Western Europe did not appear as a competitor, was accordingly dependent and asked for little say in the matter, but instead left the leadership role to the United States without question."[43] In the 1970s the United States was unable to recreate the Europe

---

[42] Giuliano Garavini, *After Empires: European Integration, Decolonization and the Challenge from the Global South, 1957–1985* (Oxford University Press, 2012), 185.

[43] Fabian Hilfrich, "West Germany's Long Year of Europe," in Schulz and Schwartz, eds., *Strained Alliance*, 241.

of the American Century at its high point, even if the shape of the new transatlantic order was unclear. While Western Europe could not create the cohesion, autonomy, and independent global presence that many European leaders wanted, the seeds of Europe's later integration, autonomy, and global presence were sown in that decade. The Atlantic was widening.

10   Renewed conflict and surprising collapse

At the beginning of 1989, political calm, as cold and gray as the weather, hung over Eastern Europe; by early summer striking political changes were underway. In June a coalition led by the independent trade union Solidarity swept the Polish elections, and roundtable negotiations established the non-communist Polish Republic with Lech Wałesa at its head. Next came Hungary, where the long-demanded reburial of Imry Nagy, prime minister during the 1956 uprising, brought thousands into the streets, and negotiations established a multiparty government. On November 9 East Germany opened the Berlin Wall, thousands of East and West Germans sang, danced, and celebrated on top of that hated symbol, and the Socialist Unity Party quickly stepped down. In November and December Czechoslovakia's Velvet Revolution brought the noted dissident and literary figure Václav Havel to power. As the year ended Ceauşescu's notoriously repressive regime in Romania was overthrown by force, and with much less fanfare, the Bulgarian leader Todor Zhivkov resigned, and the country began a halting transition to parliamentary democracy.

With the exception of Romania, regimes collapsed and Communist parties retreated rather than violently resisting protest movements, the demands of prominent dissidents, or the examples of neighboring states. Of more importance, the Soviet Union did not oppose these revolutions or block the reunification of Germany. Nor did it survive them, for in 1991 communism collapsed and the multinational Soviet Union dissolved. The ideological struggles, political geography, and economic and cultural competition that had structured European-American relations in the second half of the twentieth century vanished – to the surprise of direct participants and observers alike.

What were the causes of these dramatic transformations in Europe, ones comparable to those that had occurred between 1917 and 1920? Was communism's collapse inevitable or contingent, a result of structural contradictions or ideas and human agency? Did the United States win the Cold War, as so many Americans triumphantly claimed? Or was it a supportive but secondary actor in a European drama in which the Soviets played the leading role? To answer these questions, we need to look not only at 1989, the *annus mirabilis*, as Pope John Paul II called it, but also at the preceding decade.

The 1980s began with renewed superpower hostility, the so-called "second Cold War," and conflicts within Europe and across the Atlantic about Euromissiles, economic sanctions, and American interventions in the global South. By mid decade, however, there was partial reconciliation between President Ronald Reagan and General Secretary Mikhail Gorbachev around nuclear disarmament. As the United States sought to reassert its dominance over the Soviet Union and within the Atlantic alliance, Western Europe continued to pursue détente with Eastern Europe and deepen economic and political integration within the expanding European Community. As the Soviets loosened their hold on Eastern Europe and embarked upon reform at home, governments across the Communist bloc grappled with escalating economic crises. Both the American Century and the Cold War order continued to erode, but until 1989 no one anticipated the demise of either.

The collapse of communism was a European or, more specifically, an Eastern European drama. National actors and issues shaped the overthrow of old regimes, but all communist countries suffered from failing economies, growing debts, and declining legitimacy. These alone would not have led to communism's downfall, however, without new ideas and a charismatic new leader. Reagan's much vaunted toughness toward what he called the "evil empire" is often credited with ending communism and the Cold War; in fact, it retarded change in Eastern Europe. Gorbachev's "new thinking," as his policy approach was labeled, and search for "a common European home" created the environment in which the transformation of neighboring states and the USSR could occur, even as they brought consequences he never intended. Only when the revolutions of 1989 had succeeded, did the United States and Western Europe join in to construct the framework for Europe's post-Cold War order. The place of America in it was by no means clear, for Europe continued to take control of its own destiny.

Toward a second Cold War

The eighties opened inauspiciously in the United States, which for a decade had been buffeted by economic crises, rancorous political divisions, and contentious disputes with its European allies. The humiliations of the Iranian hostage crisis compounded America's bitter loss in Vietnam; defense officials warned of a missile gap that endangered national security, and bestselling historians like Paul Kennedy predicted that the United States, like all empires before it, would inevitably decline. In this atmosphere of pessimism, Ronald Reagan was elected president with a campaign urging Americans "to recapture our dreams ... regain that unique sense of destiny and optimism that had always made America different from any other country in the world."[1] He promised to reverse America's perceived decline, restore the economy, reassert United States military dominance over the Soviet Union, and restore its undisputed leadership in the Atlantic alliance. Aggressive neoliberal economic policies at home and assertive anti-communism abroad were the core tenets of Reaganism.

Reagan did not start the second Cold War. As we saw, Carter had increased the military budget, modernized nuclear weapons, responded aggressively to the Soviet invasion of Afghanistan, and tried to discipline Western Europeans to follow suit. Superpower détente was dead before Reagan took office, but he did enthusiastically embrace a hard-line stance toward the Soviet Union and leftist movements in the Third World. Convinced that Soviet power had grown in Europe and outside, he increased the military budget by 35 percent in the first half of the decade in order to produce more B1 bombers, MX Intercontinental Ballistic Missiles, and Trident submarines and develop stealth bombers.[2] Historians disagree about whether Reagan was a warmonger or a proponent of peace through strength, whether he wanted nuclear superiority or disarmament, whether he intended to bankrupt the Soviet Union by forcing it to increase its defense spending or believed that the Soviets, given their economic problems, would made concessions if America were assertive. At various times his statements and actions lent support to each of these contradictory positions. To Soviets and Western Europeans in the early eighties, however, he seemed to be embarking on a dangerously confrontational path.

Although the Politburo worried about American rhetoric and military buildup, it was in no position either to respond in kind or make concessions. Sclerotic leadership, mounting economic problems, and the deepening quagmire in Afghanistan fostered paranoia and paralysis. In the early 1980s the economy and government stagnated as Brezhnev's health declined. After his death in 1982, Yuri Andropov, who was deeply

[1] Melvyn P. Leffler, *For the Soul of Mankind: The United States, the Soviet Union and the Cold War* (New York: Hill and Wang, 2007), 345.

[2] Beth A. Fischer, "United States Foreign Policy under Reagan and Bush," in Melvyn P. Leffler and Odd Arne Westad, eds., *The Cambridge History of the Cold War*, vol. III: *Endings* (Cambridge University Press, 2010), 270–71.

suspicious of Reagan's policies, ruled until 1984, when his death brought another geriatric apparatchik, Konstantin Chernenko, to power for scarcely a year. Negotiation and policy innovation came only with the election of Gorbachev to head the Communist Party in 1985.

America's Western European allies were equally suspicious of Reagan's policies, albeit for different reasons from the Soviets. Western Europe remained committed to its version of détente, for West Germany, France, Italy, and Britain had developed deep economic, cultural, and political ties to Poland, Czechoslovakia, Hungary, and the GDR. Many countries had refused to boycott the Moscow Olympics or impose economic sanctions on the Soviets. *Ostpolitik* benefited both Eastern and Western Europe, and America's allies saw no reason to abandon it because Reagan preferred containment or confrontation. The second Cold War had not begun as a transatlantic project and did not develop as one in the first half of the 1980s.

Four issues were at the heart of the worsening relations between the United States and the Soviet Union and within the Atlantic alliance: Euromissiles, Star Wars, the Polish crisis, and wars and proxy wars in the Third World. They raised divisive questions about the arms race and disarmament, national security, and military and economic interventions. They illustrate the complexity of late Cold War conflicts and the limits of the superpowers' abilities to control their spheres of influence.

Euromissiles and Star Wars

In the seventies agreements about disarmament had been central to Soviet-American détente but marginal to *Ostpolitik* and the Helsinki Accords. In the early eighties the superpowers fought bitterly over missiles and antimissile defense, and European governments and publics demanded a voice on these issues. The Soviet stationing of intermediate-range nuclear missiles within striking distance of Western Europe and American plans for a Strategic Defense Initiative (SDI) or Star Wars, as it was quickly dubbed, triggered bitter disputes between the superpowers and within the Atlantic alliance.

In 1979 NATO approved its controversial dual-track decision, according to which West Germany, Italy, Britain, Belgium, and the Netherlands agreed to receive 464 intermediate-range Cruise and 108 Pershing II missiles, commonly referred to as the Euromissiles. Simultaneously, NATO was to pursue negotiations with the Soviets on arms limitation and reduction. The United States had long wanted to modernize its nuclear forces in Western Europe, but governments there had been reluctant. By the late 1970s, however, Western European leaders grew worried that superpower negotiations on strategic nuclear weapons might lead the United States to either ignore European security or leave Europe open to a limited nuclear war. When the USSR deployed modernized intermediate-range SS-20 missiles in the Western Soviet Union, the United States increased pressure on its NATO allies to take new weapons, and Western European leaders came to view these Euromissiles as a token of America's commitment to Western Europe's defense, which many felt had waned due to Vietnam, economic crises, and détente. Germany, Italy, and Britain responded most enthusiastically, despite a lack of clarity about whether deployment would have priority, as the United States wanted, or negotiations, as the Europeans preferred, and about when the missiles would actually be installed. Only in 1981 did the United States set 1983 as the date to deploy the new missiles.

While Western European governments knew they faced growing social movements against nuclear weapons and nuclear power, they were unprepared for the deluge of protest that followed the dual-track decision. As the British government instructed its citizens on how to "Protect and Survive" in the face of nuclear war, the Campaign for Nuclear Disarmament, which morphed into the transnational European Nuclear Disarmament, ridiculed its recommendations and urged people to "Protest and Survive." And protest they did. In the fall of 1981 over 1.8 million people of all ages and classes took to the streets in West Germany, Italy, the Netherlands, Belgium, and Finland. Some were veterans of 1968, others were new to protests; many were Social Democrats or in Italy Communists, and many others were associated with church-based peace movements. While a majority of Belgians had supported Euromissiles in 1980, by late 1981 over 80 percent were opposed. By 1985 3.75 million Dutch out of a population of 14 million had signed a petition against deployment. Women from across the British Isles, fearing "for the future of all our children and for the future of the living world," set up a peace encampment outside the American air base and missile site at Greenham Common. They protested there continually from 1981 until the missiles were finally removed in 1992.[3] In 1982 1 million people gathered in New York's Central Park to endorse the United States Nuclear Freeze movement and support the UN special session on disarmament.

United States officials did not understand how scared Europeans were about the possibility of nuclear war. Once again very different experiences with past wars helped create diametrically opposed attitudes toward

[3] John Prados, *How the Cold War Ended* (Washington, DC: Potomac, 2011), 81–82.

prospective ones. Western European leaders recognized the deep anxiety pervading their nations but were torn by the conflicting demands of security and the Atlantic alliance on the one hand and swelling domestic protest on the other hand. The West German and British governments put down demonstrations, often brutally, claiming that terrorists and communists had infiltrated them. The West German domestic intelligence agency, for example, made films of all protests, peaceful or not, and its head claimed that the peace movement was manipulated and funded by the GDR and represented a danger to the constitution.[4]

It proved easier to disperse demonstrators and deploy missiles than to restore Cold War ways of thinking. The peace movements across Western Europe and the United States, as well as the much less visible one in East Germany, challenged Cold War conceptions of the enemy. They criticized American policies as strongly as Soviet ones and rejected the idea that nuclear wars, even "limited" ones, were survivable, let alone winnable. Some favored a freeze on nuclear weapons, others total disarmament, but all demanded a say on what many Europeans viewed as a life and death issue. Rethinking was going on among politicians and experts as well. In 1982 the Independent Commission on Disarmament and Security, which was chaired by the Swedish Social Democrat Olaf Palme and had members from Western European socialist parties and peace institutes, issued a provocative report that advocated replacing the concept of national security with "collective security" and "non-offensive defense." It insisted that nuclear weapons were unusable, nuclear war unwinnable, and nuclear disarmament essential. This clear rejection of the Cold War consensus shaped Western European political attitudes and by mid decade those of Gorbachev as well but found little resonance in the United States.[5]

Indeed, Reagan was taking American policy on national security in a very different direction. In addition to increasing military budgets and expanding weapons programs, his defense advisors developed plans for waging war, including limited nuclear ones. Most controversially, in 1983 Reagan outlined plans for a missile shield to protect the United States from any and all Soviet nuclear weapons with laser technologies. Debate abounds about why Reagan embraced SDI, a program whose technical feasibility was dubious and whose costs promised to be astronomical.

[4] Gerard Braunthal, *Political Loyalty and Public Service in West Germany: The 1972 Decree against Radicals and Its Consequences* (Amherst: University of Massachusetts Press, 1990), 166–67.

[5] Geoffrey Wiseman, "The Palme Commission: New Thinking about Security," in Andrew F. Cooper and John English, eds., *International Commissions and the Power of Ideas* (New York: United Nations Press, 2005), 46–75.

Pressure from the military and Senate may have shaped his pursuit of absolute security, so too may concerns about his declining popularity and a desire to counter the Nuclear Freeze movement. Some posit that a visit to NORAD, the North American Aerospace Defense Command, shocked him into realizing that the United States had no defense against Soviet missiles. Others emphasize that he was terrified of nuclear war, even as he pushed the arms race, and believed, in his words, that SDI was "a means of rendering these nuclear weapons impotent and obsolete." Reagan acknowledged that "defensive systems have limitations and raise certain problems and ambiguities. If paired with offensive systems, they can be viewed as fostering an aggressive policy and no one wants that."[6]

Yet that was precisely how the Soviet Union and America's Western European allies, who had not been consulted in advance, viewed the announcement of SDI. Star Wars threatened to militarize outer space and violate the 1972 ABM Treaty, which permitted the United States and the Soviet Union to each have a missile defense installation at only one site. Star Wars planned to protect the entire country. If Star Wars succeeded, it would undermine deterrence; instead of MAD, America would have guaranteed first-strike capacity. It would no longer have to concern itself with Soviet actions and might loose interest in defending Western Europe. The Soviets protested SDI for much of the decade, but Western Europeans ultimately accepted it, while still claiming to defend the ABM Treaty and MAD. They agreed with Reagan's closest ally, British Prime Minister Margaret Thatcher, who admonished him that "It would be unwise to abandon a deterrence system that has prevented both nuclear and conventional war."[7]

Poland and proxy wars

Superpower interventions abroad proved every bit as contentious as nuclear weapons. The thorny issue of Soviet involvement in its satellites and the appropriate Western response came to the fore once again. Of equal importance, Soviet and American direct military interventions in the Third World as well as covert support for diverse contending factions there persisted. As in the past the Cold War was much hotter and more

---

[6] John Prados, "The Strategic Defense Initiative: Between Strategy, Diplomacy and United States Intelligence Estimates," in Leopoldo Nuti, ed., *Crisis of Détente in Europe: From Helsinki to Gorbachev, 1975–1985* (London: Routledge, 2009), 97. Ronald Reagan, Star Wars Speech, March 23, 1983, http://pierretristam.com/Bobst/library/wf-241.htm.
[7] Sean Kalic, "Reagan's SDI Announcement and the European Reaction: Diplomacy in the Last Decade of the Cold War," in Nuti, ed., *Crisis of Détente*, 102.

deadly in the global South than in Europe. How did interventions – and noninterventions – shape European-American relations?

Let us begin with Poland, the European country that loomed largest at the decade's beginning as at its end. Since the 1950s Poland had experienced repeated protests by workers, students, intellectuals, and the Catholic Church, and another round occurred in 1980–81. Pope John Paul II's 1979 visit during which he urged his fellow countrymen not to compromise with communism laid the groundwork for protest as did the growing cooperation between illegal trade unions and the intellectual dissidents, who formed KOR, the Committee for the Defense of Workers. But it was the regime's inability to continue borrowing abroad to support consumption at home and its decision to raise meat prices that sparked a wave of strikes, the occupation of the Lenin Shipyards in Gdansk, and the formation of the unofficial trade union Solidarity in the summer of 1980. Although the protesters were deliberately cautious – advocating "a self-limiting revolution," as its leaders termed it – General Wojciech Jaruzelski, the prime minister, feared the worst and asked for Soviet intervention. In a first indication of changing Soviet policy toward the bloc, the Soviet minister of defense replied, "The Poles themselves must solve the Polish question. We are not prepared to send troops."[8] Intervention would have been militarily risky, politically damaging, and above all far too expensive. Jaruzelski settled for proclaiming martial law in December 1981 and throwing numerous political prisoners in jail.

Reagan condemned these actions and immediately imposed economic sanctions. As he told the National Security Council, "we should quarantine the Soviets and Poland with no trade or communications across their borders." Western European allies should be told to join us or "risk estrangement."[9] Joining would mean not buying Soviet gas or providing parts for the Soviets' planned gas pipeline to Western Europe and not allowing European subsidiaries of American companies to do so. The return to a policy of severe trade limitations reflected Reagan's staunch anti-communism, and it entailed few material risks, for the United States, unlike Western Europe, had little trade and investment in Eastern Europe and no need for Soviet gas.

Western European governments condemned martial law, and the EC urged Jaruzelski to negotiate with the church and Solidarity and release political prisoners, but no state imposed sanctions. Even Thatcher, who

---

[8] Constantine Pleshakov, *There is No Freedom without Bread! 1989 and the Civil War that Brought Down Communism* (New York: Farrar, Straus, and Giroux, 2009), 122.

[9] Douglas Selvage, "Politics of the Lesser Evil: The West, the Polish Crisis and the CSCE Review Conference in Madrid 1981–3," in Nuti, ed., *Crisis of Détente*, 42.

Illustration 23 Strike by Polish Solidarity at the Gdansk shipyard, 1980.

applauded Reagan's "bold strategy to win the Cold War," pushed legislation through parliament saying British firms could ignore Reagan's call
for compliance. Western Europeans resisted sanctions for both economic and political reasons. The 1973 oil crisis had shown that they
needed alternative energy sources, and Soviet ones were the nearest and
most promising. Sanctions would endanger jobs and profits for the many
Western European firms that were involved in the pipeline project or
traded and invested heavily in Poland and the Soviet Union. As French
Foreign Minister Claude Cheysson rhetorically asked Chancellor
Helmut Schmidt, "Should we punish ourselves with sanctions just
because there are developments in Eastern Europe that one cannot
accept?" Finally, the allies, who once again had not been consulted in
advance, saw no reason to endanger détente by punitive actions. As a
1982 United States State Department report noted, not only European

governments, but also "The public remains firmly in favor of détente." Western European governments did not believe that détente artificially prolonged the life of communist regimes or that Reagan's hard line would influence the Polish situation. And when Jaruzelski lifted martial law and released political prisoners in 1986, it was due largely to pressure from Western Europe, not from sanctions, which in any case had been lifted in 1982.[10]

Soviets and Americans continued their involvements in Africa, Asia, and Latin America. Sometimes they offered economic and military aid to long-standing capitalist or communist allies, such as Vietnam and Cuba or Egypt and Mexico; at other times, and more problematically, they supported regimes and movements whose politics and practices were murkier and more compromised. Adhering to the zero-sum logic of the early Cold War, each superpower objected to the other's interventions while refusing to discuss its own; Western Europe wanted no involvement with any of them. Afghanistan and Nicaragua provide prime examples of such contested interventions.

The Soviet invasion of Afghanistan in December 1979 on behalf of the weak and unpopular Communist government there provoked not only strong United States condemnation but also covert American aid to the anti-communist and Islamist Mujahedeen. Indeed, according to former Carter advisor Brzezinski, United States aid began before the invasion and "had the effect of drawing the Russians into the Afghan trap." Afghanistan quickly became the Soviet Union's Vietnam – a grueling war against tenacious guerillas that was costly in lives and money and deeply unpopular at home. Negotiated solutions proved elusive but abandoning an ally would threaten Soviet credibility. The United States repeatedly demanded Soviet withdrawal but found little support from its European allies. If the United States had lived with the Soviet invasions of Hungary and Czechoslovakia in a region vital to United States and European security, they reasoned, surely they could live with Soviets in marginal Afghanistan without escalating the Cold War. Having lost their colonies, Western Europeans no longer viewed the Third World in zero-sum terms.[11]

---

[10] Prados, *How the Cold War Ended*, 24. Werner Lippert, "Economic Diplomacy and East-West Trade during the Era of Détente," in Nuti, ed., *Crisis of Détente*, 196. Marilena Gala, "From INF to SDI: How Helsinki Reshaped the Transatlantic Dimension of European Security," in Nuti, ed., *Crisis of Détente*, 119.

[11] Brzezinski interview in *Le Nouvel Observateur*, January 15–21, 1998. John W. Young, "Western Europe and the End of the Cold War," in Leffler and Westad, eds., *Cambridge History of the Cold War*, III, 291–93.

United States policies in Central America were no more popular with Western Europeans. In the wake of Vietnam, the United States sought to avoid direct engagement against leftist movements and governments, preferring less expensive and less politically controversial proxy wars. Wrongly insisting that the Nicaraguan Sandinistas were totalitarian and a threat to the United States, the Reagan administration funded and armed the right-wing Contra forces that had backed the previous dictator and mined Nicaraguan harbors, devastating the economy. Nicaragua charged that the mining violated the laws of war and won in the International Court of Justice in The Hague, but the United States refused to recognize the Court's jurisdiction or pay the fine. According to the reigning views of American UN ambassador Jean Kirkpatrick, traditional authoritarian regimes fostered stability and American interests, while totalitarian ones were a threat to national security. Since funding the Contras was illegal, Reagan's advisors devised a scheme to sell arms to the Islamic Republic of Iran (a proclaimed enemy with which the United States had no diplomatic relations) in order to funnel aid and arms to the Contras. When the Iran-Contra Affair was exposed in 1986, it caused a firestorm of protest in the United States and intensified the already strong Western European criticism of American support for the brutal and reactionary military forces in Nicaragua and the repressive dictatorship in Guatemala.

Disagreements about Poland, Afghanistan, and Central America contributed significantly to worsening Soviet-American relations but did not create fundamental divisions within the Atlantic alliance. Despite popular and governmental criticism of American policies, NATO was never endangered; Western Europe accepted Euromissiles and SDI, and Britain and France joined the United States as part of an international peacekeeping force in Lebanon. The Cold War contained dissent among allies, yet recurring disputes about the meaning and value of détente, the desirable forms of European security, and the efficacy of sanctions were steering Western Europe and America in different directions. So too were differing attitudes toward the global South, as the Third World was increasingly called. Unlike Americans and Soviets, Western Europeans did not automatically impose Cold War categories on complex disputes involving national liberation, social justice, and increasingly, religion and culture. They opposed unilateral military adventurism, whether direct or by proxies. Among Social Democrats there was strong interest in North–South dialogue about a more equitable division of global economic resources, as indicated by such institutions as the Independent Commission on International Development, which Willy Brandt chaired.

Intensification and abrupt end

In 1983 many in Europe feared the second Cold War might become hot, even nuclear. In March Reagan delivered his "evil empire" speech against the Soviet Union, followed by the SDI announcement. By midsummer the Soviet Central Committee wrote to its Warsaw Pact allies that there was "a destabilization of the whole system of intestate relations, the increase of the arms race and a serious increase in the threat of war." Two-thirds of the Soviet population agreed. At the end of August the Soviets shot down Korean Air Lines 007, killing all aboard, after it crossed into Soviet airspace. The United States was shocked and angered. In October the United States invaded the tiny Caribbean island of Grenada to save it from the purported threat of communism, an action garnering harsh criticism not only from the Soviets but also Western Europeans, especially the British, whose former colony it was. That same month, the United States deployed the Euromissiles and left both the Intermediate Nuclear Force talks and the Strategic Arms Reduction Treaty (START) talks. In early November NATO staged its Able Archer maneuvers, a routine exercise which, however, included a new scenario about the possible use of nuclear weapons. The Soviet leadership thought an attack was imminent; determined to avoid a repetition of the German attack in 1941, it put its nuclear forces on high alert until the exercise ended in mid November. Reagan was shocked at what he saw as Soviet overreaction, but Robert Gates, the deputy director of the CIA, admitted, "We in the CIA did not really grasp how alarmed the Soviet leadership might be."[12]

Reagan's hard line escalated tensions without producing the desired change in Soviet policy. In the early 1980s Soviet leaders debated three possible responses: maintaining weapons parity, unilaterally reducing forces and pursuing strategic sufficiency, or third, negotiating with the West on mutual disarmament, but they pursued none of these. The military budget stayed steady and there was no effort to emulate SDI, but nor were there unilateral reductions in nuclear or conventional forces. Reagan may have wanted an interlocutor in the Kremlin, as some of his biographers claim, but his confrontational policies and provocative rhetoric made it harder for the Soviets to change policy or seek negotiations. In addition, the United States, which had little trade and investment in the Soviet Union, could not exert economic pressure.

---

[12] Beatrice Heuser, "The Soviet Response to the Euromissiles Crisis," in Nuti, ed., *Crisis of Détente*, 139. Prados, *How the Cold War Ended*, 59.

After the ratcheting up of tensions in 1983, the second Cold War in Europe (but not in the Third World) rapidly deescalated. Reagan led the retreat. In his 1984 presidential campaign he proudly noted: "It's morning in America again"; he continued to push his anti-union and anti-welfare domestic policies but toned down his foreign policy rhetoric, modernized the hotline between the White House and the Kremlin, and proposed a ban on chemical weapons. Reagan may have been sobered by the 1983 war scare or by seeing *The Day After*, an American film depicting what Lawrence, Kansas, would look like after a nuclear attack. Or practical concerns like losing the midterm congressional elections and the Iran-Contra scandal may have pushed him to change course.

The soft line would not have been any more effective than the hard one, however, had not a new leader with new ideas come to power in the Kremlin. Realist and neorealist scholars of international relations argue that power differentials determine policy responses; economic problems at home and military weakness in relationship to the United States around the globe dictated that the Soviets would make concessions. But the Soviets had faced military inferiority and economic crisis before and responded differently. In 1985, however, a combination of acute economic problems, new ideas developed by younger elites, and Gorbachev's election as head of state opened the way for a partial renegotiation of Soviet-American relations.

Like his predecessors, Gorbachev was a loyal Communist who was educated entirely within the Soviet Union and had worked his way up the party hierarchy in Stavropol before being elected to the Politburo. Unlike them, however, he represented a younger generation, who had been adolescents rather than adults during World War II. He was educated in law rather than engineering, had read widely in Western as well as communist works and traveled to the West with an open mind. He was part of a younger Westernizing elite, whose members were scattered about the academic establishment and government and wanted to end Soviet autarky and political isolation, reshape foreign policy, and adopt Western technology. The "new thinking" of this loose group profoundly shaped Gorbachev's approach to foreign and nuclear policy on the one hand and domestic affairs on the other.[13] And the two were inextricably intertwined for Soviet reformers, who believed that excessive military spending and imperial overreach in Eastern Europe and the Third World stood in the way of dealing with slow economic growth, low productivity, and

---

[13] Robert D. English, *Russia and the Idea of the West: Gorbachev, Intellectuals and the End of the Cold War* (New York: Columbia, 2000), 127, 141–47.

technological backwardness at home. Let us turn first to security policy, however, for that most directly impacted relations with the United States.

Shortly before coming to power, Gorbachev gave a speech to the British parliament, emphasizing that the most pressing problem facing the world was "the prevention of nuclear war." He subsequently, if not always coherently, laid out the changes in Soviet policy necessary to attain that goal. Foreign policy had to be deideologized, that is talk of two camps and class struggle on a global scale had to end, and ideas of common security, such as those proposed by the Palme Commission and the Pugwash Conferences on Science and World Affairs, had to be explored. The United States and the Soviet Union had to deescalate the arms race, and the USSR should settle for sufficient security rather than pursuing parity. Although he remained mired in Afghanistan throughout the decade, he agreed with Andropov's 1980 statement that "The quota of interventions abroad has been exhausted."[14]

Deeds followed words. In 1985 the Soviets announced a unilateral moratorium on nuclear testing at a time when the United States would not even discuss the issue. A year later, Reagan and Gorbachev held their famous summit in Reykjavik at which they developed a personal rapport and shared their intense dislike of nuclear weapons but were unable to negotiate an arms deal. Gorbachev proposed reducing strategic ballistic missiles by half and removing all medium-range missiles from Europe as a first step toward eliminating all nuclear weapons. Reagan agreed in principle and to most details, but SDI was the stumbling block. Gorbachev insisted it had to stop, but Reagan and his advisors, many of whom were appalled by the prospect of eliminating all nukes, refused.[15] The summit was a failure, but Gorbachev was reassured that the United States had no war plans.

Even though the Americans remained committed to SDI, the Soviets increasingly viewed it as a futile project that should not block unilateral reductions or more modest negotiations. In 1987 the United States and the USSR hammered out the Intermediate Nuclear Forces (INF) Treaty, under whose terms the nearly 2,000 SS-20s and over 800 Euromissiles would be removed from Europe by 1991. It was less a victory for the United States than one for people on both sides who were committed to reducing weapons and tensions. Western European leaders, however,

---

[14] Vladislav M. Zubok, *A Failed Empire: The Soviet Union in the Cold War, from Stalin to Gorbachev* (Chapel Hill: University of North Carolina Press, 2007), 267.

[15] Memorandum of Conversation between President Ronald Regan and General Secretary Mikhail Gorbachev, Reykjavik summit, October 12, 1986. In Prados, *How the Cold War Ended*, 215–17.

Illustration 24 President Reagan and Soviet General Secretary Gorbachev
at the Reykjavik summit.

were ambivalent about the INF Treaty, even though it did not affect
French and British nuclear weapons. They felt most comfortable with a
balance of forces in Europe that produced a stable standoff, and no one in
1987 remotely imagined how different Europe would look by the time the
missiles were withdrawn. In 1988 the Soviets unilaterally began reducing
their conventional forces in Eastern Europe and implementing the
START. On February 1, 1989 Gorbachev announced that the remaining
Soviet troops would be withdrawn from Afghanistan.

In key respects the Cold War was over even before the revolutions of
1989 began, and Gorbachev was mainly responsible for ending it by
revamping Soviet security policy and unilaterally reducing arms and
troops.[16] He did so in pursuit not only of better relations with the
United States but also of a transformed Soviet Union that would be
situated in a "common European home." The events of 1989–91 were
to show that the former was much easier to attain than the latter.

---

[16] Matthew Evangelista, "Explaining the End of the Cold War: Turning Points in Soviet
Security Policy," in Olav Njølstad, ed., *The Last Decade of the Cold War: From Conflict
Escalation to Conflict Transformation* (London: Frank Cass, 2004), 131.

The roots of revolution and collapse

The rapid rise and demise of the second Cold War in Europe was primarily a story of the Soviet Union and the United States with Western and Eastern Europe providing theaters of projected war and sites of governmental ambivalence and popular anxiety and protest. The Soviet Union and Eastern Europe dominated the events of 1989, with Western Europe and the United States playing relatively minor roles. What transpired was a story of structural contradictions and the dwindling ideological appeal of socialism, of social movements, scared elites, and a charismatic but flawed Soviet leader, who unleashed forces he could not contain. The Eurocentric character of 1989 is one more indication of the erosion of American influence.

Soviet and Eastern European economic problems were not the sole or sufficient cause of communism's collapse, but they were a necessary one. Reagan's policies of confrontation and then conciliation had virtually no influence on their development. Romania's austerity strategy and East Germany's unending competition with West Germany, for example, were rooted in national politics. The major problems – debt, trade imbalances, and technology lags, all of which had begun in the seventies, were shared across the bloc. Escalating debts were the most visible symptom of crisis and growing dependency on the West. Poland, Hungary, and the GDR led the way in borrowing from Western European and Japanese banks, although Romania and Bulgaria had sizable debts as well. (The United States lent little to this part of the world, particularly after the 1982 Mexican default and ensuing Latin American debt crisis.) Poland accumulated $41.8 billion in debt, Hungary $20.3 billion, and the GDR $26.5 billion. Sheer debt totals were a cause for acute concern, but debt service was positively crippling for countries without convertible currencies. By the late 1980s it ate up 40 percent of Hungary's hard currency income, 45 percent of Poland's, and 75 percent of Bulgaria's.[17] The very borrowing that was necessary to fund current consumption and acquire new technology threatened to inhibit both.

As debts grew the ability to repay them shrank, for the Soviets were in an ever weaker position to extend loans or subsidize oil and demanded more in return from their Eastern European neighbors. In 1974, for example, Hungary had to export 800 buses to obtain 1 million tons of Soviet oil; by the mid 1980s, 4,000 buses were necessary. In 1982 the Soviets would

[17] Zubok, *Failed Empire*, 326. Ivan T. Berend, *Central and Eastern Europe, 1944–1993: Detour from the Periphery to the Periphery* (Cambridge University Press, 1996), 230–31.

only extend a loan to the GDR if it redirected more trade to the Soviet Union; instead the East Germans secured a 1 billion DM loan from the Federal Republic.[18]

Both Eastern Europe and the Soviet Union sought to increase trade with the West, and intra-CMEA trade diminished. By decade's end only Czechoslovakia and Bulgaria traded more than half their exports within the Communist bloc. Yet trade with the West was not on beneficial terms, for few Eastern European countries produced goods that Western Europeans wanted to buy or that could compete elsewhere with East Asian goods. Yugoslavia, for example, sought in vain to produce a car that would be exportable to the West. The Soviet Union was somewhat better positioned because it had oil, lumber, and gold to sell, but being a primary commodity exporter hardly fit the image of the advanced industrial economy it strove to be.

The inability to export manufactured goods to capitalist economies, in turn, resulted from the widening technology gap. Even the most advanced Eastern European countries like the GDR and the Soviet Union failed to develop a domestic computer industry and the new manufacturing and service sectors that used information technology. Indeed, they even lacked the well-developed telephone infrastructure necessary to support these. Such technologies were crucial not only for the production of new consumer goods but also for the next generation of military hardware. Most communist regimes clung to "socialist Fordism"[19] and their inefficient, centralized command economies. Countries like Hungary had moved toward a mixed-market socialist system but fared little better due to debts, a shortage of foreign investment, and a concern with political reform more than economic innovation. Eastern Europe remained relatively marginal to the increasingly interconnected world economy. No European communist country was willing or able to use repression on a massive scale; nor were they able to revive their Fordist production systems and plug them into the global economy by means of Western investment or joint state-capitalist ventures, the authoritarian hybrid model that the Chinese pioneered after communism had collapsed in Eastern Europe.

Debt, trade, and technology problems sent communist economies on a downward spiral. For East Central Europe as a whole, growth dropped

---

[18] Stephen Kotkin, "Kiss of Debt," in Niall Ferguson, Charles S. Maier, Erez Manela, and Daniel J. Sargent, eds., *The Shock of the Global* (Cambridge, MA: Harvard University Press, 2010), 87. Hans-Hermann Hertle, "Germany in the Last Decade of the Cold War, 1979–89," in Njølstad, ed., *Last Decade*, 270.

[19] Charles Maier, *Dissolution: The Crisis of Communism and the End of East Germany* (Princeton University Press, 1997), 93.

from 3.9 percent in 1973 to 1.9 percent in 1987. Individual economies suffered much worse. Hungary's growth stopped completely in the early eighties, and the Polish and Yugoslav economies actually shrank. Soviet economic growth declined from 4.1 percent in 1986 to 1.5 percent in 1989 (and down to −12 percent in 1990). In 1980 Soviet GDP per capita was only 37 percent that of the United States, midway between the highest figure of 52 percent for the GDR and the lowest of 24 percent for Romania among the communist countries. Slow growth was not exclusively a communist problem; average growth rates were no higher in Western Europe, but EC countries fared much better in comparison to America and Japan, both of which were booming. West German GDP per capita stood at 83 percent of America's, most nations were in the mid to high 70 percent range, and only Spain with 64 percent and Finland at 67 percent fell below.[20]

Eastern European economies heavily subsidized basic necessities such as housing, health, education, and childcare, which lessened the gap with the United States somewhat but not with social democratic Western Europe, which offered better social benefits. Communist regimes failed most miserably in the area of consumer durables. By the 1980s ownership of TVs, washing machines, and refrigerators in the GDR nearly equaled that in France, but car ownership lagged far behind.[21] The GDR, how-ever, was the tenth or eleventh largest economy in the world and the most advanced in Eastern Europe. Consumer durables increased more slowly elsewhere in Eastern Europe and were often of poor quality; cars and telephones were in very short supply everywhere.

The Soviet Union faced additional debilitating problems. Oil prices, whose astonishing rise in the 1970s had bolstered the economy, fell equally dramatically at decade's end and remained low thereafter. Agriculture suffered from low productivity, and the Soviet Union contin-ued to be the world's largest grain importer. Defense spending officially accounted for 16 percent of the state budget, but some estimate that it took up to 40 percent and accounted for 15–20 percent of GDP. Of equal importance, extensive social programs, essential to the regime's legiti-macy, were increasingly costly. And then there were the burdens of empire – loans and subsidies to Eastern Europe and the cost of stationing

---

[20] Berend, *Central and Eastern Europe, 1944–1993*, 223. Stephen G. Brooks and William C. Wohlforth, "Economic Constraints and the Turn toward Superpower Cooperation in the 1980s," in Njølstad, ed., *Last Decade*, 96. Maier, *Dissolution*, 94. www.bls.gov/fls/intl_gdp_capita_gdp_hour.htm#table01. Figures are for 1979.

[21] Gerold Ambrosius and William H. Hubbard, *A Social and Economic History of Twentieth-Century Europe* (Cambridge, MA: Harvard University Press, 1989), 248.

a few million troops there, subsidies and special trade deals with Cuba and Vietnam, and funds for leftist movements in the Third World.[22]

Multiplying economic difficulties did not, however, automatically produce protest or spell the demise of communism. Protest and dissent, where they appeared, were responses to a lack of political rights and freedom of thought and movement as much as a lack of consumer goods. But did the Helsinki Final Act and the expanding human rights movement in Eastern and Western Europe and America pose fundamental problems for communist states? From the mid 1970s on, the EC was convinced that the human rights provisions of the Helsinki Accord were a useful means of exerting pressure on Eastern Europe. United States leaders had been ambivalent about the Helsinki process before 1975, but Carter embraced it wholeheartedly and Reagan invoked human rights to condemn Communist behavior and plead for better treatment of dissidents. (He did not, however, defend human rights in Latin America, but instead supported their most egregious violators in Guatemala, Chile, and elsewhere.) The Helsinki human rights movement, a loose network of Western non-governmental organizations (NGOs), Eastern activists, national government bodies like the United States Human Rights Commission, and the regular CSCE follow-up meetings, publicized the Helsinki human rights norms, monitored compliance with them, and publicly shamed violations of them, above all by the Soviet Union.

The impact of these efforts on the practices of communist governments and the emergence of dissident movements, however, remains a matter of dispute. Some insist that human rights advocacy was instrumental in altering government policies in Eastern Europe and eroding the Cold War order there. Others more cautiously and persuasively posit that the Helsinki process spread new international norms but only influenced government policies when Western European states demanded better behavior from countries like Poland in return for material aid. Of necessity Gorbachev had to acknowledge human rights once he sought rapprochement with Western Europe, which was so strongly identified with them. Human rights interacted with détente, behind which lay complex ideas, economic interests, and material needs, to shape the last years of the Cold War order in Eastern Europe.[23]

---

[22] Prados, *How the Cold War Ended*, 109–10. Zubok, *Failed Empire*, 299. Brooks and Wohlforth, "Economic Constraints," 89–91.

[23] Sarah B. Snyder, *Human Rights Activism and the End of the Cold War: A Transnational History of the Helsinki Network* (Cambridge University Press, 2011), 11–13. Rosemary Foot, "The Cold War and Human Rights," in Leffler and Westad, eds., *Cambridge History of the Cold War*, III, 445–65. Daniel C. Thomas, *The Helsinki Effect: International Norms, Human Rights and the Demise of Communism* (Princeton University Press, 2001), 220–56.

Yet, neither official Helsinki monitoring nor human rights advocacy within or outside Eastern Europe was able to ignite substantial and successful protest movements. They could publicize and shame but not punish or produce reform. In the late seventies and early eighties, dissidents mobilized around human rights in Poland and in Czechoslovakia with Charter 77, but those regimes repressed protest and continued to violate human rights, as did the Soviet Union, which had not anticipated that Basket III of the Helsinki Final Act would be taken seriously. Except for Poland, opposition movements were minuscule or nonexistent, while human rights monitoring was probably more visible in the West than the East. Dissidents such as Havel urged people to "live in truth" rather than to demand political rights and power. In countries like Czechoslovakia, Hungary, and the GDR, few supported their governments with enthusiasm, but many acquiesced to regimes that tried to provide more consumer goods and space for private activities while demanding less and less in the way of ideological commitment or political participation. Across most of Eastern Europe and certainly in the Soviet Union, civil society was less a cause of 1989 than a product of it. Human rights discourse and advocacy provided some of the language used by the protest movements which sprang up suddenly in 1989, helping to shape postcommunist regimes – albeit more so in countries like Czechoslovakia than in ones like Romania and the Russian Federation.[24] They were not the principle cause of communism's demise. It was Gorbachev's effort to reform the ailing Soviet economy that began the unraveling of socialism around the bloc.

Rational plans or impossible dreams?

Gorbachev's "new thinking" aimed not only to diminish the dangers of nuclear war but also to reform the ailing Soviet economy – and it was economic change more than democratic reform that dominated Gorbachev's agenda. According to Gorbachev, perestroika or restructuring called for "the revival and development of the principles of democratic centralism in running the national economy . . . and the overall encouragement of innovation and socialist enterprise." It was to combine "the achievements of the scientific and technological revolution with a planned economy" and "means priority development of the social sphere aimed at ever better satisfaction of the Soviet people's requirements for good living

[24] Stephen Kotkin, with a contribution from Jan Gross, *Uncivil Society: 1989 and the Implosion of the Communist Establishment* (New York: Modern Library, 2009), xiv. Pleshakov, *No Freedom without Bread*, 56–57, 66.

and working conditions."[25] This was an ambitious but amorphous and contradictory program that produced diverse measures to end economic corruption, raise productivity, improve work discipline by curbing alcohol consumption, create more autonomy at the factory level, and increase investment in heavy industry. All were imposed from above, many were unpopular, and most proved destabilizing. Gorbachev sought to introduce market elements, first as a subordinate part of a planned economy, and then, by late 1989, as the major but not only economic regulator. In so far as Western thinkers and politicians shaped perestroika, European Social Democrats, such as Felipe Gonzalez of Spain, were more influential than any Americans.

Political liberalization was slower and more inconsistent. In 1985–86 Gorbachev did appoint several people open to political reform. In the wake of the Chernobyl nuclear disaster in April 1986, where government secrecy and bureaucratic complexity inhibited an effective response, he augmented perestroika with glasnost or transparency, which allowed limited freedom of speech and information. In 1987 he permitted the noted dissidents Andrei Sakharov and Yelena Bonner to return to Moscow and announced to the Central Committee that "Perestroika itself is only possible through democracy."[26] In March 1989 the Soviet Union held its first contested elections for a new legislative body. These encouraging developments emerged with little pressure from the United States or Western Europe. They did not, however, indicate a steady move toward democratization, for the Communist Party retained its "leading role," elections were not multiparty, and Gorbachev imposed many liberal reforms via the authoritarian power he wielded as general secretary. His intent throughout was to revitalize the Soviet Union and strengthen the position of a reformed Communist Party within it, not to undermine either.

Foreign policy was to serve the ends of domestic reform by transforming relations with the United States but more importantly with Western Europe and the Warsaw Pact allies. As early as 1984 Gorbachev had broached the rather inchoate idea of "Europe as our common home," perhaps from a growing commitment to universal values, perhaps in the hope of sowing dissent between the United States and its European allies. Within a few years, he refined his vision by arguing that Europe is "our essential partner" in trade and economic aid, in cultural exchanges, and in security. As Gorbachev told the PCI general secretary in 1988, "we think

---

[25] Mikhail Gorbachev, *Perestroika*, quoted in www.historyguide.org/europe/perestroika.html. Accessed June 13, 2011.
[26] Archie Brown, *The Gorbachev Factor* (Oxford University Press), 166.

of ourselves as Europeans."[27] In 1988 the EC and CMEA issued a joint declaration, laying the basis for trade and economic cooperation. Western Europe was appealing for many reasons. It continued to promote détente and provide aid. The EC had become an economic giant that surpassed the Soviet Union, and it mixed economic efficiency and prosperity with social democratic welfare policies. Western Europe both suggested a third way and was a potential counterweight to the United States.

While seeking closer relations with Western Europe, Gorbachev put more distance between the USSR and Eastern Europe. In the mid 1980s he told his Warsaw Pact allies that relations should be equal and voluntary, and each state should be responsible for its own situation. This was a clear repudiation of the Brezhnev Doctrine, which called for strict adherence to Marxism-Leninism and justified Soviet intervention in case of deviations. It was followed in 1988 by the withdrawal of half a million Soviet soldiers and six tank divisions from Eastern Europe and the promise of more to follow. The Red Army was becoming defensive. Gorbachev's actions reflected his priorities – cooperation with Western Europe and economic reform at home. He embraced the lesson first learned with Poland in 1981 and driven home by Afghanistan: military interventions were economically destructive and politically counterproductive at home and abroad.[28]

Soviets at the time, like later historians, differ widely in their assessment of Gorbachev's initiatives. Some admired both his specific policies and his evolution from Communist to reform socialist and post 1989 to social democrat. Others viewed him as naïve, romantic, and messianic; still others as erratic and contradictory. All concur that Gorbachev did not set out to be a revolutionary but rather the savior of communism. His attempted reforms created instability and insecurity without, however, improving industrial efficiency, raising state revenues, or curbing corruption. He wanted to end the Cold War but not communism or the Soviet Union, yet he was the essential actor in the demise of all three.

The radical consequences of reformism

Between June and December 1989, the old order in East Central Europe was swept aside. Liberal democracies, with multiparty parliamentary

---

[27] Marie-Pierre Rey, "Gorbachev's New Thinking and Europe, 1985–9," in Frédéric Bozo, Marie-Pierre Rey, N. Piers Ludlow, and Leopoldo Nuti, eds., *Europe and the End of the Cold War: A Reappraisal* (London: Routledge, 2008), 28–29.
[28] Archie Brown, "The Gorbachev Revolution and the End of the Cold War," in Leffler and Westad, eds., *Cambridge History of the Cold War*, III, 253–55. Prados, *How the Cold War Ended*, 189. Leffler, *For the Soul*, 421.

regimes and non-communist governments, sprang up. Trade unions were legalized, a free press established, and religious toleration introduced. Protesters toppled statues of Marx and Lenin, and new governments dismantled the secret police. Political parties barely existed, civil society was fragile, and visions of the desired economy and society were rudimentary, yet, in the euphoria of the moment, it was the magnitude of the changes that impressed and inspired.

These dramatic transformations were a response to long-term economic problems and dwindling political legitimacy. They were sparked by events in Poland, the only country with organized mass movements and a developed civil society. It provided a model of protest and deliberation – the famous roundtable negotiations between communist governments and new contending political forces – that other countries followed. In each case a combination of specific domestic forces and grievances and the contagion effect of neighboring uprisings spread change. Poland also provided the model for Soviet behavior.

The Soviets played a crucial role in the success of the 1989 revolutions by virtue of what they did not do. For reasons principled and pragmatic, Gorbachev chose not to intervene. Not in Poland when Solidarity won the elections and Wałesa became president. Nor in the GDR as thousands of East Germans fled to the West through Hungary and Czechoslovakia and demonstrators flooded the streets. Indeed, in early October, Gorbachev urged the Central Committee of the East German Socialist Unity Party to initiate reform, arguing "It is important not to miss our chance here . . . Life itself will punish us if we are late."[29] Nor did he resist changes in Hungary and Czechoslovakia, the sites of earlier infamous interventions. Without such restraint 1989 would not have succeeded. Gorbachev was overwhelmed with problems at home, for economic reform was failing and the gap between promises and achievements aroused popular ire. Liberals wanted more reform, and neo-Stalinists hoped to reimpose a hard line while non-Russian minorities demanded autonomy or independence. Gorbachev was also committed to non-intervention and had told his fellow Communist rulers that. After Georgian government forces violently repressed a nationalist demonstration in Tbilisi in April 1989, Gorbachev banned the use of force within the Soviet Union. The massacre of Chinese protesters in Tiananmen Square in June of 1989 can only have reinforced his determination not to go down that road, even though East German leaders recommended doing so.

---

[29] Record of Conversation between Mikhail Gorbachev and Members of the CC SED Politburo October 7, 1989, www.gwu.edu/~nsarchiv/NSAEBB/NSAEBB290/index.htm.

The United States was virtually absent from the East European stage. Reagan had argued for change in Eastern Europe and in a 1987 speech in Berlin demanded, "Mr. Gorbachev, tear this wall down," but his rhetoric had no impact. In 1989, George H. W. Bush succeeded him as president and immediately sent Kissinger on a secret mission to Moscow, suggesting cooperation in managing any changes in Central Europe. Gorbachev refused and Bush advisors Dick Cheney, James Baker, and Condoleeza Rice, who favored a more confrontational stance, shaped subsequent policy. Although initially unsure how to react to escalating unrest, in June 1989 Bush traveled to Poland, where he received a lukewarm reception, and Hungary, where he got an enthusiastic one. In neither place did he provide the hoped-for economic aid; this time there would be no Marshall Plan. The EC approved of this policy because Western Europe wanted to provide and control aid and felt Eastern Europe would not be able to absorb large sums, given the lack of market institutions. The Poles, however, were deeply disappointed when they asked the United States for $10 billion and got $100 million instead. The Hungarians got even less – $25 million in aid plus Peace Corps volunteers and a cultural center. By contrast, Egypt, the second largest beneficiary of United States aid was receiving $968 million and Israel even more.[30]

In July Bush attended the G7 meeting in Paris, where he urged Europeans to reschedule the vast Polish and Hungarians debts and provide aid to them. In addition he blocked any sanctions against China for the Tiananmen massacre, arguing that "the United States-Chinese relationship was too important to world peace." From then until late 1989, the United States stood on the sidelines. As Bush told Gorbachev, "I have conducted myself in ways not to complicate your life. That's why I have not jumped up and down on the Berlin Wall."[31] Gorbachev was grateful, for he had complications enough.

Gorbachev and his supporters underestimated both the fundamental character of the changes underway in Eastern Europe and the costs of nonintervention. In late 1988 Gorbachev had proclaimed before the UN that "freedom of choice is a universal principle" for all peoples,[32] but he did not anticipate the choices Poles and Hungarians or Lithuanians and Ukrainians would make. He imagined reformed socialist nations, in which Communist parties would continue to play a role, not capitalist ones in

---

[30] http://usgovinfo.about.com/od/historicdocuments/a/teardownwall.htm. Pleshakov, *No Freedom without Bread*, 166.
[31] Pleshakov, *No Freedom without Bread*, 173. Leffler, *For the Soul*, 450.
[32] Brown, *Gorbachev Factor*, 225.

which Communists would be marginalized or outlawed. If they chose to leave the Warsaw Pact, he expected them to become neutral, like Finland. Rather than NATO expanding eastward, he envisioned the CSCE as the basis for pan-European security. If German reunification occurred, it would be the culmination of a slow process of European integration, not its first act.[33] Nothing went according to Soviet hopes, beginning with Germany.

The day after the Berlin Wall fell on November 9, Chancellor Helmut Kohl pledged West Germany's commitment to the Atlantic alliance, European integration, and Franco-German cooperation. A few weeks later and without consulting his allies, he gave his controversial ten-point speech, promising aid to the GDR and calling for an eventual federation of East and West Germany. Gorbachev called it a diktat, and Western European leaders, shaped by their World War II experiences, were also hostile. As Thatcher exclaimed to a December 1989 EC meeting, "Twice we've beaten the Germans! And now here they are again!"[34] If unification were to come, Mitterrand wanted further European integration as a counterweight, while Thatcher hoped NATO would serve the purpose.

Fast-track reunification followed, largely because Kohl persuaded Bush that it was sound and necessary. Bush and Secretary of State James Baker had experienced the Pacific War, not the European theater; they saw Germany as a reliable Cold War ally, not a potentially dangerous European hegemon. America's most significant contribution to the transformations of 1989 was to legitimize and promote Kohl's plans and thereby redraw the map of Central Europe. After much negotiation, the Two-plus-Four Treaty was signed by both Germanys and the four occupying powers in September 1990. It united East and West Germany, recognized once again the Oder-Neisse line as the eastern border and allowed a united Germany to be in NATO. This was not the German solution Gorbachev envisioned, but the fact that it resulted from a four-power agreement and that plans for further European integration, including developing the European Monetary Union, were moving forward made it more palatable. So too did the Federal Republic's promise of a DM 12 billion loan to help with the cost of

---

[33] Zubok, *Failed Empire*, 326. Svetlana Savranskya, "In the Name of Europe: Soviet Withdrawal from Eastern Europe," in Bozo, Rey, Ludlow, and Nuti, eds., *Europe and the End*, 45–46. Prados, *How the Cold War Ended*, 93.

[34] Mary Elise Sarotte, *1989: The Struggle to Create Post-Cold War Europe* (Princeton University Press, 2009), 82.

removing and reintegrating the Soviet troops in East Germany and a DM 3 billion interest-free credit line.[35]

The promised aid could not revive the declining fortunes of either Gorbachev or the Soviet Union. The economy plummeted downward, and nationalists in the Baltic States, Armenia, Georgia, and across Central Asia took to the streets demanding autonomy or independence. Conservative hard-liners attacked Gorbachev for pushing democracy and marketization too quickly; reformers accused him of dragging his feet. As non-Russian nationalities pushed for independence, many Russians insisted force should be used to keep the Soviet Union intact. Gorbachev's policies became more erratic. In mid 1990 he launched a 500 Days program that called for rapid marketization and the privatization of industry as well as greater power to the Soviet republics; in the fall he slowed reform. By year's end only 17 percent of Soviets supported him, down from 52 percent a year earlier.[36] Even this evaporated in 1991, as rivals staged a failed coup and Latvia, Lithuania, and Estonia declared their independence, to be followed by Armenia, Georgia, Moldova, and the Central Asian republics. Bush had wanted gradual change in the Soviet Union rather than its destabilizing and precipitous collapse, but the United States had not provided aid in 1989, and both the United States and the G7 were unwilling to do so in 1991, given the deteriorating situation. At year's end Gorbachev resigned and the remaining parts of the Soviet Union became the Russian Federation.

Gorbachev had hoped that the Soviet Union would "return to Europe." He envisioned an economically integrated Europe that was committed to what he called "universal values" and would take care of its own security. German reunification disrupted these hopes, but so too did the appeals of Western Europe. Havel was initially sympathetic to Gorbachev's vision, but the Hungarians wanted to join the EC and NATO, and the Poles waffled. Soon all looked west. For their part, Western Europeans were absorbed with their own integration project. They approved of the East European revolutions and were relieved to incorporate a united Germany but had no roadmap for how relations with East Central Europe or the former Soviet Union should evolve.

Absent through much of 1989, the United States nonetheless claimed its legacy, advocating a new Atlanticism rather than a Europe that looked to itself. In December 1989 Secretary of State Baker gave a speech in

---

[35] Helga Haftendorn, "German Unification and European Integration Are but Two Sides of One Coin: The FRG, Europe and the Diplomacy of German Unification," in Bozo, Rey, Ludlow, and Nuti, eds., *Europe and the End*, 136–43. Sarotte, *1989*, 192–93.

[36] Brown, *Gorbachev Factor*, 271.

Berlin, the site of so many American proclamations about their desired relationship with Europe. He called for a "new architecture" that would include "old foundations and structures" like NATO and the continued construction of the EC. "The architecture should reflect that America's security – politically, militarily, and economically – remains linked to Europe's security."[37] "The United States," he concluded, "is and will remain a European power." In the ensuing decades, however, American power in Europe would be substantially redefined and diminished.

[37] James Baker, "Upheaval in the East," Dec. 13, 1989, Nytimes.com/1989/12/13/world/
upheaval-east-excerpts-baker-s-speech-berlin-us-role-europ-s-future.html?

11   A widening Atlantic

The year 1990 marked the beginning not only of a new decade but also of a new post-Cold War order. Perhaps it marked "the end of history," in Francis Fukuyama's oft-quoted phrase, for the great ideological battles of the twentieth century among fascism, communism, and democracy were over, and liberalism appeared to have triumphed. Capitalism reigned globally, social democracy was on the defensive, and across the globe right-wing political and economic ideas were gaining adherents. The "evil empire" had collapsed, the United States was militarily unchallenged, and no enemies were in sight to disturb the new pax Americana. After a decade of troubles, the American economy had rebounded, while its European and Japanese counterparts languished. Europe, all of Europe, seemed ripe for full incorporation into an American-dominated global order.

The ensuing two decades, however, were less a story of convergence and cooperation between Europe and the United States than of divergence, disagreement, and at times overt hostility. Economically, politically, and culturally a multipolar global order replaced the bipolar one; only in military terms did the United States continue to reign supreme and alone. Unlike in the late nineteenth and early twentieth centuries, however, the powerful poles are no longer located only in the North Atlantic region. Globalization, measured in the movement of commodities, capital, people, ideas, and cultural products, has returned to levels not seen since before World War I, but the United States and Western Europe are no longer at the center of all exchanges and networks. Manufacturing and finance are dispersed around the globe, and the rise of China is but the most visible symbol of shifting power relations. The United States is once again a nation among nations, even if has great difficulty acknowledging and accepting its diminished role.

In 1989 the political and economic geography of Europe changed, eliminating the constraints on European autonomy imposed by the Cold War. Europeans have increasingly articulated their own aspirations, developed their own economic, political, and cultural projects, and controlled their own destiny. This is most evident in the proliferation of European

Union institutions and policies and in the expansion of the EU itself. Europe, which was an idea shared only by a few in the first half of the twentieth century and which emerged primarily as an economic entity after 1945, has become a much more visible presence not only economically but also politically, legally, and culturally – and outside of Europe as well as within. The definition of a European identity remains contested, but its existence, alongside national affiliations and in opposition to identification with the United States or the Atlantic community, is indisputable.

European states have maintained their particular varieties of capitalism, and even though these have been modified in the face of economic crises and globalization, they remain in crucial ways distinct from the increasingly neoliberal form that has triumphed in the United States and the UK. The European social model with its diverse social policies, generous benefits, and universal coverage persists despite doubts about its viability from within Europe, especially from the UK, and above all from the United States. Nowhere is the transatlantic gap wider than in conceptions of society and social rights. American goods, capital, and mass culture continue to flow into Europe, but they no longer arouse either the hopes or fears they had earlier. The Americanization debates that haunted the twentieth century are over, as a more confident Europe defines itself in terms of itself.

The United States is still the largest single national economy, but its economic power, measured in terms of manufacturing, trade, and foreign investment is eroding and its debts and deficits are rapidly growing. Europe has reached comparable levels of private consumption while providing many more public goods than America does. The United States is no longer at the cutting edge of technological innovation and productivity as it once had been. Throughout much of the twentieth century, America was the model of modernity (or, if one counts the Soviet Union, one of two models) against which Europe measured itself and from which it selectively appropriated and adapted production methods and management techniques, commodities and technologies, advertising and marketing. America no longer plays that role for European states.

A new Europe

The expansion of the EC made the most significant contribution to the widening of the Atlantic, for new institutions were created, new policies implemented, new countries joined, and a more robust European identity emerged. Some of these developments had roots in earlier decades but came to fruition after 1989; others were a response to the opportunities created by the collapse of the Cold War order. There was an intensification of European economic integration, moves toward greater political cooperation, and the extension of the EU eastward, all of which absorbed the attention of European leaders, enabled Europe to act more autonomously, and positioned it to play a larger role on the global stage. The acceleration of European integration had begun in the 1970s in response to the destruction of Bretton Woods, structural economic crises, and policy disagreements with the United States. It continued in the mid 1980s with the Schengen Agreement and the Single European Act (SEA). In 1985 Germany, France, and the Benelux countries created a territory without internal borders in which people could move without visas or passports and customs inspections. By 2007 all EU members, except the UK, Ireland, Cyprus, Romania, and Bulgaria, were part of this Schengen Area. In 1986 the SEA began the process of creating an internal market in which goods, capital, people, and services would circulate without restrictions. It also encouraged greater cooperation on worker health and safety, research and technical development, and environmental protection.

In 1992 integration took another leap forward with the Treaty on European Union, commonly referred to as the Maastricht Treaty, which completed the single market, opened the way for political integration, and called for the establishment of a single currency by 1999. In 1994 the EC was officially renamed the European Union (EU), and Austria, Finland, and Sweden joined. In 1998 the European Central Bank was established, and in 2000 eleven of the EU's fifteen members adopted the euro as a common currency. By 2010 twenty-four countries had, including three from Eastern Europe, while Britain, Denmark, and Sweden are still using their national currencies. Efforts to ratify a European Constitution were put on hold when French and Dutch voters rejected it, reflecting a continuing European ambivalence about how much and what kinds of sovereignty should be ceded to transnational institutions. In 2009, however, the Treaty of Lisbon provided a more comprehensive legal framework for the EU that was intended to make it more democratic and transparent as well as more efficient and to enhance "Europe as an actor on the global stage."[1] Although Europeans were preoccupied with negotiating the policies and institutions necessary for intensified integration, this did not preclude enlargement, as many at the time argued it would.

Expansion eastward was not a priority for the EU in the 1990s, but Eastern European states desperately wanted inclusion, for it promised expanded markets and access to technology and loans and would symbolize a return to Europe. The EC/EU was attractive and near, while the

---

[1] http://europa.eu/lisbon_treaty/index_en.htm.

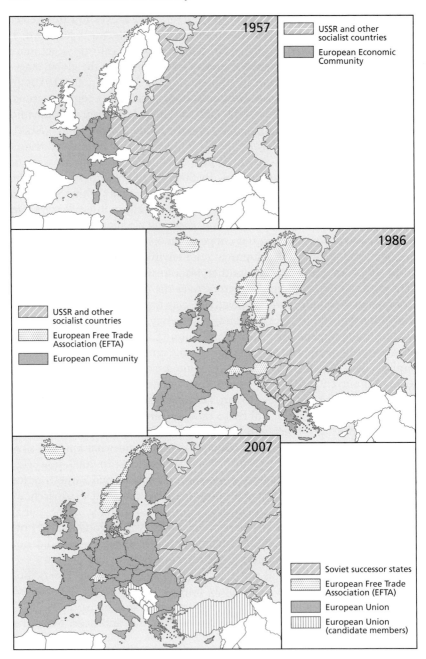

Map 3 European integration

United States was distant and uninterested. But enlargement proved slow, for in order to join, Eastern European countries had to meet the conditions of political stability, democracy, and a functioning market economy and agree to the EU's terms of membership. Only in 2003 did the Czech Republic, Estonia, Hungary, Latvia, Lithuania, Poland, Slovakia, and Slovenia along with Cyprus and Malta join, while Bulgaria and Romania became members in 2005. As the EU moved eastward, it assumed a position of dominance over economies there; it was an empire by invitation, much like the one the United States had established in Western Europe a half-century earlier.

These multiple changes served to knit the EU member states closer together. As at the turn of the previous century, the bulk of European trade was within Europe, both intra-EU and between EU members and those outside. By the 1990s, even before expansion eastward, over 60 percent of trade by the fifteen EU member countries was with one another, as opposed to 30 percent in the 1960s. Over two-thirds of trade by the Czech Republic, Poland, and Hungary, which were candidates for EU membership, was with the EU, and the EU was responsible for over 80 percent of investment in Eastern Europe. Although American goods flowed into Russia in the early 1990s, that trade dwindled by mid decade due both to Russia's acute economic crisis and growing economic nationalism. In transatlantic trade Europe was a more important partner for the United States than the reverse. As had been true throughout the twentieth century, Europe accounted for a larger share of world trade than the United States, but both were challenged by the emergence of China as a global economic player.[2]

Foreign direct investment continued to flow in both directions across the Atlantic and in increasing volumes, just as it had before World War I and from the 1960s on. The United States was the largest recipient of EU fdi until 2005 when non-EU European nations received 35 percent versus 33 percent for America and 23 percent for Asia. The United States continued to be the largest foreign investor in Europe, although its dominance was not as great as in the immediate post-1945 period. Through the European Neighborhood Policy, the EU established or expanded bilateral relations with countries in North Africa and the Middle East as well as with the successor states of the Soviet Union. Although assigning itself a global role, the EU has focused primarily on its relations with the

---

[2] Ivan T. Berend, *Europe since 1980* (Cambridge University Press, 2010), 177. Barry Eichengreen, *The European Economy since 1945: Coordinated Capitalism and Beyond* (Princeton University Press, 2007), 331. Stephen Lovell, *The Shadow of War: Russia and the USSR, 1941 to the Present* (Oxford: Wiley-Blackwell, 2010), 311.

expanded Mediterranean region and states bordering the Russian Federation. The EU has never considered Russia as a potential member or Neighborhood Policy partner. For the EU America was one economic partner among many rather than the dominant source of investment and trade that it had been in the two decades after 1945.[3]

By the time the EU had expanded to twenty-seven members in 2005, its population was larger than that of the United States. While its absolute GDP was slightly smaller, when GDP is adjusted for purchasing power parity, the EU was slightly ahead of the United States. In 2005 four of its members, Germany, France, the UK, and Italy, were among the ten largest economies, while Russia, after collapsing catastrophically in the nineties, was the tenth largest. American GDP per capita was $44,362 versus only $27,394 for the entire EU, but that wide gap between Europe and America came mainly from the incorporation of the struggling transition economies of Central and Eastern Europe. Europe, in short, became a major economic player; few in the first decades after 1945 would have predicted this.[4]

For Europeans the widening and deepening of the EU has raised contentious issues about political sovereignty, national identity, the EU's democratic deficit, and the economic costs and benefits of membership to countries of different sizes and with varied levels of economic development and financial stability. For the United States the only question was whether a transformed EU helped or harmed transatlantic relations and American interests. In the mid 1980s the United States did not take the SEA seriously, but once it was ratified, policymakers and the press feared a "fortress Europe" might emerge. After 1989 American administrations viewed expanded integration more favorably, seeing it as a way for Europe to contain a reunified Germany and fund reconstruction in the East, which the United States could not afford to do. Although President Clinton failed to pressurize Europe into ceasing to trade with Iran, Cuba, and Libya, he and subsequent United States leaders worried less about economic policy disagreements than about diplomatic and military ones.

From the mid 1990s on, there was talk of a new Euro-American economic partnership. In 1995 the United States and the EU signed the New Transatlantic Agenda, one provision of which called for "the promotion of economic relations and expansion of world trade ... and

---

[3] *European Union Foreign Direct Investment Yearbook 2007* (Luxemburg: European Commission, 2007), 27. Tony Judt, *Postwar: A History of Europe since 1945* (New York: Penguin, 2005), 788.
[4] http://politicalcalculations.blogspot.com/2007/11/2006-gdp-ppp-eu-vs-us-smackdown. html. www.earth-policy.org/datacenter/xls/indicator2_2006_2.xls. Eichengreen, *European Economy*, 408.

building bridges among our business, civic and academic communities on both sides of the Atlantic." A TransAtlantic Business Dialogue was established to explore the creation of a transatlantic common market, and in 2007 European Commission President José Manuel Barroso, German Chancellor Angela Merkel for the EU and United States President George Bush signed a Framework for Advancing Transatlantic Economic Integration between the European Union and the United States of America. Increased consultation has resolved some economic disputes, but it has not settled conflicts about tariffs, especially agricultural ones, or about intellectual property rights, monopolies, and genetically modified foods. A transatlantic free trade zone, let alone full economic integration, is nowhere in sight. The United States wants maximum openness to European markets but does not want to sacrifice any of its sovereignty.[5]

Europeans in the making

Has this proliferation of EU institutions created a shared European culture and identity in addition to national ones? Answers vary within and across countries, but a few generalizations can be risked. There are increasingly robust European cultural circuits and exchanges as well as distinctive attitudes and practices that have created a European identity, even if it is thinner than national ones. Economic integration and cultural exchanges within Europe have made Europe less open to American influences than it was in the first postwar decades.

Many forces have contributed to an emerging European culture and identity. There are Europe's distinctive varieties of capitalism and the European social model, which will be discussed below. Of equal importance are the experience and memory of World War II and the Holocaust, which are shared by countries across Europe, whatever their diverging postwar histories. These have burdened Europeans with responsibility for genocide, war crimes, and collaboration and encouraged national and transnational projects of coming to terms with the past. They have also made Europeans ambivalent about nationalism, wary about the use of force, and hostile to the militarism that had characterized the European Great Powers in the first half of the twentieth century. The very processes of Americanization, especially the spread of American popular culture, contributed to making Europeans more like one another. Whether they embraced, rejected, or redefined rock 'n' roll, Hollywood films, Coke,

---

[5] www.eurunion.org/partner/summit/Summit9712/nta.htm. http://ec.europa.eu/enterprise/policies/international/cooperating-governments/usa/transatlantic-economic-council/.

and jeans, these provided a shared set of products, experiences, and references. Even at the high point of the American Century, however, they did not, as we have seen, make even the most seemingly Americanized countries like Germany a mini United States, for products and ideas also moved among European countries and are increasingly moving within Europe rather than across the Atlantic. Intra-European tourism has grown exponentially since the 1960s and now includes the former communist East as well. Business people and workers move with ease across borders, where they find similar economic regulations and enjoy the social entitlements of the country in which they work. Educational exchanges have proliferated, and the Bologna Process, begun in 1999, is coordinating and standardizing the curriculum and requirements of national university systems across Europe. The aim is to facilitate the movement of students and faculty among EU universities and prepare them to pursue careers anywhere in the EU. Some national newspapers are read across Europe, and TV goes beyond national borders. There is the popular Eurovision Song Contest and a shared love of soccer. These have not supplanted national or class cultures and identities but rather coexist with them.

While Europeans continue to come to the United States to study and work, just as they did in the first post-World War II decades, they now do that in other European countries in increasing numbers. Global migration has escalated markedly since the 1960s, but in the transatlantic world it resembles neither the pre-World War I exodus from Europe to the United States nor the interwar and immediate postwar flow of refugees to America. Europe, above all Western and Northern Europe, has become a mecca for migrants and asylum seekers. Non-EU Europeans move to Western Europe in search of work, persecuted minorities, such as the Roma, seek less repressive conditions in places like Italy and France, and political refugees, especially from the Middle East, seek safety in countries like Sweden and Germany. The overwhelming majority of migrants, however, come from North Africa, sub-Saharan Africa, or former colonies in Asia and the Caribbean. America has become a land of immigration once again, but its documented and undocumented migrants come overwhelmingly from Mexico, Central America, and China. Both Europe and America are becoming much more racially, ethnically, culturally, and religiously mixed as globalization, political conflict, and climate change push and pull workers and their families along new migratory paths.

Yet neither the experience of intensified immigration nor the challenges of multiculturalism are bringing them closer together. Many Europeans and Americans are deeply ambivalent about the changing character of their societies and their economic dependence on workers from the global South, but different imperial and colonial histories, conceptions of citizenship and national identity, and constructions of race lead to distinctive responses. Take the transatlantic preoccupation with Islam. Although many Europeans share with Americans a discomfort about the growing presence of Muslims, states define the perceived problem differently. France sees them as a threat to the state's commitment to *laïcité* with its rigorous enforcement of the separation of church and state and banning of religious symbols in public, above all the full-face veil. The Dutch insist that Muslims refuse to assimilate to social and sexual norms, and many Germans, including Chancellor Merkel, insist that multiculturalism has failed, even though the possibility of citizenship for foreign workers has only existed since 2000. In Europe Muslims are seen as a challenge to national identity and shared social norms; in America they are viewed as a threat to national security and the Christian identity of the United States, which many insist on despite the legal separation of church and state.

Europe and America began to diverge in other ways in the 1970s and 1980s that profoundly shaped everyday life, politics, and self- understandings. First, whereas Europe became increasingly secularized, the United States moved in the opposite direction. Both the vast expansion of the religious right in America and the colonization of political language, policies, and institutions by fundamentalist religious views occurred in the last Cold War decades and persisted beyond. Regular church attendance remained high, evangelical churches grew at the expense of mainstream ones, and religiosity was viewed as the necessary basis of morality by preachers, politicians, and the growing evangelical populace. Western Europe became "the exceptional case" in matters of religion.[6] Although many European countries have state churches, regular church attendance has remained low, evangelical sects are small and marginal, and the language of politics remains resolutely secular. Religion has revived strongly in some Eastern European countries but is not instrumentalized for political ends as extensively as in the United States.

Germany provides an instructive example of these differences. In constitutional theory, church and state are more separate in the United States than in Germany, where churches get federal funds and religion is taught in the schools. The United States never had a political party comparable to the CDU/CSU, which is officially committed to Christianity and has close ties to both the Protestant and Catholic churches. In the 1950s and early 1960s, Germany seemed as religious as America, if not more so. Both

---

[6] Grace Davie, *Europe: The Exceptional Case: Parameters of Faith in the Modern World* (London: Darton, Longman and Todd, 2002).

shared large Protestant and Catholic church memberships, and religiosity and respectability were closely associated. In both countries religious rhetoric was a key element in anti-communism. (In West Germany religious rhetoric also featured prominently in Christian Democratic attacks on excessively materialistic, morally lax Americanism as well.)

In recent decades, Germany has become more secularized, even if official church membership has not declined significantly. Religion does not permeate everyday life, nor does it pervade the speeches of politicians. Perhaps most importantly, fundamentalism of either a Catholic or Protestant sort has not taken root. Whereas two-thirds of Americans go to church weekly, only 20 percent of West Germans and 14 percent of former East Germans do. The religious language of America's leaders, the pervasive religiosity of American society, and the ever more pronounced intertwining of church and state, even as their separation is proclaimed, find no counterpart in Europe. In an early 2003 article, *Der Spiegel* expressed a deep European skepticism about President Bush's linking of his Christianity to his desire to reorder American global influence. It worried – rightly, as it turned out – that Bush's religiously based radicalism would be used by Vice President Dick Cheney and Secretary of Defense Donald Rumsfeld for expansionist power politics, justified as a divinely ordained mission. Although religion could be instrumentalized, *Der Spiegel* acknowledged, one could no longer understand America unless one took it seriously. The article, replete with pictures of Bush addressing evangelical Christians in front of a towering painting of Jesus and of prayers before cabinet meetings, revealed how difficult such understanding is, for Europe's secular visions of society and politics are far removed from those of a religiously transformed America.[7]

The rise of the religious right and its growing political influence in America is related to the cultural backlash in the wake of the civil rights movement, the sexual revolution, second wave feminism, and America's defeat in Vietnam. Many Americans invoke religion to challenge the findings of science on everything from evolution to climate change and to advocate for family values, conservatively defined. Gender anxieties became linked to political and economic ones, and politicians and popular movements sought to recreate the conservative sexual order of the 1950s, dismantle the welfare state, and curb big government. They simultaneously attacked Keynesianism, secularism, multiculturalism, feminism, homosexuality, and the liberalism alleged to foster them. While by no

[7] (no author), "Krieg aus Nächstenliebe," *Der Spiegel*, August 2003, 91–99.

means free of disagreements over issues of sexuality, family, and feminism, Western European nations were not swept up in culture wars over the issues that proved so divisive in America, such as abortion, the teaching of evolution, and gay marriage. In the 1970s and 1980s the often-bitter controversies about divorce and abortion in countries like Italy did not become linked to attacks on the welfare state or the rejection of modern science. Europeans by and large came to accept sexual liberalization, high divorce rates, and low birthrates, although homophobia is a growing problem in Eastern Europe. They did not link cultural concerns to neoliberalism as Americans did. Both Europeans and Americans insist they are committed to families and children, for example, but as the head of Norway's Christian Democrats Valgard Haugland explained:

We have decided that raising a child is real work. And that this work provided value for the whole society. And that society as a whole should pay for this valuable service. Americans talk about family values. We have decided to do more than talk; we use our tax revenues to pay for family values.[8]

American movies still dominate the European market; there are McDonald's restaurants from Madrid to Moscow, and Abercrombie and Fitch has opened a store on the Champs Elysées in Paris. Since 1989 East Europeans have had access to everything from fast food and clothing to *Playboy* and American TV programs. Mass consumption spread in the East as it had earlier in the West, but it took on distinctive national forms and was no longer associated primarily with the United States. To be sure, there have been some protests against American goods. For example, French farmers led by José Bové attacked and dismantled a McDonald's restaurant, viewing it as a symbol of industrialized food and globalization for which the United States was held primarily responsible. For most Europeans, however, American goods and American culture were consumed without the fear of losing their national identity that had haunted so many earlier. On the one hand Europeans were confident about their ability to pick and choose among American products, use them in distinctive ways, and assign them particular meanings. On the other hand, Europeans were drawing from multiple sources within Europe, across the Atlantic, and in the Middle East, Africa, and Asia to enrich their cultures, expand their cuisines, and alter their listening, reading, and viewing habits. Like Americans through much of the twentieth century, Europeans view

[8] T. E. Reid, *The United States of Europe: The New Superpower and the End of American Supremacy* (New York: Penguin, 2004), 152–53.

cosmopolitan consumption as a way to enrich their identities without destroying their essence.[9]

While the United States is a favorite tourist destination for Europeans, they have a differentiated view of American culture and increasingly criticize American politics. A 2003 BBC poll showed that nearly two-thirds of the French, Russian, and British interviewees described Americans negatively as arrogant but positively as free. The British and the French, but not the Russians, viewed American music, TV, movies, and products (food aside) favorably, even as they judged their own country as overall more cultured, as Europeans did throughout the twentieth century. Whereas a majority of Americans praised the traditional family, only 15–20 percent of Europeans did. While many Europeans enjoy and approve of American values and goods, surprisingly few – only 21 percent of Russians, 15 percent of the British, and 7 percent of the French – wanted to live there. (Yet, 96 percent of Americans assume that most non-Americans are eager to do so.)[10]

Europeans no longer look to America as the model of modernity, as they did in the post-World War II decades. An amorphous yet powerful concept of Americanism and the more concrete processes and products of Americanization no longer provide the terms and parameters in which Europeans debate their own future. Americans no longer enjoy the unrivaled level of consumption and prosperity that they did in the 1950s and 1960s; European homes have long since acquired the same appliances and amenities. Indeed, in parts of Europe these are of higher quality and more environmentally friendly, and many European goods find markets in the United States. Politics, economics, and everyday life are seen in terms of a real and imagined Europeanization. The era of American cultural hegemony in Europe is over.

Toward neoliberalism?

As Europe became more economically integrated, politically coordinated, and culturally autonomous, did national economies and the EU nonetheless converge on the neoliberal economic model pushed so strongly by the United States and the UK? Many insisted that European autonomy and

---

[9] www.bbc.co.uk/bbcfour/documentaries/profile/jose_bove.shtml. Emily S. Rosenberg, "Consumer Capitalism and the End of the Cold War," in Melvyn P. Leffler and Odd Arne Westad, eds., *The Cambridge History of the Cold War*, vol. III: *Endings* (Cambridge University Press, 2010), 490.

[10] "What the World Thinks of America," Poll taken May–June 2003, http://news.bbc.co.uk/1/shared/spl/hi/porgrammes/wtwta/poll/html/default.stm.

Americanization, now defined as neoliberal globalization, could, indeed must, go hand in hand if Europe were to thrive. One of Thatcher's favorite slogans was "There is no alternative" – to the liberalization of markets, the deregulation of manufacturing and finance, the privatization of state-owned enterprises, to small government and balanced budgets. Market fundamentalists on both sides of the Atlantic praised free markets, free trade, and free investment and sought to commodify not only goods, services, and financial instruments but also everything from intellectual property to basic necessities like water. Keynes was dismissed and Hayek embraced by those seeking to impose the Washington Consensus, as these policy prescriptions were called, in social democratic Western Europe and the formerly communist East as well as elsewhere around the globe. Countries on both sides of the Atlantic did liberalize their economies, but to very different degrees. Both distinctive European varieties of capitalism and the European social model have persisted, albeit with modifications.

The United States continued to abandon its remaining Fordist mass-production industries, with the exception of the downsized automobile sector, and outsourced the manufacturing of clothes, shoes, appliances, computers, etc. to East and Southeast Asia, Mexico, Central America, and the Caribbean. While European countries moved out of coal, iron, and steel, they have retained more manufacturing. Northern Italy, for example, turned to small-scale industries, characterized by flexible specialization, while Germany retained its traditional mix of mass production and decentralized, small and medium-sized firms that utilize skilled labor to produce quality goods. Late developers like Finland became leaders in new industries like cell phones. Manufacturing has played an especially prominent role in Eastern Europe, for from the mid 1990s on Western European firms eagerly invested in modernizing old factories or constructing new ones in order to produce a variety of consumer durables, using skilled but comparatively low-cost labor.[11]

Europe did follow the United States lead and eliminate all controls on capital flows. The SEA laid the basis for the creation by 1992 of a fully integrated EU market in which capital, as well as goods and labor, moved unimpeded. This was a marked break with past practice, which had placed limits on capital flows and thus capital flight in order to promote nationally specific industrial and social policies. Although the EU eliminated many regulations on finance and trade, the United States remained the most deregulated economy.

---

[11] Berend, *Europe since 1980*, 210–13.

The European financial sector did not develop on a scale comparable to that in the United States, where finance and real estate dominated the economy after the turn of the century and banks and hedge funds developed ever new, more opaque, and highly leveraged investment vehicles like collateralized debt obligations and credit default swaps. Millions of risky subprime mortgages fueled an unprecedented American housing boom. Europeans, with the exception of countries like Iceland, moved later and more hesitantly into these new financial products. While there were housing booms and later busts in some of the more neoliberal European countries like England, Spain, and Ireland, mortgage markets in much of Europe remained more regulated, thereby limiting risky mortgages. Mortgage debt as a percentage of GDP was 70 percent in the United States in the first five years of the new century, a figure higher than in all European countries except the Netherlands and Denmark. Americans saved less and consumed more, often borrowing to do so. While European savings rates declined in Sweden, the UK, and Italy, they did not in France and Germany, the two largest European economies. Household credit as a percentage of disposable income in 2005 ranged from 18 percent in Poland and 34 percent in Italy to 70 percent in Germany and 112 percent in Spain; in the United States it was 132 percent.[12]

The United States, long suspicious of Western European state-owned enterprises, recommended extensive privatization from the 1980s on. Although countercyclical spending and planning had been more important than nationalized businesses in the postwar European economic model, Britain, France, and Italy had sizable state sectors and everywhere utilities and transport were government-owned. That changed dramatically; in the nineties alone European governments sold off $400 billion worth of banks, factories, and utilities. Thatcher led the way when in the eighties she privatized British Airways, British Aerospace, and British Telecom as well as utilities, railroads, and public housing. In 1985 she broke the miners' strike and closed many nationalized mines. Public sector employment shrank from 27.4 percent in 1981 to 18.1 percent in 2003. Public spending, which had reached 45 percent of GDP in 1980, dipped below 35 percent in 1990, only to rise again to between 35 and 40 percent for the next two decades. The newly privatized utility firms were not more profitable; the main beneficiaries were the new owners and the financial overseers of privatization, not the taxpayers.

---

[12] Saskia Sassen, "The Return of Primitive Accumulation," in George Lawson, Chris Armbruster, and Michael Cox, eds., *The Global 1989* (Cambridge University Press, 2011), 68, 73.

Between 1981 and 1983 French President Mitterrand tried to buck the neoliberal trend by nationalizing banks and corporations, thereby doubling the size of the state sector, but capital flight led him and his successors to reverse course and reprivatize both newly nationalized enterprises and long-standing ones. Italy privatized ENI, the state oil firm, as well as TV and radio.[13]

Reacting against the failures of socialism, Eastern Europeans embraced the doctrine of privatization much more enthusiastically than Western Europeans, but actually privatizing communist economies proved difficult. Small firms could be handed over to their workers with relative ease, but it was hard to find buyers for large ones, which were technologically outmoded and often produced goods no one wanted to buy. In many cases, former managers or former high party and state officials took over large firms, thereby "stealing the state" in the words of one analyst. Czechoslovakia set up a voucher system intended to enable every citizen to buy stock in privatizing companies, but it was scandal-ridden, and most people sold their vouchers for immediate cash. Poland and Hungary favored the "shock therapy" of rapid privatization that American economists like Jeffrey Sachs recommended but could find few buyers in the early 1990s. Only in reunified Germany did the government sell off state industries rapidly and at bargain basement prices. Some governments, like Romania's, did not even try, keeping over 60 percent of industries in state hands.[14]

In response to slower growth, rising unemployment, business pressure, the admonitions of neoliberal economists, and globalization, European economies did move in a more liberal direction. Yet, fully liberal market economies did not develop, and faith in the market as the ultimate arbiter of all relations, economic, social, political, and personal, did not triumph.

Coordinated market economies

Distinctive European varieties of capitalism existed throughout the twentieth century, as we have seen. Although death by convergence on the American model had been repeatedly predicted, especially in the 1950s and again in the 1990s, European economies have retained production regimes, industrial relations, forms of governance, and value

---

[13] Jeffry A. Frieden, *Global Capitalism: Its Fall and Rise in the Twentieth Century* (New York: Norton, 2006), 399. www.ukpublicspending.co.uk/downchart_ukgs.php?year=1900_2010&state=UK&view=1&expand=&units=p&fy=20. Judt, *Postwar*, 541–43.

[14] Steven L. Solnick, *Stealing the State: Control and Collapse in Soviet Institutions* (Cambridge, MA: Harvard University Press, 1998). Judt, *Postwar*, 689.

commitments that differ substantially from those in the United States and Britain. The Anglo-American model is labeled liberal or stock market capitalism, while European economies are called coordinated market capitalism or welfare capitalism or they are disaggregated into a Nordic or statist model on the one hand and a continental social market or corporatist one on the other hand. Some of the distinctions are long-standing, others a recent product of the neoliberal turn in Britain and America.

European firms often behave differently from American ones. They have long-term and loyal relations with suppliers and customers, and managers and owners frequently sit on the boards of firms close to them. All this fosters trust and cooperation and limits practices, such as hostile takeovers, that are widespread in America. Capital is more patient, for firms are more likely to secure financing through banks with which they have long-term relations rather than via the stock market, although the proportion of bank financing is declining.[15] In the 1990s roughly 40 percent of stock in the 500 largest firms in the United States and the UK was held by large financial institutions rather than by families or non-financial shareholders; only 15–18 percent was for comparable firms in France and Germany.[16]

Business and labor are more organized in Western Europe than in America and bargaining between them and with the state is more institutionalized. In Germany, for example, industry and labor are organized in autonomous, self-administered bodies, whose roles are spelled out legally. Firms are governed by the participation of labor and management in works councils. While codetermination is not as extensive in other Western European countries, similar institutions exist in Northern and Western Europe, and the state is frequently more involved in vocational training as well as in worker retraining. Conditions are more varied in Eastern Europe. Corporatist bargaining of a Western European sort has emerged in Slovenia but not elsewhere. While Poland, Hungary, and Romania experienced high strike rates at various points in the 1990s, labor was unable to institutionalize workers' interests.[17]

Wage bargaining is coordinated at the plant, industry, and national levels, and in 2000, collective bargaining agreements covered between 70 percent and 95 percent of workers in continental Western Europe, with only Germany (68 percent) and Switzerland (40 percent) falling

---

[15] Eichengreen, *European Economy*, 419–20.

[16] Andrew Glyn, *Capitalism Unleashed: Finance, Globalization and Welfare* (Oxford University Press, 2006), 56.

[17] Stephen Crowley and Miroslav Stanojević, "Varieties of Capitalism, Power Resources, and Historical Legacies: Explaining the Slovenian Exception," *Politics & Society* 39/2 (2011): 268–95.

below. By contrast only 30 percent were covered in the UK and a scant 13 percent in the United States. Collective bargaining was weak in most Eastern European countries during the troubled 1990s. Over the following decade, collective bargaining became more decentralized in Western Europe and emerged at the local and company levels in Eastern Europe. By 2009 coverage rates ranged from 100 percent in Slovenia and the nine- tieth percentile in France, Sweden, Norway, Austria, and Belgium, to 63 percent in Germany and 44 percent in the Czech Republic. Poland, Hungary, Slovakia, and the UK were at 35 percent, while Estonia with 22 percent and the United States with 13 percent brought up the rear. European collective bargaining coverage was extensive whether union den- sity was high as in Sweden and Denmark, moderate as in Belgium, Italy, and Norway, or at very low American levels as in France. High coverage encouraged more solidaristic wage policies that narrowed the gap between the highest and lowest paid workers and facilitated wage restraint. Workers across Europe enjoy much higher levels of employment protection than do American ones. The United States traded job security for labor market flexibility, while European countries made the opposite choice.[18]

Distinct institutions and policies reflect and reinforce value differences. Western Europe has developed a more socially embedded model of capitalism in which economic transactions and institutions are supposed to serve noneconomic ends as well as economic ones and in which economic relations are bolstered by social ties. The maximization of shareholder returns is not their sole raison d'être. In the words of one French commentator, "In America, money is the goal and things are the means to achieve it, while in Europe our goal is to achieve things, with money as the means." The entrepreneur enjoys much higher social esteem in America than in Europe. While Americans see the state and the market as antithetical, most Europeans accord the state an essential economic role in building infrastructure, promoting economic integration, preserv- ing the environment, and providing health and education. At issue in transatlantic economic debates, argues a leading German economic his- torian, are not just markets and profits but the very "rules of the game of economic life." A *"Kulturkampf"* or clash of civilizations is occurring among the most developed capitalist countries. Nowhere is that more evident than in social policy.[19]

[18] Jonas Pontusson, *Inequality and Prosperity: Social Europe vs Liberal America* (Ithaca: Cornell University Press, 2005), 26. Danielle Venn, "Legislation, Collective Bargaining and Enforcement: Updating the OECD Employment Protection Indicators," *OECD Social, Employment and Migration Working Papers*, No. 89 (2009).

[19] Michel Serres, cited in Michel Albert, *Capitalism vs Capitalism: How America's Obsession with Individual Achievement and Short-Term Profit Has Led It to the Brink of Collapse* (New

Persistence of the European social model

From the 1980s on social programs on both sides of the Atlantic were under increasing pressure from slow economic growth, an aging population, globalization, and a widespread preoccupation with containing inflation, no matter what the cost to jobs. Conservative politicians and neoliberal economists in the United States and Britain launched an across the board attack on social rights and benefits as economically damaging, politically objectionable, and morally corrosive. What could not be completely eliminated should be shrunk and privatized. Families and individuals should be responsible for their welfare, not the "nanny state." In the face of real economic pressures and ferocious ideological assaults, however, most European countries defended their postwar welfare states. Whether they continued to emphasize social citizenship and similar benefits for all as Scandinavian countries did or relied on social insurance and differential entitlements as most Western and Southern European states did, all defended their commitments to universal coverage, social solidarity, and the state's central role in securing social welfare. Britain is the exception here, but even Thatcher did not privatize the National Health System. Europeans do not view private goods and services as a priori better than public ones, nor the market as always better than the state. The transatlantic social gap widened substantially, for it was no longer just the size of programs and benefits that was at issue but the very existence of social rights and a safety net.

Spending on social programs provides one indicator of these differences. From 1980 on Western and Northern European countries spent a higher proportion of their GDP on social programs than the United States; from the mid 1990s so did Spain, Portugal, and Greece, and after the late 1990s the Czech Republic, Slovakia, Poland, and Hungary did as well. In 1980 no European country spent a smaller proportion of GDP on social programs than America's 13.1 percent; in 2001 only Ireland did worse than America's 14.6 percent. By contrast Sweden spent over 27 percent in both years, France increased from 21.1 percent to 27.2 percent, and Italy moved from 18.4 percent to 23.9 percent in the same two decades. Even the neoliberal UK moved from 17.3 percent to 21.5 percent. An aging population drawing pensions and rising unemployment account for part of these increases as do universal health coverage in Europe and Medicare and Medicaid in the United States. Public social spending per capita, however, was slightly less in Ireland and

York: Four Wall Eight Windows, 1993), 75. Werner Abelshauser, *Kulturkampf: Der deutsche Weg in die Neue Wirtschaft und die amerikanische Herausforderung* (Berlin: Kulturverlag Kadmos, 2003), 8.

Iceland than in America and over a $1,000 per capita less in Spain, Portugal, and Greece. If private social spending, which is especially high in the United States, is included, total social spending on both sides of the Atlantic is closer together. But not everyone can afford to participate in private social programs for retirement or health care. And neoliberal countries like the United States, which have high private social spending, also have a much higher percentage of means-tested assistance and a lower proportion of the population covered by sickness, unemployment, and pension benefits than do societies with low private spending.[20]

As in the past, healthcare was a key area of transatlantic difference. Both East and West Europeans regard healthcare as a social right and a social good rather than as a commodity. The average sickness and health insurance benefits in the fifteen Western European EU members in 2005 were €1,900 per person, far above the €300–400 in Eastern Europe, but across Europe states paid 80–90 percent of health expenses. In the United States, by contrast, the government pays for only 44 percent of health costs and over 46 million Americans or 15 percent of the population have no health insurance. Moreover, total private and public healthcare spending has increased more rapidly than in Europe and accounts for a larger percentage of GDP.[21]

Differences abound in other areas as well. In education the United States spends more, but a higher percentage of that is private. In Europe the educational system from preschool through university is overwhelmingly state-funded and free or very low cost, except in England. Old-age pensions present a mixed picture. United States public spending is high, but there are proposals to cut social security benefits, and Americans have long relied on a mixture of social security and private retirement plans provided by employers or state and local governments. These defined-benefit plans are either being eliminated completely or replaced by defined-contribution plans, whose benefits depend on the stock market. European states provide guaranteed pensions, but these are now being supplemented by mandatory pension insurance and in some places by private pensions as well. Everywhere the retirement age is being raised.

---

[20] Willem Adema and Maxime Ladaique, "How Expensive Is the Welfare State?" *OECD Social, Employment and Migration Working Papers*, No. 92 (2009): 3, 23. Peter Baldwin, *The Narcissism of Minor Differences: How America and Europe Are Alike* (Oxford University Press, 2009), 71. Pontusson, *Inequality and Prosperity*, 145, 147.

[21] Berend, *Europe since 1980*, 264–67. www.cms.gov/NationalHealthExpendData/02_NationalHealthAccountsHistorical.asp#TopOfPage. Baldwin, *Narcissism of Minor Differences*, 41–43. www.emaxhealth.com/1506/cdc-number-americans-without-health-insurance-coverage-increases.

Nearly all Western European countries replace more of the net income of sick employees than does the United States. The same is true for those who are unemployed short or long term, although Britain and Germany have lowered unemployment pay and imposed increasingly stringent work requirements over the past two decades. No European country has reformed aid to needy mothers and children along the lines of the American Temporary Aid to Needy Families, which limits benefits to sixty months over a person's lifetime and imposes work requirements on mothers. Both European countries that encourage mothers to stay home, like Germany, and those that encourage them to work, like Sweden and France, continue to spend much more on family policy than does the United States.[22]

The results of these systemic differences are profound. The United States has become a low-tax nation for both corporations and individuals. While Western European and American corporate tax rates were similar until the turn of the century, United States ones dropped sharply thereafter. Western and Northern Europe have higher personal income tax, especially for the wealthy, while income tax in the United States and in most Eastern European countries is less progressive. In 2004 tax revenues were equivalent to two-fifths of GDP in the EU-15; in America the figure was one-quarter. In 2007 the United States spent the smallest percentage of its national budget on social protection of any developed country – one-fifth versus two-fifths for Sweden and Germany and nearly that for Britain. If health, education, and general public services are added in, the American figure remains lower than any European country except the Czech Republic.[23]

Europeans pay more taxes but they get more benefits, and this translates into more equality and intergenerational mobility and less poverty. It also creates a broad societal investment in social rights and state social policies. Although income inequality has risen in all OECD countries since the 1980s, the distance between the top 10 percent and bottom 10 percent has grown fastest in the United States. Only Russia comes close in terms of inequality. In 1980 the average American CEO earned 42 times more than the average worker; in 2001 he or she made over 400 times more, while in Britain CEO compensation was 25 times greater, in Sweden 14 times, and in Germany and Switzerland 11 times. Measured in terms of income, the United States has poverty rates comparable to

---

[22] Adema and Ladaique, "How Expensive," 43.
[23] Glyn, *Capitalism Unleashed*, 165. Berend, *Europe since 1980*, 265. Sabina Dewan and Michael Ettlinger, "Comparing Public Spending and Priorities Across OECD Countries," www.americanprogress.org/issues/2009/10/oecd_spending.html.

Western and Northern Europe, but after taxes and transfer payments are factored in, it has the highest rates. The United States has the highest infant mortality rate of any developed country. Life expectancy is nearly equivalent in the EU and the United States, but this masks longer life expectancy in most Western European countries and considerably shorter ones in Eastern Europe where health systems collapsed after 1989.[24]

Different social models reflect the relative importance assigned to alternative values – risk versus security, the individual versus society, opportunity versus equality, the market versus the state. In the early and mid twentieth century, Europeans paid little attention to American social policy and were deeply ambivalent about American mass consumption and mass culture. By the century's end the latter had been incorporated into the daily life of people across Europe. Disagreements now concern the state and societal context in which capitalist consumer economies will continue to develop. Europe and America increasingly articulate divergent visions of the good life and a just society. Indeed, in the United States and Britain the concept of society has been evacuated, for the "ownership society" that is promulgated is profoundly individual or at most familial; the state is only considered legitimate in its military and national security instantiations.

While many American liberals admire the European social model, conservatives like the political commentator Irving Kristol rejected it in toto. Europeans, he argued, have "feminine-maternalistic" welfare states, which seek to protect people and enable them to avoid risks; they impede economic growth, limit military expenditures, and do their "best to emasculate the spirit of nationalist patriotism in all nations of Europe." The alternative is the American "masculine, paternalistic" welfare state, which tries to do for its citizens what fathers try to do for their children, that is make them "grow up to be self-reliant, self-supporting and able to cope with a recalcitrant world."[25] Although some Europeans have argued strongly that generous welfare states must be jettisoned in the interests of economic competitiveness and productivity, and most recognize the need to rationalize and trim their social policies, few want to emulate the American model and the values underlying it.

---

[24] www.nationmaster.com/graph/eco_inc_equ_un_gin_ind-income-equality-un-gini-index. Pontusson, *Inequality and Prosperity*, 48. Michael Hennigan, "Executive Pay and Inequality in the Winner-take-all Society," August 7, 2005, www.finfacts.com/ireland businessnews/publish/article_10002825.shtml.

[25] Irving Kristol, "The Two Welfare States," www.aei.org/article/the-two-welfare-states-issue/. A version of the article appeared in the *Wall Street Journal*, October 19, 2000.

Inconclusive competition

Instead of convergence on the United States neoliberal model, there has been transatlantic competition between distinctive European and American varieties of capitalism and social policies. None, however, have been able to recapture the Golden Age of the 1950s, 1960s, and early 1970s. The United States was not able to restore its former hegemony; Western European states could not revive the growth and employment rates of the postwar recovery and modernization, and the new capitalist economies of Eastern Europe failed to deliver on the enormous hopes placed in them. In the wake of the 2008 financial crisis, countries on both sides of the Atlantic faced ongoing deficits and national debts. They found themselves in a multipolar world, which the North Atlantic no longer dominated.

Take growth. The American economy grew substantially faster than European ones in the 1980s, but growth plunged to near zero in the early 1990s, zoomed up to almost 5 percent during the information technology boom, and plunged again during the 2001 crash before recovering to a respectable 3 percent by 2005. Between 1980 and 2000 real GDP per capita growth averaged 2.1 percent in the United States as opposed to 1.9 percent for Western European countries. Yet, the United States did not outperform all European economies. Ireland, Spain, and Portugal, for example, grew substantially faster from the early 1990s on, and Sweden grew at modestly higher rates from the mid 1990s on. Eastern Europe was a special case, for post-1989 attempts at rapid liberalization and privatization led industrial production to drop by half and GDP by a third; unemployment shot up and the standard of living declined. It took a decade for Poland, the Czech Republic, Slovenia, Hungary, and Slovakia to begin growing again and still longer for the Balkans, Romania, Bulgaria, and Russia. Overall, American economic expansion was steady but not spectacular, for the high-tech boom, which so many Europeans envied, was offset by the net decline in exports. The dramatic success story of these decades lay not in the Atlantic world but in China, whose vast economy grew at double-digit rates from the late 1990s.[26]

The United States gained on the productivity front. By the 1990s Western and Northern European productivity had come within 80–90 percent of America's but then fell back to 65–75 percent. Some attribute

---

[26] Pontusson, *Inequality and Prosperity*, 5. Eichengreen, *European Economy*, 319–20. http://Data.worldbank.org/indicator/NY.GDP.MKTP.KD.ZG. Berend, *Europe since 1980*, 197–99. Glyn, *Capitalism Unleashed*, 132–33.

American gains primarily to the financial sector and to changes in retail and wholesale trade, such as Wal-Mart. Others credit higher United States investment in research and development in electronics and aerospace, often defense related. European firms, by contrast, focused more on micro inventions and improvements in the chemical, machinery, and textile industries. Many European governments supported ailing industries in the 1980s and early 1990s before promoting high-tech firms and research and development with subsidies and tax breaks.[27]

United States unemployment exceeded Europe's through the 1970s, but by the late 1990s European unemployment ranged from 7.3 percent in the UK to over 12 percent in Italy, while it was only 5 percent in America. Thereafter, United States rates remained lower than Western and Northern European ones but only slightly. In Eastern Europe, however, unemployment averaged 12–20 percent in the early 1990s and remained at 10–13 percent in Hungary, Poland, and Russia thereafter. In some areas of the Balkans, two out of every five workers were unemployed. As disturbing as the sheer number of European unemployed was the fact that after the turn of the century a large number (up to one-third in France and one-half in Germany) were long-term jobless. Analysts disagree about whether lower American rates reflected a more robust economic model or resulted from very high rates of incarceration, which removed many of the least educated and skilled from the labor market. Some attribute higher European rates to more generous social benefits, others to excessive regulation that limited job creation. In Germany reunification ended the possibility of employment for many in the former GDR.[28]

The Washington Consensus preached the virtues of small government, reduced national debts, and no deficit spending, yet debts and deficits were common on both sides of the Atlantic, among countries endorsing neoliberalism and those resisting it. The United States national debt rose steadily as a percentage of GDP from around 40 percent in the mid 1980s to over 60 percent in the mid 1990s and remained there, except for a brief drop at decade's end. By 2007 government debt averaged 58 percent of GDP in the EU and 66 percent in the euro area, which was slightly above the 60 percent criteria prescribed in the Maastricht Treaty. This masked wide national variations; France and Germany hovered around the average, for example, while Sweden and Ireland were well below and Greece

---

[27] Glyn, *Capitalism Unleashed*, 78–79. Eichengreen, *European Economy*, 257–61. Berend, *Europe since 1980*, 169.

[28] Pontusson, *Inequality and Prosperity*, 70, 72. Berend, *Europe since 1980*, 198.

and Italy far above. Hungary and Poland had substantial debts, but many Eastern European countries did not.[29]

Balanced government budgets were a particular United States preoccupation but seldom an accomplished fact; Reagan ran substantial deficits, as did both Bush presidencies and only Clinton managed a surplus. By 2007 the annual deficit was 1 percent of GDP. European deficits were higher than United States ones in the 1980s and again in the late 1990s but lower in between. The Euro area mandated that deficits not exceed 3 percent of GDP, but even the most prosperous and stable countries like Germany and France had difficulty meeting that criterion consistently. In 2007 the average EU deficit was 0.8 percent of GDP and for the Euro zone 0.6 percent, While countries such as Sweden, the Netherlands, Finland, Spain, Ireland, and Denmark ran a surplus, Germany and France had modest deficits, Greece, Italy, Portugal, Hungary, and Poland more serious ones. If crises struck, even the most neoliberal governments intervened to limit damage. When the Long Term Capital Management hedge fund collapsed in 1998, for example, the American Federal Reserve pressured banks to bail it out; in the 2001 crash it stepped in again.

And then came the 2008 financial crisis, which began in the United States with the collapse of the subprime mortgage market, spread to American banks and brokerage firms, and then moved to Europe and around the globe. An American and European recession followed. By 2009 the United States debt had shot up to 80 percent of GDP and the deficit had risen to 10 percent. In the EU average deficits were 6 percent of GDP, and national debts spiraled out of control in Ireland, Iceland, and Greece. By 2011 the global economy was once again in danger, and this time the debt crises in the Euro zone led the way. Growth remained flat, unemployment continued to climb, and fears of a lost decade abounded on both sides of the Atlantic.[30]

As in the 1930s and 1970s, there is no agreement about how to handle the crisis. In 2008–9 the United States, Britain, and many continental governments bailed out banks on an unprecedented scale. There was much talk of the return of Keynes, but as deficits and debts continued to rise, politicians on both sides of the Atlantic began prescribing austerity at home and for countries like Greece and Italy, which were in severe financial straits. In the United States, Congress refused to raise taxes, fund infrastructure projects, or revive employment programs like the

---

[29] http://epp.eurostat.ec.europa.eu/cache/ITY_PUBLIC/.../2-22042010-BP-EN.PDF. www.usgovernmentspending.com/federal_deficit_chart.html.

[30] www.usgovernmentspending.com/federal_debt_chart.html.

CCC. In Europe, more has been done to protect jobs, but the most prosperous countries like Germany have been reluctant to consider issuing Eurobonds that would stabilize weak countries but also increase the interdependence of states in the Eurozone. Economists, politicians, and pundits debated whether Greece, and perhaps Spain, Portugal, and Italy, would default and whether the euro would survive.

In the face of mounting crises and uncertainty about effective cures, it is an open question whether European states can defend their social policies. Prime Minister David Cameron in Britain has no intention of trying, advocating instead "the Big Society" in which national programs have been slashed and individuals and local communities are to be somehow empowered to care for themselves. In the United States the assault on social programs is targeting Medicaid, Medicare, and Social Security, but nothing comparable is occurring on the continent. As in the 1930s, Europe and America have blamed one another for their economic problems, each insisting that the other was not doing enough or not doing the right thing. From the perspective of late 2011, the future is uncertain on both sides of the Atlantic, and the current prolonged crisis is not bringing them closer together.

12   Imperial America, estranged Europe

Transatlantic divergence turned into stark disagreements when foreign policy issues like the mission of NATO, the response to ethnic cleansing in Yugoslavia, and above all the American war in Iraq were on the agenda. After 1989 America was the only military superpower. Indeed, by the late 1990s it imagined itself and was seen by people like the French Foreign Minister Hubert Vedrine as a "hyperpower," which dominated in all categories of power.[1] Yet, despite its vast military spending and dazzling arsenal of weapons, after the turn of the century, the United States became bogged down in multiple limited wars that it could neither win nor extricate itself from. These wars severely damaged the American economy and disturbed transatlantic relations. Western European states oscillated between vehement criticism of American interventions and reluctant and, in American eyes, insufficient support, while Eastern European states offered verbal endorsements but little practical help.

As America became more interventionist and unilateralist, much of Europe remained committed to multilateralism and more hesitant about military interventions within Europe or outside. United States interests have shifted away from Europe toward the Middle East, Central Asia, and China, while Europe has focused primarily on the expanding EU and the broader Mediterranean region. The American empire of bases, its distinctive post-1945 imperial innovation, continued to exist, but the United States, like Britain before it, found that empire is economically costly and politically corrosive without enhancing national security or stabilizing vast regions of the globe.

While European anti-Americanism was hardly a new phenomenon, it took on new forms in the wake of the Iraq War. Earlier anti-Americanism had been couched in anti-capitalist, anti-modern, and sometimes anti-democratic terms and reflected economic and cultural anxieties; after 2001 its emphasis was political, its target foreign policy. The new anti-

---

[1] *New York Times*, Feb. 5, 1999.

Americanism accepted modernity, capitalism, and consumerism but reflected transatlantic differences about international relations and national security as well as desirable economic models and social values. Most United States politicians and the media condemned European critics and ignored their message, for they expected deference to American leadership and gratitude for what the United States had done a half-century ago. As Europe and the United States became increasingly absorbed in diverging national and global projects, transatlantic exchanges diminished and grew abrasive. A war gap joined the market gap and the God gap.

Unipolarity and its discontents

The collapse of communism and reunification of Germany raised as many questions about the international order as they solved. What sort of superpower would the United States be in a new unipolar world? Would it retain a commitment to multilateralism and adhere to international institutions or succumb to unilateralism and the temptations of empire? Would an increasingly integrated Europe be a partner to the United States as countries like Britain favored or a counterweight to American might as the French hoped? Without the Soviet presence and the binding ideology of anti-communism, would the transatlantic alliance hold together?

The first test of transatlantic cooperation after the successfully resolved debates about German reunification came with the Gulf War of 1991. Launched by the United States after Iraq's President Saddam Hussain invaded Kuwait and refused to withdraw, it caused few serious divisions in the Atlantic alliance. Saddam was the clear aggressor, Europe like America worried about oil supplies, and both a UN resolution and a broad coalition backed the war. Of equal importance, it ended quickly, entailed few American or European casualties, and required no costly occupation. Yet, in the run up to the war there was bitter wrangling in Europe about whether war was necessary or diplomacy might prevail; over who should provide troops, who would command them, and what the war's ultimate purpose would be. While the French supplied both troops and money and Britain men and *matériel* in generous amounts, Germany (as well as Japan) footed a large portion of the bill but refused to send troops, citing constitutional prohibitions on operations outside the NATO area. Hungary and Sweden sent medical supplies, Italy and other Western European countries ships and a few planes. American critics were particularly disappointed in Germany, impatiently admonishing its leaders to grow up and assume the adult responsibilities of a fully sovereign nation. America had facilitated German reunification, and it was the rankest ingratitude for Germany not to support America in its hour of need; money alone was insufficient thanks. No longer concerned about potential German militarism, Americans complained bitterly about a feminized anxiety that pervaded Germany, an overwrought fear of war and inability to overcome past traumas.

The Gulf War foreshadowed the issues and the area that would dominate American foreign policy and trouble transatlantic relations a decade later, but it was Europe itself that was the focus of contestation in the 1990s. Three issues dominated debates about defense and security policy: troop levels, the Atlantic alliance, and NATO. With the Cold War over, the United States dramatically reduced its military presence in Europe, which had long been a serious financial burden. The quarter of a million American troops in Germany shrank to under 70,000 over the course of the 1990s. Tens of thousands of American soldiers left Italy and Britain, and at least half of the forces in Portugal, Greece, and the Netherlands were withdrawn.[2] These sharp reductions had adverse economic impacts in those countries and raised questions about whether European and American interests overlapped.

Politicians and pundits, government officials and academics on both sides of the Atlantic made repeated efforts to redefine the relationship of Europe and the United States. These began with Secretary of State Baker's December 1989 call for a new transatlantic architecture that would link American and European security interests; this in turn harked back to Kissinger's 1973 appeal for a new Atlantic Charter. In 1990 the United States and the EC signed the Transatlantic Declaration, which mandated consultation on multiple levels. It marked a new stage in American recognition of the EC and a willingness to deal directly with it rather than just bilaterally with the member states. In 1995 the American government and the EU signed the New Transatlantic Agenda (NTA), which expanded consultation and called for joint action not only on economic issues but also on the political goals of "the promotion of peace, stability and democracy and development around the world." The precise meaning of these capacious terms and the methods to achieve them were not spelled out. The NTA also called for cooperation in "combatting pollution, drug-trafficking, and organized international crime." The NTA was a response to growing EU cohesion and efforts to define shared policies around defense and security issues; it reflected America's desire to retain a voice. It was also a response to the war in Bosnia and the problems of European and American cooperation there. The NTA functioned better as

---

[2] www.heritage.org/research/reports/2006/05/global-us-troop-deployment-1950–2005.

a forum for resolving transatlantic economic disputes than managing security ones, as both the Bosnian and Iraq wars would show.[3]

NATO was central to restructuring troop levels and rethinking the Atlantic alliance. During the Cold War, NATO's purpose was, according to Lord Ismay, its first secretary general, "to keep the Americans in, the Russians out and the Germans down." What if anything could its purpose be when the Soviets were gone, the Americans withdrawing, and the Germans securely integrated into Europe? While the United States was less interested in Europe after 1989, it was determined to remain, as Baker put it, "a European power." It saw NATO as a means to preserve America's military presence in Europe while mobilizing European resources for American ends and getting Europeans to share burdens more equitably. The United States had long dominated NATO and wanted to continue to do so at a time when European integration was accelerating not only around economic and monetary issues but also around security and defense policy.

The EC had failed to develop a common defense policy in the 1950s when France vetoed the European Defense Community; it raised the issue again in the 1970s with the European Political Cooperation, and again when the EU was formed. The 1997 Amsterdam revision of the Maastricht Treaty elaborated the goals of a Common Foreign and Security Policy, which was to include humanitarian and rescue missions, peacekeeping, and the deployment of combat forces in crisis management. Security concerns focused on the EU borders, and it was not clear how far beyond them interventions might occur. The United States could not curb these developments but sought to contain them by securing the future of NATO.

Expanding NATO was the first step. As a 1995 NATO study argued:

With the end of the Cold War, there is a unique opportunity to build an improved security architecture in the whole of the Euro-Atlantic area . . . without recreating dividing lines. NATO views security as a broad concept embracing political and economic, as well as defense, components . . . NATO remains a purely defensive Alliance whose fundamental purpose is to preserve peace in the Euro-Atlantic area and to provide security for its members.

NATO was to remain neither purely defensive nor restricted to the Euro-Atlantic region, but it did enlarge, and ahead of EU expansion, thereby giving priority to the goal of "strengthening and broadening the transatlantic partnership" over that of "reinforcing the tendency toward integration and

---

[3] "The New Transatlantic Agenda," EU-United States Summit Facts Brief No. 2, www.eurunion.org/partner/summit/summit9712/nta.htm.

cooperation in Europe."[4] The Czech Republic, Poland, and Hungary joined in 1999, Bulgaria, Estonia, Latvia, Lithuania, Romania, Slovenia, and Slovakia did so in 2004, and Albania and Croatia in 2009, as enlargement moved NATO ever closer to the borders of the former Soviet Union. Russian leaders from Boris Yeltsin through Vladimir Putin to Dmitri Medvedev were extremely upset by NATO's expansion and its plans to install missile defense sites in Eastern Europe, arguing that such actions inhibited any friendship with the United States and threatened Russia's legitimate sphere of influence.

Bosnia, Kosovo, and humanitarian interventions

The disintegration of Yugoslavia provided an opportunity for NATO to redefine its mission, even as the resulting brutal conflicts exacerbated European-American tensions. Yugoslavia, the most independent and open communist nation in Europe, fell victim to escalating economic problems, ethnic conflicts, and Serbian ambitions. In 1991 Croatia and Slovenia declared their independence; while first Germany and then the EU recognized the new nations, France and the United States defended Yugoslavia's territorial integrity. A year later Bosnia-Herzegovina broke away. Secession by this multiethnic region fueled bitter warfare among Serbs, Croats, and Bosnian Muslims that was marked by atrocities on all sides, but especially the Serbian one. Over 3 million refugees fled northward to seek asylum. Recently reunited Europe faced a destabilizing and brutal war on its periphery.

While the EU and the UN intervened to try to restore peace in Bosnia, the United States refused to help. "We have no dogs in this fight," said Secretary of State Baker in 1991.[5] Ex-Yugoslavia was Europe's problem, but the EU and the UN were unable to control the situation there. In 1993 UN special envoy Cyrus Vance, who had been secretary of state under Carter, and EC representative Lord Owen, who was a former British foreign secretary, proposed a negotiated settlement that would partition Bosnia, but the Clinton administration refused to sanction the Vance–Owen Plan because it made concessions to Serbian aggression and ethnic cleansing. As the war continued, UN peacekeepers were unable to prevent an escalation of ethnic cleansing that culminated in the 1995 Serbian murder of over seven thousand Muslim men and boys in Srebrenica and

---

[4] "Study on NATO Enlargement," NATO, September 1995, chapter 1, www.nato.int/docu/basictxt/enl-9501.htm.
[5] Soeren Kern, "Why the New Transatlantic Agenda Should, But Won't, Be Reformed," 2005, http://kern.pundicity.com/54533/new-transatlantic-agenda-reform.

mass rapes of Muslim women. Europe was once again the site of mass murder, and this prompted a United States-led NATO bombing campaign, which was the first offensive use of NATO forces. American firepower quickly defeated the Serbian forces, and the United States brokered the Dayton Accord, which, like the Vance–Owen Plan, partitioned Bosnia between Muslims and Croats on the one hand and Serbian aggressors on the other. The Americans controlled the NATO peacekeeping force for the next decade, ceding responsibility to the Europeans only in 2005. At decade's end, the United States and its NATO allies launched another air war, this time against Serbian persecution of Albanians in the Yugoslav province of Kosovo.

The wars in ex-Yugoslavia aroused intense debate in the United States and Europe. Intervention where United States interests were not directly threatened remained controversial in America, for despite the success of the Gulf War, many had not forgotten Vietnam. Europeans, still scarred by memories of both World War II and the Holocaust, viewed the prospect of renewed conflict with dread, even if many saw it as necessary. Controversy was particularly intense in Germany, for Bosnia marked the first use of German forces outside the area of NATO. Balkan refugees in Germany and the plight of the Kosovo Albanians in 1999 evoked memories of the 1945 expulsions of Germans from Eastern Europe and reminded Germans of the horrors of war. Bosnia and Kosovo created an acute conflict between two basic postwar German commitments – "Never again war" and "Never again Auschwitz." The Social Democratic-Green government gave priority to the latter and sent German warplanes to bomb Belgrade in 1998.

Bosnia and Kosovo showed that Europe could not manage its problems on its own, for key states disagreed on policy and the EU lacked military power. Aware of its weakness, the EU articulated a common security and defense policy and in 1999 announced the formation of a European Rapid Reaction Force to which the member states would make available over sixty thousand troops. The United States reluctantly tolerated this development, but Secretary of State Madeleine Albright insisted that there be no de-coupling of the European Defense and Security Policy from NATO, no duplication of capabilities, and no discrimination against non-EU NATO members like Turkey. The United States drew its own lessons from its Balkan involvement. Even though it dominated both the wars and the peace settlements, United States military commanders felt that operating within NATO and consulting its nineteen members excessively constrained American forces. Unilateralism might be a preferable option.[6]

---

[6] Gabriel Kolko, "The Crisis in NATO: A Geopolitical Earthquake?" *Counterpunch*, Feb. 18, 2003, www.counterpunch.org/kolko02182003.htm.

In Bosnia and Kosovo, the United States and NATO pioneered a new mission – militarized humanitarian interventions to preempt or stop human rights violations – and outlined a new division of labor in which the United States would lead military campaigns and dictate the peace, while its European allies would be responsible for peacekeeping, clean up, and reconstruction. The militarized defense of human rights would be invoked as the reason or rationalization for interventions elsewhere, but human rights did not prove to be as compelling a mobilizing ideology as anti-communism had been. It was applied inconsistently; while intervention to defend the rights of Bosnian Muslims was being debated, for example, those of the victims of the 1994 genocide in Rwanda were ignored. And it was difficult to distinguish humanitarian interventions from those aiming at regime change or resource control. For Americans it proved much easier to rally against Islamic radicalism after the al Qaeda attacks on the World Trade Center and Pentagon in 2001.

9/11 and the long war

In the immediate aftermath of 9/11, there was an outpouring of European sympathy, solidarity, and support for the United States. Citizens held candlelight vigils; states promised cooperation in the fight against terrorism; the French proclaimed "We are all Americans"; and for the first time, NATO invoked its self-defense clause. A shocked and understandably self-absorbed United States appreciated Europe's support, which it regarded as self-evident and appropriate, but President George W. Bush rejected any joint military response to the terrorist attack, recruiting help only from Britain. Operation Enduring Freedom seemed to defeat the Taliban swiftly and decisively, and a UN International Security Assistance Force, which NATO ran from 2003 on, took over peacekeeping and reconstruction in Afghanistan. The transatlantic relationship seemed assured. A new period of Euro-American harmonious collaboration and mutual understanding failed to evolve, however, for the Bush administration's decision to attack Iraq aroused massive controversy.

In the wake of 9/11, President Bush had promised to combat evildoers everywhere. At West Point in June 2002 he argued: "We must take the battle to the enemy, disrupt his plans and confront the worst threats before they emerge." According to the September 2002 National Security Strategy of the United States, the Cold War had required America to practice deterrence, but it could no longer be "reactive," given "the nature and motivations of these new adversaries," the "rogue states and their terrorist clients." The National Security Council concluded:

Illustration 25 Britons mourn United States terror attack victims, September 13, 2001.

The greater the threat, the greater the risk of inaction – and the more compelling the case for taking anticipatory action to defend ourselves, even if uncertainty remains as to the time and place of the enemy's attack . . . The United States will, if necessary, act preemptively.

The United States would pursue "an American internationalism that reflects the union of our values and our national interests."[7]

Although Iraq was not involved in 9/11, the United States declared war against it in March 2003. In the preceding months, United States officials argued that Saddam had weapons of mass destruction (WMDs), was allied with terrorism and al Qaeda, and represented a threat to America. Unable to get a UN mandate to attack, the United States recruited a Coalition of the Willing to which forty-nine countries around the globe signed on, but only six – Britain, Poland, Portugal, Australia, Spain, and Denmark – provided troops. France and Germany refused to cooperate. After two months of fighting Bush declared victory, and Americans expected to go home rapidly.

European governments were divided about the necessity and legality of war against Iraq, but their citizens were not. On February 15, 2003, millions of people in Berlin, London, Rome, Paris, and other European capitals took to the streets to protest the impending attack. In Europe, as in America, there were peace flags and Bush caricatures, pleas to give peace a chance and chants of "no blood for oil." Demonstrators came not only from the ranks of usual suspects, that is the virtually dormant peace movements, left and Green political parties, universities and schools but also from church groups, trade unions, and community associations. Anxiety about war and instability, dislike of Bush, a broader critique of American foreign policy, and a desire for greater European autonomy and power mixed in proportions that are impossible to untangle.

Although the intense transatlantic animosity of 2003 subsequently subsided, relations remained uneasy. By 2005 American confidence in an easy victory had evaporated; the United States occupation of Iraq dragged on, and in 2010 over 50,000 American troops remained in that conflict-ridden and unreconstructed country. They did not depart until the end of 2011. In Afghanistan nearly 100,000 American troops (and an equal number of American-paid contractors) have been fighting alongside 40,000 NATO troops in a war that grinds destructively and inconclusively on. While Britain, Germany, Italy, France, and Poland have

---

[7] David Armstrong, "Dick Cheney's Song of America: Drafting a Plan for Global Dominance," *Harper's Magazine*, October 2002, 81. The National Security Strategy of the United States, www.whitehouse.gov/nsc, 5, 9–11.

Illustration 26 Antiwar campaigners gather in Trafalgar Square, November 20, 2003.

provided troops, their numbers have been diminishing, and many will do peacekeeping but not combat. Moreover, the cost of these two wars, which Noble laureate economist and former World Bank head Joseph Steglitz and Harvard Professor Linda Bilmes estimate will reach $3 trillion dollars, is borne overwhelmingly by America.

Although the United States was unwilling to share decision-making responsibility in Afghanistan or Iraq, there were calls for improved transatlantic relations. Prominent American and European officials signed on to the Center for Strategic and International Studies' call for a Renewed Transatlantic Partnership, and the American Council on Foreign Relations also spoke of "renewing the Atlantic Partnership." In 2005 leading security experts in the United States and Europe drew up "a Compact between the United States and Europe," arguing "the partnership . . . must endure, not because of what it achieved in the past, but because our common future depends on it."[8] Yet, improving relations proved difficult, due not only to the heated debates of 2003 but also to the enduring issues of division that underlay them.

---

[8] www.brookings.edu/media/NewsReleases/2005/20050216compact.aspx.

Anti-Europeanism

Before and after the Iraq War, American politicians and the media launched vitriolic attacks on Europeans and their ostensible anti-Americanism. The Bush administration and its many neo-conservative and mainstream supporters presented the case for war in Afghanistan, in Iraq, and against terror everywhere as a necessary and virtuous battle of good against "evildoers," and chastised "unwilling" Europeans for failing to understand the moral and civilizational stakes in the struggle. Many European governments and most of the populace West and East were selfishly absorbed in such secondary European issues as economic unification and a possible EU military force. Europeans who questioned American rationales for war were ridiculed; those who refused to join the war effort were publicly threatened with retaliation in the form of troop withdrawals, economic boycotts, and diplomatic marginalization. When Germany, France, Belgium, and Luxemburg discussed plans for the headquarters of an EU military force, a State Department spokesman belittled "the little bitty summit" of "the chocolate makers."[9] The House of Representatives mandated that its cafeteria henceforth sell only "freedom fries" instead of the now unmentionable other sort; and restaurants prided themselves on dumping their French wines. In mid and late 2003, when victory in both Afghanistan and Iraq seemed assured, Americans told NATO and the UN to reform and cooperate with the only superpower or risk becoming irrelevant. Europeans were reminded of American military might, economic prowess, and cultural influence and told that the only alternative to an American-controlled world order was chaos.

Through much of the long twentieth century, Americans had criticized Europeans as militaristic and imperialistic. Now, in a widely read article and book, Robert Kagan, a neo-conservative commentator, condemned America's allies because:

Europe is turning away from power … it is moving beyond power into a self-contained world of laws and rules and transnational negotiation and cooperation. It is entering a post-historical paradise of peace and relative prosperity, the realization of Kant's "Perpetual Peace."

While Europe had embraced the morality of the weak,

The United States remains mired in history, exercising power in the anarchic Hobbesian world where international laws and rules are unreliable and where true

---

[9] http://asia.news.yahoo.com/030903/afp/030903043915int.html.

security and the defense and promotion of a liberal order still depends on the possession and use of military might.[10]

Such depictions of America and the European other marked a dramatic reversal of the way Americans represented themselves to Europeans after 1945. Then Americans saw themselves and were seen as pragmatic, optimistic, rational, reliant on technological cures, and committed to international cooperation. Now they presented themselves as pessimistic realists, rightly skeptical of internationalism, and appropriately committed to military solutions.

Whether the defenders of American foreign policy claimed to be idealist champions of democracy and human rights or reluctant bearers of the imperial burden of restoring world order, they insisted American men were strong and tough, unafraid to make difficult decisions, eager to compete, and willing to resort to force. Europeans, once condemned for their irrational bellicosity, were told they did not understand that "fighting enemies and protecting the nation are overwhelmingly male projects." The low European birthrate was certain proof of Europeans' lack of virility, but so too was the widespread preference for negotiation and cooperation. The *New York Post* labeled France and Germany "The Axis of Weasel," and the American media was replete with references to Euroweenies, wimps, and EU-nuchs.[11]

These differing European and American positions on issues of policy and principle were bolstered by the different tales Europeans and Americans have told themselves about World War II and the reconstruction of Europe. For America World War II was the good war, the just war against totalitarian violence, the war that was the proclaimed model for the Iraq intervention. Americans insisted they won World War II more or less on their own and reminded Europeans how easily they had succumbed to the totalitarian temptation in its fascist and communist guises, how nobly America came to their rescue, and how blind Europeans were to the ostensible recurrence of similar conditions in the Middle East. The French were labeled "cheese-eating surrender monkeys."[12] The Germans were reminded of their complicity in the twentieth century's worst crimes, while the British were complimented for recognizing the need to continue a political and military collaboration solidified in World War II. As American

---

[10] Robert Kagan, *Of Paradise and Power: America and Europe in the New World Order* (New York: Alfred A. Knopf, 2003), 1 .

[11] "Real Men: They're Back," special issue of *The American Enterprise*, September 2003, 5. *New York Post*, January 24, 2003. Timothy Garton Ash, "Anti-Europeanism in America," *New York Review of Books*, February 13, 2003.

[12] Jonah Goldberg, "Chirac Envy," *The National Review* online, February 19, 2003.

politicians and the media constantly remind Europeans, American generosity continued with massive Marshall Plan aid, the maintenance of a vast American military presence, and after 1989 support for the reunification of Germany and the construction of capitalism and democracy in Central and Eastern Europe. Americans presented themselves as acting altruistically to promote European prosperity and anti-communism (while downplaying the benefits to American power and wealth). So why, American critics of Europe asked in tones of wounded surprise or indignant protest, did so many European nations ungratefully withhold political support, moral approval, and material aid?

In prosecuting the wars in Afghanistan and Iraq and pursuing the Global War on Terror, the American government both passed major restrictions on civil liberties at home with the USA Patriot Act and resorted to torture, extraordinary rendition, and the indefinite detention at Guantanamo and elsewhere of suspected terrorists and enemy fighters who were and are still denied their Geneva Convention rights as prisoners of war. While there are strong suspicions that Poland and Romania aided in the extraordinary rendition of suspected terrorists to third-party states noted for torture, most European governments and the public have condemned torture and rendition and insisted on the applicability of international law. Europeans regard terrorism as a criminal act, to be combated by intelligence, police work, and judicial proceeding, not as an ideology or movement to be countered militarily and outside national and international law.

America is the world's only empire, a term enthusiastically embraced by some but avoided by others. As the 2002 National Security Strategy emphasized, "The United States enjoys a position of unparalleled military strength and great economic and political influence." Indeed, "It possesses unprecedented – and unequaled strength and influence in the world." Before the recent wars, the United States defense budget neared the $400 billion mark; thereafter it soared to over $600 billion. The combined EU states, by contrast, spend around $150 billion. Europe has become a relative military pigmy, which was what America had been in comparison to Europe a century before. America has continued to avoid formal colonies, preferring to expand the empire of bases it began constructing during World War II. As of 2004 it had over seven hundred bases in 130 countries. Military prowess is augmented by cultural influence or soft power and by economic might, although both are declining as the world has become economically multipolar, and cultural ideas and goods flow in multiple directions. According to the 2002 National Security Strategy, America is determined to promote the "single sustainable model for national success: freedom, democracy and free enterprise" by recommending pro-growth legal and regulatory policies, sound fiscal policies, and free trade – much as it had in the early twentieth century, during the 1920s, and from the 1980s on.[13]

The United States thinks and acts like an empire with global interests; it insists that what happens anywhere is relevant and cannot understand why Europeans do not share America's perceptions of opportunities, interests, and above all threats. The American government and many citizens argue that national security is the top priority; they have been willing to sacrifice social welfare in pursuit of it, although polls in 2010 and 2011 show that a majority now want to bring the troops home and give priority to domestic problems. European states define national security differently and have made different choices about defense versus social spending. For the world's sole empire unilateralism is not only appealing but also self-evident; for Europe it is neither possible nor desirable.

Anti-Americanism

Many Americans and some Europeans insist that, as in the past, Europeans resent America for what it is and not for what it does; many others have attributed European criticism to jealousy of America's military might, economic influence, and cultural power. Still others argue that it is American policies and competing values that shape European responses to the United States. A 2002 survey by the Pew Global Attitudes Project supports the latter view, concluding that "in general, antipathy toward the United States is shaped more by what it *does* in the international arena than by what it *stands for* politically and economically." The survey also revealed that "criticisms of United States policies and ideals such as American-style democracy and business practices are also highly prevalent among the publics of traditional [European] allies"; indeed more prevalent than in Africa and Asia. Although the British, Germans, and French believed that Iraq represented a great or moderate danger in only somewhat lesser proportions than Americans did, they suspected that the United States might intervene because of oil as much if not more than for security.[14]

While Americans overwhelmingly believe that "America is a force for good in the world," Europeans – even the British – were highly skeptical, according to a 2003 BBC poll. The June 2003 Pew survey of nine European countries showed that whereas 70 percent of the British continued to have a favorable image of the United States, fewer than 50 percent of those

---

[13] National Security Strategy 2002, 1, 3, 19–20. Chalmers Johnson, "America's Empire of Bases," Tomdispatch.com, June 15, 2004.
[14] The Pew Global Attitudes Project, *What the World Thinks in 2002* (italics in original), www.people-press.org, 2–3.

interviewed in Germany, France, Spain, and Russia did. Over three-quarters of French people, nearly two-thirds of Spaniards, Italians, and Russians, and nearly 60 percent of Germans favored a more independent relationship with America. A 2003 Eurobarometer survey comparing attitudes within the fifteen EU member countries and the thirteen candidate countries (CC-13) in Eastern Europe revealed surprising agreement despite differing stances on the Iraq War and United States officials' proclaimed preference for the ex-communist "New Europe" over the "Old Europe" of the West. While a mere 23 percent in the EU thought the United States was a positive force for peace in the world, the figure for the CC-13 was only 34 percent. The CC-13 ranked the EU well above the United States on everything from fighting terrorism and poverty to protecting the environment and promoting world economic growth. By 2011 America's reputation had improved slightly, but of the seven European countries in the BBC survey, Italy was the only one where a majority viewed American influence as mainly positive. While 37 percent of Germans viewed it as mainly positive, 44 percent saw it as mainly negative; for France the figures were 46 percent and 40 percent, for America's special friend, Britain, 46 percent and 43 percent.[15]

The German philosopher and public intellectual Jürgen Habermas and the French philosopher Jacques Derrida made a more sweeping criticism of America and defense of the European alternative in a May 2003 manifesto entitled "February 15, or, What Binds Europeans Together." They argued that "'old Europe' sees itself challenged by the blunt hegemonic politics of its ally ... Many reject the illegality of the unilateral, pre-emptive and deceptively justified invasion." They defended the European social model and the EU as a form of "governance beyond the nation-state." Europe has been shaped by its totalitarian past, by the Holocaust, and by both imperialism and the loss of empire. Unlike Americans, Europeans realize that "the domestication of state power demands a mutual limitation of sovereignty, on the global as well as the nation-state level."[16]

Europeans saw the Iraq War not as an isolated American action but as part of a disturbing pattern. Europe was worried not just by the Iraq

---

[15] "What the World Thinks of America," Poll taken May–June 2003, http://news.bbc.co.uk/1/shared/spl/hi/programmes/wtwta/poll/html/default.stm. The Pew Global Attitudes Project, America's Image Further Erodes, Europeans Want Weaker Ties, March 18, 2003; June 2003, 19, 29. *Candidate Countries Eurobarometer 2003*, 37–38. BBC World Service Poll, March 7, 2011, 8.

[16] Jürgen Habermas and Jacques Derrida, "February 15, or, What Binds Europeans Together: Plea for a Common Foreign Policy, Beginning in Core Europe," in Daniel Levy, Max Pensky, and John Torpey, eds., *Old Europe, New Europe, Core Europe: Transatlantic Relations after the Iraq War* (London: Verso, 2005), 3–13.

War but also by America's hubris, its assertive nationalism, and its lack of clear priorities and refusal to compromise on any of its conservative and unilateral goals. The United States' withdrawal from the Kyoto Accord on global warming, its refusal to sign the land mine treaty or the Convention to End All Discrimination against Women, its rejection of the International Criminal Court, and its reluctance to sell anti-HIV drugs at prices the global South can afford are constantly cited in European criticisms of American policy. United States withdrawal from the ABM Treaty and the Test Ban Treaty are especially upsetting to Russia, which for all its economic problems remains a major nuclear power. Still relishing its Cold War triumph, the United States has insisted on maintaining a confrontational relationship with Russia that some describe as a "semi-cold war."[17] America defends its turn away from international accords and institutions as vital to its independence and self-interest, insisting that constraints can be accepted by smaller, weaker nations but not by the world's only superpower.

The 2003 European Security Strategy, entitled "A Secure Europe in a Better World," differed markedly in content and tone from its American counterpart. It acknowledged threats from terrorism, WMDs, regional conflicts, and failed states but insisted they must be countered by multiple strategies, not just military means. It recognized America's dominant military position and the importance of the transatlantic relationship but called for "an effective multilateral system leading to a fairer, safer and more united world."[18]

European discussions of Iraq also refer back to World War II, but the war carried different memories and meanings. Regardless of whether they were victors or vanquished, the war had extracted an enormous toll on human life, material resources, social cohesion, political institutions, cultural traditions, and moral values. Europeans experienced devastating wars on their territory twice within thirty years and on a smaller scale in the 1990s, and there had also been the costly and brutal struggles to thwart decolonization, while the United States had not known war on its own soil since the 1860s. Nationalism, past and present, had been too problematic to be celebrated unequivocally, and the romance of war that pervaded American society until Vietnam and returned with the Gulf War had no European counterpart. Europeans are wary of a speedy resort to military force, preferring containment to open conflict, nuclear arms limitation to proliferation, and multilateral negotiation to unilateral intervention.

---

[17] Stephen F. Cohen, "Obama's Russia 'Reset': Another Lost Opportunity?" *The Nation*, June 20, 2011.
[18] www.consilium.europa.eu/uedocs/cmsUpload/78367.pdf, 14.

As German Chancellor Gerhard Schroeder noted, Germany's experiences in World War II made it look at issues through a different moral prism and be extremely careful when considering the use of force.[19] Europeans are profoundly appreciative of the system of international institutions and law, which the United States was instrumental in establishing after World War II, but their loyalty is to the values and practices embodied therein, not to the changed priorities of the system's chief designer.

The 2011 NATO intervention in Libya, however, showed that Europeans are not immune from the temptation to use force. At the urging of British Prime Minister David Cameron and French President Nicolas Sarkozy, NATO intervened in support of the Libyan rebellion against the brutal dictator Muammar Qaddafi. Invoking the UN provision on the Responsibility to Protect Civilians, NATO launched an extensive bombing campaign. Far from improving transatlantic relations, however, the Libyan intervention sowed dissent within Europe and across the Atlantic. Germany refused to participate, to the annoyance of American officials, and Norway withdrew after a few months. France, Britain, Italy, and the United States, which provided the bulk of planes and bombs, anticipated a quick victory, and when that did not happen, the United States once again chastised Europeans. In his June 2011 farewell speech, Secretary of Defense Robert M. Gates railed against Europeans who "don't want to share the risks and costs" of combat missions outside Europe. He warned that "Future United States political leaders, those for whom the Cold War was not the formative experience that it was for me, may not consider the return on America's investment in NATO worth the cost." There is, he concluded, "the real possibility for a dim, if not dismal, future for the transatlantic alliance." Europeans were divided in their response to this diatribe; some advocated more burden sharing, others greater European responsibility for its own defense. Still others, like a defense expert at the European Council on Foreign Relations, insisted that not everyone shared the same risk assessment and interests. But, he complained, "we are getting used to upset defense secretaries spewing bile at regular intervals."[20]

The tropes and targets of Europe's anti-Americanism have changed substantially over the twentieth century. In a departure from the pre- and immediate post-World War II eras, politics plays a much more central role than culture. Economic critiques, which are shaped by social and

---

[19] Interview on *The Charlie Rose Show*, September 24, 2003, www.charlierose.com/archives/archive.shtm.
[20] Greg Gaffe and Michael Birnbaum "Gates Rebukes European Allies in Farewell Speech," *Washington Post*, June 10, 2011.

ecological concerns, occur on the terrain of capitalism rather than being anti-capitalist or anti-modern. With the fall of the Soviet Union and the growing economic power and unity of Europe, American anti-Europeanism has also reoriented itself. The claimed requirements of Cold War anti-communism can no longer be invoked to critique and cajole; the relegation of Europeans to the status of feminized or childish junior partners is no longer rhetorically persuasive or politically productive. American anti-Europeanism alternates between trying to deploy anti-terrorism as it once did anti-communism, appealing to Realpolitik, and ridiculing Europe's idealism and anxiety as immature and unmasculine. In a reversal of earlier positions, America is now a debtor state and needs to appeal for aid, while many European states equivocate or refuse. This role reversal has imparted a singularly shrill and emotional tone to American anti-Europeanism.

According to the former Swedish Prime Minister Carl Bildt, Europe and America once shared a common date, 1945, but now Europe's defining date is 1989 and America's is 2001.[21] While this formulation illuminates crucial aspects of the recent conflictual European-American relationship, its periodization is too neat, its implied causation too simple. The relationship between Europe and America, as we have seen, is so troubled because it is troubled by so many things, dating from so many periods. Different approaches to security and defense reinforce and are reinforced by competing economic and social models. Europe is unable to be the effective counterweight to the American hegemon that many would like, but it is not the reliable and pliable partner that America longs for. This situation is unlikely to change, for the Atlantic has continued to widen and the market gap, the God gap, and the war gap show no signs of disappearing. The American Century in Europe is over.

---

[21] Quoted in Thomas L. Friedman, "The End of the West?" *New York Times*, November 2, 2003.

Suggested readings

1 AN UNCERTAIN BALANCE, 1890–1914

Michael Adas, *Dominance by Design: Technological Imperatives and America's Civilizing Mission*. Cambridge, MA: Harvard University Press, 2006.

Geoffrey Barraclough, *Introduction to Contemporary History*. Baltimore: Penguin, 1967.

Thomas Bender, *A Nation among Nations: America's Place in World History*. New York: Hill and Wang, 2006.

Frederick Cooper and Ann Stoler, eds., *Tensions of Empire: Colonial Cultures in a Bourgeois World*. Berkeley: University of California Press, 1997.

Gary S. Cross, *An All-Consuming Century*. New York: Columbia, 2002.

Jeffrey Frieden, *Global Capitalism: Its Fall and Rise in the Twentieth Century*. New York: Norton, 2006.

Heinz Gollwitzer, *Europe in the Age of Imperialism, 1880–1914*. New York: Norton, 1979.

Daniel R. Headrick, *The Tools of Empire: Technology and European Imperialism in the Nineteenth Century*. New York: Oxford, 1981.

Eric Hobsbawm, *Age of Empire*. New York: Vintage, 1989.

Kristin Hoganson, *Consumers' Imperium: The Global Production of American Domesticity, 1865–1920*. Raleigh: University of North Carolina Press, 2007.

Matthey Frye Jacobson, *Barbarian Virtues: The United States Encounters Foreign Peoples at Home and Abroad, 1876–1917*. New York: Hill and Wang, 2001.

Tom Kemp, *Industrialization in Nineteenth Century Europe*. London: Longman, 1985.

Paul A. Kramer, "Empires, Exceptions, and Anglo-Saxons: Race and Rule between the British and United States Empires, 1880–1910," *Journal of American History* 88/4 (2002): 1315–53.

Charles F. McGovern, *Sold American: Consumption and Citizenship, 1890–1945*. Raleigh: University of North Carolina Press, 2006.

Karl Polanyi, *The Great Transformation: The Political and Economic Origins of Our Times*. Boston: Beacon, 2001.

Daniel T. Rodgers, *Atlantic Crossings: Social Politics in a Progressive Age*. Cambridge, MA: Harvard University Press, 1998.

Susan Strasser, Charles McGovern, and Matthias Judt, eds., *Getting and Spending: European and American Consumer Societies in the Twentieth Century*. Cambridge University Press, 1998.

Ian Tyrrell, *Transnational Nation: The United States in Global Perspective since 1789*. New York: Palgrave Macmillan, 2007.

William Appleman Williams, *The Tragedy of American Diplomacy*. New York: Norton, 2009.

2 WORLD WAR I: EUROPEAN CRISIS AND AMERICAN OPPORTUNITY

Ann Taylor Allen, *Women in Twentieth Century Europe*. New York: Palgrave Macmillan, 2008.

Stéphane Audoin-Rouzeau and Annette Becker. *14–18: Understanding the Great War*. New York: Hill and Wang, 2002.

Volker Berghahn, *Europe in the Era of Two World Wars: From Militarism and Genocide to Civil Society, 1900–1950*. Princeton University Press, 2008.

Alan Dawley, *Changing the World: American Progressives in War and Revolution*. Princeton University Press, 2003.

Gerald Feldman, *Army, Industry, and Labour in Germany, 1914–18*. Oxford: Berg Publishers, 2004.

Shelia Fitzpatrick, *The Russian Revolution*. Oxford University Press, 2008.

Susan R. Grayzel, *Women and the First World War*. London: Longman, 2002.

Eric Hobsbawm, *Age of Extremes: A History of the World, 1914–1991*. New York: Pantheon, 1994.

Margaret MacMillan, *Paris, 1919: Six Months that Changed the World*. New York: Random House, 2003.

Erez Manela, *The Wilsonian Moment: Self-Determination and the International Origins of Anticolonial Nationalism*. New York: Oxford University Press, 2007

Mark Mazower, *No Enchanted Palace: The End of Empire and the Ideological Origins of the United Nations*. Princeton University Press, 2009

Neil Smith, *American Empire: Roosevelt's Geographer and the Prelude to Globalization*. Berkeley: University of California Press, 2003.

Ronald Grigor Suny, *The Soviet Experiment: Russia, the USSR and the Successor States*. Oxford University Press, 2010.

Eric D. Weitz, "From the Vienna to the Paris System: International Politics and the Entangled Histories of Human Rights, Forced Deportations and Civilizing Missions," *American Historical Review* 113/5 (Dec. 2008): 1313.

Jay Winter, *Remembering War: The Great War between Memory and History in the 20th Century*. New Haven: Yale University Press, 2006.

Ronald Zieger, *America's Great War: World War I and the American Experience*. Lanham, MD: Rowman and Littlefield, 2001.

3 AMBIVALENT ENGAGEMENT

Liaquat Ahamed, *Lords of Finance: The Bankers Who Broke the World*. New York: Penguin Press, 2009.

Peter Baldwin, *The Politics of Social Solidarity: Class Bases of the European Welfare State, 1875–1975.* Cambridge University Press, 1992

Ivan T. Berend, *Decades of Crisis: Central and Eastern Europe before World War II.* Berkeley: University of California Press, 1998.

Geoff Eley, *Forging Democracy: The History of the European Left, 1850 to 2000.* Oxford University Press, 2002.

Gerald Feldman, *The Great Disorder: Politics, Economics, and Society in the German Inflation, 1914–1924.* Oxford University Press, 1997.

Wendy Goldman, *Women, the State and Revolution: Soviet Family Policy and Social Life, 1917–1936.* Cambridge University Press, 1993.

Atina Grossmann, *Reforming Sex: The German Movement for Birth Control and Abortion Reform, 1920–1950.* Oxford University Press, 1997.

Akira Iriye, *Cultural Internationalism and World Order.* Baltimore: Johns Hopkins University Press, 1997

Melvyn P. Leffler, *The Elusive Quest: America's Pursuit of European Stability and French Security, 1919–1933.* Chapel Hill: University of North Carolina Press, 1979.

Mark Mazower, *Dark Continent: Europe's Twentieth Century.* New York: Vintage. 2000.

Mary Nolan, *Visions of Modernity: American Business and the Modernization of Germany.* Oxford University Press, 1994.

Susan Pedersen, *Family Dependence and the Origins of the Welfare State in Britain and France, 1914–1945.* Cambridge University Press, 1993.

Detlev Peukert, *The Weimar Republic.* New York: Hill and Wang, 1993.

Bernd Widdig, *Culture and Inflation in Weimar Germany.* Berkeley: University of California Press, 2001.

4 THE DEPRESSION AND TRANSATLANTIC NEW DEALS

Alan Ball, *Imagining America: Influence and Images in Twentieth-Century Russia.* Lantam, MD: Rowman and Littlefield, 2003.

William Barber, *Designs within Disorder: Franklin D. Roosevelt, the Economists, and American Economic Policy, 1933–1945.* Cambridge University Press, 1996.

Thomas Ferguson, "From Normalcy to New Deal: Industrial Structure, Party Competition, and American Public Policy in the Great Depression." *International Organization* 38/1 (Winter 1984): 41–94.

John Kenneth Galbraith, *The Great Crash 1929.* New York: Houghton Mifflin, 1997.

John A. Garraty, "The New Deal, National Socialism, and the Great Depression." *American Historical Review* 78/4 (Oct. 1973): 907–44.

Peter Gourevitch, *Politics in Hard Times: Comparative Responses to International Economic Crisis.* Ithaca: Cornell University Press, 1986.

Harold James, *The End of Globalization: Lessons from the Great Depression.* Cambridge, MA: Harvard University Press, 2002.

John M. Jordan, *Machine Age Ideology: Social Engineering and American Liberalism, 1911–1939.* Raleigh: University of North Carolina Press, 2010.

Charles Kindleberger, *The World in Depression, 1929–1939*. Berkeley: University of California Press, 1986.

Jennifer Klein, *For All These Rights: Business, Labor and the Shaping of America's Public-Private Welfare State*. Princeton University Press, 2003.

Wolfgang Schivelbusch, *Three New Deals: Reflections on Roosevelt's America, Mussolini's Italy, and Hitler's Germany*. New York: Metropolitan Books, 2006.

Philippe C. Schmitter, "Still the Century of Corporatism?" *Review of Politics* 36/1 (Jan. 1974): 85–131.

Robert Skidelsky, *Keynes: The Return of the Master*. New York: Public Affairs, 2009.

Peter Temin, *Lessons from the Great Depression*. Cambridge: MIT Press, 1989.

Margaret Weir and Theda Skocpol, "State Structures and the Possibilities for 'Keynesian' Responses to the Great Depression in Sweden, Britain, and the United States," in Peter Evans, Dietrich Rueschemeyer, and Theda Skocpol, eds. *Bringing the State Back In*. Cambridge University Press, 1985, 107–63.

5 STRANGE AFFINITIES, NEW ENEMIES

Kendall E. Bailes, "The American Connection: Ideology and the Transfer of American Technology to the Soviet Union, 1917–1941." *Comparative Studies in Society and History* (1981): 433.

Shelly Baranowski, *Strength through Joy: Consumerism and Mass Tourism in the Third Reich*. Cambridge University Press, 2007.

Susan Buck-Morss, *Dreamworld and Catastrophe: The Passing of Mass Utopia in East and West*. Cambridge, MA: MIT Press, 2000.

Victoria de Grazia, *How Fascism Ruled Women, 1922–1945*. Berkeley: University of California Press, 1993.

The Culture of Consent: The Mass Organization of Leisure in Fascist Italy. Cambridge University Press, 2002.

David Engerman, *Modernization from the Other Shore: American Intellectuals and the Romance of Russian Development*. Cambridge, MA: Harvard University Press, 2003.

Klaus P. Fischer, *Hitler and America*. Philadelphia: University of Pennsylvania Press, 2011.

Douglas Forgacs and Stephen Gundle, *Mass Culture and Italian Society from Fascism to Cold War*. Bloomington: Indiana University Press, 2007.

Saul Friedländer, *Nazi Germany and the Jews: The Years of Persecution, 1933–1939*. New York: Harper, 1997.

Michele Hoenicke Moore, *Know Your Enemy: American Debate on Nazism, 1933–1945*. Cambridge University Press, 2010.

Stephen Kotkin, *Magnetic Mountain: Stalinism as a Civilization*. Berkeley: University of California Press 1995.

Stephan Kuhl, *The Nazi Connection: Eugenics, American Racism and German National Socialism*. Oxford University Press, 1994.

Stephen H. Norwood, *The Third Reich in the Ivory Tower: Complicity and Conflict on American Campuses*. Cambridge University Press, 2009.

Alec Nove, *An Economic History of the USSR*. London: Penguin, 1969.

John Scott, *Beyond the Urals: An American Worker in Russia's City of Steel*. Bloomington: Indiana University Press, 1989.

J. Adam Tooze, *Wages of Destruction: The Making and Breaking of the Nazi Economy*. London: Penguin, 2008.

Tim Tzouliadis, *The Forsaken: An American Tragedy in Stalin's Russia*. New York: Penguin, 2008.

6 FROM WORLD WAR TO COLD WAR

Cambridge History of the Cold War, Vol. I: Origins, ed. Melvyn P. Leffler and Odd Arne Westad. Cambridge University Press, 2010

Frank Costigliola, "'Mixed Up' and 'Contact': Culture and Emotion among the Allies in the Second World War." *International History Review* 20/4 (Dec. 1998): 791–805.

Carolyn Eisenberg, *Drawing the Line: The American Decision to Divide Germany, 1944–1949*. Cambridge University Press. 1998.

Richard Evans, *Third Reich at War*. New York: Penguin, 2008.

John Lewis Gaddis, *We Now Know: Rethinking Cold War History*. Oxford University Press, 1998.

Atina Grossmann, *Jews, Germans and Allies: Close Encounters in Occupied Germany*. Princeton University Press, 2009.

Tony Judt, *Postwar: A History of Europe since 1945*. New York: Penguin, 2006.

George Kennan, *Memoires*. New York: Bantam, 1965.

Warren Kimball, *Forged in War: Roosevelt, Churchill, and the Second World War*. Chicago: Ivan R. Dee, 2002.

Warren Kimball, ed., *America Unbound: World War II and the Making of a Superpower*. New York: St. Martins, 1992.

Gabriel Kolko, *Century of War: Politics, Conflicts and Society since 1914*. New York: Norton, 1994.

Melvyn Leffler, *For the Soul of Mankind: The United States, The Soviet Union and the Cold War*. New York: Hill and Wang, 2007.

Mark Mazower, *Hitler's Empire: How the Nazis Ruled Europe*. New York: Penguin, 2008.

Norman Naimark, *The Russians in Germany: A History of the Soviet Zone of Occupation*. Cambridge, MA: Harvard University Press, 1995.

Richard Overy, *Why the Allies Won*. New York: Norton, 1996; New Haven: Yale University Press, 2008.

Geoffrey Roberts, *Stalin's Wars: From World War to Cold War, 1939–1952*. New Haven: Yale University Press, 2006.

Gerhard Weinberg, *Visions of Victory: The Hopes of Eight World War II Leaders*. Cambridge University Press, 2005.

A World at Arms: A Global History of World War II. Cambridge University Press, 2005.

David S. Wyman *The Abandonment of the Jews: America and the Holocaust, 1941–1945*. New York: New Press, 2007.

Elena Zubkova, *Russia after the War: Hopes, Illusions, Disappointments*. New York: M. E. Sharpe, 1968.

7 COOPERATION, COMPETITION, CONTAINMENT

Cuban Missile Crisis website. http://www.gwu.edu/~nsarchiv/nsa/cuba_mis_cri.

Campbell Craig and Fredrik Logevall, *America's Cold War: The Politics of Insecurity.* Cambridge, MA: Harvard University Press, 2009.

Marie-Laure Djelic, *Exporting the American Model: The Postwar Transformation of European Business.* Oxford University Press, 1998.

Gösta Esping-Anderson, *The Three Worlds of Welfare Capitalism* Princeton University Press, 1990.

Guiliano Garavini, *After the Empires: European Integration, Decolonization and the Challenge from the Global South, 1964–1981.* Oxford University Press.

Abbott Gleason, *Totalitarianism: The Inner History of the Cold War.* Oxford University Press, 1997.

Michael H. Hunt, *The American Ascendancy: How the United States Gained and Wielded Global Dominance.* Raleigh: University of North Carolina Press, 2007.

Paul R. Josephson, *Industrialized Nature: Brute Force Technology and the Transformation of the Natural World.* Washington, D.C.: Island Press, 2002.

Alan Milward, *The Reconstruction of Western Europe, 1945–1952.* Abingdon: Routledge, 2003.

Thomas McCormick, *America's Half Century: United States Foreign Policy in the Cold War and After.* Baltimore: Johns Hopkins University Press, 1995.

Philip Nash, *The Other Missiles of October: Eisenhower, Kennedy and the Jupiters, 1957–1963.* Raleigh: University of North Carolina Press, 1997.

Anders Stephenson, "Fourteen Notes on the Very Concept of the Cold War," in Geróid O. Tuathail and Simon Dalby, eds., *Rethinking Geopolitics* London: Routledge, 1998.

Marc Trachtenberg, *A Constructed Peace: The Making of the European Settlement, 1945–1963.* Princeton University Press, 1999.

Odd Arne Westad, *The Global Cold War: Third World Interventions and the Making of Our Time.* Cambridge University Press, 2005.

Jonathan Zeitlin, and Gary Herrigel, eds., *Americanization and Its Limits: Reworking US Technology and Management in Post-war Europe and Japan.* Oxford University Press, 2000.

8 CULTURE WARS

Volker Berghahn, *America and the Intellectual Cold Wars in Europe.* Princeton University Press, 2001.

Susan L. Carruthers, *Cold War Captives: Imprisonment, Escape and Brainwashing.* Berkeley: University of California Press, 2009.

David Caute, *The Dancer Defects: The Struggle for Cultural Supremacy during the Cold War.* Oxford University Press, 2003.

Jeffrey W. Cody, *Exporting American Architecture, 1870–2000.* London: Routledge, 2003.

David Crowley and Jane Pavitt, eds., *Cold War Modern: Design 1945–1970.* London: V and A Publishing, 2008.

Victoria de Grazia, *Irresistible Empire: America's Advance through Twentieth-Century Europe*. Cambridge, MA: Harvard University Press, 2005.

"Domestic Dreamworlds: Notions of Home in Post-1945 Europe." Special issue of *Journal of Contemporary History* 40:2 (2005).

David Ellwood, and Rob Kroes, eds., *Hollywood in Europe: Experiences of a Cultural Hegemony*. Amsterdam: VU University Press, 1994.

Heidi Fehrenbach and Uta G. Poiger, eds., *Transactions, Transgressions, Transformations: American Culture in Western Europe and Japan*, Oxford: Berghahn Press, 2000.

Stephen Gundle, *Between Hollywood and Moscow: The Italian Communists and the Challenge of Mass Culture, 1943–1991*. Durham: Duke University Press, 2000.

Rob Kroes, *If You've Seen One, You've Seen the Mall: Europeans and American Mass Culture*. Champagne-Urbana: University of Illinois Press, 1996.

Stephen Lovell, *The Shadow of War: Russia and the USSR, 1941 to the Present*. Wiley-Blackwell Publishers, 2010.

R. Laurence Moore and Maurizio Vaudagna, eds., *The American Century in Europe*. Ithaca: Cornell University Press, 2003.

Ruth Oldenziel and Karin Zachmann, eds., *Cold War Kitchen: Americanization, Technology, and European Users*. Cambridge, MA: MIT Press, 2009.

Richard Pells, *Not Like Us: How Europeans Have Loved, Hated and Transformed American Culture since World War II*. New York: Basic Books, 1998.

Timothy W. Ryback. *Rock around the Bloc: A History of Rock Music in Eastern Europe and the Soviet Union, 1954–1988*. Oxford University Press, 1990.

Frances Stonor Saunders, *The Cultural Cold War: The CIA and the World of Arts and Letters*. New York: New Press, 2000.

9 THE AMERICAN CENTURY ERODES, 1968–1979

Oliver Bange and Gottfried Niedhart, eds., *Helsinki 1975 and the Transformation of Europe*. Oxford: Berghahn Press, 2008.

Cambridge History of the Cold War, Vol. II: Crises and Détente, ed. Melvyn P. Leffler and Odd Arne Westad. Cambridge University Press, 2010.

Niall Ferguson, Charles S. Maier, Erez Manila, and Daniel J. Sargent, eds., *Shock of the Global: The 1970s in Perspective*. Cambridge, MA: Harvard University Press, 2010.

Carole Fink, Philipp Gassert, and Detlef Junker, eds., *1968: The World Transformed*. Washington, D.C.: GHI and Cambridge University Press, 1980.

Raymond Garthoff, *Détente and Confrontation: American–Soviet Relations from Nixon to Reagan*. Washington, D.C.: Brookings Institution Press, 1994.

Martin Klimke, and Joachim Scharloth, eds., *1968 in Europe: A History of Protest and Activism, 1956–1977*. New York: Palgrave Macmillan, 2008.

Diane Kunz, *Butter and Guns: America's Cold War Economic Diplomacy*. New York: Free Press, 1997.

Frank Logevall and Andrew Preston, eds., *Nixon in the World: American Foreign Relations, 1966–1977*. Oxford University Press, 2008.

Wilfried Loth, and George Soutou, eds., *The Making of Détente: Eastern Europe and Western Europe in the Cold War, 1965–75*. Abingdon: Routledge, 2010.

Arthur Marwick, *The Sixties: Cultural Transformation in Britain, France, Italy and the United States, c. 1958 to c. 1974.* Oxford University Press, 2000.

Philip Mirowski and Dieter Plehwe, eds., *The Road from Mont Pelerin: The Making of the Neoliberal Thought Collective.* Cambridge, MA: Harvard University Press, 2009

Daniel T. Rodgers, *Age of Fracture.* Cambridge, MA: Harvard University Press, 2011.

Angela Romano, ed., *From European Détente to Détente in Europe.* Brussels: Peter Lang, 2009.

Axel Schildt and Detlef Siegfried, eds., *Between Marx and Coca-Cola: Youth Culture in Changing European Societies, 1960–1980.* New York: Berghahn Press, 2006.

Matthias Schulz and Thomas A. Schwartz, eds., *Strained Alliance: US–European Relations from Nixon to Carter.* Cambridge University Press, 2010.

Quinn Slobodian, *Foreign Front: Third World Politics in Sixties West Germany.* Durham: Duke University Press, 2012.

Jeremy Varon, *Bringing the War Home: The Weather Underground, the Red Army Faction and Revolutionary Violence in the Sixties and Seventies.* Berkeley: University of California Press, 2004.

Vladislav M. Zubok, *A Failed Empire: The Soviet Union in the Cold War from Stalin to Gorbachev.* Chapel Hill: University of North Carolina Press, 2007.

10 RENEWED CONFLICT AND SURPRISING COLLAPSE

Frédéric Bozo, Marie-Pierre Rey, N. Piers Ludlow, and Leopoldo Nuti, eds., *Europe and the End of the Cold War: A Reappraisal.* London: Routledge, 2008.

Archie Brown, *The Gorbachev Factor.* Oxford University Press, 1996.

The Rise and Fall of Communism. New York: Harper, 2009.

Cambridge History of the Cold War, Vol. III: Endings, ed. Melvyn P. Leffler and Odd Arne Westad. Cambridge University Press, 2010.

Michael Cox, "Whatever Happened to the 'Second' Cold War? Soviet–American Relations: 1980–88." *Review of International Studies* 16 (1990), 164.

Robert D. English, *Russia and the Idea of the West: Gorbachev, Intellectuals and the End of the Cold War.* New York: Columbia, 2000.

Frances Fitzgerald, *Way Out There in the Blue: Reagan, Star Wars, and the End of the Cold War.* New York: Simon and Schuster, 2001.

Timothy Garton Ash, *The Magic Lantern: The Revolution of '89 Witnessed in Warsaw, Budapest, Berlin, and Prague.* New York: Vintage, 1993.

In Europe's Name: Germany and the Divided Continent. New York: Vintage, 1994.

Stephen Kotkin, *Armageddon Averted: The Soviet Collapse, 1970–2000.* Oxford University Press, 2008.

Stephen Kotkin (with a contribution from Jan Gross), *Uncivil Society: 1989 and the Implosion of the Communist Establishment.* New York: Modern Library, 2009.

Charles Maier, *Dissolution: The Crisis of Communism and the End of East Germany.* Princeton University Press, 1997.

Olav Njølstad, ed., *The Last Decade of the Cold War: From Conflict Escalation to Conflict Transformation.* London: Frank Cass, 2004.

Leopoldo Nuti, ed., *Crisis of Détente in Europe: From Helsinki to Gorbachev, 1975–1985*. London: Routledge, 2009.

Constantine Pleshakov, *There is No Freedom without Bread! 1989 and the Civil War that Brought Down Communism*. New York: Farrar, Straus and Giroux, 2009.

Daniel C. Thomas, *The Helsinki Effect: International Norms, Human Rights and the Demise of Communism*. Princeton University Press, 2001.

11 A WIDENING ATLANTIC

Ivan Berend, *Europe since 1980*. Cambridge University Press, 2010.

Grace Davie, *Europe: The Exceptional Case: Parameters of Faith in the Modern World*. London: Darton, Longman and Todd, 2002.

Ronald Dore, *Stock Market Capitalism: Welfare Capitalism, Japan and Germany versus the Anglo-Saxons*. Oxford University Press, 2000.

Barry Eichengreen, *The European Economy since 1945: Coordinated Capitalism and Beyond*. Princeton University Press, 2007.

Francis Fukuyama, *The End of History and the Last Man*. New York: Avon, 1992.

Andrew Glyn, *Capitalism Unleashed: Finance, Globalization, and Welfare*. Oxford University Press, 2006.

Peter Gowan, *The Global Gamble: Washington's Faustian Bid for World Dominance*. London: Verso, 1999.

Peter Hall and David Soskice, eds., *Varieties of Capitalism: The Institutional Foundations of Comparative Advantage*. Oxford University Press, 2001.

Steven Hill, *Europe's Promise: Why the European Way Is the Best Hope in an Insecure Age*. Berkeley: University of California Press, 2010.

Tony Judt, *Ill Fares the Land*. New York: Penguin, 2010.

Esther Kaplan, *With God on Their Side: How Christian Fundamentalists Trampled Science, Policy, and Democracy in George W. Bush's White House*. New York: New Press, 2004.

Geir Lundestad, *The United States and Western Europe since 1945: From "Empire" by Invitation to Transatlantic Drift*. Oxford University Press, 2003.

Jonas Pontusson, *Inequality and Prosperity: Social Europe vs Liberal America*. Ithaca: Cornell University Press, 2005.

T. R. Reid, *The United States of Europe: The New Superpower and the End of American Supremacy*. New York: Penguin, 2004.

Vivien A. Schmidt. *The Futures of European Capitalism*. Oxford University Press, 2002.

12 IMPERIAL AMERICA, ESTRANGED EUROPE

Andrew Bacevich, *Washington Rules: America's Path to Permanent War*. New York: Metropolitan Books, 2010.

Dan Diner, *America in the Eyes of Germans. An Essay on Anti-Americanism*. Princeton: Marcus Wiener Publishers, 1996.

Lloyd Gardner and Marilyn Young, eds., *The New American Empire: A 21st-Century Teach-in on US Foreign Policy*. New York: New Press, 2005.

Timothy Garton Ash, *Free World: America, Europe and the Surprising Future of the West*. New York: Random House, 2004.

Godfrey Hodgson, *The Myth of American Exceptionalism*. New Haven: Yale University Press, 2009.

Chalmers Johnson, *Blowback: The Costs and Consequences of American Empire*. New York: Henry Holt, 2004.

Nemesis: The Last Days of the American Republic. New York: Metropolitan Books, 2007.

Robert Kagan, *Of Paradise and Power: America and Europe in the New World Order*. New York: Vintage, 2004.

Peter J. Katzenstein and Robert O. Keohane, eds., *Anti-Americanisms in World Politics*. Ithaca: Cornell University Press, 2006.

Daniel Levy, Max Pensky, and John Torpey, eds., *Old Europe, New Europe, Core Europe: Transatlantic Relations After the Iraq War*. London: Verso, 2005.

Anatol Lieven, *America Right or Wrong: An Anatomy of American Nationalism*. Oxford University Press, 2005.

Michal Mandelbaum, *The Frugal Superpower: America's Global Leadership in a Cash-Strapped Era*. New York: Public Affairs, 2010.

Andrei S. Markowits, *Uncouth Nation: Why Europe Dislikes America*. Princeton University Press, 2007.

Joseph Nye, *The Paradox of American Power: Why the World's Only Superpower Can't Go It Alone*. New York: Oxford, 2003.

Index